D. E. Needham
E. K. Mashingaidze
N. Bhebe

FROM IRON AGE TO INDEPENDENCE
A History of Central Africa

New Edition

Longman

Longman Group Limited
Longman House
Burnt Mill, Harlow
Essex CM20 2JE, England
and Associated Companies
throughout the World.

© Longman Group Ltd. 1974 and 1984

All rights reserved. No part of this
publication may be reproduced, stored
in a retrieval system, or transmitted
in any form or by any means, electronic,
mechanical, photocopying, recording, or
otherwise, without the prior written
permission of the Publishers.

First published 1974
New edition 1984
Second impression 1985

ISBN 0 582 65111 5

Set in Times (Lasercomp)
Printed in Great Britain by
Butler & Tanner Ltd,
Frome and London

Acknowledgements

The publishers are grateful to the following for permission to reproduce photographs in the text:

David Attenborough for page 16; BBC Hulton Picture Library for pages 34, 68, 84, 85, 86, 114 and 143; Camera Press Limited for pages 111, 175, and 195 top; Central Office of Information for page 187; Central Press Photos/Keystone for page 201; Department of Antiquities, Malawi, for page 161 top; Department of Information, South Africa for page 113 bottom; Mary Evans Picture Library for pages 27 and 83 top; Professor B.M. Fagan, University of California for page 6; Werner Forman Archive for page 46; Ghana Information Services for page 189; Hoa-Qui for pages 9 left, 9 right and 23; Illustrated London News for page 123; Keystone Press Agency for page 191; Livingstone Museum, Zambia, for page 15 left; Malawi High Commission for page 166; Malawi Information Services for page 104; Mansell Collection for page 89; Ministry of Information, Immigration and Tourism, Zimbabwe, for page 42 and 157; National Archives of Zimbabwe for pages 58, 67 top, 67 bottom, 77, 94, 97, 112, 117, 124 top, 124 bottom, 127, 129, 131, 132, 134, 137, 138, 161 bottom, 163 top, 163 bottom, 164, 168 top, 174, 176, 178, 195 bottom, 196 top, 196 bottom and 200; National Museums and Monuments of Zimbabwe for page 17 right; Popperfoto for page 17 left, 83 bottom and 186; R.S.P. Ndola, Zambia, for page 170 top; Royal Geographical Society for page 144; United Society for the Propagation of the Gospel for page 92; Zambia Information Services for pages 10 left, 32, 73, 169, 170 bottom, 179, 181, 182, 183, 188, 192 and 193; Zimbabwe Livingstone Museum for page 21.

The publishers regret that they are unable to trace the copyright holders on the following pages and apologise for any infringement caused: 10 right; 18; 28; 33 reproduced from 'Benguella to the Territory of the Yacca' (11) by Capello & Ivens; 47; 49 top and 55 reproduced from 'Dapper,' German Edition; 49 bottom, 52, 54 and 59 reproduced from: 'Africa History of a continent' by Basil Davidson; 57; 76; 79 reproduced from: 'Malawi, a Geographical Study,' by Dike and Rimmington; 87 reproduced from: 'To the Victoria Falls' by E.C. Tabler; 93; 102; 113 top and 121 reproduced from 'The Downfall of Lobengula' by Wills and Colleridge; 140 reproduced from 'Nyasaland' by Frank Debenham; 153 reproduced from 'Politics in a Changing Society' by Barnes; 160 reproduced from 'Independent African' by Shepperson and Proce; 168 bottom; 171; 184.

The cover photographs were kindly supplied by Prof. B.M. Fagan, University of California (top left); John & Penny Hubley (top right); Werner Forman Archive/Robert Aberman (bottom left); Ministry of Information, Zimbabwe (bottom right).

Contents

Part I The Iron Age
1 Bantu-speaking peoples of Central Africa *5*
2 Iron Age trade in Central Africa *14*

Part II The Growth of States in Central Africa
3 Luba-Lunda states under Songye chiefs: 1200–1400 *20*
4 Luba-Lunda spread into Zambia *25*
5 The Lozi kingdom *31*
6 Malawi people: the Kalonga and the Undi kingdoms *35*
7 South of the Zambezi *39*

Part III The Portuguese in Central Africa
8 The Portuguese in the Congo: 1482–1700 *45*
9 The Portuguese in Angola: 1575–1836 *51*
10 The Portuguese in the Zambezi and south of the valley *57*
11 The prazos and the missions to Kazembe *63*

Part IV Effects of Mfecane/Difaqane
12 The Ndebele *66*
13 The Kololo of Sebetwane *72*
14 The Ngoni *77*

Part V Nineteenth Century Traders, Explorers and Pioneer Missionaries
15 Nineteenth century traders and hunters *81*
16 David Livingstone and the exploration of Central Africa *89*
17 Pioneer Christian missions in Zimbabwe and Zambia *96*
18 Pioneer Christian missions in Malawi *102*

Part VI The Scramble, Conquest and Colonisation
19 Leopold and the establishment of the Congo Free State *107*
20 Rhodes and the occupation of Zimbabwe *111*

21 Ndebele and Shona Uprisings 1896–97 *122*
22 Lewanika and the Barotseland Protectorate *130*
23 The colonisation of Malawi *136*
24 Yao and Ngoni resistance to the establishment of British rule *142*
25 Occupation of North-Eastern Zambia *147*

Part VII Colonial Rule in Central Africa I
26 Colonial rule in Zimbabwe *152*
27 Colonial rule in Zambia *155*
28 Colonial rule in Malawi *157*
29 Early African resistance and protest *159*

Part VIII Colonial Rule in Central Africa II
30 Development and underdevelopment in Central Africa *162*
31 The growth of African opposition *167*

Part IX The Shadow of Federation
32 The shadow falls *173*
33 African opposition to Federation *177*
34 The dark years in Central Africa *180*
35 The collapse of Federation *184*

Part X Independence: struggle and achievement
36 The growth of nationalist parties in Zambia and Malawi *186*
37 Independence in Zambia and Malawi *190*
38 The liberation of Zimbabwe *194*
39 Post-colonial developments *198*

Questions *202*

Further reading *205*

Index *206*

PART I
The Iron Age

1 Bantu-speaking peoples of Central Africa

By far the largest single group of Central Africa are the Bantu-speaking peoples. The word *bantu* simply means people or human beings. The peoples of sub-equatorial Africa speak well over 400 languages and all these, except for the Khoisan languages, have very similar words for people or human beings. The following few examples will demonstrate these similarities: the Swahili of East Africa call a person *mtu* (singular) and *watu* (plural). The Nguni of Southern Africa call a person *muntu* (singular) and *bantu* (plural). The Shona of Zimbabwe in South-Central Africa say *munhu* (singular) and *vanhu* (plural).

Linguists say that the various Bantu languages may have come from one parent language many hundreds, or perhaps thousands, of years ago. It has also been suggested that this common language-parent might have come into existence in the general area between Nigeria and Cameroon.

Migrations of Bantu-speaking peoples
If the parent of Bantu languages developed in the Benue-Cross region between Nigeria and Cameroon then the various Bantu languages spoken in Central Africa and in Southern Africa must have been brought to these regions by people who had moved away from the Benue-Cross region. This movement of large groups or communities of people from one region to another is usually referred to as *migration*. The ancestors of the Bantu-speaking peoples may have migrated to Central Africa in search of pasturelands, good agricultural areas, water or such things. We do not think that the people moved in whole communities. Possibly young men were first sent to far away places to look for new areas. They would disappear for a long time, perhaps, before returning with news about new areas. Heads of families and clan leaders would study such reports carefully before any decisions were taken. If the decision was to move to the new lands the young men who had been there would lead the way. Even then only some members of the families moved to the new places, while others remained in the old area for several years. The whole process of migration and the Bantu occupation appears to have taken many generations. We do not know exactly when the migration began and when it ended. Linguists, historians and archaeologists are still not agreed on a single explanation of this movement.

A factor creating difficulties in tracing the movement of the early Bantu speakers to what is now Bantu-Africa is that between the suggested region of origins and Bantu-speaking Africa lies a vast and thick forest region. It is argued that since the ancestors of the Bantu-speaking people may have already become keepers of cattle and grain growers, the thick forest region might have created problems for them during their journey through it. For instance, the tsetse fly might have killed their cattle, while the acidic soils of the forest region did not allow them to grow food crops, especially grain. It is suggested, however, that the Bantu-speakers used the numerous rivers that cut through the tropical

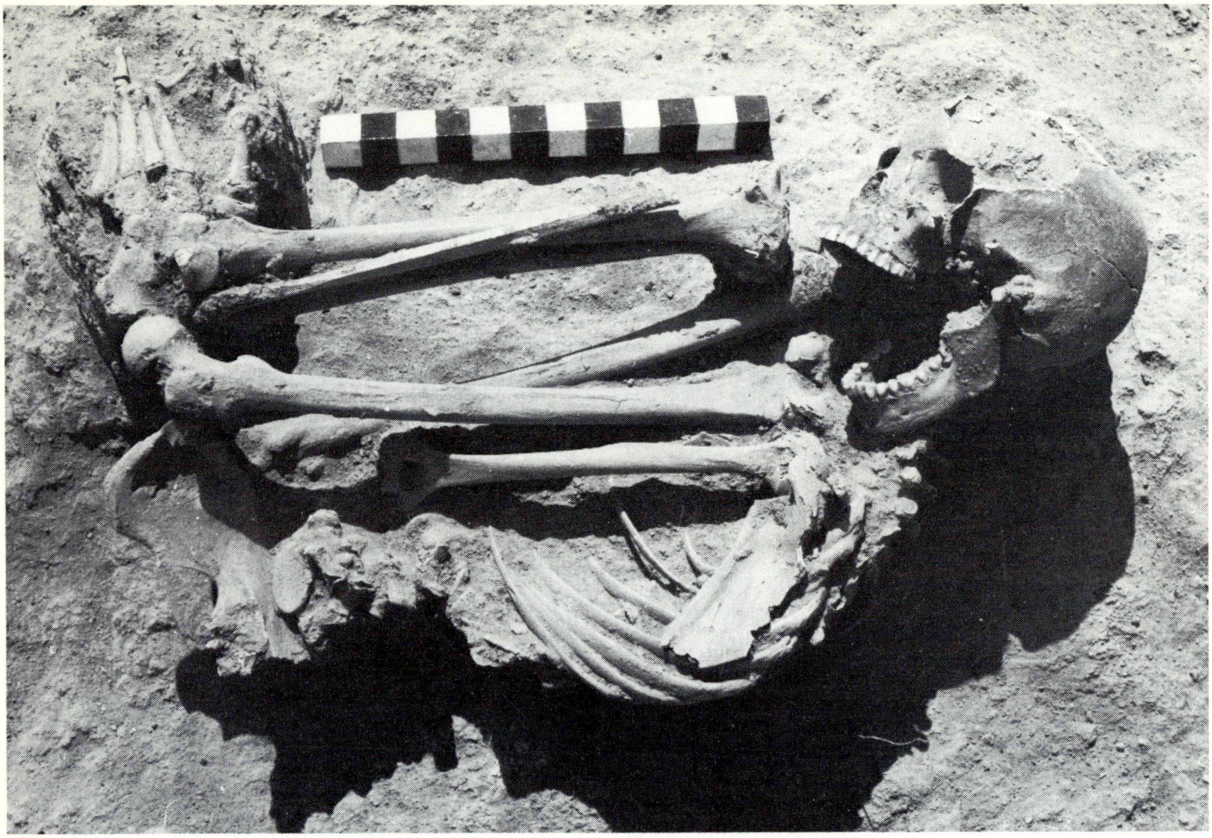

Iron Age burial from Isamu Pati, Zambia, about AD 1000

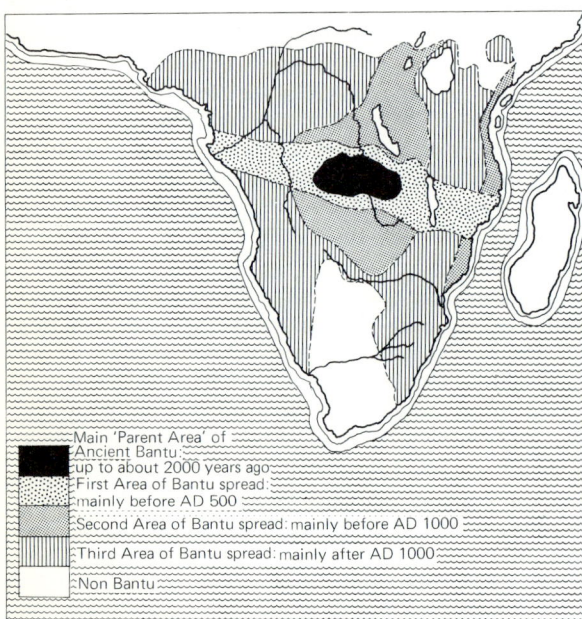

Possible migrations of Bantu-speaking peoples before about AD 1500

forest, travelling along them to the healthy and beautiful grasslands to the south of the forest.

Yet another view suggests that the ancestors of the Bantu-speakers might have travelled southwards, and then eastwards along the northern edges of the forest, and then southwards again until finally entering the savannah region south of the forest. This same view holds that the Bantu-speakers might not have developed as a distinct linguistic group until they had arrived and established themselves in the savannah area somewhere around northern Katanga (now the Shaba province of Zaire). This area would have therefore been the cradleland from which the Bantu-speaking peoples later spread themselves throughout the rest of Bantu-speaking Africa.

Today these people fall into three broad divisions: the Western, the Eastern and the Southern Bantu-speakers (see Map 1.1). These are linguistic divisions only. The Bantu-speakers met and mixed with other groups both during their long migration and when they settled in their respective areas in Central and Southern Africa. In Central and South-

6

ern Africa they found Stone Age San and Khoikhoi peoples. These are called *Stone Age peoples* because they made their tools and weapons from stones and wood. One important outcome of the meeting of the two groups is that the two language groups began to borrow from each other. For example the clicks now found in such Southern Bantu languages as Sotho, Zulu and Xhosa have Khoi-San influences.

Food production in Central Africa

One of the most revolutionary developments in the story of mankind was when man discovered ways of producing his own food rather than relying on his immediate surroundings to provide it. This meant the domestication of certain plants and animals which were to provide the greater part of man's diet. Before they discovered ways of producing their own food our great-grand ancestors were hunter-gatherers living from hand to mouth and were constantly on the move in search of wild berries, edible roots and wild animals. The domestication of food crops and animals brought about far-reaching changes to their way of life. That is what is meant by the phrase 'revolutionary development'. For instance, people were no longer dependent on their immediate surroundings to provide them with food and they also stayed in one place far longer tending their crops. They could build permanent homes and establish larger communities. With larger settled communities came the need to make laws and rules to control the people and the available resources for the benefit of everybody.

When Europeans came to Central Africa about 500 years ago the peoples of the region were already producing their own food and living in large communities including complex political states. How the knowledge of food production came to Central Africa is still unclear. What seems certain, however, is that although some food crops belong to Central Africa, the actual knowledge of producing food began somewhere in the Middle East and later reached Egypt in North Africa. By about 6000 BC the peoples of the Lower Nile owned cattle, sheep, goats etc. and were also growing their own rice, barley and wheat. The knowledge of food production spread to the west and to the south through the Sahara region, which enjoyed wet conditions.

Possibly Central Africa had to wait for several thousands of years before food producing knowledge arrived. Perhaps the knowledge of raising cattle and other domestic animals travelled faster than that of growing food crops and some people, such as the Khoikhoi, acquired the knowledge of keeping animals to the exclusion of crop farming. The San, however, opted to remain hunter-gatherers.

Since neither the Bantu-speakers nor the Khoisan left written records it is difficult to date with any certainty the arrival of food production in Central Africa. However the pre-literate inhabitants of Central Africa left behind useful information. For example, archaeologists (those who dig and study ancient settlements) have found many settlements believed to have once belonged to Bantu-speaking communities. Places on which human settlements once stood are known as 'sites'.

Early Iron Age sites

We usually differentiate between sites occupied by people who possessed the knowledge of making tools from iron and those who used stone and wood in making their tools. Those with evidence of the use of iron are known as *Iron Age* sites and those without are called *Stone Age* sites.

How do we know whether a particular site was occupied by iron-using people? Historians depend on the investigations of others, especially archaeologists. Archaeologists study human remains, remains of houses, pieces of broken pots, tools, weapons, bones of animals, waste matter from iron smelting, food stuffs – anything at all about the way of life of the occupants of old sites.

It seems that it was not until about AD 300 or AD 400 that iron-making was practised in Central Africa. It also appears therefore that the beginning of the Central African Early Iron Age coincided with the introduction of food production in the region. Early Iron Age sites have also been closely associated with certain types of pottery found at some sites in East, Central and Southern Africa. It has also been suggested that the makers of this pottery were food-producing and Bantu-speaking iron users.

Archaeologists describe pottery found in Central Africa according to its appearance, shape and whatever decorations are found on it. Two broad divisions of the pottery have been made: the *dimple-based* and the *channelled* pottery. The dimple-based pottery derives its name from the dimple or depression on the bottom of the pot. This type, however, is not so common in Central African Early Iron Age sites. It is more widespread in East Africa.

The channelled pottery, so called because of the characteristic grooves that decorate it, was found to be more widespread in Central Africa. We should now attempt an identification of some Early Iron Age sites of Central Africa.

Burial of man of about 28 years from Ingombe Ilede, Zambia. The skeleton lay in an extended position and was buried with many grave goods, including the items labelled in the picture:

1, 2 Hammerheads, 3 Iron razor, 4 Sheafs of copper trade wire, 5, 6 Iron spike, 7 Iron tongs, 8 Bronze bar.

The disc-like objects around the neck of the burial are Cohus *shells from the East African coast. Rows of copper bangles adorn the limbs. The scale is 12 inches long. (Excavations by J. H. Chaplin, 1960)*

Early Iron Age sites in Zaire and Zambia

Many archaeological sites are known to exist in Zaire's forest and savannah regions. But very little work has been done in these areas. The most important site was discovered south of the Congo forest at Tshikapa on the upper Kasai river. This site is in an area suitable for both agriculture and cattle raising. The Tshikapa pottery is mainly dimple-based, making this site the most southwestern dimple-based pottery industry so far discovered. Tshikapa is also within the area regarded

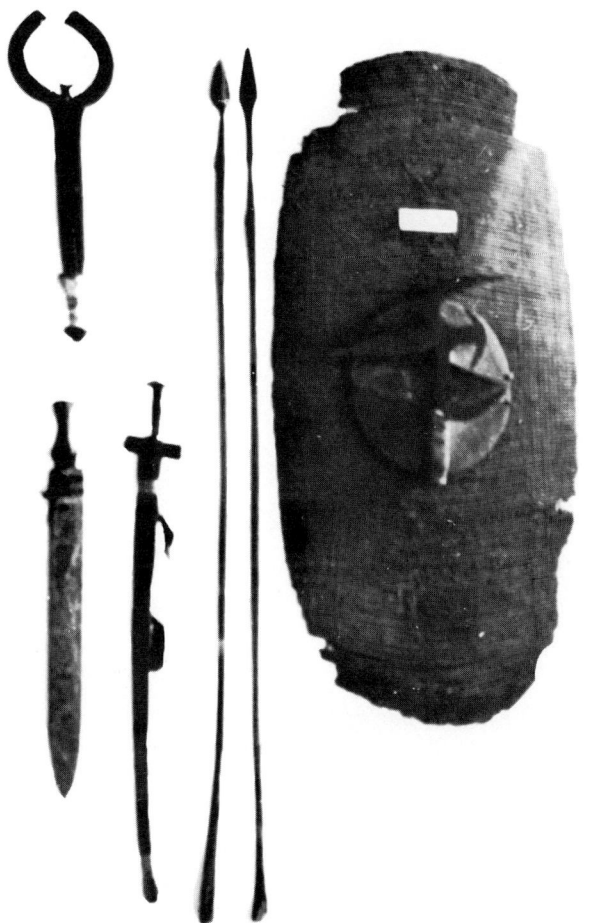

Iron age weapons

Another site was at KaLambo Falls on the southern tip of Lake Tanganyika. Here dimple-based pottery, iron slag, remains of pole and mud huts and other pieces of information were found. The pottery included dimple-based pots and undecorated bowls similar to the type of pots associated with Stone Age people and found at rock shelters in the Northern Province of Zambia. It seems that the Kalambo site was occupied more than once, or perhaps for a very long period, as there were layers or levels of occupation. The first occupation may have taken place during the fourth century AD.

Because most of the Kalambo pottery had grooved decorations, it was described as 'channelled ware', a term later adopted for most of the pottery found in Zambia. Another type of pottery was found between Zaire's Shaba province and Zambia. Archaeologists have named the group of sites found here after Lake Kisale on the upper Lualaba. A number of burial places have been dug up and funerary pots, vessels, copper and iron objects, glass beads and cowrie shells were recovered. As glass beads and sea shells do not belong to the Central African interior, it may be assumed that they reached this area by way of trade with the east coast.

as the cradle-land of the ancestors of the Bantu-speakers. Unfortunately no date has been established for the Tshikapa pottery and this makes it difficult to say whether the pottery should be associated with the Early Iron Age period.

Thanks to archaeological work carried out in recent years in Zambia, there is now information on a number of Early Iron Age sites in that country. The first important discovery was made at Machili in the Western Province, where pottery and iron objects were found in many soil pits. These objects were tested by radiocarbon dating, a method used by archaeologists to estimate roughly how old the remains of old cultures are. The tests established that there were Iron Age people at Machili during the early centuries of the Christian era (AD 96–212). Another site was found at Lusu, southwest of Machili, on the upper Zambezi. The charcoal and pottery at Lusu produced dates slightly older than those yielded by Machili.

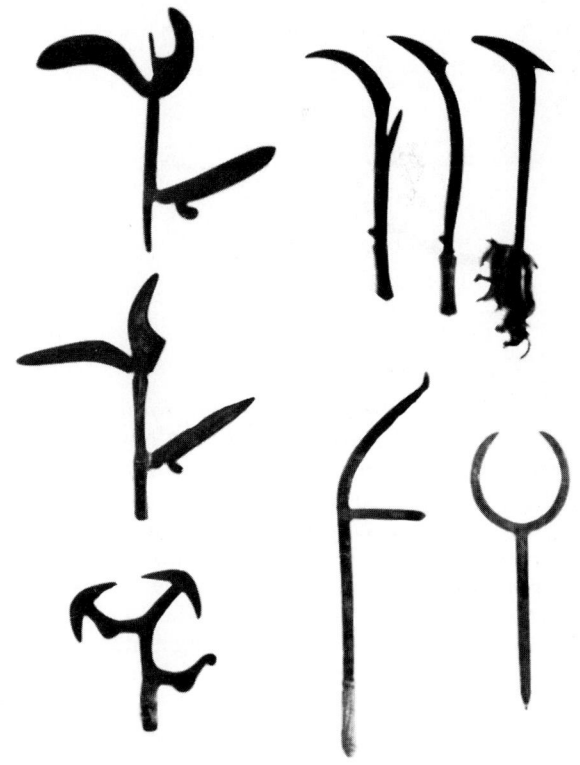

Iron age tools

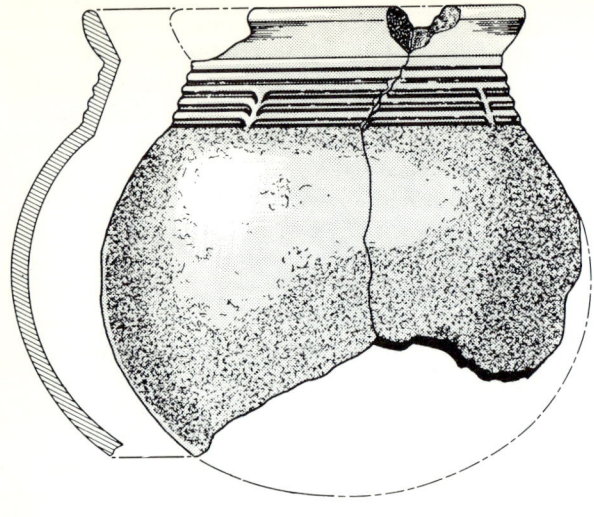

Furnace for smelting from Chipembe in Zambia

Iron age clay pot

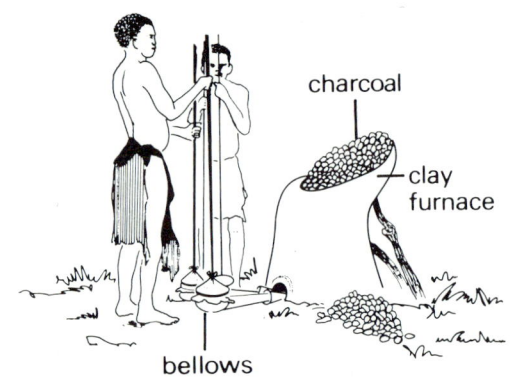

Fourteen sites have also been found on the headwaters of the Kafue river on the Copperbelt. At Chondwe, the main settlement, 'comb-stamped' pottery dating from about the eighth to the tenth centuries, has been found. Fragments of copper have also been found, although not enough to suggest any large-scale copper trading at this time. Further sites have been found in the Lusaka area (Kapwirimbwe) and in the Livingstone area, at Kamadzulo and Dambwa. At the last two sites, copper, iron and pottery were found. At Kapwirimbwe iron-smelting furnaces, spear-heads, iron razors and rings, necked vessels and bowls were also found.

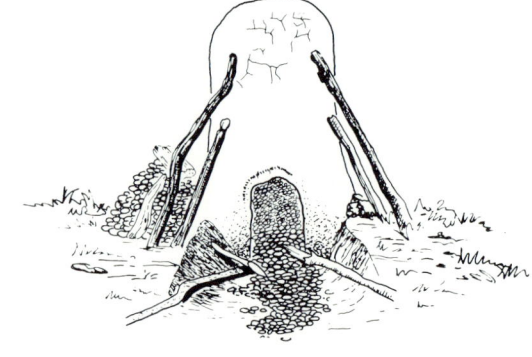

Iron age smelting process

Studies of the Zambian Early Iron Age by archaeologists reveal several other characteristic features. There is a general agreement that not only is the Zambian pottery similar to that of other parts of Central Africa, it also bears resemblances to that of East Africa.

Early Iron Age sites in Malawi
Archaeological investigation has been carried out at a number of places in Malawi. It would appear that the Malawian Early Iron Age was somewhat different from that of Zambia as its pottery was similar to that found in East Africa. This is certainly true of the pottery found at Mwavarambo Village in the Karonga District. The pots are globular in shape with 'comb-stamping' and a red-black finish. This type of pottery was also found at the Phopo hill site near Lake Kazuni. The Phopo hill site has been dated to the third century AD. There is evidence that the iron industry was a very important element of Phopo Hill culture. The same ware has also been found on the Nyika plateau at Chowo rock, a place associated with ancient iron workings.

Yet another type of pottery has been found in southern Malawi near the southern tip of the lake, at Nkope Bay. The pottery here is like the Gokomere and the Ziwa ware of Zimbabwe. Copper and iron were used by the inhabitants of the Nkope Bay settlement. It must be noted that the Nkope Bay site is close to the Mozambique border and it is possible that the settlement extended into Mozambique. The Early Iron Age people of Nkope Bay and the neighbouring areas seem to have been hunters and fishermen. Iron hoe-heads also suggest cultivation. There is, however, no evidence that pastoralism was practised.

There is also evidence that Early Iron Age Malawians might have had trade contacts with the east coast. In 1970 a blue glass bead and a cowrie shell were found at an archaeological site on the upper Shire at Matope.

Early Iron Age sites in Zimbabwe
Iron Age research has been carried out in Zimbabwe for over a century, but more attention seems to have been on the Zimbabwe Ruins. Even here more interest was on the Later Iron Age rather than on the Early Iron Age. There are, however, many Early Iron Age settlements in Zimbabwe, the best known of which are Gokomere, Ziwa and Mabveni. Archaeologists' attention to the Early Iron Age settlement at Gokomere began in 1937. The pottery found there was different from that of the Shona inhabitants of the area. The stamped and grooved

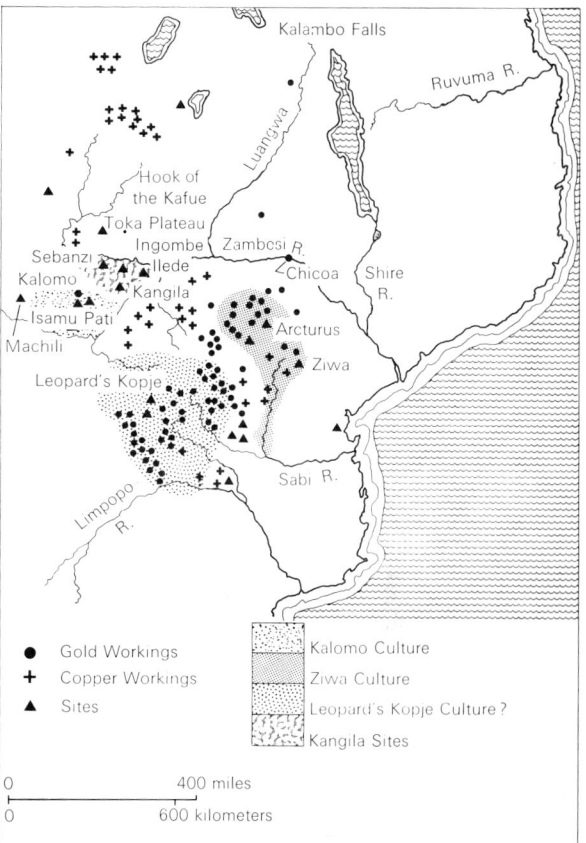

Iron age sites in Central Africa

decorations were similar to the pottery found in East Africa and across the Zambezi.

In the Chivi District to the west of Great Zimbabwe were found a number of Early Iron Age sites, the most notable of which is Mabveni. The Mabveni pottery was given various dates in the second, third, sixth and seventh centuries, all of which are comparable to those of Gokomere and some Zambian Early Iron Age sites. The earliest Iron Age deposit at Great Zimbabwe, called Zimbabwe I by archaeologists, has yielded dates ranging from the fourth to the sixth century AD. This is the same dating as the Gokomere site. Pottery similar to that at Gokomere was also found as far south as the Limpopo valley area at Malapati, and as far west as the Hwange Game Reserve.

In the eastern districts of Zimbabwe a distinct cultural tradition was found represented by the Ziwa site in the Inyanga area. The Ziwa pottery differs from that of Gokomere in its decorations and also in its certainly better and finer quality. Radiocarbon dates have been obtained for the Ziwa pottery in the fourth, ninth and tenth centuries AD.

It has been suggested that some of the Ziwa-type sites in the area could be associated with the ancient gold mining industry.

The successor to the Gokomere phase of the Zimbabwean Early Iron Age was found in the southern and western parts of the country, and is known by the clumsy name Leopard's Kopje I. Leopard's Kopje I peoples of Zimbabwe built their settlements in places with rich soils and near ancient gold mines. Their pottery has some similarities with Gokomere ware. For instance, it has stamped-decorations. Leopard's Kopje I has been dated between the eighth and the ninth centuries AD. Leopard's Kopje I was followed by Phase II.

Leopard's Kopje II settlements were usually situated in the dry savannah grasslands in southern and western Zimbabwe. Some sites, such as Bambandyanalo, were found as far south as across the Limpopo. Homes were usually built in the shelter of rocky hills. Rough stone walls were used to divide villages. Leopard's Kopje II's pottery tradition bore very little resemblance to that of Gokomere. The common forms of decoration consisted of incised, dragged and stylus impressions. There were also undecorated beakers, figurines of women and domestic animals, especially cattle. These probably represented a new pottery industry or even a new culture which was strongly pastoral. It has been suggested that a new and strongly pastoral culture was affecting Zambia almost at the same time. This has made some people speculate that the second phase of Zimbabwe Leopard's Kopje culture and Zambia's strongly pastoral culture are related. It has also been observed that the figurines of women in the Leopard's Kopje II pottery have certain characteristics of San artistic influence. It is possible that Leopard's Kopje II pastoralists contained a substantial Khoikhoi element which was perhaps being gradually integrated within the Bantu-speaking population of mixed farmers. Leopard's Kopje Phase II has given a number of dates, the tenth and eleventh centuries being the most common.

The Central African Early Iron Age: concluding remarks

The coming of the knowledge of ironworking to Central Africa is closely associated with the early pastoral and crop cultivating settlers. These mixed farmers built large settlements or villages consisting of huts made of poles and mud, and with hardened floors. The huts had thatched roofs and were similar to the huts built by modern Bantu-speakers of Central Africa. The period from about the second to about the tenth centuries seems to have witnessed Early Iron Age occupation, especially in Zambia, Malawi and Zimbabwe. This occupation took the form of villages which were situated far apart. The Early Iron Age food producing communities found hunter-gatherer communities which they either gradually absorbed or forced out of the areas of occupation.

The pottery of Central Africa, in spite of local variations and changes, and in spite of differences some of which are fundamental, shares many strong similarities, just as it bears similarities with that of East Africa.

The Later Iron Age

It is, of course, not possible to give a definite date for the change over from the Early Iron Age to the Later Iron Age. If the Early Iron Age lasted until around the end of the tenth century and the beginning of the eleventh century, then the Later Iron Age must have begun some time during the twelfth to the thirteenth century.

The main characteristics of the Later Iron Age in Central Africa include the development of a more specialised pastoral economy spreading across central Zambia southwards on both sides of the Kalahari. Populations grew fast during this period especially in eastern Zambia, Shaba (Katanga), in parts of the Congo Basin and south of the Zambezi on the Zimbabwean high veld. Larger communities emerged, encouraging more efficient ways of exploiting the area's natural resources for the benefit of growing societies. Material evidence from Later Iron Age settlements in Zimbabwe, Zambia and Malawi also bear witness to the technological advancement achieved during this period.

Later Iron Age in Zimbabwe
The area stretching from the Zambezi in the north to the Limpopo in the south, and from the Mozambican channel in the east to the fringes of the Kalahari in the west (south Central Africa) seems to have developed faster than the rest of Central Africa in some respects. This area was in a particularly favourable position regarding natural resources such as good agricultural and pastoral conditions, mineral wealth and ivory. Added to that was the fact that a great part of south Central Africa was easily accessible to good external trade through the east coastal markets. No doubt, as will be seen later, these favourable conditions contributed not only to the development of a rich material culture but also to the growth of large and complex political units in the area – especially in Zimbabwe.

In terms of material culture the Later Iron Age in Zimbabwe is represented by the latter part of Phase II of Leopard's Kopje and especially by Phase III. The latter part of Phase II and Phase III became very widespread. Although the centre was in south-west Zimbabwe in the dry grasslands around Khami, settlements have also been found hundreds of miles away from there. For example, to the south across the Limpopo were Bambandyalo and Mapungubwe. To the west sites have been found as far as Botswana.

The peoples of Leopard's Kopje II and III appear to have been strongly pastoral and agricultural in their economy, although hunting continued to be important. The agricultural industry is confirmed by the grindstones and hoe heads which have been found. In some cases even grain seeds have been discovered.

Later Iron Age in Zambia
Related to Zimbabwe's Leopard's Kopje culture is the Kalomo culture of Zambia. This culture is represented by a group of settlements found in the area roughly bounded by Mosi-o-Tunya, the Gwembe valley and Bulozi, with the areas around modern towns of Kalomo and Choma forming the centre of the settlement. Like their Zimbabwean contemporaries, the Kalomo peoples lived in large communities. While the peoples of Leopard Kopje's II and III built their homes among rocky hills, those of Kalomo built theirs on mounds which were abandoned from time to time and re-occupied.

The early phase of Kalomo is represented by the Kalundu and the Gundu mounds. Isamu Pati seems to have been occupied a little later. The pottery at Kalundu was well decorated and it consisted of pots and spherical bowls. The pottery at Isamu Pati is even better in quality. Here globular vessels, perhaps for containing water, milk and beer, have been found. The people of Isamu Pati owned cattle and it seems that their huts were built around a central cattle enclosure or kraal. They also grew crops because remains of seeds have been found. It would appear, however, that wooden tools were more commonly used than iron in land cultivation.

Another culture developed and flourished much later on the Toka Plateau at Kangila not far from the modern town of Mazabuka. Kangila seems to

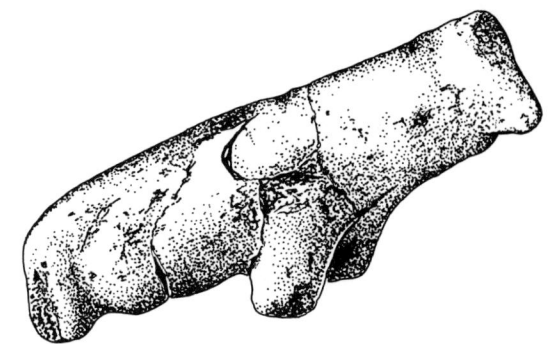

Clay model of an ox from Kangila near Mazabuka

have been predominantly pastoral and this has led some people to think that the people of the Later Iron Age might be the ancestors of the cattle-keeping Tonga of southern Zambia. The pottery found at Kangila tends to support this. The pottery is bag-shaped and mostly undecorated. The Kangila bowls are shallow with an incised motif on the shoulders resembling Tonga pottery found in the Kafue Basin.

Later Iron Age settlements have also been found at Basanga and at Mwanamapa in the Namwala district; also at Sebanzi hill, on the edge of the Kafue flats. Some of these settlements were occupied up to as recently as the eighteenth century, although most of them belong to earlier periods in the eleventh to thirteenth centuries.

Later Iron Age in Malawi
Later Iron Age settlements have also been found in Malawi. One of the best known of these was found at Mwamasapa, in the Karonga district. Here remains of pole and mud huts, pottery, iron objects, glass beads and remains of grain seeds were found. The pottery was different from any found in Malawi. It was thin, gourd-shaped and with a long neck.

Pieces of pottery believed to be of Ngonde origin have been found at Mbande hill. Along with this ware were also found a piece of blue and white porcelain, and glass beads similar to those found at some Leopard's Kopje sites in Zimbabwe. At Kaperi hill in the southern region of Malawi a pole and mud structure, perhaps a hut, was found together with pieces of pottery.

2 Iron Age trade in Central Africa

The system of exchange between peoples of different areas within the same region is known as *local* or *regional trade*. Grain, salt, game meat, fish, iron ore, hoe and axe heads, baskets and pots were exchanged and carried from one part of Central Africa to another, and between Central Africa and other regions of Africa, throughout the Early and the Later Iron Ages. This exchange was arranged because such items were not necessarily found in the same amounts throughout the region. For example it is known that salt and iron ore were not evenly spread in Central Africa; there were areas that did not have these and which had to depend on their neighbours for them. In time a number of exchange or trade centres, developed in some areas throughout Central Africa. Archaeologists have found and investigated some of these Iron Age markets, especially in Zambia, Zimbabwe and Malawi.

There is also sufficient evidence to show that some Central African trade centres maintained relations with peoples and centres out of the region, especially by way of the east coast of Africa. It is also clear from archaeological evidence that this trade was specialised, i.e. dealing with special goods. This kind of trade is usually known as *external trade, long distance trade*, or *inter-regional trade*. Unlike local trade which involved goods necessary for livelihood, external trade seems to have been predominantly concerned with luxury and ornamental goods. It included items like gold, copper objects and ivory which were exchanged for foreign valuables such as beads, weapons and tools, porcelain and sea shells.

Most Iron Age centres were probably involved in both regional and inter-regional forms of trade. In some cases the need to control foreign trade contributed to the development of large states and the growth of political authority for certain individuals in the areas involved in trade. Evidence of well-established foreign trade relations or contacts has been found at two main centres in Central Africa: Ingombe Ilede in Zambia and Great Zimbabwe in Zimbabwe, both of which seem to have conducted their external trade through the east coastal trading city states.

Ingombe Ilede

Not only did regional and external trade help in distributing goods and food to areas which did not produce them, it also brought into contact areas far apart. For instance, fragments of copper wire have been found at Dambwa not far from Livingstone. Livingstone is not a copper-producing area and thus it is possible that this copper had come from the Kafue area in Zambia, or even from Western Zimbabwe's Gwaai district. Both these areas are very far away from the Dambwa area. This is a clear demonstration of the far-reaching nature of Central Africa's Iron Age trading relations.

Until about the eleventh century Iron Age Zambia does not seem to have had any external trade contacts. The main item of regional trade was iron ore. Ivory was to become just as important later, possibly because of an increased demand for it in India and China. Merchants from the East, especially from India, came to Africa in search of African products and they brought with them goods from their own parts of the world which found their way into the African interior. At Ingombe Ilede, on the north bank of the Zambezi not far from Kariba, quantities of foreign goods have been recovered from graves. This is also true of Isamu Pati which we have already mentioned. Cowrie shells, glass beads and necklaces have been found at both these sites.

Ingombe Ilede is probably the richest burial place not only in Zambia but in Central Africa as a whole. It probably started as a local trade centre but later developed into an important market place for foreign trade as well. This latter development is usually attributed to Ingombe Ilede's relations with Mashonaland in Zimbabwe. Some historians have even suggested that when Ingombe Ilede was reoccupied during the fourteenth and fifteenth centuries it was functioning as an outpost of the Zimbabwean trade. Iron hoe-heads, tongs, cotton cloth, cowrie shells and copper objects were among the things found in some of the graves. They suggest that copper came from across the Zambezi in the Lomagundi district of Zimbabwe. Since Ingombe Ilede exercised control over the salt pans in the Lusitu river valley it was in a position to use salt to buy ivory and slaves from neighbouring areas. It was these slaves and ivory which the people of Ingombe Ilede used in order to buy foreign goods from merchants who came up the Zambezi valley about twice every year. A large baked mud floor found at Ingombe Ilede seems to confirm that regular markets were held there.

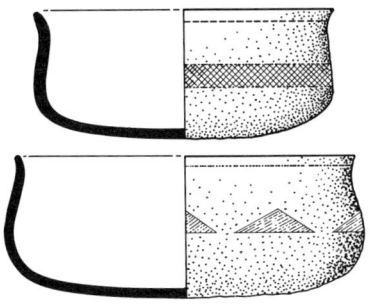

Bowls from Ingombe Ilede with comb-stamping on the sides

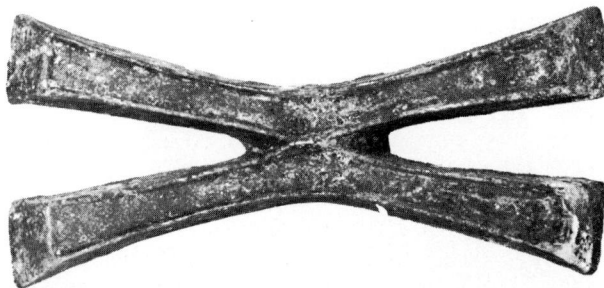

Copper cross ingot such as found in Ingombe Ilede graves

Very richly decorated skeletons have been unearthed and it has been suggested that they may have been those of chiefs. One of them was brilliantly dressed, with red, yellow and blue beads made of gold and glass round his waist and neck. His cloth was made of cotton and bark-cloth. He also wore bracelets made of copper and gold and had two wooden amulets of Islamic origin – possibly from the east coast of Africa. The man was buried with a variety of copper-working tools at his side. These included hammers, gauges and tongs. There were also bales of copper wire which might have been used in the manufacture of bracelets.

In other graves were copper crosses, ceremonial gongs, hoes, beautiful bowls and pots, needles, shells and beads. If these rich graves were those of chiefs then these chiefs must have also been middlemen in the trade with the Swahili traders from the coast. Although it is likely that cotton was grown at Ingombe Ilede, there is no evidence that the people of Ingombe Ilede knew how to spin. This is also the case throughout the rest of Central Africa before the twelfth century AD.

Ingombe Ilede was finally abandoned in the sixteenth century, although trade in the area continued. Thus, the Portuguese traveller, Fernandes was to speak of the 'Kingdom of Mobara' in 1514, which seems to have been a reference to the Tonga people of the Zambezi. According to him the people of Mobara traded copper ingots for Shona goods.

Great Zimbabwe

The Shona centre of Great Zimbabwe flourished because of favourable conditions found in the area. Agriculture and cattle-keeping were successfully carried out in many parts of Zimbabwe, and especially on the high veld. There was enough mineral wealth in the form of gold, iron ore and copper. Ivory too was easily obtainable. A great part of southern Central Africa was easily accessible to international trade through the east coast. Although we are not certain about when and how Zimbabwe's external trade began, we know that by the eleventh century there was in Zimbabwe a powerful and organised trading society founded by the Shona ancestors. Even at some Early Iron Age settlements such as Mabveni, Gokomere and Ziwa evidence of external trade has been found. The greatest source of Iron Age trade in Zimbabwe was the ancient city of Great Zimbabwe near the modern town of Masvingo.

This great centre is now known as the Zimbabwe Ruins because its founders, ancestors of some of the present Shona people, abandoned it about 500 years ago. Its stone buildings and its great walls have been destroyed although a great part of the city is still in a remarkable condition. Today Great Zimbabwe is uninhabited. It is preserved as a valuable cultural centre and a tourist attraction. Every year hundreds and hundreds of both local and foreign tourists go to see and admire what has certainly been the finest and highest achievement of Shona civilisation.

Great Zimbabwe covered over 60 acres of land and consisted of two complexes of dry stone buildings (the builders used no mortar). The two complexes have been named (by the Europeans) the 'Acropolis' and the 'Temple' respectively. The

An aerial view of Great Zimbabwe

Acropolis is made up of a number of enclosures or small buildings and the Temple consists of a large number of stone buildings most of which are surrounded by a stone wall 32 feet high and 17 feet thick. When the country of the Shona was invaded and occupied by the British towards the end of the nineteenth century some of the enclosures were named after early white visitors to the ancient Shona settlement. By far the most impressive part of the ruins is the 'Conical Tower', measuring 30 feet high and 18 feet in diameter.

In early accounts of Great Zimbabwe by European writers the establishment of the city of Zimbabwe and the development of the civilisation associated with it, were attributed to non-Africans. These writers have suggested such people as the Phoenicians, Jews, or even some unknown and forgotten whites were responsible for the city. However the work of historians, archaeologists, and Shona traditions and, of course, sixteenth century Portuguese records have now shown clearly that Shona ancestors built Great Zimbabwe. Great Zimbabwe was in fact one of many such stone towns and cities of the Shona Iron Age, although it was the largest and the most spectacular of them.

The name Zimbabwe comes from the Shona *dzimba dzamabwe*, meaning stone buildings. It appears that in time the name Zimbabwe assumed a special and restricted meaning, which was the chief's or the king's place or centre. Great Zimbabwe was therefore the king's dwelling place. It is also possible that other *dzimba dzamabwe* such as, for example, Chisvingo, Nhunguza, Nhava ya Tumbare, Danangombe, Nalatale etc. were chiefs' or kings' dwellings.

There had been an Early Iron Age Settlement at Great Zimbabwe's site before the establishment of the stone buildings. It seems that this earlier settlement flourished on the hill top – on the Acropolis – during the third and fourth centuries AD. It was then abandoned for almost 600 years to be re-occupied sometime around the eleventh century AD. But it was not until about the end of the twelfth or early thirteenth century that stones were used to build houses. The greatest period of stone building at Great Zimbabwe was during the fourteenth and fifteenth centuries. It was also at this same time that the gold trade was being extensively developed.

Great Zimbabwe and trade

One of the most assorted finds of Iron Age trade goods in the Central African interior was made at Great Zimbabwe in 1903. The goods, which included various local and imported items, were found buried in a corner of one of the enclosures. Some of the goods were dated to the thirteenth and fourteenth centuries. Among these goods were Persian bowls, Chinese dishes, Near-Eastern glass of the 13th and 14th centuries, an iron spoon, an iron lamp-holder, copper chains, copper rings and a copper box.

It has been suggested that these foreign goods may have been brought to Zimbabwe by a trader or traders, and that since they could not be used for daily purposes in the house, they could have been brought as presents or gifts for Great Zimbabwe chiefs to help create good trade relations. There were, however, other goods which were undoubtedly for trade. These included a variety of glass beads (yellow, green and blue in colour), brass wire, sea shells, iron wire, axe and hoe heads and chisels. Local goods or objects included ivory, iron gongs, gold wire and beads, soapstone dishes and other things too. This list of trade goods shows that not only did the people of Great Zimbabwe have trade contacts with such areas as China, India, the Middle East and the Near East, but also that their African trade contacts were just as wide. For example, the

The 'Conical Tower', part of the fortification system at Great Zimbabwe. Note that no mortar is used in the building

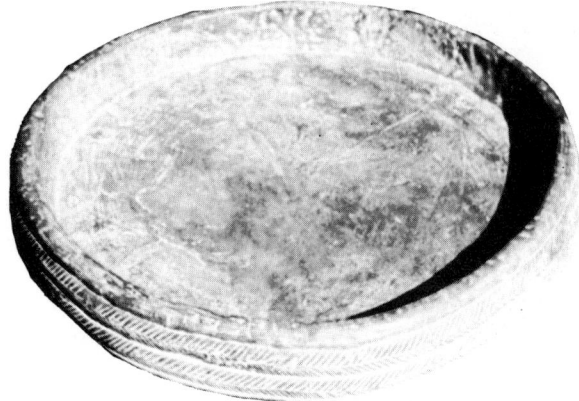

Soapstone dish of the Zimbabwe culture

iron gongs were African in origin but were certainly not made in Zimbabwe. Most likely they were West African. They have also been found in one or two Ingombe Ilede graves. This is not surprising as Ingombe Ilede and Great Zimbabwe had trade contacts during the Later Iron Age period. Copper objects identifiable with Ingombe Ilede have also been found at other Zimbabwean sites such as Chamnungwa, away from Great Zimbabwe. It would appear, therefore, that the people of Great Zimbabwe were involved in both the regional and the inter-regional types of trade.

Great Zimbabwe's rise to prominence was not limited to the economic sphere. In addition to trade goods other articles were also recovered some of which were clearly ornamental. They included soapstone birds sitting on decorated monoliths and various soapstone figurines and figures. Seven or eight soapstone birds have been found at Great

Soapstone bird (the fish-eagle) found at Great Zimbabwe and used to interpret the voice of Shiri ya Mirari

Zimbabwe only and nowhere else in Central Africa or in any part of Zimbabwe. They have not been identified with any known birds: perhaps the person who carved them did not intend to depict any specific birds.

It has, however, been speculated that the above carvings, including the mysterious soapstone birds, were Shona religious symbols. The birds are thought to have played an important role in the religion of the Shona ancestors. It has been suggested that Shona priests at Great Zimbabwe used the soapstone birds to interpret the voice of *Shiri ya Mwari, Hungwe Shirichena*, bird of bright plumage. Shiri ya Mwari or God's Bird, has been identified as the fish-eagle, which probably used to be common in the area around Great Zimbabwe. If this suggestion is correct, Great Zimbabwe may have been a cultural centre of great religious importance – possibly the spiritual headquarters of the Shona ancestors.

Great Zimbabwe might have been important for other reasons besides being a cultural and religious centre. It may have been a military centre although nothing about its great walls suggests this. As the control centre of Shona trade, the ancient city was well-placed. Great Zimbabwe lay on the edge of the major gold-producing areas of south-western Zimbabwe or Matabeleland and on the shortest and most direct line between them and the east coast. It is possible that a combination of religious and economic factors made a great contribution towards political and administrative centralisation by early Shona rulers. The rulers were backed by economic interests and religious institutions both situated in Great Zimbabwe between centres of production to the west and marketing to the coast on the east.

At the height of its glory and greatness, Great Zimbabwe must have been very rich. The art of weaving was known and some people at Zimbabwe wore locally woven cloth. It is also possible that contact with the Swahili people from the east coast led to the acquisition of other skills. A great deal of improvement on the stone buildings and walls was made, especially during the late fourteenth and early fifteenth centuries. Regularly coursed walls were built and this period also saw the building of the 'Conical Tower' and the outer walls.

Decline and abandonment of Great Zimbabwe

Peace and stability were necessary for the achievement of the vast material progress at Great Zimbabwe. Until most of the Zimbabwe-type ruins which are scattered in the country are fully investigated we shall not be in a position to judge how widespread this peace was. We shall also not be able to say whether most people of Zimbabwe or only a small minority benefited from this prosperity. But it is clear that the period of peace and prosperity at Great Zimbabwe was followed by decline and ultimate abandonment of the stone-city. Shona traditions attribute this abandonment to a severe shortage of salt. Salt must have been an important item of trade in Zimbabwe. However severe the shortage, it alone could not have led to the abandonment of Great Zimbabwe. It has been suggested that the salt shortage mentioned by Shona traditions may indicate a general shortage in food supplies, pastures, fuel and other resources not only at Great Zimbabwe but in the city's immediate neighbourhood as well. This general shortage may have disrupted people's way of life and trade.

The general reduction of natural resources in the area must have been a gradual process which reached dangerous levels towards the middle of the fifteenth century. At that time the ruler of the land decided to move in search of better areas. Shona traditions identify this man as the Mbire ruler Mutota who, says tradition, led his people to the Dande area in the north of Great Zimbabwe. A new

Zimbabwe (or even Zimbabwes) may have been built although it never achieved Great Zimbabwe's great fame and greatness. It has been suggested that the Ruanga and the Nhunguza ruins found in the general area to which Mutota is said to have moved could have been built at that time. There are also several other smaller ruins in the area.

The Dande area in the Zambezi Valley was rich in natural resources including salt, ivory and grazing. It was also well placed for trade as it lay in the region between Ingombe Ilede and the Swahili trade centres at Tete and Sena. Dande stood on the edge of the Mazoe valley, a major tributary of the Zambezi River linking the Zimbabwean goldfields and heartland with the Lower Zambezi trading settlements. The Mwene Mutapa empire, established after the move to the Dande area, later developed this important trade route to full capacity. The Portuguese also later established their trading posts in the area at Dambarare, Bocuto, Massapa and Ruwanze or Luanze on the upper Mazoe.

By the late fifteenth century Great Zimbabwe had been completely stripped of its wealth, trade, political importance and cultural significance. According to tradition, political control in the area had passed to Togwa, one of Mutota's dependents in charge of the Mbire province. Togwa was later reduced in power by another dependent, Changa, a Rozvi in charge of the Guruhuswa province to the west and south of Great Zimbabwe. The Changa house later founded a completely new Shona dynasty – the *Changamire* dynasty closely associated with the founding of the Changamire empire which will be discussed later. However, with the establishment of the Changamire rule in the south, Great Zimbabwe's links with the Mwene Mutapa in the north were gradually severed. The Rozvi rulers of the Changamire state did not live at Great Zimbabwe – they built their own less spectacular stone centres or *madzimbabwe* in the western part of the new empire. It is possible though that Great Zimbabwe functioned for some time as a religious centre.

PART II
The Growth of States in Central Africa

3 Luba-Lunda states under Songye chiefs: 1200–1400

By the eleventh century AD most of Central Africa had been populated by various peoples among whom were metal-using crop cultivators and cattle-keepers. These were the ancestors of modern Bantu-speaking peoples of Central Africa. They settled in small village communities under village leaders or chiefs. It is clear that the villages were far apart and usually separated by large stretches of land roamed by wild animals. Probably because of this separation each of the communities developed its own way of life, its own peculiar customs, religious beliefs and system and, in some cases its own dialect too. Such differences should not, however, be exaggerated as there were more similarities than differences and many contacts existed between the various communities. For example, there were systems of exchanging goods and skills, as well as intermarriage.

The period stretching from about 1000 AD to about the sixteenth century witnessed gradual but very fundamental changes among the peoples of Central Africa. Some villages were developing into larger political units deserving to be called chiefdoms, kingdoms and in some cases even empires. Factors and forces responsible for the formation of larger states in the region are not altogether clear. Historians can only speculate about them. Certain features seem to be characteristic of this period of the history of Central Africa. It was the time of the rise and decline of large Bantu-speaking states, and when population movement on a large scale led to the formation of states by leaders of warrior groups.

The process of state formation probably began earlier than the eleventh century, reaching a very high level in the eighteenth and nineteenth centuries. It is important to point out that the process was entirely internal and independent of any significant outside influences.

The second characteristic feature of Central African history during that period were the striking similarities as well as differences between the social, political, religious and economic systems of the various societies. Thirdly, there seems to have been a great deal of surplus food production among the various peoples. Not only did this encourage a system of internal and external exchange already discussed, it created an opportunity for certain ambitious individuals to exert control over larger areas. As communities became larger numerically, and as more people became involved in a greater variety of economic activities, more effective systems of governing communities were required to replace family or village heads. Men of greater power and authority rose to prominence and in most cases these men were respected and even feared as holders of special spiritual or religious powers.

The following chapters will look at specific cases in the development of large state systems in Central Africa.

The Congo savannah land is a spacious country sufficiently watered by its many rivers. This land, especially the eastern part including the Shaba or

Katanga area, has been occupied by food-producing communities for nearly 2000 years. Some authorities think that the Congo grasslands were one of the earliest homes of many Bantu-speaking peoples of Central Africa. It is thought that the idea of governing through chiefs possibly had its origins in this area as early as the eighth century or even earlier. Certainly by the eighth century the peoples living in the Shaba region were living under chiefs and by the thirteenth century the states had become even larger. It is possible that the early chiefs made their impact as organisers of trade in copper and ivory. Long-distance trade had already begun in the area as is demonstrated by the presence of copper and iron objects, belts, pins and other items recovered at an archaeological site near Lake Kisale (see page 9).

By AD 1300 there were well-established chieftainships in three parts of the Shaba area: around Lake Kisale and Upemba; near Kisangani; and in the wooded country to the north-east where the Bolia people lived. Population pressure and the resultant shortage of farming land and pastures had already caused fights between the region's chiefs. Such a situation encouraged the development of larger political units, with military leaders emerging and organising larger defensive chieftainships, especially in the eastern grasslands. The most important of these military chieftainships was Luba.

The origins of Luba are not clear. What is known is that the chieftainship developed among the farming and hunting communities of the Lake Kisale area. Since there are no written records to tell us what exactly happened, we rely on what the people of the area say, that is oral traditions.

The Katanga cross

According to one such tradition, a group of people known as Songye who came from the north settled on the Lubilasha river. They were led by a man whose official title was the *Kongolo*. According to the tradition, the first Kongolo married the woman-ruler or queen of the Kalundwe. The children of the marriage inherited from both their mother's and their father's sides. The Songye chiefs later sent raiding and conquering bands to the east in search of salt and palm oil. As time went by the name of the state changed from Kalundwe to Luba, and Luba included many conquered areas that had been incorporated. The capital of the larger Luba state was moved to Muibele near Lake Boya. More conquests were organised from Muibele until the Luba state became a large kingdom. It included the people living between the Lubilashi and the Lualaba.

The Songye rulers of Luba became more powerful than any of their Kalundwe predecessors and they controlled a larger area than the Kalundwe chiefs had ever ruled. In the Luba state the Kongolo, or king, alone had the final word on matters concerning warfare, and he alone controlled long-distance or external trade. He was assisted in carrying out his work by a number of officials.

The Songye rulers governed Luba until some time around the fifteenth century when they lost their power in a way similar to how they had gained it two centuries earlier. In the fifteenth century a more powerful group, the Kunda, also from the north, arrived in the area and settled east of Lake Kisale. It is not known exactly how the Kunda replaced the Songye as rulers of Luba. According to local traditions these newcomers under their chief, Mbili Kiluhe, arrived from across the Lualaba and were well received by the reigning Kongolo, Mwana. Tradition also relates how Mwana gave Mbili Kiluhe two of his sisters to marry. One of the sisters bore Mbili Kiluhe a son, Kala Ilunga. Kala Ilunga grew up among his mother's people and became a very able fighter who won many major battles and wars for the Kongolo. Later he claimed the Luba kingdom from the Kongolo arguing that he was entitled to it by matrilineal descent (i.e. through his mother). The Kongolo would not recognise this claim and, instead, he tried to have Kala Ilunga killed. Kala Ilunga however managed to escape across the Lualaba. He later came back with a stronger army and defeated his uncle, Kamwana, whom he killed. Ilunga then declared himself king of Luba and thus began the Kunda dynasty. The Kunda monarchy was to rule Luba until the nineteenth century.

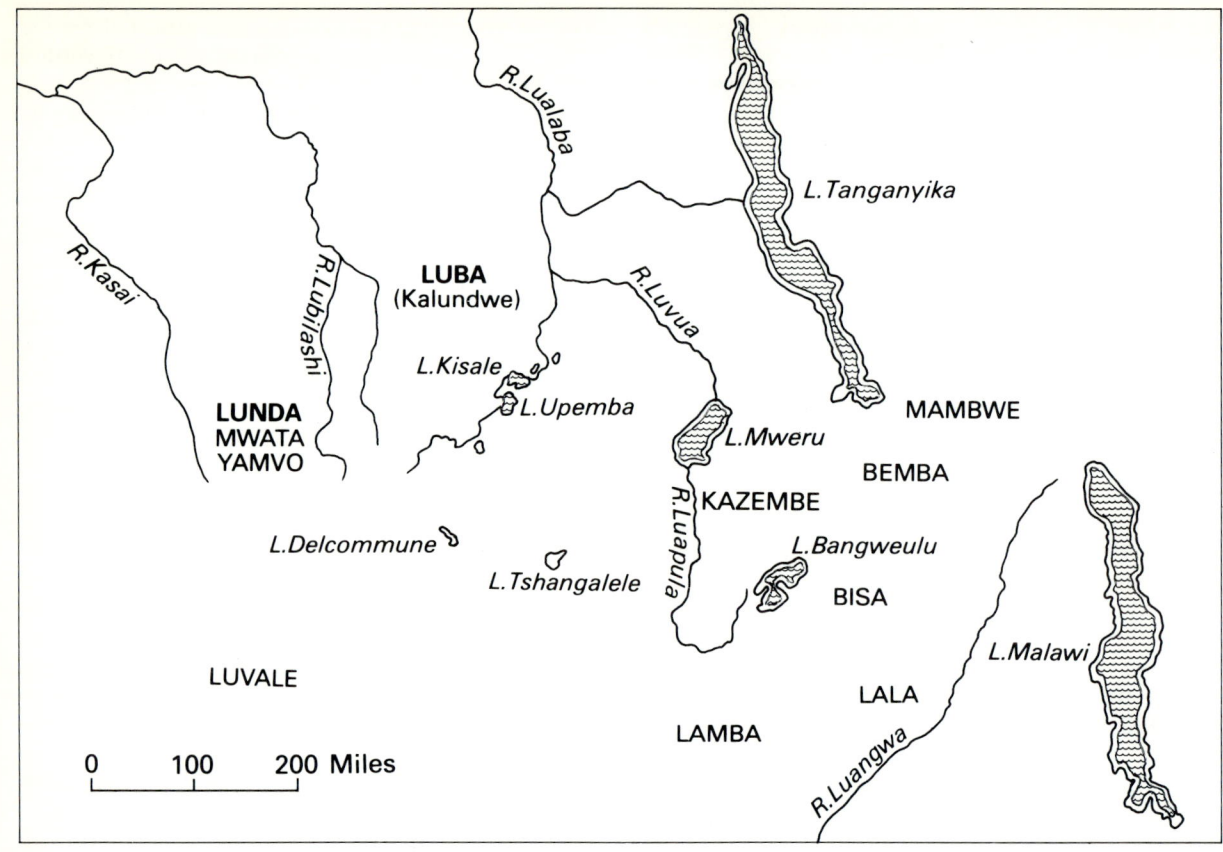

The Luba-Lunda peoples

Luba under Kunda rule (fifteenth–nineteenth centuries)

The Kunda continued territorial conquest and brought more people into the Luba kingdom, including peoples to the west of Lake Kisale. Eventually the Kunda rulers became even more powerful than any of their predecessors, Kalundwe or Songye. They were more successful especially in organising trade and in their system of collecting tribute from their subjects. Under Kala Ilunga and his successors Luba enjoyed a great deal of expansion. The Kunda did not build an empire; they built a kingdom, bringing the conquered peoples under their own rule as much as possible.

It is thought that the process of state-building in Luba reached a very high degree during the Kunda period. Kala Ilunga and his successors tried to maintain a centralised administration in Luba. Thus the king presided over a very strong government because he was himself a powerful ruler. He assumed a new traditional title and was no longer known as Kongolo but as the *Mulopwe*. Under Kunda rule, the Mulopwe alone had the final word on matters of war, and he controlled external trade. The Mulopwe was also a religious figure with sacred spears and was associated with special religious ceremonies. He ate and drank alone in a secret place. His food was cooked on fires made by rubbing together a pair of sacred fire sticks.

The Mulopwe had many officials and chiefs to help him in running his government, who were officially called *balopwe* (the plural of mulopwe). They lived at the king's court rather like government ministers and civil servants in a modern government. They were in charge of various departments and sections of the Mulopwe's administration. The main department was the army and the police, looking after order and peace as well as defending the kingdom from any external forces. This department was headed by a mulopwe known as the *twite*. There was a special department looking after the Mulopwe's sacred spears and such matters as pertaining to the king's sacred or spiritual being. The mulopwe heading this department was the *inabanza*. The third important department acted as the king's mouthpiece. This was the responsibility of the *sungu*, who passed the king's orders, laws and decrees to the people. Then there was a special mulopwe, the *nsikala*, ready to act for the king if the latter was, for any reason, unable to do his work; or to act as king after the death of the king and until a new king was put on the throne. This provision of the Kunda constitution was probably made in order to minimise the disruption of government after the death of the king, and also to ensure the continuation of government processes in the event of any succession dispute.

There were, of course, other departments which were similarly filled up by the king's officers. All the balopwe or chiefs were, and had to be, related to the king. In this way political power was kept in the hands of a small group of families. There was a clear chain of command from the lesser chiefs to the village headmen. Provincial rulers were above district chiefs from whom they demanded tribute on behalf of the Mulopwe.

When the king or Mulopwe died he was buried in a dry river bed with some of his wives and servants. His successor had to build his own new capital and the old capital was left in the charge of a priestess, becoming a special religious centre or shrine. All the balopwe or chiefs serving under the deceased king were required to resign their positions formally so that the new head of state could appoint his own chiefs and high officials. Naturally this usually led to dissatisfaction among officials and some old chiefs were reluctant to give up their positions. Sometimes the ambitions of young men who had hoped to become chiefs were not satisfied. Some of these discontented elements left the kingdom in disgust, taking with them their supporters to look for new areas where they could establish their authority. One such man was Kibinda Ilunga, the man credited with the founding of the Lunda kingdom.

The Lunda kingdom

One of the most important results of Luba state-formation was the process of westward expansion, which was directly or indirectly responsible for the emergence of the Lunda state. This was some time around the middle of the sixteenth century, during what is generally known as the second Luba kingdom. According to one tradition, Kibinda Ilunga (possibly a brother of the ruling Luba Mulopwe, Ilunga Walefu) left Luba at the head of a strong military band. He had been frustrated in his ambitions to be king. He and his people travelled westward until they finally settled on the banks of the Kasai river among the Lunda people. At that time the Lunda were subsistance farmers living in small communities or villages. They made iron tools and pots, and were good fishermen too.

Although there was no political centralisation and each village was independent of its neighbours, there was however a kind of senior chief among the various chiefs. He wore a special copper bracelet, a *lukano*, which was decorated with human nerves and elephant sinews. His role was not political but rather ceremonial. According to tradition, when Kibinda Ilunga arrived in the Lunda area the senior chief was a woman, Lueji. It is not clear what happened when Kibinda arrived. It would appear that he married Lueji and discovered later that his wife could not bear him children. Accordingly he married another woman, Kamonga, who bore him a son – Lusengi. Lusengi later became ruler of his mother's people and introduced measures for the creation of a larger kingdom under a central government. Lusengi was succeeded by his own son, Naweji, who conquered more Lunda people and brought them under his rule. Naweji and his successors assumed a new official title, being known as *Mwata Yamvo*, meaning lord of the viper, or master of wealth.

Naweji, who must have come to the throne round

A Luba mask

about 1600, is remembered as *Mwata Yamvo I* and it was he who laid down the foundations of what later developed into an empire. By 1600 or immediately after that date the Lunda state had brought under its rule many chiefdoms in the area. Many neighbouring non-Lunda areas were also conquered although no doubt some of them voluntarily put themselves under the Mwata Yamvo. Perhaps it should be noted that although in some ways the Mwata Yamvo state was similar to that of Luba, there were also differences between them. The Mwata Yamvo had a capital where government officials who assisted him resided, just as the Luba king's balopwe, at the Luba capital. The Lunda capital was at Mussumba. The Mwata Yamvo, just like the Kongolo or the Mulopwe, had no standing army but a small police force to keep order and to assist the chiefs in the collecting of tributes. While the Luba rulers seem to have tried to build something like a kingdom, Mwata Yamvo's state was more like an empire. All conquered chiefs, Lunda and non-Lunda, were given new titles and became the Mwata Yamvo's chiefs. Villages were grouped into administrative districts each under an official known as the *kilolo*. Over the kilolo was a commissioner called the *yikeazy*. This officer was usually appointed to take charge of kilolos whom the Mwata Yamvo did not trust. As in the Luba state, all the people appointed to high positions had to be the king's relatives. In this arrangement, known as the system of 'positional succession', it was pretended that the successor actually became his predecessor by taking his name, title, house and family possessions.

Another important characteristic of the Lunda state was its tendency towards conquest and expansion. No doubt this was motivated by a desire on the part of the Mwata Yamvos to control large areas for their ever-growing population. Trade was yet another reason behind expansion. The Portuguese on the west coast provided a sure market for Lunda ivory, copper and slaves. There was a market on the East African coast as well. Trade brought beads, spirits, clothes and firearms to Mwata Yamvo's land. The larger the territory under the Mwata Yamvo's control the better the trading, because chiefs in the conquered areas were required to pay tribute in the form of ivory, copper, slaves, salt and labour. These goods were important in the Mwata Yamvo's trade with the Portuguese and with the Swahili ports on the east coast.

There is no doubt that some chiefs grew tired of paying tribute to Mwata Yamvo and they decided to emigrate to distant places; to the west, east and south. Oral tradition refers to some of Lueji's brothers who left their land because they would not accept what they regarded as Luba domination when Kibinda Ilunga and his immediate successor established their dynasty among the Lunda people. These early emigrants went in search of new lands. One of Lueji's 'brothers' was Kinguri who is said to have led his band of followers into Angola. It is said that he and his people later settled in that land where they became known as the Imbangala. Their leader, Kinguri, was killed in a battle with the Mbundu, but under his nephew, Kasanji, they reached the west coast. Some time between 1612 and 1630 they returned to the east in search of fertile land. They finally settled near the Kwango river where they established a kingdom called Kasanje.

Yet another of Lueji's 'brothers' also led his followers southwards during the same period. The band split into several small groups of which the Luvale and the Chokwe are most well known. These groups brought Lunda ideas of centralised chieftainship to Zambia where they settled.

4 Luba-Lunda spread into Zambia

The spread and migration of Luba and Lunda elements into Zambia during the seventeenth and eighteenth centuries brought to that country Luba-Lunda systems of government. The migrants were shifting crop cultivators in search of new farming lands. The sparsely populated Zambian territory was ideal for Luba-Lunda settlement. In many areas there were still some Stone Age societies and very few Bantu-speaking communities when the Luba-Lunda migrants arrived. Among the few Bantu-speaking communities were the Tonga in the southern province of Zambia; the Ila and the Sala in the north; the Totela occupying the southern part of the Western Province; the Nkoya, Mbelwa and Lukolwe in the west and north-west; the Nsenga and related groups in the central, eastern and northern provinces; and the Fipa, Sekumu and Bwile in the northern and Luapula provinces. All these groups were matrilineal, except the Lungu, Mambwe and the Namwanga who had come from East Africa.

A number of factors were behind Luba and Lunda migration into Zambia during the seventeenth and eighteenth centuries, and these were mainly economic, political and social. In the Shaba area (Katanga) home of both the Luba and the Lunda, the population was still growing fast, causing shortages of arable and pastureland. The situation seems to have become more critical as a result of wider acceptance of new agricultural crops brought by the Portuguese on the west coast. The new crops included maize, groundnuts, cassava, and others. By the seventeenth century most Katanga cultivators had accepted and were successfully growing these crops in their fields. Either because they had to be grown on more fertile land, or because they exhausted the soil more quickly than traditional crops, they created a great deal of pressure on available land.

Land pressure was an economic problem which in turn created social hardships and political problems for Luba-Lunda rulers and their states. Some people felt that the solution lay in emigrating to other areas where opportunities might be better. Other people left their areas for reasons which were purely political. This was true of conquered chiefs who moved to Zambia where they thought they might be able to maintain their political independence. No doubt some chiefs and their people emigrated in order to escape being punished by Luba-Lunda rulers after unsuccessful rebellions. There were many reasons for emigrations. We have, for instance, referred earlier to a number of bands who left their homelands after they had lost in succession disputes. It has also been suggested that a lot of migrants might have left because they were suspected of being witches. Some like the Bemba and the Bisa left after family quarrels. The slave trade also forced many people to flee their original homes in the Shaba or Katanga area.

Many migrants were not chiefs in their original home areas. But a good number became chiefs after settling in Zambia. This was true of the Senga, for instance, who became chiefs over the Tumbuka in the Lundazi area although they had been Luba commoners in their own land. As no centralised chieftainship had existed among the Tumbuka it was the Senga who introduced it from the Shaba area.

The various migrant groups that settled in Zambia founded different types of political states. But these new states generally followed the Luba-Lunda pattern already discussed in the last chapter. In each of the new states there was a central ruler-chief or king ruling a particular territory, although the borders of that area were not always clearly defined. The chief or king possessed both political and religious powers in his area. Below him were lesser rulers or chiefs and headmen from whom he collected annual tribute in grain, meat, fish, iron tools and weapons, copper, pots, baskets, mats, ivory, salt and slaves. In return the king provided his people with judicial, religious and military services.

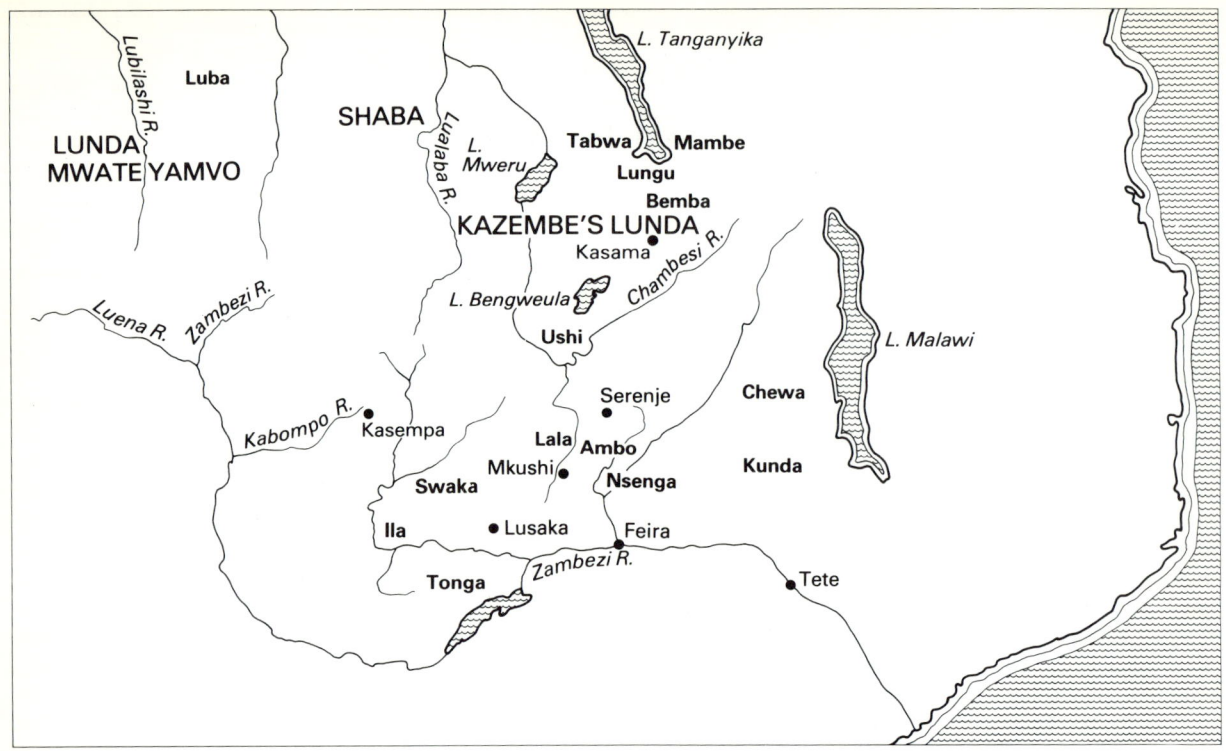

Expansion of the Luba-Lunda into Zambia

To a great extent therefore the Zambian system of chieftainship depended on trade. The ruler re-distributed the tribute goods collected from the lesser chiefs and headmen to whatever areas that lacked wealth. In this way he assisted in building up local trade in the various parts of his kingdom. This local trade was eventually linked with external or long-distance trade because goods such as cloth, guns, and beads were re-distributed to lesser chiefs and headmen by the king to ensure their loyalty. When the kingdom was enlarged by peaceful means or by conquest it was usually to increase the volume of trade goods.

Lunda expansion into Zambia

The group of Lunda who left their land in the early 1600s under the leadership of a man called Chinyama finally settled on the Luena river, a tributary of the Zambezi. Here they found and brought under subjection an earlier Bantu-speaking people – the Mbelwa. Most of these people left their country and went to settle in the Nkoya district east of Bulozi. The Lunda settlers founded the Luvale chieftainship under Chinyama and his successors. They increased their territory by conquest. At the height of their power the Luvale chiefs ruled a country which included parts of Zaire and Angola, as well as Zambia's Bulovale, Mwinilunga and Kasempa areas.

The Luvale rulers continued to use Chinyama as their official ruling title but they never built a truly centralised kingdom. Instead many semi-independent chiefs emerged. The Chinyamas' method was to take men from villages that accepted them as over-lords, and then strengthen such political ties through marriage. They also created many smaller chieftainships. Political marriages and especially the Luvale's strong system of family relationships, going back many generations and covering a wide geographical area, encouraged a sense of unity among the Luvale people.

The Luvale were fishermen and therefore they spent most of their time in the Zambezi river valley. Accordingly they were better placed to develop trade contacts with the west. For instance trade relations were developed with the Imbangala to the west. By the eighteenth century they had become very successful slave traders.

The parent-state of Mwata Yamvo was probably at the height of its success and prosperity around the 1680s during the reign of Mwata Yamvo Muteba. He promoted external trade, through which he obtained firearms. Muteba obtained these firearms by selling many slaves. The Mwata Yamvo empire enjoyed a great deal of expansion during this time and ultimately reached Zambia under Muteba and his sons and successors. Ishinde, one of the sons, established a kingdom east of the Zambezi, and to the north-east in the Mwinilunga district and in parts of Angola another of the sons, Kanongesha, set up a chieftainship. Farther to the north and to the east, Musokantanda also set up his own chieftainship in the districts of Solwezi and Kasempa.

Most of the Lunda chiefs who settled in Zambia tended to remain in contact with one another and with the Mwata Yamvo state. Contacts among them and with Mwata Yamvo helped these chiefs in their efforts to be successful traders. They did have many difficulties however in their new areas. Very often the areas were small, remote from trade routes and lacking in natural resources. They also had problems in establishing centralised authority among people who did not know anything about their state system. But some areas had very favourable conditions. This was true of the area in which the kingdom of Kazembe was established.

Kazembe's kingdom

The state of Kazembe was one of the most successful and most important offshoots of the Lunda state of Mwata Yamvo. The Kazembe state was also to become one of the biggest and most important Central African kingdoms in the eighteenth and nineteenth centuries.

Some time about 1680 Mwata Yamvo Muteba sent one of his war lords or generals to conquer areas to the east of his state. The man chosen to lead this important expedition was Mutanda Yembe Yembe. The area to be conquered was in Shaba and was rich in salt, copper and other resources. Yembe Yembe was also instructed to establish control over trade between the new area and the lower Zambezi region. A certain Chinyanta, however, told the Mwata Yamvo that Yembe Yembe was being disloyal to him and was keeping some of the tribute due to the king to himself. Yembe Yembe killed Chinyanta for having made that report to the Mwata Yamvo. But Yembe Yembe was also himself killed by the Mwata Yamvo's army. The king was so grateful to Chinyanta that he rewarded him posthumously by giving Ngonda Bilonda, Chinyanta's son, a special title of *mwata kazembe*. Ngonda Bilonda was also sent to continue the Lunda eastward expansion begun by Mutanda Yembe Yembe. All this happened about 1700.

However Ngonda Bilonda is said to have drowned in the Luapula river while carrying out the mission. He was succeeded by Kanyembo who became Kazembe II. A new state had been founded and by about 1725 Kanyembo was the ruler of a vast kingdom to the east of Lualaba and mainly in the Luapula valley area. Mwata Yamvo gave Kazembe II all the insignia of a Lunda king, including a knife, staff, belt, beads, rings, dress, and a cutting of the *mutaba* tree to be planted at his new capital. Around 1740 Kazembe II defeated the Ushi in the Luapula valley, and then the Chungu of the Mukulu, Chibwe of the Chishinga, and a group of Iron Age fishermen known as the Shila. The Shila had themselves defeated another Iron Age people, the Bwilile, and had then come under the control of the Bemba chiefs Nkuba and Mununga. In about 1760 the mutaba tree was planted at the village of the defeated Shila chief, Katele.

The expansion of Kazembe's Lunda had, by Lunda standards, been fairly rapid. For this there are good historical reasons. Kazembe's Lunda were not just adventurers like so many other Lunda migrants: they were more like an official colonis-

Kazembe as seen by the Portuguese, 1831

ation party, expanding from the established kingdom of Mwata Yamvo, and backed by its political system and trade contacts to the west. They were skilled fighters and had a powerful army, military discipline and Portuguese guns. The people whom Kazembe's Lunda conquered were, on the other hand, militarily weak and politically disorganised.

The Lunda expansion to the east was completed by Kazembe III, Ilunga Lukwesa, who conquered Nsama's Tabwa, some of Mporokoso's Lungu, and Nkuba's Shila near the capital. Nkuba, though a defeated chief, was given an important ritual position in Lunda society. This demonstrates one of the important attractions of Lunda rule: that defeated chiefs could retain their power as owners of land, though at a price. The price was that they had to pay tribute, supply labour to Kazembe, trade only through the Kazembe's capital, and put up with Lunda aristocrats appointed to supervise them, collect tribute from them, distribute presents among them and make sure that their people remained loyal.

Under Kazembe III the kingdom stretched from the borders of Mwata Yamvo on the Lualaba to include southern Shaba (Katanga) as far as the Luapula and beyond into Zambia. It was an area rich in natural resources. From the Luapula and Lake Mweru came fish; from the Luapula came salt. In Shaba (Katanga) the Lamba and Sanga were copper-producers, while on the plateau to the east the Chisinga and Ushi were iron-workers. Kazembe's tribute included iron, copper, salt, slaves, ivory, and food. Trade was well organised and at first Kazembe benefited in that he was remote from the centres of Portuguese and Swahili trade. Kazembe III, however, began making trade contacts with these foreigners. Salt, copper, iron and slaves were all exported. By 1800 Kazembe's capital was the centre of trade routes crossing the continent. To the west these trade routes passed through Mwata Yamvo to Angola; to the east, through Bisa and Yao territories to the Swahili ports of Kilwa and Zanzibar. From the west came guns and woollen goods; from the east, Indian cloth, beads and other manufactures. Kazembe redistributed the cloth and beads, whilst keeping the guns firmly in his own hands.

Luba migration into Zambia

Lunda expansion into Zambia was well organised under recognised leaders. Luba movement, on the other hand, had very little cohesion and was the result of individual efforts. The Luba migrated mainly into the northern, central, copperbelt,

Bwile salt-makers' camp near Puta. Salt was used extensively in trade

Luapula and eastern provinces of Zambia. The Kaonde of the Kasempa district, though a Luba offshoot, came under a Lunda chief. The Lala, Lamba and Ushi chieftainships had their origins in Luba. Kankoma, the Lala chief, established control in the Sereje and Mkushi districts, and from this development grew the Swaka and Ambo peoples. People escaping from Lala control became chiefs among the Soli and other groups in the Lusaka and Feira areas. Similarly the Kunda fleeing from the Ushi kingdom defeated Chewa and Nsenga peoples and set up a number of chieftainships in the Chipata area. Fugitives from the Bemba and Bisa groups similarly established the Shila chieftainship around Lake Mweru and other chieftainships among the Mambwe and the Namwanga in the Isoka and Mbala districts.

Origins of the Bemba

Bemba traditions are not in complete agreement about the origins of the founders of Bemba chieftainships. Some say that the founders were of Luba origins and others say that they were Lunda. A popular view, however, favours Luba origins. According to this view the earliest Bemba chieftainships in the Kasama and Chinsali districts were Chiti Muluba, also known as Mukulu the Great, and Nkole wa Mapembwe. The two leaders were of the crocodile clan – *bena ng'andu*. It is thought that they might have come from a Luba state west of Lake Mweru. They settled on the plateau between the Luangwa and the Luapula, and became chiefs of iron-working peoples such as the Musukwa of Malopwe and Kaleleya. This was probably around 1650. They called their new land Lubemba. Since the inhabitants of the areas were loosely organised, they were too weak to oppose the new settlers.

Compared to the founders of the Kazembe state, the founders of the Bemba chieftainships were at a disadvantage. They were, unlike the Lunda, mere breakaway groups of adventurers starting in small ways. While the Lunda founders of Kazembe relied on Mwata Yamvo's wealth, well tested political and administrative methods, and on the powerful military machinery of Mwata Yamvo, the rulers of Lubemba had to rely on themselves. Another point to mention in comparing the two groups is that while the rulers of Kazembe tried to establish centralisation, the Bemba chiefs did not establish any centralised chieftainships. Instead a number of small independent chieftainships like Chitimukulu, Nkolemfumu, Nkulu and Nkweto were established. Although not a paramount political leader at this stage, Chitimukulu was the most important Bemba leader because he was a religious figure with powers over the whole land or Lubemba. After about 1770 the Chitimukulu's powers began to increase and by the nineteenth century the Chitimukulu was a fairly powerful political authority. But he was not as strong as the Kazembe, since Bemba strength was based more on cooperation between the semi-autonomous chiefs than on a high degree of political centralisation.

Compared with Kazembe's Lunda, the Bemba made fairly slow progress between 1650 and 1800. There were reasons for this: poor environment, a lack of natural resources, a decentralised political system, and a lack of any significant external stimulus. The soil on the plateau was poor, so farming was difficult. In order to cope with the problems of a poor soil, the Bemba learnt the practice of *chitemene* (a form of slash-and-burn agriculture), probably from the Mambwe, but through shortage of water they could support only a small population. The Bemba did not keep a lot of animals, especially cattle, because of the tsetse fly. Only a very small number of goats were reared. Furthermore, there was no iron in Lubemba. The Bemba had to buy tools from the Lungu to the north. There was therefore a shortage of trade goods in the area and the only real means of expansion was through warfare. Warfare was also encouraged by the fact that succession to the Chitimukulu chieftainship was generally decided by civil war.

Having become proficient in warfare, the Bemba began to expand in the nineteenth century. Expansion took place to the north and west at the expense of the Lungu and the Mambwe. New chieftainships were created, the most important being Mwamba and Makasa. The Makasa chieftainship was given to Chitimukulu's son. Since the Bemba were a matrilineal people the son could never become Chitimukulu himself. Other new chieftainships were given to a number of chiefs as rewards for services rendered; possibly a factor tending to make Bamba leaders more enterprising. One of the most enterprising was the Mambwa chief, by the middle of the nineteenth century the most important chief after Chitimukulu. He also waged his own wars of expansion.

In the 1830s the Bemba directed their campaigns against the Bisa to their south. The campaigns were aimed at seizing control of the trade between the Bisa and the Lunda.

Origins of the Bisa
The Bisa occupied the area south of Lubemba. The two groups are said to have been related according to tradition. The founders of the Bisa people belonged to the mushroom clan – *bena ng'ona*, related to the crocodile group or the *bena ng'andu* to which the Bemba leaders belonged. In fact the *bena ng'ona* are said to have broken away from the *bena ng'andu*. They settled in the Chinama area of the Mpika district under their leader, Mwansabamba. Mwansabamba sent his relatives and subordinates out to conquer more lands. As a result of these conquests the Bisa soon had roughly five times as much land as the Bemba, mainly around Lake Bangweulu and on the Lukulu river at the southern edge of the plateau.

The Bisa were soon selling ivory to the Portuguese at Tete. By 1800 they were growing Portuguese crops such as maize, cassava and sweet potatoes. They rapidly became one of the most important trading peoples in Central Africa. For this they were well situated, as they lived near both wooded country and Lake Bangweulu. They also found a powerful trading partner in Kazembe and good trade relations were maintained with the Yao at the southern end of Lake Malawi. By 1800 Bisa traders were in the country of the Chewa. By the mid-nineteenth century they were exporting ivory to the east coast from Lamba country, where they met caravans from Angola. In 1856 the missionary explorer, David Livingstone met them on the middle Zambezi trading ivory for cotton goods from the Portuguese in Mozambique. The English explorer and traveller, Richard Burton, reported in 1860 that the Bisa were well-known in Zanzibar. In the 1880s the Bisa chief, Kambwili, set himself up as a trader at Chiwanda in the Luangwa valley.

Bisa trade, however, differed from that of the Lunda in that it was in the hands of individuals rather than under the control of the chief or king. It was never tied to the chieftainship. Bisa chiefs did not distribute goods in return for tribute as did the Kazembe. In Bisa country there were few goods that could have been used as tribute, and the main chief, Mwansabamba, had little political authority outside his own area, though occasionally tribute was given to him on account of his religious importance. Bisa society, like that of the Bemba, contained a number of semi-autonomous chiefs such as Matipa, Mangulube, Mukungule, and Chibesakunda.

Several groups broke away from the Bisa. The Tambo moved north-east under chief Katyetye, and for many years they were under the influence of Mwenimalali, a Bisa chief at Chinsali. The Senga, another breakaway group, went to live in the Muchinga hills. When the Senga were attacked by the Bemba, they moved farther to the Luangwa valley.

5 The Lozi kingdom

Another important Zambian kingdom was that of the Lozi. The Lozi were previously known as the Luyi or Luyana, meaning people of the river. According to a popular Lozi tradition Mboo, the founder of the Lozi royal house, was born of a union between Mbuyu or Mbuywamwambwa and Nyambe (God) when the latter used to reside in the land of Bulozi. The Lozi or Luyi also claim to be the first inhabitants of Bulozi; that is the 160 kilometre long flood plain of the Zambezi in the western province of Zambia. In other words tradition holds that the Lozi royal family came into being in Bulozi and that the Lozi aristocracy has always lived in that area. The tradition gives the Lozi rulers divine origins which may perhaps obscure their true origins. But for the Lozi rulers this was important as it strengthened their claim to be kings of the Lozi people.

Divine beginnings or not, there is evidence suggesting that Lozi origins lie somewhere in the Shaba or Katanga area – somewhere among the tributaries of the Congo River. They probably travelled along the Kabompo some time soon after 1650 until they finally settled in the western province of Zambia. When the Lozi arrived in Bulozi they were probably a small group under the leadership of Mulambwa. Mulambwa was later succeeded by his daughter, Mbuywamwambwa who, it seems, was forced to give up her position in favour of her own son, Mboo. It was Mboo, therefore, who became the first male ruler of Bulozi and assumed the traditional title of *litunga*, or king.

During Mboo's reign the Lozi expanded their authority to other peoples through the litunga's relatives. Ilishua, for instance, established himself at Mashi with his sons Kaputungu and Mulombwe. Mwanambinyi conquered the Subiya and the Mbukushu. He set up his capital at Imatonga, and his followers became known as the Kwandi. His son, Mulia, made more conquests. Mange, possibly a nephew of Mboo, conquered the Nkoya of the eastern forest and his people became known as the Kwanga. By now both the Mange and Mwanambinyi chieftainships were more or less independent.

Lozi expansion continued under Mboo's successors, but the tendency towards decentralisation was ended. Litunga Ngalama brought the Mange and Mwanambinyi chieftainships back under royal control, and a secessionist movement among the Subiya was also suppressed by the litunga, Ngambela. The Totela, Shanji and Mashi were similarly brought under royal control. By 1800 the Lozi had built one of the most centralised states in pre-colonial Zambia. Many peoples to the west were under direct Lozi control, while others to the south and east were paying tribute to the Lozi king. Tribute generally consisted of cattle, land, or labour on public works projects such as building fish dams.

Lozi economy and growth of the chieftainship
Unlike most of Zambia's people, the Lozi were not shifting cultivators. They moved only during the annual floods, and this move was only from villages in the valley to villages on the surrounding hillsides. The litunga had two capitals – Lealui in the valley and Mongu in the hills. He moved from one to the other in a ceremonial canoe known as the *nalikwanda*.

The valley or the plain was a fairly fertile area because the Zambezi's annual floods covering it brought rich soil. This gave rise to reasonably good harvests to feed a large population. The Lozi grew corn. Later maize was also grown. Maize, according to Lozi tradition, was introduced by Namushi of Nkwenda. The Lozi also grew a relish called *sibuyuyu*, a sort of grass with seeds like rice. They also kept cattle, most of them taken from the Tonga and the Ila. Being remote from the long-distance trade routes, the Lozi nonetheless carried on a great deal of local trade. The valley people sold fish, grain and baskets to the people of the forest, and in return they bought goods made of wood, iron and barkcloth. Trade fairs were held in winter months.

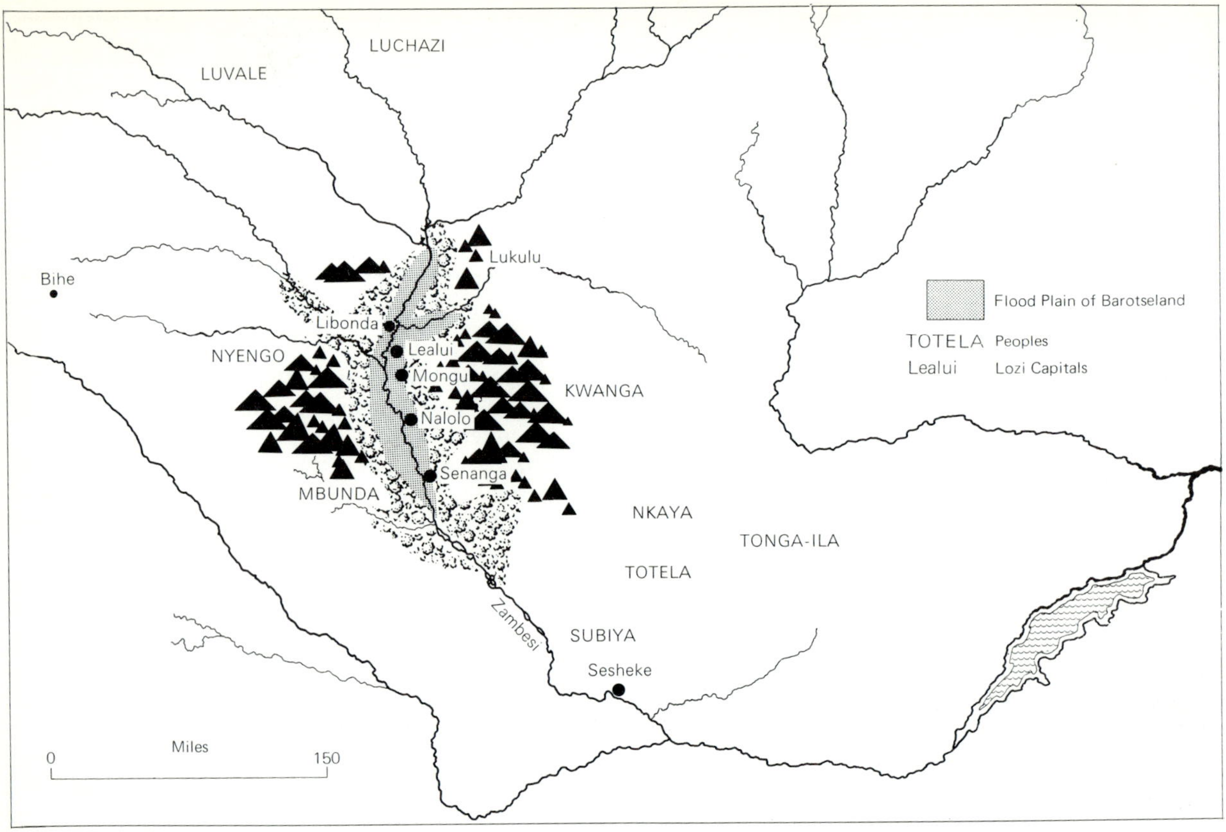

The Lozi Kingdom

Nalikwanda of the Litunga of Barotseland

Lozi political tradition. A councillor instructs headman and his followers on the principle of good rule

It may have been this emphasis on trade that persuaded the litunga to strengthen central control. The Lozi adopted a communications system based on canoes. Administrators could therefore move more easily than in, say, Bemba country. To increase unity between the two main parts of Bulozi, the flood plain and the woodland, the government used a system known as 'groupings'. There were two types of grouping: the sector for administration and justice, and the storehouse for the collection of tribute and the recruitment of communal labour. This had a unifying effect as not only the Lozi, but people from all over the kingdom could take part.

As in other Zambian societies, however, the Lozi chief had religious as well as political powers. It was believed that he ruled with his predecessors' authority. In many ways the dead kings were more important than the living kings. They provided the contact between the litunga and God, Nyambe. In times of famine the litunga consulted the dead kings (his predecessors) who, it was believed, passed on the prayers and requests of the litunga to Nyambe. The people made sacrifices to Nyambe in seeds, cattle, hoes and spears. Nyambe was believed to be all-powerful, and it was because of his relationship to Nyambe that the litunga was thought to have supernatural powers.

The importance of the Queen Mother was a significant similarity between the Lozi and the Luba-Lunda people. The king's sister was also important, as in Luba-Lunda societies. There was a council made up of chiefs and members of the royal family. Below this, in Lozi society, came the lesser chiefs, the rest of the Lozi people, and finally the conquered peoples. The Lozi did not treat the conquered peoples as slaves, nor did they admit them as equals. All sections of the community paid tribute to the chiefs, who therefore led wealthy, comfortable lives.

There were, however, several weaknesses in Lozi society. In the south, there was opposition to the ruling family. A female chief was established there to strengthen royal control, but the opposition remained. There was also friction between the Lozi and the conquered people, and between the people of the valley and those of the woodland.

Litunga Mulambwa 1780–1830

Mulambwa was the tenth and possibly the greatest of the early litungas. His reign saw a number of important developments, including innovations in the economy brought about by the building of the mounds. Mulambwa is also most remembered for his law reforms and the introduction of a legal code binding on the whole Lozi kingdom. His new laws were designed to deal with such matters as thefts, adultery and compensation for men killed in war. It was litunga Mulambwa who introduced the law whereby a man caught stealing was given some cattle, on the theory that men steal only because of need. There was also during Mulambwa's reign, opposition to slave-raiders who came from Bihe in Angola. This opposition may have been based on the fact that the Lozi needed slaves themselves to work on the flood plains.

There were two external factors during Mulambwa's time which, but for Mulambwa's skill in dealing with them, could have disrupted Lozi society. The first was the immigration of the Mbunda into Bulozi from Angola under their leaders Mwenyi Chiegele and Mwenyi Kandala. The immigrants came seeking refuge in Bulozi, which Mulambwa granted them. He settled them on the border area between his people and the Luvale (see page 26) so that the immigrants would provide a buffer between Bulozi and the slave-trading Luvale. The Mbunda settled near Mongu and in the eastern forest from Manitome to Liamutinga. Here in their new area they served Mulambwa very well and they proved to be loyal subjects and efficient warriors. They introduced new weapons such as the *lukana*, a fighting axe, and the bow and arrow. With these weapons they helped defend the country against the Luvale in the eastern forest, against the Nkoya on the Luena river, and against a number of groups around Lake Ngami.

The Mbunda also brought new food crops such as millet and cassava, and a small type of yam called *sikuswani*. They were skilled in the use of magic and medicines, providing healing services to the Lozi society. They were also good entertainers: the Makishi dances were introduced into Bulozi by the Mbunda.

The bow and arrow. Originally a weapon used by the Bushmen, it was brought into Barotseland by the Mbunda

Immigration into Bulozi continued bringing such people as the Mbowe, the Chokwe and the Luchazi. In spite of these new people coming to settle in the country the Lozi kingdom was able to maintain a measure of stability and development reaching the height of its success around 1830. It was about this time that Mulambwa died. The kingdom experienced no serious external disturbances until the late 1830s or early 1840s when, as will be seen later, it was invaded by the Kololo, a Mfecane or Difaqane group from Transorangia under its leader, Sebetwane (see Chapter 13).

6 Malawi people: the Kalonga and the Undi kingdoms

Origins of the Malawi people

By AD 1000 small groups of Bantu-speaking cultivators had established themselves around Lake Malawi alongside earlier inhabitants who were hunter-gatherers. More immigrants from Shaba (Katanga) joined, especially in the late thirteenth century. They brought with them ideas of centralised chieftainship and formed the various groups of the Malawi and related peoples: the Chikunda, Chipeta, Zimba, Mbo, Ntumba, Mang'anja, Nyanga, Nyasa, Nsenga etc. All these, except Nsenga, spoke Nyanja – the 'language of the Lake'. They occupied most of the land between the Luangwa and the Shire, from Lundazi in the north to the Zambezi in the south. Small chieftainships were established such as Lundu and Kapwiti in southern Malawi, Changamile on the Dedza plateau and in the Ncheu district, Chulu in the Kasungu and Lundazi districts, Mkanda in the Mchenje and Chipata districts, and Kanyenda in the Dowa and Nkota-Kota districts.

It is not clear if any fighting took place between the new settlers and the Chewa peoples. There is, however, some indication that the Chewa groups welcomed the newcomers who became chiefs over them. It may have been felt that the new political system was better than the old one in that it created order, a new system of justice and a number of economic services such as the collection of tribute, organisation and control of trade, and the redistribution of goods to local headmen. Some of the new chiefs were also skilled magicians and medicine men who were feared, respected and admired by the people whom they led.

By about 1500 the Malawi chiefs had begun to unite among themselves. The movement towards unity was largely due to three factors: an increase in the production of iron and iron goods, the ivory trade with the Swahili ports on the east coast (the Malawi chiefs seem to have taken over some of the trade previously belonging to Ingombe Ilede – see pages 14–15), and the influence of religion. The Kalonga family, for instance, were regarded and generally accepted as living representatives of the ancestors who had led the Malawi people from Luba. There is, however, some doubt whether Kalonga had led the people all the way from Luba, or whether the title *kalonga* was bestowed upon the leader of a Phiri clan at some time. The Kalonga family were nonetheless believed to possess rain-making powers; the Mang'anganja rain-making cult of Mbona was tied to the Lundu chieftainship, and the Makewana rain-cult near Lilongwe was controlled by the Undi chieftainship.

Malawi under Kalonga chiefs

Towards the end of the sixteenth century the Kalonga family began to increase their power and influence. A more unified chieftainship was created. This caused opposition and resentment leading in the 1580s to the breaking away of the followers of Lundu who moved to the south to create a separate state – Bororo.

The most powerful of the Kalonga chiefs was Masula, who ruled from about 1600 to 1650. He formed an alliance with the Portuguese in East Africa. In 1608, for instance, he sent 4000 warriors to assist the Portuguese in suppressing a revolt against Mwene Mutapa Gatsi Rusere. In return, the Portuguese helped Masula to suppress Lundu's rebellion. Relations with the Portuguese were, however, not always as friendly as this. Sometimes Masula did not prevent attacks on the Portuguese caravans which were passing through his territory or trading in his land, probably because the attitudes of the Portuguese were usually unfriendly. Masula was a daring man. In 1623, for instance, he attempted without success to take over the Mwene Mutapa kingdom where Portuguese influence was very strong. Masula captured a large amount of gold in the campaign.

Masula's aim in the daring campaign against Mwene Mutapa was to control the long-distance trade in ivory which would enable him to buy cotton

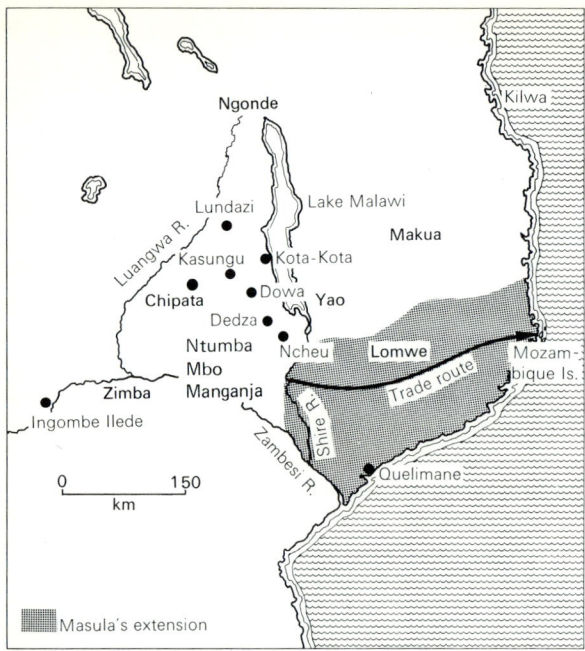

The Kalonga Kingdom

cloth and other manufactures to make gifts to some of his powerful supporters. The Portuguese had prevented him from gaining this control in the south, so he turned his attention to the north. By 1635 he had extended his influence through the Makua and Lomwe territory to Mozambique Island, and his armies, numbering about 10 000, were threatening the Portuguese port of Quelimane. The Malawi people's empire lasted in this area for 50 years. It was a large, prosperous empire, and Masula had plans for its further expansion and development. After his death, however, the empire began to decline and fall apart.

Break up of the empire

Unlike the Luba-Lunda rulers, Masula did not succeed in building up a centralised political state. Some time in the sixteenth century Undi, the defeated candidate in a succession dispute, left the kingdom, taking with him many followers which included female members of his and the Kalonga families. One of the women taken was Nyangu, a very important person who was Kalonga's mother or sister. This left Kalonga with no way of ensuring the succession of his own family, and with no close supporters of the Phiri clan. It meant that he would have to rely on his cousins of the Banda clan. Kalonga's position was now very weak. He had very little support, and two major breakaway states were growing strong outside the Kalonga state; those of Undi and Lundu. There were also some minor chiefdoms, like that of Mkanda.

In the eighteenth century traders such as the Yao preferred to deal with these separate and local chiefs rather than with Kalonga. To make matters even worse, Kalonga's territory was no longer on the main trade routes, and the Yao gradually replaced the Malawi as main traders. Another reason for the decline of Kalonga's state was the failure of the Mbona rain cult to create real unity among the Chewa people. Finally, the Kalonga chieftainship depended too much on the personality of the reigning Kalonga, and Masula's successors did not have his qualities and abilities. By 1700 Kalonga was losing respect and the decline continued until the killing of the last Kalonga by the Yao in the 1860s.

Undi's kingdom

Having broken away from Kalonga, Undi went to establish his own kingdom somewhere south of Katete in Zambia's eastern province. He established his capital at Mano and began to spread his influence and control throughout the Katete and Chadiza areas. Conquest and political expansion continued and by about 1700 Undi had brought Mkanda's Chewa, the Nsenga of Petauke, and the Chewa of Tete under control. At its height, Undi's state was vast, including the eastern province of Zambia, part of Mozambique's Tete province and part of Malawi. Undi controlled the important Chewa rain-making shrine of Makewana in the Lilongwe district and the rain-making shrines in the Luangwa valley area. He was also recognised by the Mwase chiefs in the Lundazi area as their king. By keeping power largely in the hands of his own Phiri clan, Undi achieved a great degree of political centralisation, although it is doubtful whether his kingdom was much more than a federation of semi-independent chieftainships.

A number of factors seem to have combined to bring about a relatively rapid rise of the Undi kingdom. It must be borne in mind that although in many respects similar to Luba-Lunda state systems, the development of the kingdom of Undi was not directly influenced by events in the Shaba or Katanga area. Its rise was due to a number of factors; the area under Undi's control was relatively well watered and fertile – a large population could therefore be sustained easily. There were a number of natural resources in the area such as salt, iron ore, clay, good pastures, wood, ivory and even gold. Most of these resources were important items in external trade which was carried out with the

Swahili on the east coast and with the Portuguese in the Zambezi valley area. The third factor in the rise of the kingdom was traditional religion.

Undi's aim in building a vast kingdom was to increase his tribute of ivory which he in turn sold to the Portuguese and the Swahili traders. The Portuguese gave him cloth, beads and other European manufactures, some of which he distributed to his people through their chiefs. At first the Portuguese came in small numbers and stayed for short periods. When they found that there was gold in the area however, they and their Chikunda agents came more often and stayed longer. Their numbers also increased and they carried out illegal gold-digging in order to avoid giving Undi his share of the gold. In response to these illegal activities by the Portuguese and their agents, Undi closed the mines for some time, but was soon compelled to admit that the Chikunda were important to him as well. Without Portuguese trade goods brought to his country by the Chikunda, Undi had no way of receiving sufficient tribute from his people. He therefore had to re-open the gold mines. This time he was careful to put some of his own people among the diggers in order to make sure that he received his share of the gold.

After about 1700 the Portuguese went even further in their very disruptive activities in Undi's country. Their settlers began to take land from the local chiefs. Undi could do very little to check this trend. In the past he had ensured the loyalty of his lesser chiefs by providing them with religious, legal, and economic services, but now such services had become so insignificant that they counted for nothing. For this reason his chiefs were making separate agreements with the Portuguese on trade and even land. Whatever trade monopoly he might have possessed in the past, and whatever power he had had to demand tribute from his people, were now seriously weakened. The Chikunda made matters even worse by carrying out illegal hunting expeditions to kill elephants in the Undi country. Traditionally Undi was entitled to one tusk from every elephant killed in the country, but the illegal Chikunda hunters disregarded this practice and thus deprived Undi of a major source of revenue. The result was that Undi no longer had the means to buy and re-distribute cloth and beads to his people. Thus his political influence upon them was dangerously undermined.

At this time there was a big demand for slaves and these slaves were being bought from subordinate chiefs. This growing demand for slaves resulted in increased conflicts and warfare in the kingdom because wars provided slaves. Larger numbers of people were being accused of witchcraft and sorcery so that they could be sold as slaves. As chief fought against chief, travel in the Undi area became very unsafe. The Swahili slavers also joined the Portuguese and Chikundas in the slave-raiding campaigns. Undi's kingdom became more and more unstable and the prospect of final collapse drew nearer. Portuguese settlers began adding political power to their economic influence. Some of them were establishing their own independent states within Undi's territory. This was true of the Pereira family. Similar developments were taking place elsewhere in the kingdom; for instance in the Nsenga area around the Portuguese trading post of Zumbo on the Zambezi land was being taken by individual Portuguese traders.

Undi's decline was hastened by internal factors, such as the lack of a standing army and a strong civil service; poor communication systems serving a vast state; divisions between Undi's political and Makewana's spiritual powers; and the personal weaknesses of individual Undis. It was these internal factors that were exploited by the Portuguese and their Chikunda agents. Finally, around 1870, the Ngoni came and settled among the Nsenga and destroyed whatever had remained of the Undi state.

The Tumbuka-Kamanga peoples

The Tumbuka-speaking people living to the north of the Undi state consisted of many groups. There were cultural and even religious differences among the groups. The Tumbuka groups occupied small territories each dominated by certain clan groups. Among the leading clans were the Luhanga and the Mkandawire. Around 1700–50, probably because of disturbances in Zambia and Tanzania, there were migrations into the Tumbuka area from north, west and east. The immigrant groups soon gained political control, although they adopted Tumbuka languages. They were small Tumbuka chieftainships though some, like Luhanga and Mwacidika, gained influence over a number of sub-chiefs.

The Tumbuka area was relatively peaceful and there seemed to be enough room for everybody. There was therefore no need for the establishment of strong centralised administrations or governments. There was no system of taxation or tribute, though the chief might be given a leopard-skin or a lion-skin as a special tribute.

Around 1770–80 a group known as the Balowoka came from across Lake Malawi and settled at Nkhamanga. They were probably Yao traders from Kilwa looking for ivory which was plentiful in the area. In return for ivory the Balowoka supplied the local people with beads and cloth. The Balowoka were accepted by the Tumbuka because they were honest and generous in their business. They also made no effort to interfere with Tumbuka customs. The most famous among the Balowoka traders was Mlowoka, who was both friendly and intelligent. He made alliances with chiefs and gave them presents of blue and black cloth turbans. Local chiefs therefore gained a lot of prestige and material goods, while Mlowoka also gained a great deal of economic control over the Nkhamanga-Henga-Phoka areas. He married into the Luhanga clan, which dominated the central Nkhamanga plain, an area rich in elephants and situated on the main trade route to the Bisa country in the west. Mlowoka's supporters were also placed in strategic positions to take advantage of the area's ivory supplies and to ensure the safety of the trade routes.

Mlowoka was not trying to build a kingdom. Neither he nor any of his supporters ruled the Nkata Bay area or the Mzimba district to the south. Nor did they control the Ngonde to the north. They were traders, and the area which they controlled was essentially a trade route. They are said to have brought unity among the Tumbuka, but this was not really the case. Mlowoka himself had very little political power; even when he married into the Luhanga, the Luhanga chief Mubila retained his political control. It is true that around 1805–10 when Mlowoka and Mubila died, they were both succeeded by Mlowoka's son, Gonapamuhanya. This double succession gave Gonapamuhanya both political and economic control and he became the first chief to be known by the title of *chikulamayembe*. Chikulamayembe Gonapamuhanya was powerful enough to introduce a system of taxation consisting of one tusk for every elephant killed in the area. But even he had to make do with limited political power. For example, judicial authority and power remained in the hands of sub-chiefs and there was never a centralised religion.

So there was no great break with the past even during the rule of Chikulamayembe Gonapamuhanya. Chikulamayembe's influence was not so much political or religious, as economic. His control over the chiefs was very loose. Some of the chiefs, such as Katumbi and Mwahenga, set up their own independent chieftainships. Local chiefs received tribute and it was entirely up to them to pass some of it to Chikulamayembe. Chikulamayembe also had the authority to settle disputes between minor chiefs, for example, between the Phoka leaders.

The Chikulamayembe had a trade monopoly but he was militarily too weak to maintain it. As a result other traders came to the area to do business with the people. First the Nyirenda family came, then slave traders from the east coast also came, and it was they who actually destroyed the Chikulamayembe's monopoly and dealt directly with chiefs and headmen under him. They sold beads and cloth to them. This weakened the Chikulamayembe's influence and he, like the Undi, was finally defeated by Mbelwa's Ngoni.

Ngonde chieftainship

The area north of Lake Malawi was one of the great crossroads of Central Africa, with successive movements of people over many centuries. Chiefs and their peoples were often of different stock, and even among one people there could be many chieftainships. Only among the Nyakyusa-Ngonde peoples were related chiefs able to establish control in areas where different languages were spoken. The Nyakyusa-Ngonde peoples came from Bukinga, high in the Livingstone mountains. Both groups probably originally had the 'age-system' that survived only among the Nyakyusa. Every 30 or 35 years there was a ritual in which fathers handed over power, land and cattle to their sons, and the leading members of the older generation became priests.

The main Ngonde chief was the Kyungu. He and his followers came from north-east of Lake Malawi. They settled on Mbande hill near Karonga some time in the fifteenth century. They drove out the Fipa chiefs including Simbobwe, a well-known elephant hunter in the area. At first the Kyungu was a religious leader living in seclusion in an enclosure on the summit of a hill. He was believed to possess rain-making powers, and was a symbol of fertility. He was often smothered if he became ill because a healthy Kyungu was necessary to ensure the fertility of women and successful harvests.

The first Kyungu and, presumably Simbobwe himself or one before him, was also an ivory trader. He imported cloth, metal, porcelain, and pots which he redistributed to his supporters. In this, the Kyungu was simply taking over an ancient trade. Glass, beads and other trade items have been found at Mwasampa and Mwenepera hill dating from the thirteenth century. The volume of trade was probably small then, and most of the ivory was sent to the north. This pattern changed later. Goods were then sent across the lake, and in the nineteenth century the amount of trade increased as slaves were sold in addition to ivory. Firearms became the main import. This was probably the most prosperous period in the history of the Ngonde chieftainship.

7 South of the Zambezi

The area and early peopling
We should now turn to historical developments in the southern part of Central Africa, also known as South-Central Africa. This includes that area bounded by the Zambezi in the north, the Limpopo in the south, the Mozambique channel in the east and, to the west, stretching as far as the fringes of the Kalahari desert. In the early centuries of the Christian era this area was occupied by iron-using crop-cultivators and pastoralists. Early Iron Age settlers, already identified as Bantu-speakers, either displaced Stone Age communities living in the area or they intermarried with them. In time more and more Iron Age cultivators arrived and settled so that by the period running from the eleventh century to the fifteenth century the area became predominantly Bantu-speaking and food-producing.

Among the early settlements of people were the Zimba of Malawi and Mozambique, the Tawara and the Sena of Zimbabwe and Mozambique, the Tonga of the Zambezi valley area, the Karanga/Shona of Zimbabwe's high veld, and many others. All these groups are mentioned in the writings of the Portuguese of the sixteenth and seventeenth centuries. Today these people are divided into even more numerous sub-groups with different names and even speaking widely different dialects, making it difficult to think of them as having the same or similar linguistic and cultural origins. This diversity provides strong evidence that these peoples have been established in the area for a long period of time, since no group who had recently arrived and settled in the area could possibly have acquired such variety.

The cultural and especially the economic diversity among the communities in South-Central Africa has also been attributed to the factors of climate and geography of the sub-region. Thus, for instance, the Shona of the Zimbabwe high veld practised a kind of mixed economy. Cattle, goats and sheep were raised in the western parts of the country where the rainfall is unreliable but sufficient to ensure the growth of good pastures. In the central, northern and eastern areas of Zimbabwe where rains are good and the soils reasonably fertile, people were predominantly crop-producing, although animals were also raised. The Zambezi valley area and the belt of land along the east coast of Mozambique are hot and humid. The soil is in many places fertile. Such conditions favoured the growing of food crops, especially fruit and vegetables. Hunting and fishing were also very important economic activities among the people living in these areas – the Tawara, Sena and related groups. Pastoralism was made difficult by the presence of the tsetse fly in these areas.

We have seen that this part of Central Africa also contained a variety of minerals, especially iron ore and gold. Thus from early times mining and the production of iron articles were important economic activities in the area, though somewhat specialised and therefore limited to certain people or individuals in society.

These favourable economic conditions contributed greatly to the important political developments in the area.

Political developments: the rise of Shona state systems
Good economic conditions ensured successful harvests and the accumulation of surpluses in grain, animals and other forms of wealth by people. This and the growth of population were probably among some of the major factors encouraging certain individuals to assume for themselves positions of leadership. In particular little chieftainships emerged on the Zimbabwe high veld. This was the beginning of the growth of the large states. Large-state formation was especially rapid among the Karanga or Shona people and led to the rise of the Mwene Mutapa dynasty. It was the Mwene Mutapa dynasty which went on to found the Mwene Mutapa state.

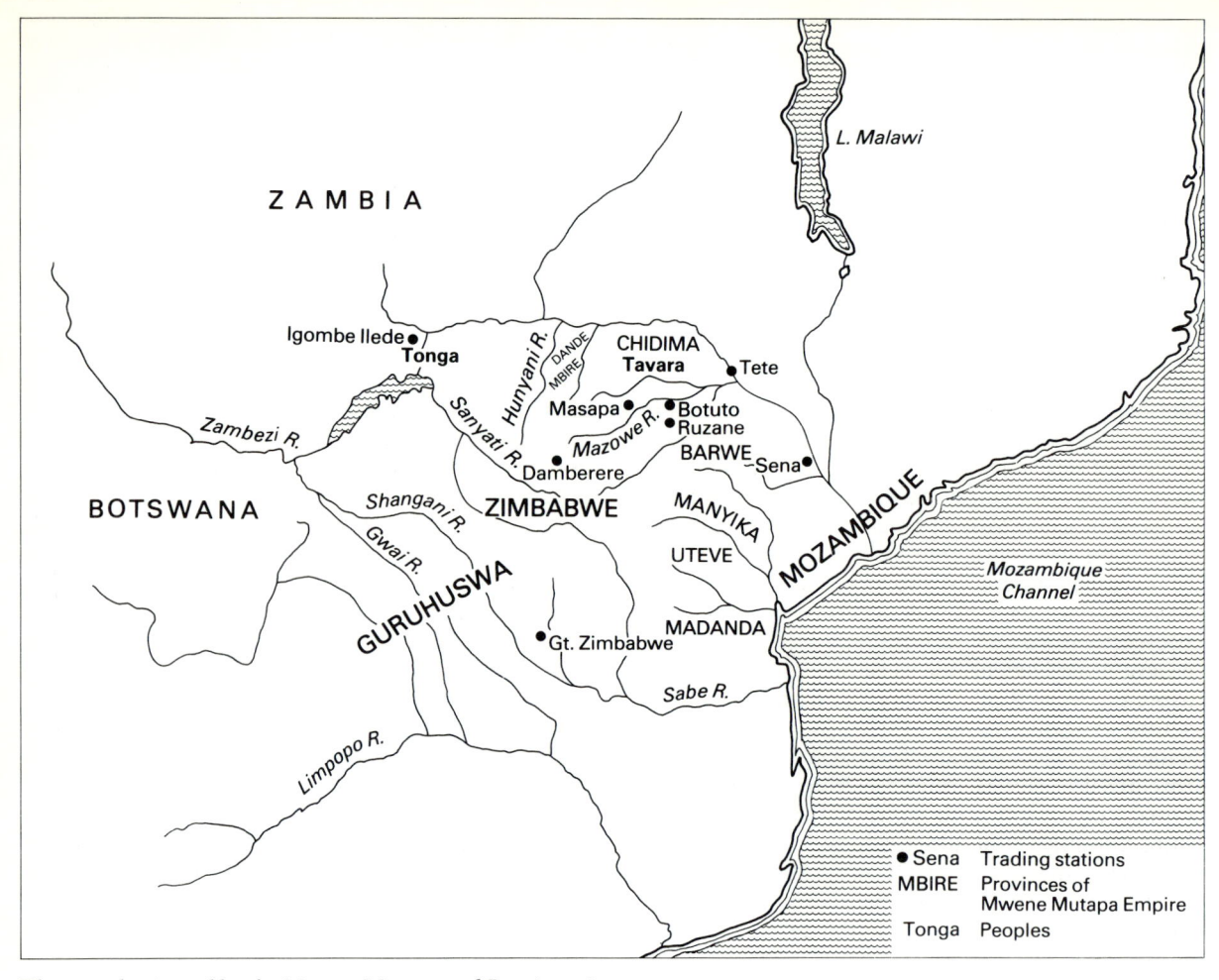

The area dominated by the Mwene-Mutapa and Rozvi empires

The Mwene Mutapa state

One of the most difficult questions in studying the rise and development of the state of Mwene Mutapa is to identify the real factors behind its beginning. A successful agricultural and pastoral economy, the availability and effective exploitation of minerals and the accessibility of the area to international trade through the east coast, were certainly very important factors. So were the presence of politically ambitious individuals among the Shona, and the role of Shona traditional religion and its leadership. Perhaps there were other factors of which we have no knowledge. What we know, however, is that by about the fourteenth century, or perhaps earlier, the process of political centralisation had begun among some Shona-speaking groups. It is likely that even at this early stage one of the chieftaincies was already becoming more powerful than its neighbours.

Since there are no written records we can only rely on traditions among the Shona people themselves. There are several, if not many, traditions about the beginning of the Mwene Mutapa state. One of them mentions the name of Chikura about whom very little is known. He is thought to have been the first chief to have a lot of control over a number of chiefdoms. Even then his influence and authority were limited to the Guruhuswa area with its centre at Great Zimbabwe. Guruhuswa was very excellent agriculture and cattle country, creating a mixed economy.

The next well known ruler, probably Chikura's successor, was Nyatsimba Mutota of the Mbire line. It was under Mutota that political control was extended to the south and to the north to include most of the Mbire province. Mutota probably ruled some time between 1420 and 1450. He seems to have been a man of great ambitions, ideals and a remarkable political and military leader. During his reign military conquests were made upon peoples in the west, some say as far as the Limpopo-Shashe confluence. It was during the reign of Mutota Nyatsimba that the Mwene Mutapa dynasty was actually born. He therefore became the first bearer of the title. He led his band of conquerors to the north towards the Zambezi valley and the Mozambican lowlands. To the west his army is said to have gone as far as the fringes of the Kalahari Desert, although it is very unlikely that his control in these distant areas was ever established on a regular basis.

It is not known why Mutota had adopted such an expansionist policy. A number of possible reasons have been suggested. One is that after years of settlement the area around Zimbabwe in particular, and Guruhuswa in general, might have become too exhausted and it was becoming increasingly difficult to feed and support the growing human and animal population. Military conquest and expansion seemed to be the only reasonable solution to this problem. One oral tradition, for instance, mentions a 'severe shortage of salt' experienced by the people around Great Zimbabwe. It is possible that this severe shortage of salt symbolised a general and widespread shortage of supplies which was threatening the very existence of the community at Great Zimbabwe. Another tradition also refers to a hunting expedition or expeditions being led by Mutota to distant areas. One such expedition took Mutota and his men as far to the north as the Dande-Chidema region in the Zambezi valley. Here the hunters were greatly attracted by the abundance of natural resources; the soil was fertile and there was also much salt. Mutota and his men were so impressed, according to the story, that they decided to stay on. This area was occupied by the Tawara and Korekore groups of the Shona-speaking people of Zimbabwe.

Whether Mutota and his Karanga people were peacefully accepted by the Korekore and Tawara of the Dande and Chidema area is not known. In the tradition there is evidence to suggest that there was some resistance, but that Mutota and his people were very successful in the fighting that followed. The Tawara and the Korekore were so impressed that they nick-named Mutota, *Mwene Mutapa*, meaning 'owner of conquered lands or Master-pillager'.

It has also been suggested that Mutota pursued a military policy because he had been advised to do so by resident Muslim or Swahili traders at Great Zimbabwe. The traders wanted Mutota to establish control over as much land as possible so that their trade would benefit. They were particularly interested in the ivory-rich Zambezi valley area. This suggestion does not, however, have any backing from oral traditions. Yet a third possibility is that Mutota was simply an ambitious ruler who wanted more territory for himself and his people.

We shall never know the real motives behind Mutota's activities which led to the creation of a vast empire, the Mwenemutapa state. What is clear is that economic, political and military considerations all combined to influence Mutota's expansionist system. His move north brought disaster for Great Zimbabwe. The stone city soon lost its long-standing role as the centre of political and economic control. Instead the new centre of the now larger empire was established in the Dande area on the edges of the Zambezi valley. This area, bordering the middle Zambezi River, was not far away from Ingombe Ilede across the river. The Mwene Mutapa were bound to benefit from the trade between Ingombe Ilede and the trading settlements of Tete and Sena in the Lower Zambezi. Dande put the Shona rulers into a remarkable position to control this trade in their own interests, and eventually to eliminate Ingombe Ilede's people from the trading.

New trade routes were also developed, the most important of which was the Mazoe river. This major tributary of the Zambezi linked the Shona gold-bearing regions with the main trade centres of Tete and Sena in the Lower Zambezi. When, in the sixteenth century, the Portuguese took over Tete and Sena they found this route the key to the success of their trade with the Shona. Indeed it was so important that a number of trading posts were established along it, especially on the upper reaches of the Mazoe: at Dambarare, Bocuto, Massapa and Luanze.

But the Mwene Mutapa empire was short-lived and it never succeeded in controlling as much wealth as had Great Zimbabwe in the south. Nor did the Dande-controlled state seem to have made Great Zimbabwe's cultural and technological achievements. True, about five different *madzimbabwe* (stone centres) have been found in the general Dande-Chidema area, and they can be dated during the period coinciding with the development of the Mutapa empire in the area. The most well-known of these are Ruhanga or Ruanga and Nhunguza. But neither of these matches the achievements of Great Zimbabwe.

Mutota, or Mwene Mutapa I, died in about 1450. He was succeeded by his son, Matope, who reigned from about 1450 to 1480. As Mutota had not completed the conquest of the Zambezi valley area,

Reconstructed family dwellings around a pit structure at Inyanga

this task fell upon Matope. He was so successful in this that at the time of his death he was by far the most powerful ruler in Central Africa south of the Zambezi. His territory is said to have included the area roughly from the Zambezi in the north to the Limpopo in the south; and from the Mozambique Channel in the east to the fringes of the Kalahari in the west.

But between them, Mutota and Matope had created an empire too vast for them and their successors to keep together. Its survival depended on a number of conditions including an efficient system of communication between the various parts of the empire and the Mwene Mutapa's court, and also between the various areas themselves. The Mwene Mutapa would also have to create a more effective administrative machinery assisted by a powerful state army. In addition, it was essential to have the goodwill of the subjects and their local rulers. Because of their abilities and remarkable personal qualities, Mutota and Matope seem to have succeeded in maintaining the empire. But their successors did not have Mutota's and Matope's qualities and abilities. Because of this the Mwene Muta state was almost bound to disintegrate.

System of government

The centre of the government was the Mwene Mutapa and his court. The court was run by a team of officials responsible for the various departments. The officials included the chancellor, court chamberlain, the military commander, head drummer, head doorkeeper, and the chief cook. There were also chief priests living at the court. The Queen Mother, the king's sister and the nine principal wives of the king were also very important persons in the administration of the Mwene Mutapa's headquarters.

There were many lesser officials, such as pages, who were sent to the king by chiefs and nobles as an expression of their loyalty to the throne. The most important of the chiefs and nobles in the state were, as will be seen, the rulers of the two main provinces of Guruhuswa and Mbire. Also important were the kings of Uteve, Barue and Manyika.

Shona religion was closely related to the political system of the Mwene Mutapa empire. The Shona believed in Mwari: God and Creator of mankind, the earth and everything on it – living and non-living. They also respected a variety of spiritual beings including the spirits of family ancestors (*vadzimu vemisha*), and clan and national ancestral spirits (*mhondoro*). The mhondoro in particular were involved in the political system of the Shona. These spirits spoke to the people, and they could be spoken to, through special human mediums known by the Shona as *masvikiro* (plural) and *svikiro* (singular). The ancestors continued to have a great deal of interest in the affairs of the living. They were believed to be able to intercede between Mwari (God) and the living in times of crisis and need. Clan and national mhondoro could also intervene during a dispute concerning succession to political positions such as those of chiefs and kings, and they could intervene in inter-clan disputes. Shona priests, usually from the Rozvi groups, provided an effective means of communication between the king's headquarters and the various parts of the empire, as they regularly travelled between these areas and the court. Thus through them the king was kept informed about events throughout the empire.

Break up of the empire
Matope died around 1480 and was succeeded by the less able and inexperienced Nyahuma, his own son. Nyahuma was younger than some of his chiefs, such as the rulers of the two southern provinces of Guruhuswa and Mbire – Changa and Togwa respectively. The loyalty of the two important provincial rulers could not be taken for granted, even though both of them might have been related to the Mwene Mutapa. When Mutota moved to Dande he left these two in charge of the empire in the south, including Great Zimbabwe itself where some of the principal wives were left. But Changa and Togwa had their own personal political ambitions. Indeed in 1490, during the reign of Nyahuma, they rebelled against the rule of the Mwene Mutapa. In this they were, no doubt, encouraged by the knowledge that Nyahuma was young and inexperienced in the matters of state. In addition the communication systems in the empire were not very efficient; they knew that Nyahuma's armies could not be everywhere.

The force behind the rebellion was Changa and for some time the two rebels worked together. After Nyahuma was defeated and killed the ambitious Changa declared himself emperor and overlord, establishing the *Changamire* ruling house, which later replaced the Mwene Mutapa dynasty on the Zimbabwean high veld. Changa's rule was, however, short-lived because he was himself killed by Nyahuma's successor and son in 1494. Nyahuma's successor, Chikuyo Chomunyaka or simply Chikuyo, was to rule from 1494 to about 1530. But he did not recover full control of the whole empire. Changa's son and successor claimed most of Guruhuswa and Mbire. Eventually he even took over Uteve and Madanda, leaving the Mwene Mutapa with only the Dande area and Chidema. Special alliances seem to have existed between the Mwene Mutapa state and the kingdoms of Barue and Manyika. This meant that the Mwene Mutapa state with which the Portuguese were to deal from the sixteenth century onwards was not the original one. It was a much smaller and weaker state which remained after the breaking away of the most important areas.

The Portuguese certainly did not find a vast Mwene Mutapa empire still in existence. At the time of their arrival into the interior in the sixteenth century the Mwene Mutapa empire had been split into the greatly reduced Mwene Mutapa chieftaincy in the north, and the emerging Changamire state, comprising Guruhuswa and much of Mbire. It would appear that the new state was being governed by Changa's son, Dombo or Changamire II.

The Rozvi empire of Changamire
After a successful rebellion against the Mwene Mutapa by Changa and his successors, the Rozvi rulers, also known by the title *mambo*, established their own dynasty, the Changamire dynasty. The Changamire territory, which had initially consisted of Guruhuswa and Mbire, later included most parts of what is now Zimbabwe. Relations between the Changamire and the Mwene Mutapa during the early decades of the establishment of Changamire were characterised by warfare. There were also other conflicts taking place within each of the two states. These included civil wars and succession wars, as well as fights between the Swahili traders and the Portuguese for the control of the long-distance trade between the coast and the interior. However, in spite of all these difficulties, Changamire emerged stronger and victorious. While the Mwene Mutapa state had entered a period of decline which would end in its final disintegration and collapse, the Changamire state developed rapidly once the initial difficulties had been overcome. This was because of the wise leadership of some of the mambos and, perhaps more importantly, because of the strong economy.

The economy of the Changamire state
At the height of their power, the Rozvi mambos controlled territory which included most of Zimbabwe. The centre of the empire was situated in Guruhuswa, known as Butua by the Portuguese.

With its dry grasslands and low trees, Guruhuswa was excellent pastureland. Thus the Rozvi rulers and their people raised large herds of cattle, goats and sheep. The central and northern parts of the empire were good for both crop and animal farming.

Agriculture and pastoral farming were therefore the backbone of Shona economy under the Rozvi rulers, as they had been before under the Mwene Mutapa. This point needs to be emphasised because there is often a misleading impression created about the importance of gold in the economies of the Mutapas and the mambos. Indeed, according to Portuguese records, the Shona spent so much time looking after their herds and working in their grain fields that gold mining suffered.

Everybody who could afford to owned cattle. The largest owner was, of course, the mambo himself. He had cattle, goats, and sheep all over his empire. There were those who could not afford cattle of their own. Such people looked after other people's animals under a system known in Shona as *kuronzera*. This system still operates today among the Shona people of Zimbabwe. It allowed a man to keep another man's cattle; he was free to consume the milk, use manure and the cattle in any way, but could not dispose of any of the animals without the authority of the owner. He was required to report to the owner any births or deaths among the animals. As the biggest cattle-owner, this system meant that the king had many people related to him through the distribution of his cattle.

Pottery, blacksmithing, weaving and basketry were among some of the important economic activities. The iron industry, probably very specialised, was mainly for the production of tools and weapons such as hoes, axes, razors, arrows, spears and knives. Weaving and spinning concentrated on a special cloth known as *machira*. All these activities were necessary for the production of items which were required for everyday use. Often there was enough surplus for local exchanging or internal trading between families and villages, as well as between the various areas in the empire.

Gold mining and big game hunting were also pursued, but on a smaller scale. This kind of trade did not concern the majority of the people. They were connected with external trade; that is trade with the east coast or with the Portuguese on the Zambezi.

PART III
The Portuguese in Central Africa

8 The Portuguese in the Congo: 1482–1700

The Kongo Kingdom

Some time around 1400, or perhaps earlier, a kingdom was established in the territory stretching from the Congo River to the Dande River, and from the Kwango to the Atlantic Ocean. The founders of this state were migrants from the little chiefdom of Bungu in the north, not far from the modern town of Boma just across the Congo. The area was inhabited by the Ambundu and the Ambwela. Under their leader, Wene, the immigrants conquered and occupied the plateau around Mbanza, or San Salvador as it was later called by the Portuguese. They made alliances with the leading lineages in the area through political marriages. For example, Wene himself married the daughter of a man who held spiritual rights over the land. The *Mani*, as this important man was officially called, was thus a kind of earth priest. The Mani later accepted Wene as political overlord and Wene assumed the official title of *ne Kongo* or *Mani Kongo*, 'the Lord of Kongo'.

The Mani Kongo began the task of building a large kingdom by military conquest. Mpemba, Nsundi, Mbamba and Soyo, all of which were to be important parts of the kingdom, were conquered. So also were the kingdoms of Mpangu and Mbata to the east. Strictly speaking, however, the kingdom of Kongo was a confederacy of these six provinces, in which the rulers of these parts played important political and administrative roles. It was their responsibility to collect tribute from their provinces and this tribute provided the Mani Kongo with revenue. The tribute consisted of slaves, ivory, hides, palm-cloth known as *raffia*, and *nzimbu*, a special sea shell. The Bakongo were skilled copper and iron workers. They made excellent mats, baskets, pots and raffia clothing and they were also expert hunters. The Bakongo were agriculturalists growing millet, sorghum, vegetables and a variety of fruit. Cattle, sheep, pigs and fowl were raised too. It is clear, therefore, that the economy of the kingdom was sound.

Arrival of the Portuguese

In 1482 the Mani Kongo, Nzinga Kuwu, received reports about unusually huge *mindele* – whales – which had been sighted close to the coast on the south bank of the Congo. These turned out to be Portuguese ships under the command of Diogo Cao. Diogo Cao and his people had heard of a large and wealthy kingdom in the interior, but they had decided to sail farther south, leaving only four members of the party at the coast. The four men proceeded to Mbanza, the Mani Kongo's capital. In the meantime Diogo and the rest of the expedition returned to the spot where they had arranged to meet with the four ambassadors to Mbanza. But the four had not arrived from the interior because Nzinga Kuwu had detained them. Diogo therefore decided to capture four Bakongo whom he found at the coast and took them as hostages to the Portuguese king. In Portugal, King John II had the four Bakongo converted to Christianity, educated and taught them to speak and write the Portuguese

45

A Portuguese soldier of the 16th Century

language. He also used them to learn about the kingdom of Kongo.

Diogo Cao led another expedition back to Africa in 1484/5. He took the four Bakongo back to their country. He also carried gifts and presents for the Mani Kongo from King John. Nzinga Kuwu was pleased to see his four subjects back in good health and now fluent in the Portuguese language. He released the four Portuguese whom he had held hostage since 1483. They too had been well looked after as royal guests. The Mani Kongo too had used the opportunity to learn from them as much as he could about Portugal and the Portuguese king. Their accounts were now being confirmed by the stories from his own returning subjects. It is clear that the king of Kongo was favourably impressed with what he had learnt about Portugal, as he now decided to establish an embassy in Lisbon. Thus when Diogo Cao returned to Portugal he took with him Nzinga Kuwu's ambassador and his staff. The Mani Kongo also sent to Lisbon a number of young Bakongo to be educated in Portuguese schools. It had been arranged that their school fees would be paid in the form of gifts to the Portuguese king. The Mani Kongo asked King John to send him missionaries, teachers, builders, and carpenters as well as tools.

The embassy returned to Kongo in 1490 with Portuguese teachers, missionaries, blacksmiths, masons, bricklayers, and agricultural experts as well as necessary tools. The commander of the fleet which brought the Portuguese experts was Rui da Sousa. On the way to Mbanza the party went through Soyo where da Sousa converted and baptized the chief of that province.

The work of converting the Bakongo to Christianity began immediately after the party's arrival at Mbanza. A church was built at the capital and in June 1491 Nzinga Kuwu was baptized and became King John I of Kongo. Many Bakongo, most of them members of the nobility and the aristocracy, were converted with their king.

In that year, war broke out between the Kongo kingdom and the Tyo (Teke) living in the area around Stanley Pool. The Portuguese joined the war to assist the Kongo forces and the enemy was defeated. Rui da Sousa returned to Portugal the following year leaving the various Portuguese workers to continue with their mission. In the meantime two Germans brought a printing press to Mbanza and more youths were sent to Santo Eloi College in Portugal for education and training.

At first the Portuguese were more interested in spreading Christianity than in the politics of the Kongo kingdom. Slow progress was made until 1494, when divisions and differences began to develop at the Mani Kongo's Court because of the emergence of two factions. These were the anti-Portuguese and the pro-Portuguese groups. The king had gone back to his traditional way of life, possibly as a result of the anti-Portuguese faction's activities and influence upon him. But one of the king's sons, Affonso, and the Queen Mother were devoted Catholics and in favour of the work of the Portuguese in the kingdom. The hostilities between the factions became so bad that Affonso was compelled to leave the capital in about 1495. He went to settle in the Nsundi Province. But he maintained contact with Lisbon from the Nsundi country and it is said that priests were even sent to him from Lisbon in 1504.

Affonso I's attempts at westernisation

Nzinga Kuwu died in 1506 and his death was followed by much political disagreement between Affonso and his brother, Mpanzu a Kitima, who had been leading the anti-Portuguese faction at Court. Both of the sons wanted to succeed the late king. Before his death, Nzinga Kuwu had named

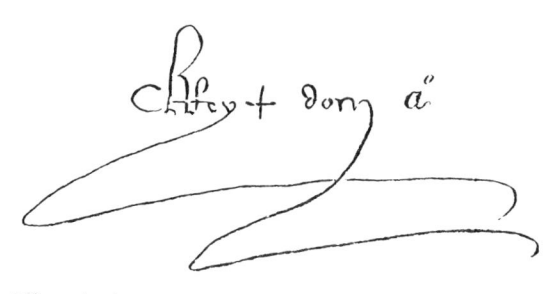

Affonso's signature

Affonso as his successor and the electors had been accordingly briefed. But Mpanza a Kitima had a strong army and was already in occupation of Mbanza. He also had the backing of the traditionalists and many provincial rulers. However, in the war that followed he was defeated and executed by Affonso, who had the support of all the Portuguese in the country. Affonso succeeded his father as Affonso I of Kongo.

Affonso was a Catholic convert and a great admirer of the Portuguese way of life. He spoke the Portuguese language and was familiar with Portuguese customs and history. He also wore European clothes. When he came to power he made known his intention to make the Kongo a Christian state and to introduce the Portuguese culture throughout the kingdom. In these efforts he had the support of Manuel I, the new king of Portugal. Affonso asked Portugal for aid to develop his country, and Manuel gave him his full support. Moreover, Manuel was only too glad to see such a large African state becoming Christian. Thus from 1506 to 1512 many expeditions were sent to Kongo from Portugal, for which Affonso paid in slaves, copper, ivory and other forms of wealth.

Portuguese-Kongolese relationships, however, soon met with unexpected difficulties. Most of the people sent to Kongo lived like rich nobles, despising and ill-treating the Africans, whom they were supposed to teach. The attitude of the governor of the Portuguese-occupied island of Sao Thome was also an important factor in the failure of Portuguese-Kongolese efforts to Europeanise Kongo. He was always uncooperative because the island had enjoyed a trade monopoly in Kongo and it stood to lose if the cooperation between Kongo and Portugal continued. Sao Thome's government also hampered communication between Portugal and Kongo in order to frustrate the plans of the two kings. In the meantime, the Portuguese in Kongo were refusing to recognize Affonso I's authority over them. In 1510 Affonso asked Manuel to send a representative to Mbanza to work with him in order to control the resident Portuguese population, most of whom were involved in the destructive slave trade. Manuel sent Simao da Silva to Kongo in 1512, who brought a document containing instructions for the development of the Kongo Kingdom. This document was known as the *regimento*.

The regimento affirmed that the Catholic kings of Portugal and Kongo were brothers. The Portuguese king would assist his African brother to establish the Catholic faith throughout the Kongo Kingdom. The document also gave an outline of the role of da Silva, Manuel's representative, who was given a code of Portuguese laws which Affonso might consider adopting for his kingdom. This would assist in transforming the Kongolese legal and court system completely. Da Silva was to be Portugal's ambassador to Kongo and as such he would also advise Affonso in military matters. He was also judge over all the Portuguese living in Kongo and had authority to expel any Portuguese who, by his behaviour, caused the name of Portugal to be held in disrepute. All the services rendered to Kongo were to be paid for in ivory, copper, and slaves.

The regimento also stipulated that trade between Kongo and Portugal would be organised according to the ways acceptable to Portugal, that is on the basis of royal monopolies which cut out all private intermediaries. Finally, da Silva was to collect as much useful information as possible about Kongo's geography and politics. He was specially instructed to explore the Rio Zaire (the Congo River).

Why westernisation failed

The attempt to create an African Christian state did not succeed. The reasons for this failure seem to be connected with the regimento and also with the various groups of people involved in its implementation.

Firstly, the plan for introducing modernisation in Kongo was too ambitious. In addition, the regimento's projects were not clear in how change was to be achieved in Kongo. Moreover, da Silva, the man in charge of the programme, died before he had had a chance even to meet the king of Kongo. He was succeeded by Alvare Lopez.

Secondly, not everything in the regimento was acceptable to Affonso and his officials. Affonso was prepared to try to build schools, churches and technical institutions. This is because he had specifically asked for these improvements. But plans which he found unacceptable were either altered or completely rejected. Manuel's laws, for instance, were found to be unacceptable to Affonso and were accordingly rejected before they were tried. Thus the Kongolese legal system and the organisation of the Kongolese court remained unchanged.

The third factor explaining the failure was that there were not enough Portuguese workers in Kongo. Moreover, the Portuguese in Kongo were not united in their effort to implement the regimento. For instance many of them cooperated with the Sao Thome traders and government. In fact Alvare Lopez later fell under the influence of the Sao Thome group which was trading in slaves. Thus thousands and thousands of people of Kongo were taken away as slaves to Sao Thome where they worked on the sugar plantations.

An equally important factor against efforts to westernise Kongo was the attitude of the majority of the people in the Kongo Kingdom. These people were suspicious of the cooperation between their king and the Portuguese king. The slave trade of the Sao Thome traders did not help matters. Even after taking over the administration of Sao Thome in 1532 the Portuguese government failed to stop the slave trade in Kongo. Affonso made numerous appeals to the Portuguese king to put a stop to the activities of his subjects in Sao Thome, but with no success. When no help came from Lisbon, Affonso appealed through the Head of the Catholic Church, the Pope in Rome. The Pope wrote to the Portuguese king, but to no avail.

Affonso's problems were made more difficult by Manuel's successor, John III who reigned from 1521 to 1557, and who had very little interest in the Kingdom of Kongo. John's replies to Affonso were always very late and unhelpful. With no backing from Portugal, Affonso's standing in his country was being seriously undermined and his authority weakened. Affonso's son, Henrique, was made bishop of Kongo, but even he too could not stop the activities of the slave traders. Moreover some of the Portuguese priests were participating in the slave trade and neglecting the schools and church work. Affonso died in 1543, tired, thoroughly disillusioned, and completely cut off from his people.

Collapse of the Kongo Kingdom
Affonso's death was followed by a civil war between his son, Pedro, and Diogo, a nephew. Diogo won the succession war and by 1545 he was on the throne as Diogo I of Kongo. He had popular support and was backed by the pro-Lisbon faction of the resident Portuguese population. Like Affonso I, he also favoured modernisation, including the system of royal monopoly in trade. This was aimed at cutting out the influence of the Sao Thome traders, making Diogo unpopular among the pro-Sao Thome faction of the Portuguese population in Kongo. But his efforts to carry out some of Affonso's modernisation programmes failed because by now the power of the king had been badly eaten away.

A group of Jesuit missionaries arrived in Kongo in 1548 and within four months they had converted and baptized 2100 persons. Schools had been built and about 600 pupils were in regular attendance. Three new churches, including that of San Salvador, were built. But before long, the Jesuit missionaries were also involved in the slave trade and politics. Four years later, in 1552, they left the country. They were succeeded by another Jesuit group in 1553. But these too failed in their work.

The slave trade and the hostilities of the Portuguese in Kongo continued to threaten the king's authority and the stability of the kingdom. The Sao Thome traders had now moved to Ndongo in the south of the kingdom. Here they operated a profitable trade in slaves with local rulers. The Portuguese supporters of the Lisbon government that had remained with Diogo I persuaded him to declare war on Ndongo in 1556. The ruler of Ndongo, the *ngola*, as he was called, asked the Portuguese in his province to assist him against Diogo's army and was able to defeat Diogo's forces. The result was the increase of the slave trade from 1557. In addition, Diogo's Portuguese supporters deserted him and began to move southwards to Ndongo. Eventually relations were established between Portugal and Ndongo, which were to lead in time to the establishment of the Portuguese colony of Angola.

Diogo I's death in 1561 was followed by a civil war. Once again the Portuguese took sides and succeeded in imposing upon the elders Affonso, Diogo I's son, as king. But Bernado, another son of Diogo, killed his brother. Strife followed in which many Portuguese were killed. Trade was badly disrupted as no ships could reach Mpinda, the Kongolese port. On the other hand, trade was increasing in Ndongo, to Bernado's anger. Ndongo's rebellion against Kongo was now becoming a reality. Relations between Kongo and Portugal were bad and they became worse when the Portuguese Queen Mother, Catherine, rebuked Bernado for having murdered Affonso II.

During a battle with Tyo (Teke) in 1567, Bernado was killed and was succeeded by Henrique I. But the latter too was killed during the same war in 1567. His successor was Alvare, his wife's son by another man. The new king managed to create peace in the kingdom, but not for long because Kongo was invaded by the Jaga. These ferocious fighters, using

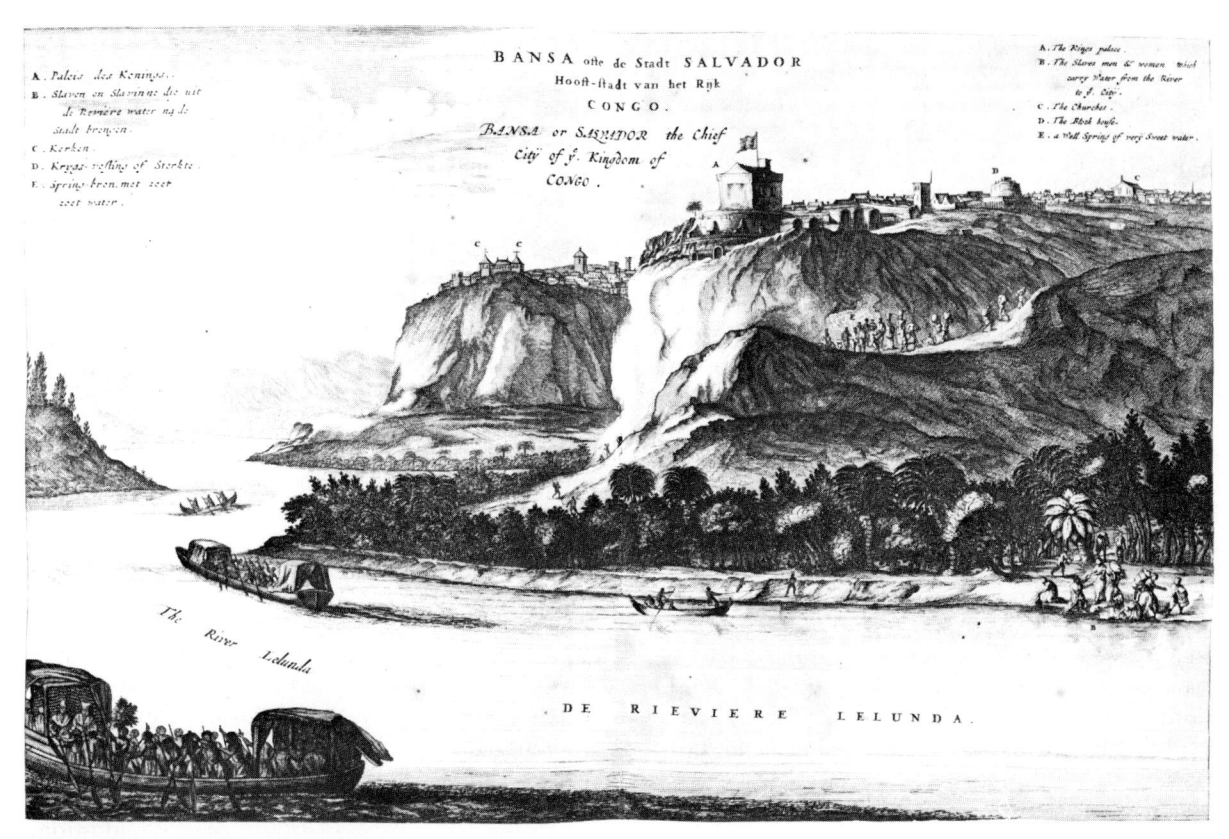

Mbanza (San Salvador) later destroyed by the Jaga

King Alvare of Kongo receiving Dutch ambassadors

swords, javelins and shields, completely destroyed Mbanza (San Salvador). The king and the resident Portuguese were forced to become refugees on an island in the lower Congo. From there Alvare appealed to Portugal for assistance. The Portuguese king sent a military expedition to drive the Jaga out of Kongo in 1571. The expedition then occupied Kongo for four years, reducing the kingdom into a vassal state. But Portugal was now more interested in the new colony of Angola.

The Mbundu of Ndongo (Angola) added to Kongo's problems by capturing many people from southern Kongo and selling them to Portuguese slave traders. The Mani Kongo was too weak to protect his subjects. He had been abandoned by many Portuguese, except those who had married local women. His country was extremely unstable and there were civil wars between the two factions in Affonso's family, the Kimpanzu and the Kimlazu.

In 1665 the Portuguese invaded Kongo and by that time well over 15 000 Kongolese were being taken out of the country as slaves. On 29 October 1665 the Mani Kongo, Antonio I, and many of his nobles and chiefs were killed by the Portuguese at the battle of Mbwila. Then followed a period of unprecedented instability during which one king after another was assassinated. It was, therefore, only a matter of time before the final collapse of the kingdom.

Christianity, which had seemed successful in the early years of the contact between Portugal and Kongo, was struggling for survival; after 1676 not a single bishop was found in Kongo; by 1700 all of San Salvador's twelve churches were in ruins. Although there were missionaries in Kongo and Christianity survived until the nineteenth century, Christian influence was very small. The Portuguese had completely failed to establish a Christian state along Portuguese lines in Africa in four centuries. The slave trade had frustrated all the efforts to introduce change in Kongo. It had interfered with the work of teachers, missionaries and every kind of expert sent to Kongo from Portugal. Antonio Barosso has correctly summed the position in the following words:

'At the side of the missionary who carried salvation was the buyer of men, who destroyed the ties linking father to son and mother to daughter.'

9 The Portuguese in Angola: 1575–1836

Ndongo

The main group in Ndongo were the Mbundu. The small kingdom of Ndongo was founded some time towards the end of the fifteenth century by Mbundu subsistence farmers who grew millet, sorghum and bananas and kept livestock. The ruler of Ndongo was known by the title, *Ngola*. Ndongo was less centralised than its more powerful northern neighbour, Kongo. In fact the Ngola used to pay annual tribute to the Mani Kongo before the Portuguese moved to Ndongo in the middle of the sixteenth century. Traditionally, Ndongo's trade was mainly in salt. But this changed in the sixteenth century when the Ngola began to sell slaves to the Sao Thome traders in return for cloth, alcohol and tobacco. In this way he increased his political authority and his state claimed more territory too. By 1556, when Ndongo broke away from Kongo, the Ngola was ruling a vast area between the Lukala and the Cuanza rivers.

For a long time the Portuguese were not interested in Ndongo. For instance the Ngola invited Manuel I to send missionaries, technicians and merchants to his country in 1519. The Portuguese sent an expedition, not to do what the Ngola had asked the Portuguese to do, but to hunt for silver mines. The expedition failed to find any silver. From the 1540s the Portuguese began to be more interested in Ndongo. Traders from Sao Thome were making frequent visits to Kabasa, the capital. An official expedition which included four Jesuit missionaries was sent to Ndongo in 1560 under the leadership of Paulo Dias de Novães. This mission does not seem to have achieved its main objective, trade and mission work. In fact Dias de Novães was detained at Kabasa for five years. During this period he was used by the king as an adviser. Most of the Jesuit priests died and Father Gouvea, the survivor, was reduced to a state of slavery by the Ngola.

Breakthrough and preparation for colonisation

In 1565 Kiluanji Kukakwango, one of the Ngola's chiefs, rebelled against his king. To put down this rebellion the Ngola needed Portuguese military assistance and in order to get this he released Dias de Novães. He sent him back to Portugal with presents and gifts for the Portuguese king, from whom he asked military assistance against the rebel chief. For his part, de Novães was keen to return to Ndongo because he believed that huge deposits of silver existed in the interior. He had also seen that Ndongo had a very profitable slave trade and had wanted to take part in it. He sought a special trade monopoly in Ndongo and with the help of the Jesuits obtained a *donatario* from the king of Portugal. This document gave him rights and

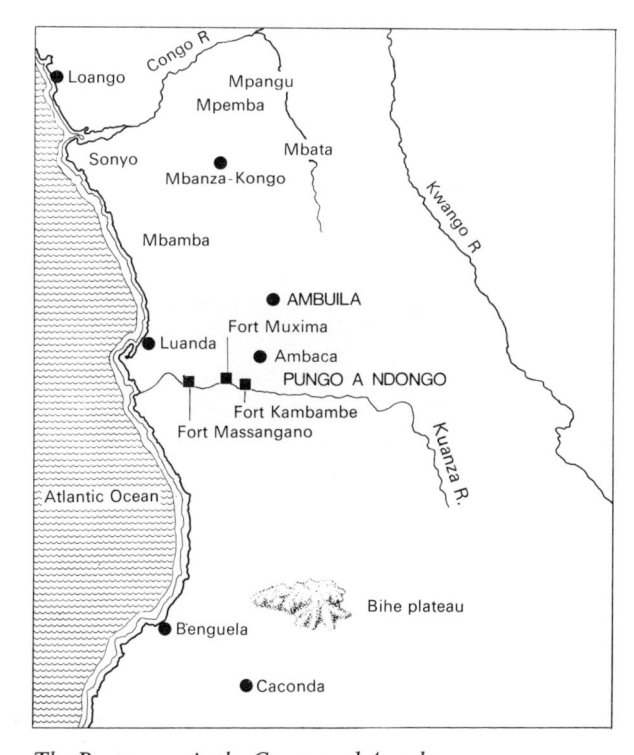

The Portuguese in the Congo and Angola

powers to colonise Ndongo at his own expense. The donatario also entitled Dias de Novães to take the southern part of Ndongo as his personal property, in addition to being governor of the whole of the new colony of Angola during his lifetime. He was to take with him an army of 400 soldiers and 100 Portuguese families to enable him to establish the new colony effectively. These families, the nucleus of the new settler society, were to be provided with seeds and agricultural implements.

Colonisation

Paulo Dias de Novães and his people arrived on the island of Luanda in February 1575. By 1576 the colonising party had moved to the mainland to establish the port of Luanda. There were many factors favouring the Portuguese colonisation of Angola. There was the death of the Ngola in 1575 and the subsequent war of succession. Even after a successor had been elected, he became too preoccupied with internal unrest to be able to fight the Portuguese. Secondly, although Kongo still regarded Ndongo as its province, it was unable to intervene in Ndongo at that time. As already pointed out, Kongo was still occupied by the Portuguese military expedition (see page 50).

De Novães, however, went ahead preparing for war with the Ngola. He built forts at a number of places, including one on the Cuanza river and he was joined by more Portuguese colonists. In 1579 he advanced towards Kambambe along the Cuanza. The Ngola killed all Portuguese traders residing at Kabasa and sent his forces to meet De Novães's army. Reinforcements were sent from Portugal and in 1583 the Portuguese won major battles against the Ngola's forces. New forts were established, including the Massangano Fort on the Lukala-Cuanza confluence. However, Portuguese advance towards Kambambe was still vigorously opposed by the Ngola's army.

Paulo Dias de Novães died in 1589 and was succeeded by Luis Serrao, who carried on with his predecessor's efforts to colonise the rest of Angola. He was very severely beaten by the Ngola's forces in 1590 at the famous battle of Ngoleme a Kitambu. Unfortunately, however, the Ngola and his allies did not follow their remarkable victory with further attacks on Portuguese strongholds at Massangano and Luanda.

Meanwhile the slave trade was benefiting greatly from these wars. For example, about 2500 slaves a year were being exported through Luanda during the period 1575 to 1587; 7500 a year from 1587 to 1591. Many Angolans were also killed in these wars.

But the Portuguese also suffered. By 1591 nearly 2000 men had been lost and in that year only 300 remained. Diseases, war and desertion accounted for these losses. Thus reduced in numbers, the Portuguese were forced to rely heavily upon African auxiliary troops, who could not always be completely trusted as they might defect to the Ngola's side. Indeed, the prospects of the new colony were very bleak. Neither Portuguese settlers nor missionaries could carry out their work. The only significant economic activity was the slave trade. Politically, Portuguese colonial rule had not yet been established on any regular or permanent basis.

Establishment of Portuguese colonial rule

It was clear that the Portuguese government had to take direct control in order to prevent the Angola venture from becoming an expensive failure. This was vigorously opposed by Dias's settlers, soldiers and missionaries who already possessed land and other forms of property. Indeed, when the first governor-general, Francisco d'Almeida, revoked all the land grants in 1592, there was an open revolt. The governor-general was expelled from the colony

Francisco d'Almeida, the first Governor-General of Angola

as a result of demands by the settlers, missionaries and traders. His successor brought with him reinforcements and succeeded in establishing colonial rule in Angola. Within a short time he had moved to the side of the settlers and was greatly opposed to control from Portugal.

The Angolans continued with their military resistance against Portuguese rule. The war spread to many areas and the Jaga had joined in the resistance. In 1603 General Manuel Cerveira Pereira, ruthless and greedy, but an able man, was appointed as interim governor-general. In 1604 he managed to occupy Cambambe but was disappointed to find no silver there. The Ngola sued for peace and an agreement was signed. But when the new governor-general arrived he arrested Pereira on charges of conspiracy with the enemy. The war continued and it became even more cruel and destructive. Slave traders were following the troops, since the commander, Bento Banha Cardoso, invited them to do so. In 1615 Pereira, who had been sent back to Portugal in 1604, was sent to Angola once again to act as interim governor-general. He was instructed to conquer what was referred to as the Kingdom of Benguela. He defeated the Ngola's forces in 1616 and built a fort at Ambaca on the Lukala river. From there he sailed to Benguela in 1617, the same year in which the Ngola died.

Then followed campaigns by the Portuguese to break Ndongo up completely. By 1619 this objective had been achieved. In that year the Ngola's capital, Kabasa, was overrun and the Ngola himself was forced to flee to an island while over 100 of his chiefs were massacred in cold blood. The Jaga who had sided with the Portuguese caused untold damage to property and killed many people. The brutality and ruthlessness of the campaigns was such that the Pope was compelled to put pressure on Lisbon to recall Pereira. Pereira's successor was sent to Angola with orders to arrange peace with the Ngola. A peace agreement was signed in 1622 by which the Ngola was allowed to return to Kabasa. The agreement also required him to free all the prisoners of war. The negotiator of this peace treaty was the Ngola's sister, Nzinga Nbandi, known as Anna Nzinga, and the signing of the treaty was a major personal diplomatic victory for her. Most of the agreement terms were, however, not immediately implemented and for this reason the relationships between the Mbundu and the Portuguese remained unsatisfactory.

The Ngola died in 1623 under mysterious circumstances and it was rumoured that his sister, Anna Nzinga, had poisoned him. This rumour was supported by the fact that the two had had conflicting views about the Portuguese in the country. Nzinga favoured a tough line in government relations with the Portuguese. She succeeded her brother and became Queen Nzinga of Ndongo. She immediately warned the Portuguese at Luanda that unless they honoured their side of the 1622 peace agreement with her brother, she would go to war with them. This warning reached Luanda when the biggest threat to the new colony was the Dutch whose warships were preparing to attack Luanda. Also at this time there was no Governor at Luanda who could take quick decisions. The Dutch did attack Benguela in 1623 and Luanda in 1624, destroying many Portuguese ships.

Nzinga prepared to attack Luanda by entering into an anti-Portuguese alliance with the Jaga and other neighbouring states. Propaganda was also addressed to *kimbares* (African soldiers in the Portuguese forces), whom Queen Nzinga wanted to rebel against the Portuguese government in Luanda. She admitted into her protection any slaves running away from their Portuguese masters. Chiefs in the areas held by the Portuguese were also invited to rebel and join Ndongo in a war against the Portuguese colonialists.

The Portuguese at Luanda decided to take Nzinga's threats more seriously. Thus they warned her that she should send back all the slaves and African soldiers that had sought refuge with her people or face the consequences. She did not comply with this demand. But while the Dutch threat was still there the Portuguese could not send an army against Ndongo. Instead, they used divide and rule tactics to weaken Nzinga's power. They incited Aidi Kimanji, a chief related to the late Ngola, to rebel against Nzinga and proclaimed him successor to the Ndongo throne. Nzinga attacked Aidi and an army was sent from Luanda to help the puppet. Nzinga was forced to flee her island stronghold in 1626, and the Portuguese installed their own puppet as Ngola Philip I of Ndongo. Their efforts to capture Nzinga were unsuccessful, however, and she returned to her island stronghold in November 1627 since the Portuguese had to return to Luanda which was facing an attack from another African group. After the departure of the Portuguese, Aidi lost what little support he had had, since most Mbundu chiefs began to re-identify themselves with Nzinga, the heroine of their anti-Portuguese campaigns. The Portuguese declared war on her and instructed that she should be captured, dead or alive.

It was while Anna Nzinga was running away from the Portuguese that she defeated and captured

Nzinga negotiating with the Portuguese. The Portuguese refused her a seat, so she called one of her attendants to sit on as shown

the kingdom of Matamba. Matamba was used as the new base from which she organised further resistance against the establishment of Portuguese colonial rule. She strengthened her position by entering into alliances with the rulers of the Kasanje Jaga, the Imbangala, Kissama and Ovimbundu. The most important of these alliances was one with the Jaga of Kasanje which enabled her to establish her position in Matamba from where she effectively harassed the Portuguese and their puppet, Aidi. In 1641 the Portuguese determined that they should rid themselves of Nzinga once and for all, but the Dutch captured Luanda before this could be done.

Dutch invasion and Brazilian influence in Angola

Luanda was captured by the Dutch in August 1641. Four months later Benguela also fell to the invaders. The Dutch-Portuguese war on the coast of western Central Africa was an extension of the struggle between Protestant and Catholic Europe. The Dutch (Protestants) also wanted slaves for their estates in South America. The people of Angola however used this opportunity to drive the Portuguese out of their land. Ndongo, Kasanje and a number of other chiefdoms combined their forces to attack the Portuguese who had now fled to the fort of Massangano. From Massangano they were trying to hold off both the Africans and the Dutch. Portugal was in no position to help as she was at war with Spain. Instead the Portuguese in Angola were helped by the Portuguese colony of Brazil. The first Brazilian reinforcement arrived in 1645. The Jaga met and wiped them all out before they had reached Massangano. A second group arrived later and managed to go through to Massangano. But for the next two years it seemed as if Nzinga and the Dutch might take Massangano.

In August 1648 when Massangano was just about to fall, a Brazilian land owner, Salvador de Sa, arrived with a fleet and successfully took the port of Luanda from the Dutch. The Dutch withdrew from Lusanda and Massangano, abandoning their African allies. The Angolans were defeated and many chiefs were massacred. However, Anna Nzinga and the Mani Kongo of Kongo continued to reject Portuguese authority over them in spite of peaceful appeals and offers from Salvador de Sa.

Only the Jaga ruler of Kasange, who had been neutral during the recent fighting, cooperated with the Portuguese and became a vassal ruler. Nzinga did, however, sign a peace treaty in 1656 under which she surrendered most of Ndongo to Aidi, the Portuguese puppet, retaining Matamba and a small part of Ndongo. By the time of her death in 1663 she had been converted to the Catholic Church and a mission had been established at her capital.

The wars benefited nobody but the slave traders. Most slaves from Angola were now being sent to Brazil, which had a great deal of influence in Angola. The period from 1647 to 1667 saw a big increase in the slave trade between Angola and Brazil because all the governors of Angola during these years were Brazilians. Salvador de Sa placed a tax on every slave leaving Angola. Some of his successors, for instance Viera (1658–61) and Negreiros (1661–66), actually caused and fought wars to increase the supply of slaves being exported.

The Portuguese strengthened Angola's defences in the face of competition with the British and the French for slaves. In 1689 the fortress of Sao Miguel was completed at Luanda while more fortresses were constructed at Massangano, Muxima, Pungo and Ndongo and Kambambe. The Portuguese also pushed further inland from Benguela to Caconda and even beyond. By 1700 Portuguese influence was being felt over a very large part of Angola. Three major slave trade routes were crossing Angola.

The eighteenth and nineteenth centuries

By the beginning of the eighteenth century Luanda had become by far the largest and busiest slave port in West-Central Africa, if not in the whole of Africa. According to one estimate 3 000 000 slaves were exported from Angola during the period 1580 to 1836. This represented about 80 per cent of Angola's total trade. Over 50 per cent of the Angolan slaves went to Brazil, 30 per cent to the Caribbean and 10–15 per cent to the River Plate.

Slaves were obtained in several ways. Many were brought to Portuguese fortresses by vassal chiefs. *Pombeiros*, special trading agents, brought in their own share of slaves from the interior. These pombeiros, usually men of mixed race, received cloth, metal instruments and spirits in return. There were also organised raiding parties known as *kuata! kuata!* Yet another very important source of slaves were well populated areas given to soldiers, priests and government officials, known as *sobabas*; the owners of sobabas would demand slaves from people living on their land. There were also some wars which were deliberately provoked by the Portuguese and chiefs who took war captives as slaves. This was true, for instance, of the war against

Loango, where the French, British and Dutch traded with Mwata Yamvo

Matamba in 1739–44; the 1765 war against Hungu and Sosso; and later in the century, the war against Mwata Yamvo who had been doing business with the British, French and Dutch at Loango.

The slaves were brought to Luanda where they were kept in large warehouses or in open corrals called barracoons. From Luanda they were sent on the Middle Passage, which was the longest journey for slave ships across the Atlantic ocean between the west coast of Africa and the West Indies. This terrible journey lasted from five to eight weeks. Many slaves died of diseases, suffocation and starvation while others committed suicide.

There were both economic and political reasons why the Portuguese could acquire slaves so easily from Angola. Politically the Angolans were not united and the Portuguese deliberately created and encouraged dissension among the various people and especially between Ndongo and Matamba, among the Imbangala, the Jaga and the Sosso. The Portuguese were used to a money-based economy and the Angolans were not. The Portuguese also controlled the main source of cowrie shells and the salt-producing areas of Angola.

The slave trade was finally made illegal in 1836 by the Portuguese Prime Minister, Sa da Bandeira. Naturally there was much opposition by the Portuguese in Angola. The Luanda Portuguese defied the Portuguese Government and it was not until 1845 that Governor Pedro da Cunha was able to enforce the ban on the slave trade. Slavery was not abolished until 1858. Even then it was practised into the twentieth century, usually disguised as corrective labour.

After the establishment of Portuguese rule the Portuguese made very little or no effort to develop the new colony. Only one governor, Sousa Coutinho, tried to do so. During his governorship from 1764 to 1772 he tried to control the export of Angolan slaves. He built a shipyard at Luanda and an iron foundry on the Cuanza. A technical school was established to train Angolans. In administration Coutinho tried to introduce efficiency and honesty. But largely because of the slave trade, his efforts came to nothing. Government officials and Portuguese colonists both enjoyed high profits from the slave trade. For that reason nobody saw any need to develop Angola's natural resources.

10 The Portuguese in the Zambezi and south of the valley

Arrival on the Mozambique coast

Since the early fifteenth century Portugal had been sending exploration voyages to bring her people into contact with Central Africa. She also wanted to reach the wealthy markets of India and the Far East, and to check the spread of Islam by taking the Catholic faith to other countries. One of her expeditions was led by Vasco da Gama. It rounded the Cape of Good Hope in November 1497, making da Gama and his men the first Europeans to sail up the Indian Ocean. As they sailed along the eastern coast of Southern and Central Africa the Portuguese sailors saw a number of Swahili trading centres. The sailors visited some of the centres on the African coast before proceeding on their long voyage to India. They gathered much commercial information from these trading towns.

The Portuguese sailors returned to Portugal in 1499, having successfully found the sea route to India and, of course, having also had firsthand information about trading activities between the Central African interior and the east coast. For instance, da Gama had been informed that there was 'infinite gold' at Sofala.

Exploration was the main objective of Vasco da Gama's expedition in 1497/8. After the route to India and the Far East was established, subsequent trips were to have different objectives. During the following decade the Portuguese would try to replace the Swahili who were controlling commerce on the west coast of the Indian Ocean. Thus, the Portuguese took Sofala in 1505 and Mozambique Island in 1507. A military fortress was built at each of the places. The commanders left in charge of the

Portuguese fortress at Sofala. It has long since disappeared

posts were instructed to locate the origins of the gold and ivory reaching Kilwa via Sofala. Sofala, Mozambique Island and other coastal towns which had been thought of as mere stopping and re-filling stations for Portuguese ships on their way to India, were becoming doorways to the African interior. The main aim was to acquire African gold and ivory and use them to buy Indian and Far Eastern goods, especially spices.

The Portuguese soon learnt that most of the gold reaching the coast came from Mwene Mutapa's land. In fact as early as 1506 the Portuguese at Sofala were being visited by official embassies from the interior, including one from Mwene Mutapa. The Portuguese became more interested in establishing contact with the land of Mwene Mutapa. In 1513 Antonio Fernandez was sent to locate the country of Mwene Mutapa and to report on its gold and other resources. Fernandez may have made more than one trip to the interior. He travelled widely, visiting Barwe, Manyika, the Dande, Tawara country, Mbire or Mount Darwin, Guruhuswa (Butua), Tete, Harare and Chegutu.

Fernandez reported that he had seen or heard about regular markets in the interior attended by Swahili traders. He told of the Mwene Mutapa's village built of stones and also about traders from near Zumbo on the Zambezi bringing cross-shaped copper ingots from the Congo. It soon became clear that the Portuguese needed to establish a number of trade posts in the interior, especially on the Zambezi River. Up to the 1530s many spies, most of them *degredados* (renegades) like Fernandez, were sent into the interior to gather more information. Most of these, however, did not go back to the coast but chose instead to settle at chiefs' courts where their greed for gold, ivory, alcohol and women caused a great deal of problems for the chiefs.

The Portuguese established *feiras* (trading posts) at Sena and Tete in the 1530s. Sena and Tete on the Zambezi were aimed at pushing the Swahili traders out of the interior and leaving the Portuguese in control of the trade with African states. At first Portuguese official policy seemed to be one of non-interference in local politics in the interior. But the Portuguese traders, who were often renegades, became independent of their coastal captains and started to become involved in local African politics.

The Portuguese changed their policy after the Mwene Mutapa had killed the Jesuit missionary, Father Goncalo da Silveira, in March 1561. Father da Silveira had converted Mwene Mutapa Negomo and about 500 of his family and nobles and court officials within a month of his arrival in December

Father Goncalo da Silveira the Jesuit missionary, who converted Mwene Mutapa Negomo

1560. These mass conversions frightened Shona leaders and within two months a rumour spread that Silveira had bewitched the king. He was advised to return to traditional religion to avoid something terrible happening to him and to the country. He was also told that the white missionary was, in fact, a Portuguese spy. All these stories about witchcraft and spying seemed to be confirmed in the king's mind by Silveira's refusal to accept offers of cattle, gold and wives from the king. Silveira did not help matters by his attacks on the traditional family and marriage systems. Finally the king abandoned his faith and decreed that all his subjects who had been converted with him should follow his example. He also had Silveira killed. Silveira's body and those of 50 of his Shona followers were thrown into a river.

The death of Silveira was a turning point in the relationships between the Shona and the Portuguese, and it also affected the relationships between the Shona and the Swahili traders. The Portuguese began openly interfering in local politics. They also put pressure on the Mwene Mutapa to drive the Swahili traders out because they alleged that the traders had been party to the murder of Silveira. The Mwene Mutapa was forced to banish

Swahili traders from his country and to allow the Portuguese to establish posts at Massapa, Dambarare, Bukuto and Luanze south of the Zambezi. Massapa, established by Antonio Caiado, was very close to the Mwene Mutapa's headquarters near Mount Fura. Caiado exercised a great deal of personal influence upon the king and made an immense fortune. He was appointed Captain of the Gates and became very fluent in the Shona language. He was also given judicial powers.

First attempt at colonisation

The Portuguese also used Silveira's death as justification to colonise the Zambezi valley area. This became more than evident in 1568 at the beginning of the reign of King Sebastian, who was extremely religious and patriotic. Angered by the death of Silveira, he resolved to expel the Swahili traders, to take control of the gold trade in the Shona country and to build a Portuguese empire in the Zambezi valley area and in Mozambique. In 1569 he sent an army of 1000 to Mozambique under Francisco Barreto to drive the Swahili out of Central Africa.

Barreto's expedition was a complete failure. It arrived on the Zambezi in November 1571, at the beginning of the rainy season. Many men died from fever and most of the horses were killed by sleeping sickness. There was very little food at Sena for the expedition. In the meantime, negotiations with the Mwena Mutapa went very slowly. Barreto himself died from fever in 1573. Less than 200 of his original force of 1000 returned to the coast alive. Another attempt was made in 1574 by Vasco Fernandez Homem, who tried to reach the gold mines of Manyika and the silver mines of Chicoa. Some of the mines were reached but were found not to be as rich as had been thought. Homem lost 200 of his men in the fighting with local peoples.

Finally, the Portuguese settlements on the Zambezi were destroyed by the Zimba in 1585 and 1592 and the government decided to abandon its imperialistic ventures, for the time being at least. Instead more effort was directed towards trade and the building of alliances with some local chiefs and with the Mwene Mutapas. A remarkable opportunity was created by the death of Mwene Mutapa Negomo in 1589. Just before his death Negomo had ceded part of his land to the Portuguese on the Zambezi. After his death the Portuguese helped a puppet, Gatsi Rusere, to the throne in 1596. From that time on the Portuguese made it their business to assist Rusere in putting down any rebellion against his rule. In this way they greatly contributed to the rapid decline of the Mwene Mutapa empire.

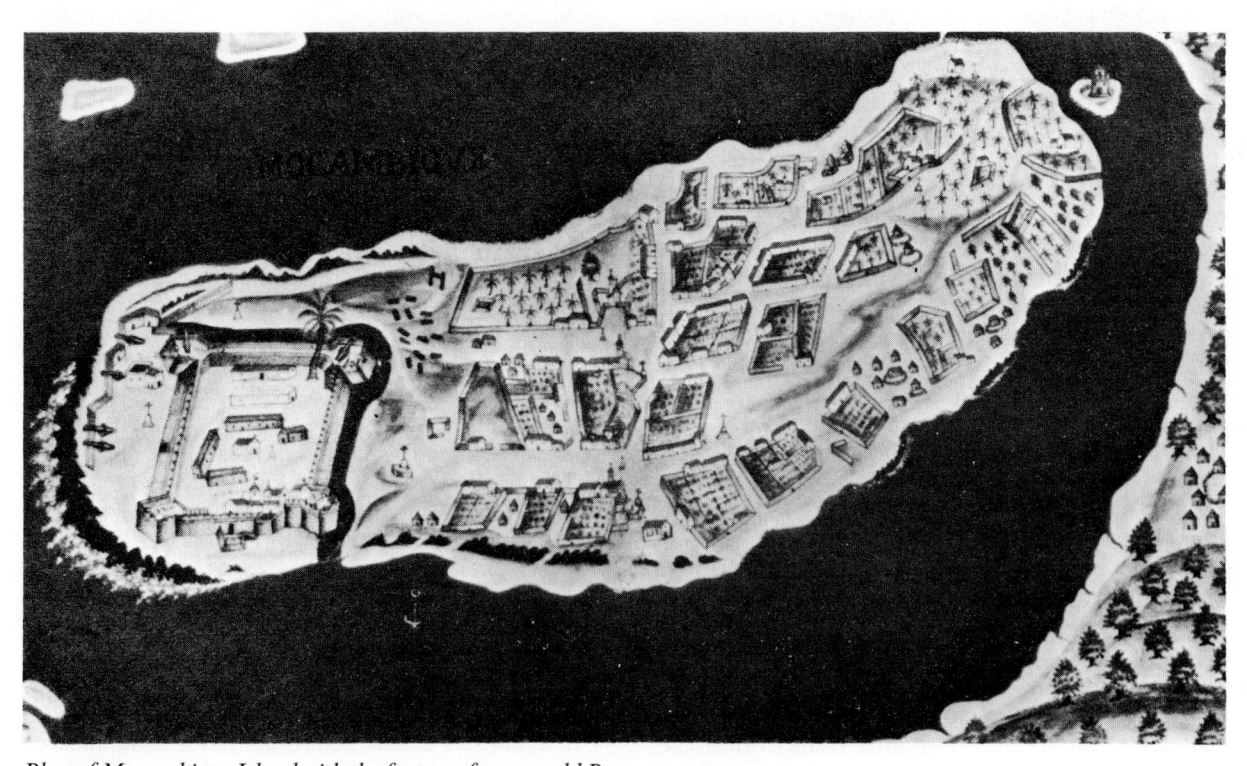

Plan of Mozambique Island with the fortress from an old Portuguese map

Mozambique after 1600

The early seventeenth century was a very profitable time for the Portuguese in the Zambezi valley. Sena, for instance, had a warehouse, a church, and a large population of 50 Portuguese, 750 Indians (Goans), and Africans of mixed races. Tete, farther on, had 40 Portuguese and many Africans, 2000 of whom had been presented to the Portuguese by the Mwene Mutapa as a special guard for the town. There were altogether over 1000 Portuguese in East Africa: soldiers, traders, explorers and missionaries. The area was divided into four main regions and the Portuguese paid tribute to the chiefs of these regions.

Another expedition, under General Nuno Alvares Pereira, was sent by the Portuguese king in 1608 to the silver mines of Chicoa. But opposition from both the Mwene Mutapa and resident Portuguese merchants at Tete and Sena who did not want government interference in their affairs meant the expedition was a failure. This conflict between the Portuguese government and Portuguese traders and settlers in the Zambezi valley was a continual problem. Pereira's mission was withdrawn after 10 difficult years.

A private expedition under Gasper Bocarro, however, was more successful. In 1616 Bocarro undertook a seven week journey from Tete to Kilwa across the Shire River, noticing that African people living north of the Zambezi were wearing bracelets made of copper. The significance of this observation will become apparent later.

The defeat of Mwene Mutapa

The puppet Mwene Mutapa, Gatsi Rusere, died in 1624 and was succeeded by Kapararaidze who was hostile to the Portuguese and wanted to reduce their influence in the internal affairs of his country. But the Portuguese had helped him to achieve the succession and therefore he was indebted to them. There had been two candidates: Kapararaidze and Mavura. The Portuguese had helped Kapararaidze, thinking he would be sympathetic to their position. But as soon as he gained power, Kapararaidze began to attack Portuguese garrisons and interfere with their trade. The Portuguese responded by using their private armies under Diogo da Meneses to fight Kaparaadze, defeating and executing him.

The Portuguese switched their support over to Mavura, who had been brought up and educated by the Dominican missionaries. Once again a puppet Mwene Mutapa was on the throne. In 1632 Mavura granted a number of concessions to the Portuguese. The Portuguese were allowed to move and trade freely in the kingdom, missionaries were given a free hand to build and teach wherever they liked, many Portuguese settlers were granted large areas of land and they gained even more later by bribery and doubtful purchases, and threats. The Portuguese were to rule these areas just as African chiefs had done, indeed they replaced African chiefs in these areas. The captain of Massapa was given authority over everyone in the area, black and white. It is clear that the 1632 agreements benefited Portuguese settlers but not the Portuguese government. That is what the settlers had always wished for.

Mavura made all these sweeping concessions because he was having to rely so heavily upon the Portuguese for the maintenance of his position as king. But this made him lose the respect of his people. He was eventually killed in a civil war in 1665 and his kingdom was split.

The Portuguese settlers and traders enjoyed some economic profit for a time. Thus the mid-seventeenth century was known as the 'golden age' of Portuguese occupation of Central Africa. For instance, Sena, the market place for Portuguese plantations, had a large population for whom four churches were built. Almost 16000 ounces of gold were exported every year. After about 1680, however, the African gold miners began to produce less gold. The Portuguese, unlike the Swahili before them, were not willing to pay a fair price for the gold. They were also arrogant in their dealing with the local people.

In 1680 the Portuguese Government opened the country to free trade, but the area was immediately swamped by Indian traders. Government control was restored in 1700. By the time David Livingstone, the British missionary explorer, passed through Tete in the mid-nineteenth century, the gold export had dropped to a mere 140 ounces a year.

Relations between the Portuguese and the Africans steadily deteriorated. Both settlers and missionaries wanted labour to work on the land which they had acquired under the concessions granted by Mwene Mutapa Mavura. They therefore used slave labour and after 1645, slaves were also being exported to the colony of Brazil. Many armed conflicts in the Zambezi valley at that time were caused by the slave trade in the area. Shona speaking inhabitants of the valley area fled to the south into the area where the Changamire's rule was being firmly established at the time.

Although the Portuguese had traded with Changamire's country they had never been allowed to gain any political control of that kingdom.

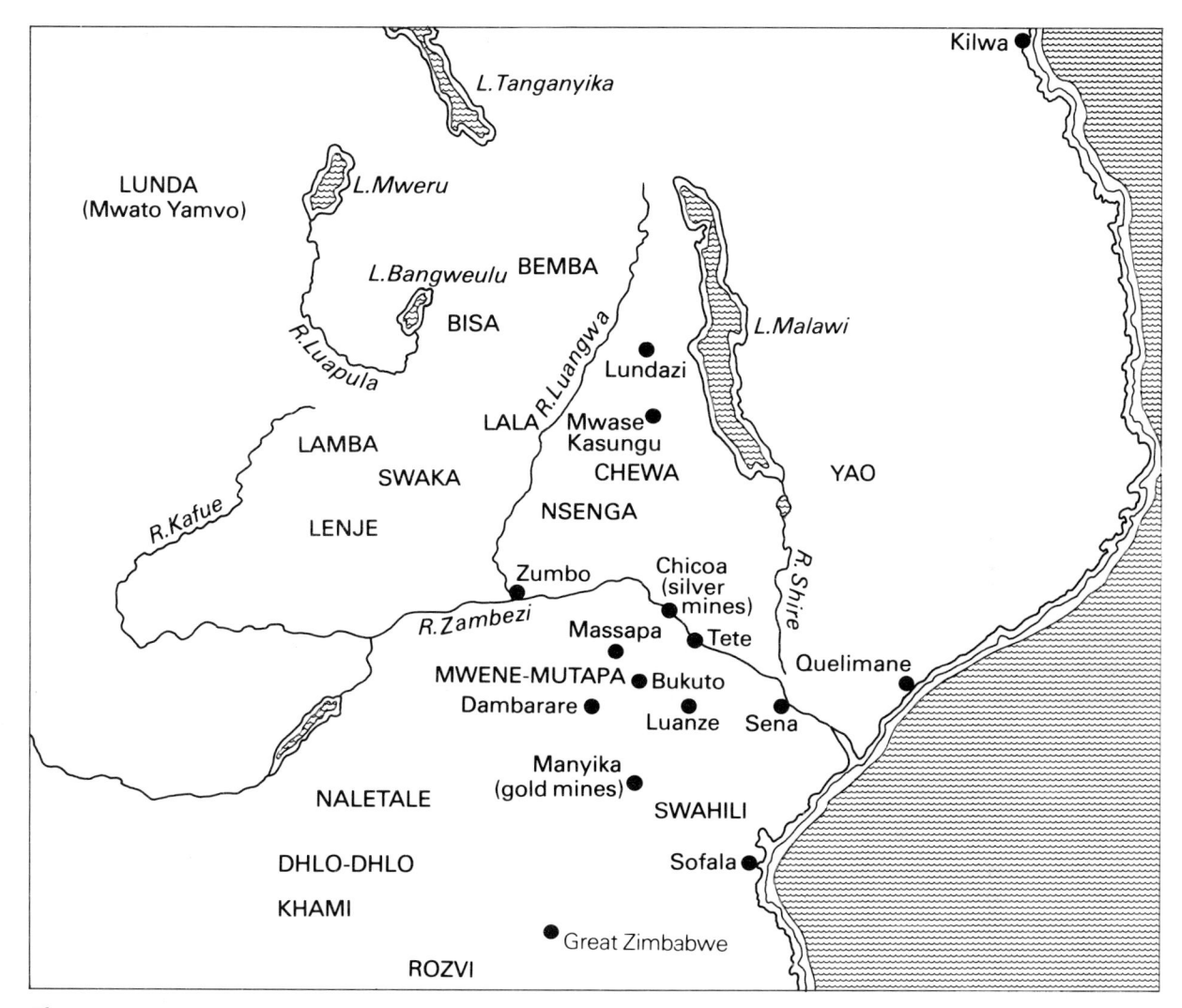

The Portuguese presence in East Africa

Changamire's trade with the Portuguese was carried out indirectly through markets or fairs in the Mwene Mutapa and other areas. Trade with the Portuguese was also done through special agents, the professional *vashambadzi*. These were usually in the employ of Portuguese masters although some of them were independent. The vashambadzi travelled between the Zambezi valley and the Shona area.

The destructive activities of Portuguese traders and settlers in Mwene Mutapa's country were well known to the Changamire or Rozvi mambos and they wanted to stop the Mwene Mutapa's experience repeating itself in their own land. Thus they adopted a policy of indirect dealing with the Portuguese. This policy had the advantage of enabling the Changamire's country to benefit from trade with the Portuguese while at the same time maintaining its political independence.

The defeat and expulsion of the Portuguese from the Zimbabwe plateau

Relations between the Shona and the Portuguese worsened to the extent that even Changamire's country to the south-west was being affected. The Portuguese were using their *chikunda* (private armies) to destroy the authority of many chiefs on the Zimbabwe high veld. With the exception of Kapararaidze and Matuzvinye, no Mwene Mutapa had attempted to rally the various chiefs behind him against the Portuguese. Most Mwene Mutapas had instead relied upon Portuguese support. This situation had given the Portuguese an opportunity to dominate the Mwene Mutapa and the Manyika kingdoms as well as that of Uteve. Even Changamire's Butua was being threatened.

The situation was now reversed during the last two decades of the seventeenth century. The Changamire rulers planned to take over the now tottering Mwene Mutapa and in the 1680s launched their attack against the Portuguese in Maungwe. The Portuguese were defeated but Changamire made no attempt to follow up his success until 1693 when he and Mwene Mutapa joined their forces against the Portuguese. It would appear that the initiative for this Changamire-Mutapa united action against the Portuguese had come from Mwene Mutapa Nyakunembire who was battling to hold his throne against Mhande, known as Don Pedro, a Christian who had the backing of the Portuguese. Changamire Dombo welcomed this initiative because he was now getting tired of the Portuguese interference near his country's northern borders. In November 1693 Changamire's forces attacked and defeated the feira of Dambarare, the main centre of Portuguese influence in Mashonaland. All the Portuguese traders there were killed. The fall of Dambarare struck so much fear into the Portuguese that the other feiras, with the exception of Manyika, were hurriedly abandoned. Massapa was burnt down. By 1694 the Portuguese had been driven out of the Zimbabwe high veld and the Changamire forces had returned to their base leaving Nyakunembire to face Don Pedro (Mhande), the Portuguese puppet, alone. In fact Nyakunembire had been expelled from his own country by Pedro. But the following year in 1695 Changamire struck the Manyika feira, destroying gold mines, missions and settlements. Many Portuguese were taken prisoners, while some were killed.

After the fall of the Dambarare and Manyika feiras the Portuguese feared that Sena and Tete might be attacked too. This, however, did not come about and the Portuguese were very relieved to learn in 1696 that the Changamire Dombo had died. His successor, who was involved in a civil war, did not follow up his father's victories. The celebrated anti-Portuguese campaigns of the 1680s and 1690s ended. Having been defeated and expelled from the Zimbabwe high veld, the Portuguese never again made any serious attempt to establish control in Zimbabwe. The Changamire was now the undisputed overlord of all the Shona areas in Zimbabwe. The Mwene Mutapa had also been swept away from the Zimbabwean high veld and all that was left for him of the Zambezi valley, was the hot and difficult area of Cabora Bassa between Tete and Zumbo. Even this small kingdom was still troubled by Portuguese interference.

11 The prazos and the missions to Kazembe

Prazos
Prazos were large land grants made to individual Portuguese settlers or traders by Mwene Mutapas and chiefs in the Zambezi valley area. Prazos were of two types; those given by African rulers in return for assistance in war, and those loaned to the Portuguese settlers by the Portuguese government. The latter were usually known as *prazos da Coroa* (Crown prazos). The prazo-holders were known as *prazeros* or *senhors* (lords). The Africans also called them the *mazungu* (*muzungos*). Prazo-holders were usually very powerful and independent. Most of the prazos were found in the area between Sofala, Chicoa and Quilimane. The most prosperous were on the south bank of the Zambezi from Tete.

Beginning of the prazo system
Mwene Mutapa's power entered a period of decline during the last decades of the sixteenth century. At the same time the Portuguese were establishing themselves in the Zambezi valley. Some of them obtained land concessions from weak Mwene Mutapas and their chiefs under very doubtful and suspicious circumstances. One of the earliest grants was made in 1589 when, before his death, Mwene Mutapa Negomo ceded land to Portuguese captains on the Zambezi. Negomo's successor, Rusere, became heavily dependent upon Portuguese military assistance. He too made land grants to the Portuguese. For instance, in 1607 he gave land to a Tete trader, Diogo Simoes Madeira and within a short time Madeira was the most powerful settler in the region leading a private force of 4000 mercenaries. Madeira was also given the chieftainship of Inhambazo. The Portuguese conquistadores (conquerors) gained more land and more power from Rusere's successor Mavura, their puppet. It is said that he was later forced to cede his whole kingdom to the Portuguese crown in 1629 as part of the price for Portuguese aid.

Sisnando Dias Bayao, another one of the conquistadors, was said to have acquired a very large area from the ruler of Quiteve as reward for military assistance. This vast territory, which was later called Cheringoma, stretched from the Pungue to the Zambezi. Yet another Portuguese, Rodrigo Lobo, was also given the area to the north of the Sofala Fort by the ruler of Quiteve.

When Portuguese settlers, traders and military adventurers obtained concessions from African rulers, whether by peaceful means or by force and deceit it was the beginning of the *prazo* system. The trend began towards the end of the sixteenth century and became more established in the seventeenth century. The Portuguese government formalised the system, by granting official recognition or land titles to individual prazeros (prazo-holders). This decision was prompted by a belief that the prazeros, who had by now become strong and independent minded, might be brought under government control by being recognised as agents of Portuguese civilisation in the region.

The prazo system worked in a manner that was bound to undermine and destroy the structures of African societies in the areas concerned. The vast land concessions deprived African communities of their land. In addition, African chiefs lost their powers and authority to the senhors who now had jurisdiction over all the people living on the prazos. The prazo-holders were now exercising the powers of chiefs. For instance they demanded all the tribute due to chiefs, and in time of war they also demanded that all the headmen under them should supply fighting men. These wars were, of course, very common as the prazeros often fought among themselves or with local chiefs. Because they demanded fighting men from headmen, they could very easily raise large private armies.

The prazeros also claimed the same ritualistic rights due to African chiefs. They insisted that they should be consulted by the Africans on their prazos before new seeds were planted and before the commencement of harvesting. They surrounded themselves with advisers, including religious leaders who helped in such ceremonies as rain-making. They also supervised the election of chiefs and headmen in their areas.

The decline of the Prazo system
By the end of the eighteenth century it was clear that the prazos had failed to function as the Portuguese government had intended them to. This was confirmed by a report written by Villas Boas Truao, Captain of the Rivers. He observed that there was no industry, commerce, or educational and religious work in the prazo areas. Furthermore, by this time most of the senhors or prazeros were not real Portuguese but people of mixed blood, a mixture of Portuguese, Goan and African. The Portuguese government tried to prevent this by passing a law that prazos da Coroa (see page 63) should pass to prazeros' eldest daughters who were required to marry Portuguese husbands. Some prazos were given to Portuguese orphans on the same conditions. But these measures did not have any significant effect on the situation.

The centres of prazos were known as *aringas* which could never be centres of civilisation, religious learning and good living. They were increasingly becoming centres of corruption and degeneration, where the senhors lived surrounded and served by slaves and the *chikundas* (slave armies) and they did as they pleased with the African women. The prazeros had their own private prisons in which many Africans were flogged, tortured and sometimes even killed for very minor offences.

Furthermore, the prazos were now being used to supply slaves who, by 1800, were the biggest export from Portuguese Mozambique. Many slaves were also being used in Mozambique itself. Brazil imported many Mozambican slaves, as did Cuba. Angola and Kongo, Brazil's main sources, were becoming inadequate by this time. During the period 1780–1800 about 10 000 slaves were exported from Mozambique annually; 15 000 annually for the period 1800–1840. The period from 1840 to 1850 saw an even higher increase, reaching 25 000 slaves a year. This increase was in spite of the ban on the slave trade in all Portuguese colonies by the Portuguese government under Sa da Bandeira in 1836 (see page 56). The ban was ignored and defied by the Governor of Mozambique who was supported by the prazeros. Under increasing pressure from other European countries, especially from Britain, the embarrassed Portuguese government authorized the ships of the British Royal Navy in 1842 to stop and search all Portuguese ships suspected of having slaves on board. But under Brazilian influence Mozambique continued to sell slaves and was threatening to declare itself independent from Portugal. This was exactly what Brazil had done earlier.

Although the slave trade declined after 1850, it continued until the 1880s when more pressure was brought to bear upon Portugal to take stronger action against Mozambique to end the shameful activities in the Zambezi valley area. Eventually, Portugal took action against the slavers and the prazo system itself was finally abolished in 1890.

The beginning of Portuguese interest in Kazembe

Although the Portuguese had settled in the Zambezi valley since the early decades of the sixteenth century, it was not until the late eighteenth century that their interest turned northwards across the river. During the late eighteenth century their position in the Zambezi valley area was beginning to be unsafe. We have, for instance, seen how the Changamire defeated and expelled the Portuguese from the Zimbabwe high veld towards the end of the seventeenth century. Some of them must have begun then to look to the north as a possible area of expansion. Indeed the economic possibilities in the north were already known to the Portuguese. African traders from the Luangwa and the Kafue valley areas had been bringing to the Portuguese ivory, copper and even gold. This trade increased during the eighteenth century. The Lenje at Zumbo sold copper to Portuguese traders which was already smelted into bars and which, when exported to India, was preferred to that from Europe. Other traders coming to Zumbo with ivory included the Nsenga, Lamba, Ambo and Lala.

To the north of Tete was Undi, which supplied gold, ivory and other valuables (see pages 36–7). The Undi gold trade brought the Portuguese into contact with Bisa caravan men bringing Kazembe's ivory to the Yao. It was after 1795 that Portuguese interest in the Kazembe state became more pronounced. It was feared towards the end of the century that the British, who had taken the Cape, might use their position to push northwards into the heart of Africa, thus separating Angola from Mozambique. The solution for the Portuguese lay in linking up their two areas (Angola and Mozambique) with the Kazembe state. Several attempts were made by Portuguese explorers to establish this link, which would also link the East African coast to the Angolan coast. The key to this scheme was the state of Kazembe, through which the Portuguese would have to pass.

The Lacerda expedition to Kazembe
The first organised official expedition to try to open the trans-African route from Mozambique to Luanda via Kazembe was undertaken in 1798 under the leadership of Dr Francisco da Lacerda, the governor of Sena. Lacerda, an experienced explorer, had assumed the Sena Governorship in 1797. He planned the trans-continental trip via Kazembe and Mwata Yamvo's country, although he was opposed by traders at Sena who were satisfied with the local slave trade. In spite of this opposition the mission began as planned in July 1798. Lacerda took with him 400 slave porters, 62 soldiers and 3 experienced guides. Two of the guides, Goncalo Pereira and his son, Manoel, had been to Kazembe's capital in 1786. Manoel had in fact brought with him the first full account of the Kazembe state. It was this account which had greatly influenced Lacerda's decision to undertake the long and dangerous expedition across the African continent in 1798.

The journey was very difficult. Half the porters deserted and those that remained with the expedition had to be whipped to keep them going. They were either unwilling to go on the expedition or were not being well treated. Women had to be brought in to carry heavy loads on very long distances. Food was scarce and this probably contributed largely to the porters' uncooperative behaviour. The Chewa, through whose country the expedition passed, were hostile. There were wars between the Bemba and the Bisa, and between the Bemba and the Lunda of Kazembe, thus making travel in those parts very dangerous.

The expedition reached Kazembe's capital on 3 October 1798 but by that time Lacerda was very ill with fever. He died on 18 October, before he had had the opportunity to meet Kazembe Ilunga Lukwesa. The Portuguese had to wait for almost two months at the capital before they could have an audience with the king. Finally, Lukwesa agreed to meet Lacerda's successor, Father Francisco Pinto. Pinto found the Kazembe very gentle and friendly. But the king would not grant the Portuguese permission to pass through his land to Mwata Yamvo's because, correctly, he regarded them as trade rivals.

Pinto had to lead his expedition back to Mozambique on a journey that was as difficult as the journey to Kazembe's. In addition to the wars, he had to contend with the rain which had begun. There was also the problem of Bisa and the Chewa, who were bitterly opposed to Portuguese efforts to interfere with their trade. Many more members of the expedition deserted. The party arrived at Tete in November 1799.

Later missions to Kazembe

The following mission, which was not official, was undertaken in 1802 from Angola by two Angolan *pombeiros*, Pedro Baptista and Amara José. They took almost nine years travelling from Luanda to Tete via Kazembe's and back. Four years of this period were spent at Kazembe's capital (1806–1810). The two men made very important observations while in the Lunda country of Kazembe. Baptista kept a diary in which he recorded details about copper mining in the country; and about a war between the Lunda and the Bisa, and between the Lunda and the Tanga Tabwa. It appears that the Bisa were at this time beginning to take over some of Kazembe's trade. Baptista and José arrived back at Luanda in 1811.

In 1824 the Portuguese acquired some land from Chief Mwase of Lundazi in the Luangwa valley area. A military garrison was posted there in 1827. The idea was to take over Kazembe's trade from the north-west. By this time, however, Swahili and Yao traders were becoming too strong and in 1829 the Luangwa valley post was abandoned.

The last Portuguese attempt to establish contacts with Kazembe was in 1831 by two army officers from Mozambique. These were Antonio Pedroso Gammitto and José Correa Monteiro and they were accompanied by about 100 slave porters. This mission, like the others, failed in its objectives. By now the Swahili traders from the east coast were becoming very important in the Kazembe trade. The reigning Kazembe, Kaleka, like Ilunga Lukwesa before him, saw the Portuguese as a threat to his own interests. He therefore refused Gammitto and Monteiro permission to cross into the copper-rich Shaba area (Katanga) and thereby link up with the Mwata Yamvo state. He also forbade them to trade with anybody except his own representatives. The Portuguese, in this, as in other expeditions, did not impress the African rulers as people who could do better trade than the coastal Swahili. They also spoilt their own position in that they always came with a huge military force as if to invade Kazembe's country. The Swahili came in small numbers and were willing to settle among the local people and even accept some of their customs. The Portuguese were arrogant in their attitudes to the African people and consequently they were rejected while the Swahili were accepted. Thus the search for the trans-continental trade route from the east coast to the west coast via Kazembe was abandoned.

PART IV
Effects of Mfecane/Difaqane

12 The Ndebele

What is Mfecane or Difaqane; how did it originate?
The rise of the Zulu nation under Shaka's leadership during the first quarter of the nineteenth century was followed by widespread wars and general disturbances not only in Natal but also in most of the southern African region and beyond as far as Central Africa and East Africa. Among the most affected were the Nguni and the Sotho speaking peoples of Southern Africa who still remember these times of great trouble as *Mfecane* (Nguni) and *Difaqane* or *Lifaqane* (Sotho). Literally these words mean the 'great crushing' or 'grinding'.

Some time towards the end of the eighteenth century two northern Nguni chiefdoms were transformed into large-scale kingdoms. These were the Ndwandwe under Zwide and Dingiswayo's Mthethwa. By about 1818 or 1819, however, the two kingdoms had been destroyed by war and new ones were emerging to take their places. The most important of these new ones were Sobhuza's Ngwane kingdom in the north and Shaka's Zulu kingdom in the south. Many smaller Nguni states fell apart completely as their people were either killed or incorporated into more powerful kingdoms. Several other groups fled the general Nguni area where a similar breakdown of the political system took place, before they settled in new areas and built new kingdoms. Three of these concern us in this book because they all came as far as Central Africa. These were the Ndebele, the Ngoni and the Kololo. The first two were of Nguni origin and the Kololo were Sotho-speaking and they originated from the west of the Drakensberg mountains. We should now discuss these groups, starting with the Ndebele.

Origins of the Ndebele
At the height of his power, Shaka, the Zulu military king, had successfully conquered and brought under Zulu rule most of the northern and central Nguni communities. Among the chiefdoms that had either been conquered by or voluntarily joined the Zulu nation, was Khumalo, led by Mzilikazi, son and successor of Mashobane.

Mzilikazi was accorded special treatment by the king. He was Shaka's most trusted and the most favoured *induna* and general. For this reason he was allowed to have his own army. He was also allowed full political control of his Khumalo section of the Zulu nation. Moreover, he had, voluntarily, joined the Khumalo chiefdom to Shaka's Zulu at the time when Shaka was fighting the Ndwandwe of Zwide; Zwide was Mzilikazi's maternal uncle and king. This Mzilikazi had done because Zwide had killed Mashobane whom he suspected of having conspired with Dingiswayo to fight against the Ndwandwe. Thus, when Shaka defeated Zwide's Ndwandwe at the celebrated battle of Mhlatuze river in 1818/19, Mzilikazi was already on the Zulu side.

Mzilikazi's revolt and the journey to a new land
As a trusted induna and general, Mzilikazi carried

An artist's impression of Shaka, King of the Zulus

successfully beaten off, but the second one went against Mzilikazi and his Khumalo army. They were thoroughly beaten at the battle of Nthumbane hill. But the Khumalo were not destroyed. Mzilikazi and many of his fighting men survived. But now they had no hope of protecting themselves and their cheifdom from Shaka's wrath except by leaving their land. Thus in about 1822, Mzilikazi led his Khumalo people northwards across the Drakensberg escarpment into the high veld. The nation-building career which was to end about thirty years later north of the Limpopo in Zimbabwe had begun.

The Khumalo's more superior military methods and strict discipline gave Mzilikazi's small band of warriors great advantage over the peoples through whose lands they passed during the northward march. By about 1822/23 they had reached the upper Olphant's river where they settled for some time to rest. Thus the new settlement was called ekuPumuleni (the resting place). EkuPumuleni was established in the Ndzundza area and most Ndzundza were later absorbed into the Khumalo nation. Raids were conducted from here into neighbouring areas on behalf of his king. Whatever booty he brought from such raids was handed over to Shaka who often rewarded his general. It would appear, however, that as time went by, Mzilikazi began to resent his inferior position under Shaka and the fact that he was working to enrich the Zulu king. He probably felt that he should carry out those raids to build up his own power and wealth. This, of course, could not be acceptable to Shaka. Indeed, the break between the two men came in about 1821 when Mzilikazi was sent on a mission to raid Sotho-speaking neighbours to the northwest of the Zulu kingdom. The mission yielded a lot of cattle which Mzilikazi decided to keep for himself instead of handing them over to Shaka. To make matters even worse he ill-treated the messengers sent by Shaka to plead with him to surrender the booty to the king. This action was understood by Shaka to be an open rebellion against him and a declaration of war on the Zulu nation. Appropriate military action was therefore necessary.

In the same year Shaka sent a regiment to punish Mzilikazi's Khumalo rebels. The first attack was

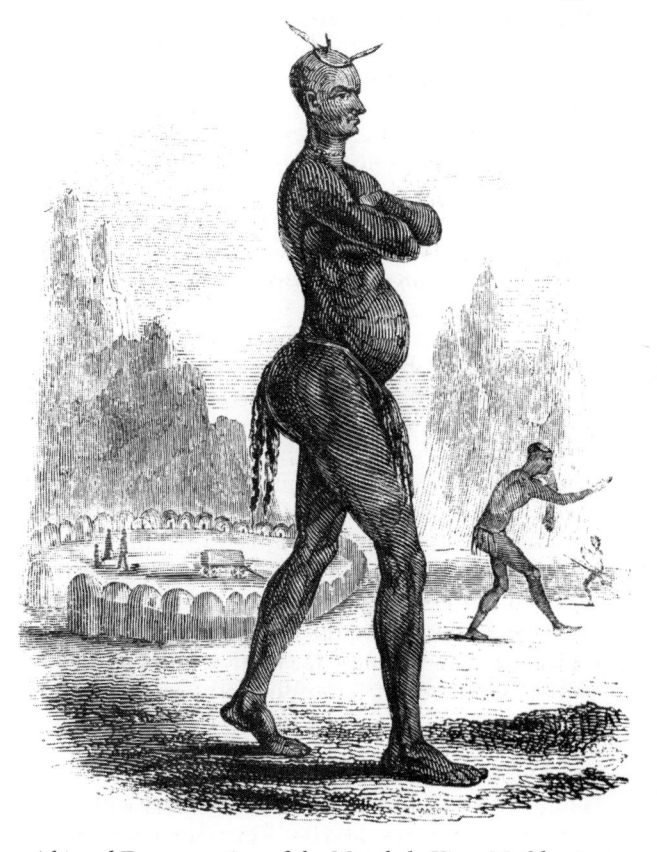

A biased European view of the Matabele King, Mzilikazi

Zulu warriors dressed for battle

bouring areas and they brought home much booty, young men and women and cattle who were integrated into the new nation, now known as the Ndebele.

EkuPumuleni was, however, not suitable for a permanent settlement because it was too close to Zululand and Shaka, who was still determined to punish Mzilikazi. Then there were the Pedi nearby who were a threat to the Ndebele. The grazing in this area was not good and especially after the serious drought of 1823/24. So ekuPumuleni had to be abandoned for a new place to the west near where Pretoria stands. By 1826 a new capital, Mhlahlandela, had been established in that predominantly Kwena land. Mzilikazi's capital was called Emhlahlandhlela, and there were other military towns such as Endinaneni and Enkungqini.

Here again, the arrival of the Ndebele brought the relative peace and prosperity which the Northern Sotho-speakers had enjoyed for generations to a violent end. During the years 1826 to the early 1830s, Ndebele regiments carried out destructive raids, not only among the communities of central and northern Transvaal, but also as far as Botswana, Lesotho and even Zimbabwe. Cattle and captives were brought from these raids to swell the Ndebele herds and to increase the nation. It was here that the London Missionary Society's pioneer missionary, Robert Moffat from Kuraman Mission, found the Ndebele king and his people in 1829, and the two men established a friendship that was to last many years.

Though excellent cattle country, the new area was far from satisfactory in other respects. It was, for instance, too close to Zululand, now under Dingane after Shaka's assassination in 1828. Dingane was just as determined as Shaka to punish the Ndebele and, indeed, in 1830 a regiment from Zululand attacked the Ndebele. Although no decisive victory was achieved by either side, the incident had left the Ndebele shaken and with a sense of insecurity. There were also hostile groups of Kora and Khoisan people to the south of the Ndebele, who might attack at any time. An attack by any of these groups might be serious because they had guns. There was also the possibility of these groups combining with Kwena people against the Ndebele. Indeed, immediately after the Zulu attack, the Ndebele were invaded by a Griqua-led force consisting of Griquas and Rolong warriors and many Ndebele cattle were captured.

Under these circumstances Mzilikazi was once again compelled to move his settlement to a new area. He had always wanted to take the country of the Hurutshe to the west, partly because it was close to his friend Moffat's mission and partly because it was good for cattle. Thus by about 1832 the Ndebele had settled around the headwaters of Marico, driving away the Hurutshe. Once again, Moffat visited his friend here. Another white visitor was Dr Andrew Smith of the Central African Expedition, who came in 1835.

Mzilikazi had hoped that his friendship with Moffat might stop Griqua and Kora from attacking his people. But he was proved wrong when in June–July 1831 a combined Tswana-Griqua force struck while the Ndebele army was away on a raiding mission against Moshoeshoe's Basotho and Moletsane's Taung in Lesotho. This attack was followed by another one, in 1834 by the Kora and the Griqua. More and more Griqua and Kora groups from the south crossed the Vaal on hunting expeditions in 1836. Then there were Boers from Potgieter's settlement in the south who, like the Kora and Griqua also came for big game hunting in the area. None of these groups sought Mzilikazi's permission to hunt in his land and accordingly the Ndebele ruler sent his army to drive them away. In the battles that followed there were heavy losses in men, women and cattle on both sides. Potgieter's Boers were forced to retreat to the south and they finally settled at Thaba Nchu in the Orange Free State.

These events indicate clearly that the Ndebele were not secure. The list of enemies was growing longer and longer and it now included Boers, Kora and Griqua who were armed with the dreaded gun. They were likely to strike again. Indeed this fear was confirmed in January 1837 when Potgieter's Boers, assisted by Griqua, Kora and Tlokwa and Rolong elements struck against Mosega, Mzilikazi's new capital. The Ndebele army was away on a raiding mission and for this reason the attackers found it easy to sack the settlement and to kill almost all its inhabitants. Meanwhile, Dingane, who still regarded Mzilikazi as a wanted runaway rebel sent yet another punitive expedition to attack Mosega. The Zulu attack was beaten off but with heavy losses in cattle and sheep. Taking advantage of the relative weakness of the Ndebele, the local Hurutshe, Griqua and other groups raided the Ndebele for cattle.

Migration across the Limpopo

These problems finally compelled Mzilikazi and his Ndebele to migrate farther north in about 1837. They moved in two groups and followed different paths. The main group consisting of old people, women and children and most of the cattle, sheep and goats left first under the leadership of Induna Gundwane Ndiweni, also known as Kaliphi. This group also included most of Mzilikazi's sons. Nkulumane, the heir apparent was also in this group, so was his brother Lobengula. The group followed a relatively direct and short route, crossing the Motloutse and the Shashe rivers. From there they went to the Mzingwane valley which they followed until they came to a place not far from the Matopo hills in western Zimbabwe. As we now know, this was a Rozvi country (see pages 43–4). The first Ndebele settlement in Zimbabwe was established here and named after Shaka's military town of Gibixhegu. In fact Gibixhegu was not far from one of the famous and most important Rozvi military strongholds, Nhava ya Tumbare.

The second migration group under Mzilikazi followed a longer route. The king was assisted by some of his senior indunas, including Magqekeni Sithole. They took a westward direction through Ngwato territory and then went further westwards still, towards Lake Ngami on the edges of the Kalahari Desert. From here they followed a north-eastward route towards the Zambezi valley. It was while he was on the Zambezi that Mzilikazi heard that the leaders of the main group, having given up any hope of ever linking up with his group, had settled at Gibixhegu and decided to make Nkulumane king in his place. The enraged Mzilikazi rushed to Gibixhegu leaving the rest of the army to cross the Zambezi and raid the Kololo in Bulozi. It is not very clear what exactly happened when Mzilikazi reached Gibixhegu. What is certain, however, is that Induna Ndiweni and his fellow chiefs, who had decided to make Nkulumane, the new king, were executed for treason. The fate of Nkulumane is not known. Some people say he was secretly killed, while others say that he was sent out of the country. Anyway, he disappeared and nobody was ever to mention his name again. But, about thirty-one years later after Mzilikazi's death, a man from Zululand called Kanda claimed to be Nkulumane and wanted to succeed Mzilikazi. His claim was not successful, however. The place where Gundwane Ndiweni and others were executed, Nhava ya Tumbare, was later called Ntaba ye Zinduna (the mountain of chiefs). Mzilikazi established his new capital at Inyati, not far away from modern Bulawayo.

Early years of Ndebele settlement in western Zimbabwe

By the 1840s the Ndebele had established themselves in their new land in western Zimbabwe, later to be known as Matabeleland. As already seen, this was a predominantly Shona-speaking area, the centre of the Rozvi state. The people the Ndebele found were, in fact, descendants of those peoples whom we have already identified as the builders of the Iron Age Leopard's Kopje culture (see page 12). For about three centuries the area had been under

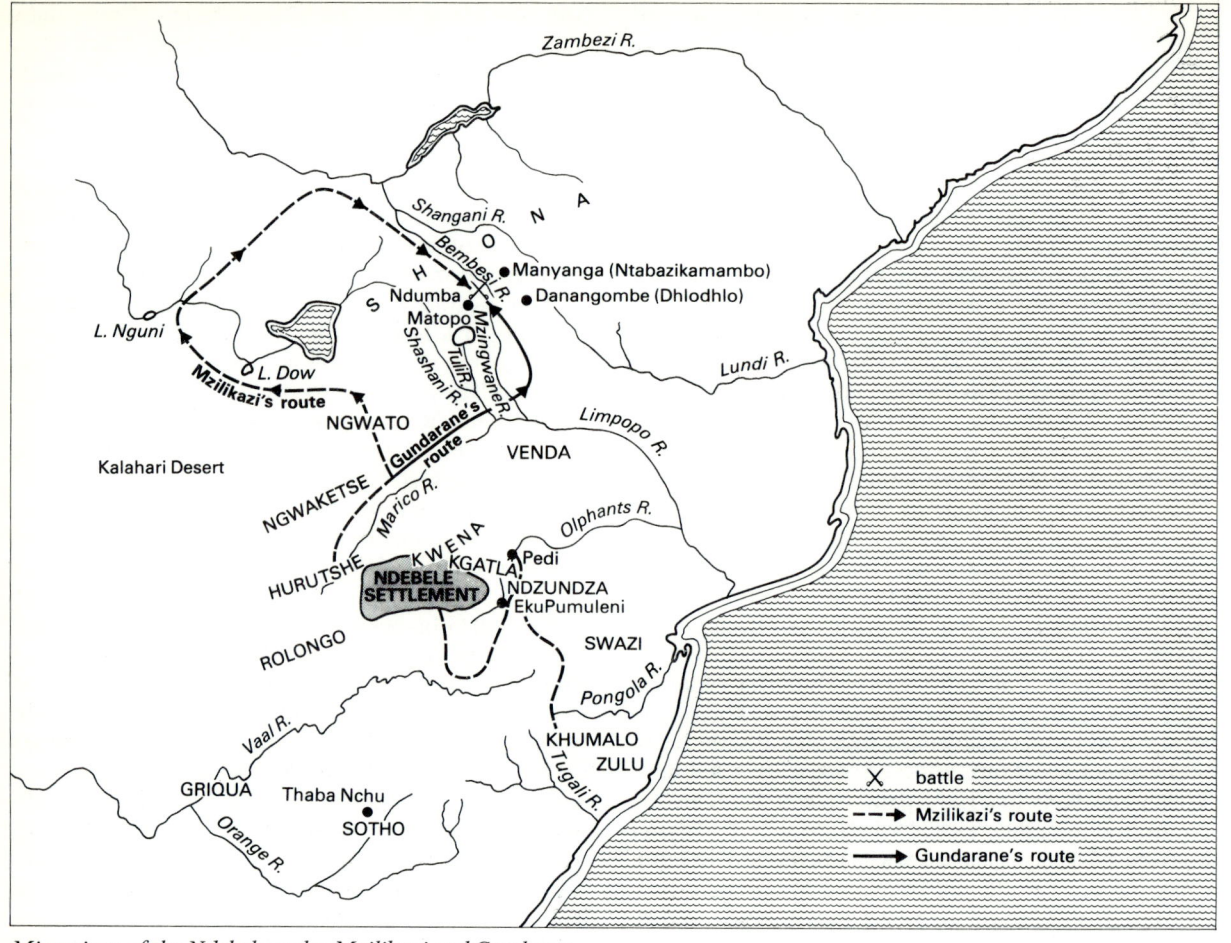

Migrations of the Ndebele under Mzilikazi and Gundarne

the Rozvi mambos of the Changamire dynasty. The Danangombe (dhlodhlo) and Manyanga (Ntaba zika Mambo) stone buildings in the area, are attributed to the Changamire period.

Mzilikazi's Ndebele were not the first Mfecane migrants to come to this part of Zimbabwe, nor were they responsible for the decline and collapse of the great Rozvi state of the Changamires. By the time of the Ndebele arrival, whatever still remained of the once powerful Changamire empire was very weak as a result of both internal and external factors. In fact by the end of the eighteenth century the kingdom had been reduced to a kind of confederacy of Shona chiefdoms. This confederacy was split into two camps in about 1800 because of civil wars and, perhaps, disputes about succession. It was at this time that Zimbabwe was invaded in 1831/32 by the Ngoni of Zwangendaba. Zwangendaba struck against Tumbare's stronghold at Nhava ya Tumbare, but was beaten off by the Rozvi general. Although the Rozvi forced the main Ngoni group to run towards what is now Mashonaland to the north-east, one group under its woman general, Nyamazana, had remained in south-west Zimbabwe. When the main group under Zwangendaba ultimately crossed the Zambezi in 1835, Nyamazana remained in the country to continue the attacks against the Rozvi. It was Nyamazana's Ngoni who, according to traditions, killed the Rozvi ruler, Mambo Chirisamhuru II, in about 1836.

Nyamazana and her people settled in the country until the arrival of the Ndebele in about 1838/39. The Ndebele found her already in control of a large section of what is now Matabeleland. It is said that Mzilikazi was so struck by the beauty of this Ngoni woman that he married her. Thus she became a Ndebele queen while her soldiers were absorbed into the Ndebele military or regimental structures.

The Ndebele settled in the western part of the

Rozvi area, a very good cattle country which was very welcome to the Ndebele who had brought with them much cattle, sheep and goats. Most Shona in this area at first fled their homes although some of them came back later and were allowed to settle under Mzilikazi. They were required to pay tribute to the Ndebele king in the form of grain and animals. Their young men and boys had to join Ndebele regiments, the *amabutho*. Mzilikazi also took positive measures to win the acceptance of his Shona subjects who otherwise continued to regard themselves as Rozvi people. The measures included military action and also peaceful methods, such as the distribution of his cattle among Shona chiefs and their people under the *ukulagisa* system, very similar to the Shona system of *kuronzera*, which we have already seen (see pages 43–4).

Ndebele society as it developed in Zimbabwe was divided into three broad sections. The first was known as the *Zansi*, mainly the original Khumalo and other Nguni elements who formed the aristocracy. Below them and second in importance, were the *Enhla*, made up of all the elements that had been incorporated into the Ndebele nation either voluntarily or forcibly in the course of the long journey from Zululand to Zimbabwe. As seen, this group included such elements as Sotho, Tswana, Kora and Griqua, with whom the Ndebele fought and from whom many young men, women and children were captured. The last group which was usually looked down upon, was the Shona and Leya and others who were collectively referred to as the *Holi* or *Hole*. Although all the people living under the rule of the Ndebele were encouraged or often required to speak the Ndebele language, as a rule marriage between the Zansi and the other groups was not encouraged. This does not mean to say there was no national unity in the Ndebele state. On the contrary, because everybody spoke Ndebele, and was officially regarded as Ndebele, there was a remarkable degree of national unity. Also the policy regarding marriage between the various sections was often violated by individual families who allowed their children to marry across the lines thus creating lasting relationships between such families.

Internal and external threats
Because of both internal and external threats to the security and stability of the nation, defence continued to be a priority in Mzilikazi's government. Military towns were established in many parts of the kingdom. At each of these centres Mzilikazi posted an *ibutho* or regiment. By 1868 when Mzilikazi died many military villages had been established and each one had its own regiment.

Mzilikazi needed a strong army to help him establish his authority in the new land. The Shona, and especially the Rozvi rulers whom the Ndebele had replaced, resisted Ndebele intrusion by military force. Such people had to be defeated and brought under control. A strong army was also needed to raid the neighbouring communities for cattle, grain, women and young men who would be incorporated into the Ndebele society. Such raids were carried out annually in the Shona areas, and to the west as far as Botswana and across the Zambezi in the north. Thus, the Leya and the Hlengwe have also made their own contribution to the Ndebele society. The independent Shona chiefdoms to the east in particular vigorously defended their areas against Ndebele invasion and tribute had to be collected from them by force.

There were also a lot of external dangers to the Ndebele nation during the early years of settlement in Zimbabwe. For instance, in about 1847 Boers from the Zoutpansbergs area in the Transvaal invaded the kingdom from across the Limpopo and they destroyed a number of outlying Ndebele villages. The Boers, under Mzilikazi's old enemy, Potgieter, were later beaten off by the Ndebele.

The Transvaal Boers were not the only source of danger to the Ndebele kingdom. There were many hunters and adventurers from the south who came into the country. Missionaries and traders also came and all the coming and going threatened the internal stability of the kingdom. Sometimes Mzilikazi dealt with them in a diplomatic way by entering into an agreement with them. For example, in 1852 he allowed the Boers to hunt in his area and in 1859 the London Missionary Society was allowed to establish a mission station at Inyati. The first mission station in Zimbabwe was established after lengthy diplomatic negotiations with Dr Robert Moffat, Mzilikazi's old missionary friend. Moffat visited Mzilikazi in 1854, 1857 and 1859. In 1867, a year before Mzilikazi's death, the white traders and travellers Karl Mauch and Hartley had found gold at Tati on the Ndebele–Ngwato border. By 1868 when Mzilikazi died, the value of the Ndebele area was already well-known among the white communities in the south. Mzilikazi was succeeded by his son, Lobengula, who inherited the problems created by external forces. The situation was complicated even more by the fact that after the death of Mzilikazi, Lobengula had to fight a civil war in order to win the succession.

13 The Kololo of Sebetwane

Origins and journey to Central Africa
The Kololo were Sotho-speaking people from the Transorangia area. They were made up of a number of elements, the more important of which were the two Fokeng groups. Their migration from the original area under chief Sebetwane was the result of Difaqane or Mfecane. Sebetwane himself was a Patsa Fokeng. The Patsa Fokeng were forced to abandon their land by attacks from the Tlokwa (Tlokoa) of Mma Ntatisi, who had taken their cattle. They fled across the Vaal river being joined by other Fokeng groups. Sebetwane's father who leading the Patsa section was killed by a hungry lion and was succeeded by Sebetwane. The enthusiastic young leader soon established his authority over the whole migratory group. Since there was no question of going back to the Transorangia area due to the unsettled conditions there, Sebetwane decided to look for a new area for his people. This had to be far away from any threats and disturbances.

Because their immediate need was to replace the lost cattle now in Tlokoa hands, they trekked westwards towards the Tlapin who were known to have much cattle. They arrived at the Tlapin capital, Dithakong in 1823 and were met and fought by the Tlapin and the Griqua. This force was too strong for the Fokeng because the Griqua had guns and fought on horseback. Sebetwane led his humiliated people northwards through Tswana-occupied territory until finally reaching the Molopo river where they defeated the northern Rolong around Khunwana. In spite of this victory, the Kololo did not remain long in this area and moved on to the country of the Hurutshe. They had no difficulty in defeating the Hurutshe, but they were themselves in turn defeated by the Ndebele of Mzilikazi, who were also on their northward march. The Kololo left the Hurutshe country and continued their journey in a north-westerly direction via Botswana. Here they found and attacked the Kgabo-Kwena and the Tshwane-Tlokoa. Sebetwane even gained temporary control of Dithubaru, the Kwena centre, before he was forced to leave the area by the Ngwaketsi. Sebatwane had already sent an advance party to the north to raid and spy on the Ngwato of the Shoshong Hill area. This was about 1826/27.

The timing of this expedition was excellent because Kgari's Ngwato were facing difficulties due to the drought of 1826/27. The Kololo struck at the Ngwato who had sought refuge in the Kutswe mountains between Shoshong and Serowe. The Ngwato had lost most of their cattle and whatever little grain they had reaped from the poor harvest of 1826/27. As soon as the Kololo invaders left, Kgari decided to go and raid the Kalanga of the Matopo area in southwest Zimbabwe in order to make good his people's losses at the hands of Sebatwane's Kololo. Unfortunately, the Ngwato were ambushed in the Matopo mountains resulting in the deaths of Kgari, several of his brothers and almost half of his force. The survivors managed to reach the Kutswe hills area some time between the end of 1827 and beginning of 1828 to be met and attacked by the main Kololo force under Sebatwane on the northward trek. As they were still too weak they were easily defeated and driven out of the hills. The area was occupied by Sebetwane's Kololo for some months before they proceeded on their northward march.

The northward march was hard as they went through the Kalahari Desert. Most of the travelling was done at night and they moved in small groups resting for some time at Lake Kamadou from where raiding expeditions were organised against the local areas. These raids were necessary as the Kololo had lost most of their cattle in the desert.

During the period 1831 to 1835 the Kololo were temporarily established around Lake Ngami. Once again, raids were organised into neighbouring areas, especially the Herero of Namibia who owned fine herds. The Herero fought them with bows and arrows.

From the Lake Ngami area the Kololo travelled across the Okavango river until they finally reached the Chobe where a temporary settlement was established at Dinyanti (Tshoroga). Here Sebetwane remained for about a year (1835–36). He defeated and ruled the Subiya fishermen and some Tswana. The Chobe valley area proved to be unhealthy and the Kololo moved on to the shores of the Zambezi which they found dominated by the Tonga. The Tonga resisted the Kololo advance but were defeated. The Kololo captured a lot of cattle, sheep and goats. A settlement was established on the Toka Plateau south of the Kafue around 1839/40. This was found to be excellent cattle land.

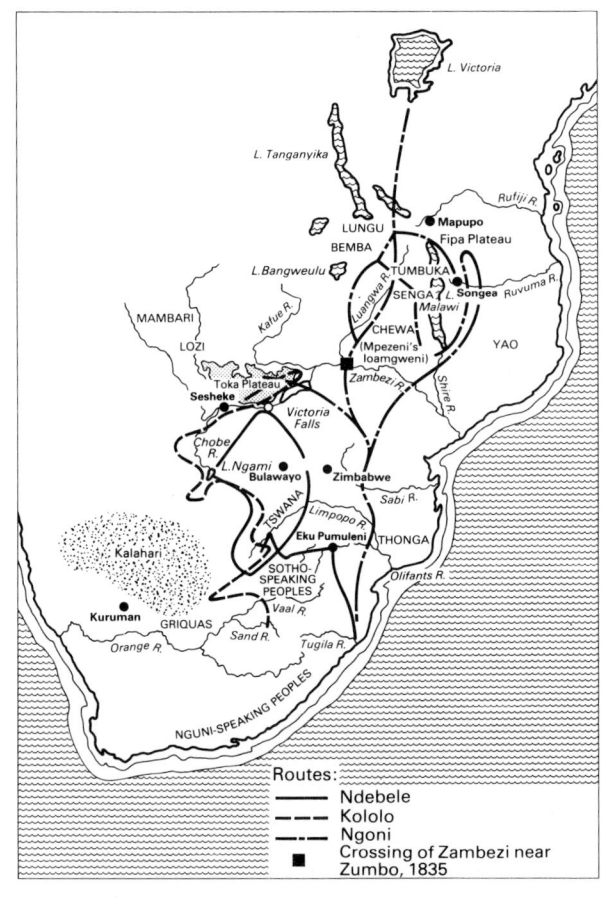

Kololo settlement in Zambia

The Kololo settlement on the upper Zambezi was not achieved without hard struggle. Having subdued most of the chiefdoms on the Toka Plateau, the Kololo crossed the difficult flood plain of the Kafue river. Canoes were used in this and local fishermen paddled them as the Kololo knew nothing about canoes. The Kololo entered the country of the Ila who resisted the intruders by force but were beaten in a battle that was fought over three days. Although very good fighters, the Ila were defeated because they were not organised into a

Left: Journeys of the Mfecane peoples

Below: The Kololo became skilful at fighting on water. The flooded Zambezi above Victoria Falls

single force. From there the Kololo reached as far as the Sala area near Lusaka. They captured the Sala religious leader, Priestess-Chief Longo. It was while they were here that a Kololo prophet warned Sebetwane against trekking farther to the east because there would be a great deal of danger, possibly from the Portuguese and their Chikunda allies in the Zambezi valley, or maybe from Swahili traders from the east coast. Instead, the prophet advised the Kololo to turn to the west where they would find a country of fine red cattle. Here Sebetwane would found a new nation among the owners of the red cattle.

Thus Sebetwane led his Kololo westwards towards the Luyi country or Bulozi, in the plains of the upper Zambezi in Zambia's Western Province. But on the way the Kololo met a Ndebele force sent by Mzilikazi to invade the Toka Plateau area. The two Mfecane groups clashed somewhere near Kalomo. The Kololo, who were joined by their women, fought bravely and beat off the Ndebele. The hill at which the fighting took place was later called by the Kololo, *Thaba ya basadi* (the women's mountain) in honour of the brave Kololo women. This war took place around 1840, probably at the time when the Ndebele force was on its way to southwestern Zimbabwe where an advance party had established itself at Gibixhegu (see page 69).

The Kololo finally arrived in the land of the Luyi or Bulozi. At that time Bulozi was ruled by its twelfth Litunga, Mubukwanu. The kingdom was very weak because of succession wars which raged for about ten years following the death of Litunga Mulambwa in about 1830 (see page 34). This was complicated by the death of the eleventh Litunga at the hands of the Mbunda. Thus when Mubukwanu emerged as the ruler, he inherited a disunited Bulozi. Sebetwane took great advantage of the disunity among the Luyi in establishing his authority in the area.

The kingdom had been split into two hostile parts, the south and the north. There was also division between the Lozi proper and the conquered subject peoples. In the battles that followed the Kololo arrival in the kingdom, Sebetwane found support among the local people as well as from the *ngambela*, all of whom disliked the Litunga. By now the Kololo had also become skilful at operating canoes and were thus able to defeat Mabukwanu's force. The Litunga was forced into exile where he later died. He was followed by many Lozi leaders and commoners. One group, for example, under Imbua went to Nyengo while another followed Sinyama Sikufela in to Lukwakwa. Most Lozi, including Sipopa, son and heir apparent, remained in the country. Sebetwane took Sipopa and all the young men of the royal line and educated them as members of the Kololo aristocracy.

Progress in the establishment of Kololo control over Bulozi was hampered by invasions from the Msene-Ngoni under Nxaba during the period 1843–45. Although the invaders were always driven away, this was done at great cost in human life and animals. The Ndebele also came in 1845 and again in 1850, but they were cleverly defeated by the Kololo. They were lured to an island where Sebetwane had left some goats and they were cut off by the rising water of the river. They were also weakened by starvation. A larger force sent equipped with canoes and instructed to establish ties with the river people was also starving and was then defeated by the Kololo. The Ndebele never tried again to invade the Kololo.

The final defeat of the Msene-Ngoni and the Ndebele did much to bring about unity in Sebetwane's new kingdom. Sebetwane's military leadership had greatly impressed many of his Luyi subjects. Trusted local chiefs were left in charge of their areas while some of them were given positions in the central government on the various state councils. Sebetwane mixed quite freely with his subjects, Kololo and Lozi. This contributed towards a spirit of trust and unity in the nation. To demonstrate his sincerity in being one with them, Sebetwane took wives from among the conquered groups. He also took measures to ensure that the Kololo language (a Sotho dialect) was spoken all over his kingdom. Sebetwane's rule was extended over most of the present Western Province of Zambia and over the Tonga areas of Kalomo and Livingstone in the Southern Province. Raids were also made into the Tonga and Ila areas of Choma, Mazabuka and Namwala in the Southern Province and in parts of Angola and Botswana, and even in north-western Zimbabwe.

Even in those areas where Kololo rule was established on a more permanent basis, Sebetwane did not force the conquered peoples to adopt the age-regiment system. He allowed the Lozi to continue their political and administrative institutions while at the same time doing all he could to encourage them to adopt his own methods. For instance, he always took care to place one or two Kololo families in every village as lords of the land. Villages were grouped into provinces under Kololo provincial governors. Subject people were encouraged to cultivate the land and they were also required to pay tribute in grain, nuts, spears, hoes, ivory, skins and canoes. Sebetwane took some of the tribute for himself and the rest was distributed among his people.

In 1850 the capital was moved from Naliele at the southern end of the upper Zambezi flood-plain to Dinyanti, an area not previously under the Luyi rulers. Strategic as well as economic considerations favoured Dinyanti as the centre of the kingdom. Strategically, Dinyanti on the Chobe river in Botswana enabled Sebetwane to defend his kingdom against any threat from the south. Perhaps for economic reasons Sebetwane was even more strongly in favour of moving the capital to Dinyanti because this was excellent cattle country. Dinyanti was also situated in the area where the wagon road from Ngamiland and the Cape ended. Beyond this point, travel was made risky by the tsetse fly which killed the oxen which pulled the traders' wagons. Dinyanti was also free from the malarial mosquito.

Sebetwane died at Dinyanti in July 1851, just after he had been visited by Dr. David Livingstone, the missionary explorer.

The end of Kololo rule in Bulozi
Sebetwane was succeeded by his daughter, Mamochisane who later abdicated in favour of her brother, Sekeletu. Unfortunately Sekeletu lacked his father's courage, intelligence and ability as a leader. He did not trust his official advisers, especially the Lozi. His councillors were chosen from among his own age-group only, but in time Sekeletu became suspicious even of these and had most of them killed. His suspicious nature increased when he became a leper. Many people, especially the Lozi, were suspected and accused of having bewitched Sekeletu.

During Sekeletu's reign, the Kololo became arrogant and they began to treat the Lozi as inferior and even like slaves. For instance the Lozi were made to do all the farm work while the Kololo waited to collect the produce. In fact after 1853 the Kololo even began to sell slaves to the Mambari slave traders from the Bihe country in Angola who were in the service of a Portuguese slave trader, Silvo Porto, who supplied them with guns and cloth to be given to the Kololo. Kololo participation in the slave trade did much to damage Kololo-Lozi relationships.

The Kololo, coming from the south, had very little resistance against malaria. This was a serious disadvantage. Some of them moved to the higher ground south of the flood plain, but most remained in the valley where the disease was becoming more widespread and rapidly weakening them.

The kingdom began to decline and fall apart. Livingstone who went there in August 1860 observed that Bulozi was by this time 'suffering grievously, and Sebetwane's grand empire was crumbling to pieces.' Sekeletu died in 1863 and his death was followed by a succession dispute leading to a civil war. The regent, Mpololo, was killed and his followers fled to the Lake Ngami area. For their part, the Lozi took this opportunity to regain their land from the now disorganised Kololo. They were also tired of Kololo misrule. Thus in 1864, they rose up in arms against their Kololo rulers. They were supported in their rebellion by groups of Tonga and the Kololo were easily defeated. Most of their older men were killed. The women, young men and children were spared and became part of the Lozi society.

It was not simply Mpololo's cruelty and the chaos that followed Sekeletu's death which sparked off the Lozi rebellion of 1864. The cause of the rebellion also emerged from the strong desire in human nature to be independent. It would appear that on the whole the Lozi did not dislike the Kololo as people, or their culture. The French missionary from Lesotho, Coillard observed that the Lozi 'always speak with affection and the highest (of the Kololo, and from the Kololo) they ... formed their ideal of the dignity, manner and power of a sovereign.' For instance the Lozi adopted the customs, manner of dressing and the language of the Kololo. They also began to call themselves Lozi instead of Luyi. Lozi rulers also supported the political centralisation maintained during Kololo rule. Political centralisation reached its greatest heights during the reign of Litunga Lewanika, as will be seen later. The Kololo had established a number of trade contacts and cattle raiding campaigns and these were continued by the Lozi rulers.

The Lozi were, however, still beset with internal differences when they regained political control from the Kololo. Each group had its own chief. Sipopa, the restored Litunga, tried without much success to establish central control. His own poor leadership contributed much to the failure of centralisation. He was killed in 1876. In March 1878 his successor, Litunga Mwanamwina II fled across the Kafue to be succeeded by Lubosi, popularly known as Litunga Lewanika. Lewanika faced opposition to his plan to reduce the powers and influence of the chiefs, some of whom had very strong private armies. He also wanted to re-introduce the land system used during the time before Kololo occupation, under which chiefs had owned too much land and again this was opposed by the powerful chiefs.

Lubosi, popularly known as Litungo Lewanika

He was temporarily deposed in 1884 but regained his position in 1885. Lewanika also fought the Tonga, Ila and Kaonde in order to create unity. However, in spite of all these efforts, opposition against him continued. In 1887 the missionary Coillard noted that the Litunga was 'suspicious of everybody, even those who brought him to power'. The main opposition came from the Sesheke chiefs. Bulozi was also threatened by the Ndebele and, in the late 1880s, by the European scramble for Central Africa.

The Kololo of the Shire River

Bulozi was not the only place with an established Kololo state. Other Kololo states were established in the Shire Highlands of Malawi. These kingdoms were founded in rather unusual circumstances and, strictly speaking, they cannot be regarded as Mfecane states. Dr David Livingstone, the missionary explorer, had been given about twenty-seven men by the Kololo ruler of Bulozi, Sekeletu, to help him as porters and guides in his journeys of exploration during the 1850s. These men were mostly Kololo although they also included other groups such as Lozi, Tonga, Subiya and Mbunda. When in 1860 Livingstone went back to Bulozi to return the men to their country, sixteen of them decided to remain in Malawi where they had married local women and founded new families. They had also acquired a few possessions including firearms. By now they were experienced in warfare. Coming from Bulozi, they also knew about Kololo political institutions.

Now, under the leadership of Kasisi and Molokwa, these men soon established themselves as chiefs over the peoples of the Shire Highlands. Unstable conditions in the area were favourable to the Kololo men. The Nganja and Yao refugees had been disorganised by slavers' activities and the invasion of the Shire Highlands area by the Maseko-Ngoni. Kasisi and Molokwa divided the area between themselves and in time two Kololo states were developed side by side in the Shire Highlands area. The two states soon established good relationships with the Yao and that strengthened their economic and political position.

Because of their special connection with Livingstone the two Kololo states of the Shire valley area were opposed to the activities of slave traders. It was also because of their connection with Livingstone that the two rulers readily welcomed the Livingstonia Mission and allowed them to establish a mission in the Shire Highlands to serve their nations.

14 The Ngoni

The Ngoni were another very important Mfecane group whose movement, like those of the Ndebele and Kololo, influenced historical developments in Central Africa. Like the Ndebele and the Kololo, the Ngoni were a mixture of various peoples united by language. They were Nguni-speaking although they acquired other languages in Central Africa. Today they are mainly found in Central Africa north of the Zambezi. They travelled to their new areas in several groups the main ones being the Jere-Ngoni under Zwangendaba; the Maseko-Ngoni first led by a man called Ngwane who was later succeeded by his son; Nxaba's Msene-Ngoni and the Ngoni of Nyamazana.

Jere-Ngoni

The Ngoni of Zwangendaba were made up of many elements of which the Jere were the largest. They came from northern Zululand. They fled their country after the Ndwandwe chief, who was also their overlord, was defeated by Shaka on the Mhlatuze River in about 1818. Zwangendaba succeeded in regrouping his Jere people and other small groups that had been dispersed by the war and were willing to accept his authority and led them northeastwards into southern Mozambique.

Although the peoples of southern Mozambique, mainly Thonga-speaking, were larger in numbers than Zwangendaba's migrants they offered very little opposition to the intruders. Moreover, Zwangendaba's people had learnt effective methods of war from Shaka's Zulu and they put them to good use during their northward trek. As they proceeded they were joined by many southern Mozambicans, especially Thonga, and in this way Zwangendaba's nation grew and his forces became more numerous and stronger. In 1826 the Jere-Ngoni defeated the Ndwandwe many of whom joined Zwangendaba and his forces became even more powerful.

In 1831 Zwangendaba met the Ndwandwe ruler, Soshangane and Nxaba, leader of the Msene-

Ngoni warrior

Ngoni. The three leaders quarreled and in the war that followed, both Zwangendaba and Nxaba were defeated by the Ndwandwe but they were not destroyed. They led their respective groups northwards. Zwangendaba's people travelled north-west towards the lower Zambezi valley area. Here they struck terror amongst the Portuguese settlers at Sena and Tete before turning southwards through the area formerly ruled by the Mwene Mutapa. In the meantime Nxaba's group, also running away from Soshangane, were entering the same area and the two clashed there in the lower Zambezi area. Zwangendaba was defeated and forced to continue his march south-westwards onto the Zimbabwean high veld. Here, as already seen, the tottering Rozvi empire of the Changamire *mambos* was nearing its end (see page 70). This was about 1832. However, the Rozvi army under its able general, Tumbare, bravely met the invaders at Tumbare's mountain stronghold, Nhava ya Tumbare (later called Ntaba ye Zinduna). Zwangendaba was successfully repelled and forced to march north-east into what is now Mashonaland, where his Ngoni caused a great deal of damage and destruction.

The Ngoni did not, however, remain long on the Zimbabwe plateau. The march continued until they crossed the Zambezi on 19 November 1835. They crossed the great river somewhere near Zumbo. However, one section of Zwangendaba's Jere-Ngoni decided to stay on in Zimbabwe, under one of Zwangendaba's chiefs a remarkable woman called Nyamazana. Nyamazana's section continued Ngoni attacks against the Rozvi and their people. It was this group that was, according to tradition, responsible for the killing of the last Changamire ruler, Mambo Chirisamhuru II, at his fortress Manyanga in about 1836.

There are many stories among the Shona relating to the way Mambo Chirisamhuru was killed by Nyamazana's people. One account says that the Rozvi king threw himself down a steep cliff to avoid being captured by the enemy. Another one says that he was captured and skinned alive. And yet another one holds that the Ngoni had been told about the fame of this great ruler and that his achievements and bravery were due to the fact that he had two hearts. Thus when Nyamazana captured Mambo Chirisamhuru she removed his heart from the body in order to prove that he had only one heart and not two as had been believed. Manyanga Hill, Chirisamhuru's fortress where he was killed, was later named by the Ngoni and the Ndebele, Ntaba zika Mambo, in memory of the last Changamire king. As already seen, Nyamazana's section of the Ngoni were later incorporated into the Ndebele of Mzilikazi and Nyamazana herself became one of the Ndebele king's queens, (pages 70–1).

The main Jere-Ngoni group, now including Tsonga and Shona elements, continued its migration northwards, settling for about four years in the Nsenga area and for another four years among the Chewa people. Then they moved northwards to the area at the source of the Luangwa on the Fipa plateau of western Tanzania. Zwangendaba established his headquarters at Mapupo and died there in about 1848.

Zwangendaba's death was followed by a succession dispute among his sons and members of the royal family. It would appear that Mbelwa, the youngest of the princes, had been chosen to succeed his father. But his elder brothers, especially Mpezeni and Mtwalo, both of whom had their own ambitions, opposed this. While the disagreement continued, one of the king's senior men, became acting leader of the Jere-Ngoni. This man was Ntabeni. Unfortunately he made the mistake of naming Mpezeni as Zwangendaba's new successor with Mtwalo as second in line. Mbelwa was banished to a new village. That only made the situation more complicated and led to the splitting of the Jere-Ngoni into five groups which settled in different areas as separate nations. The followers of Ntabeni settled in southern Tanzania as Tuta-Ngoni. Another group emerged under one of Zwangendaba's relatives called Zulu Gama, who led his group to the Songea district of Tanzania where they became known as Gwangwara-Ngoni.

The main group continued for some time under the joint leadership of two of Zwangendaba's chiefs, Mgayi and Gwaza. Gwaza showed wisdom by installing Mpezeni as leader of one group. This group later settled in the area of the Zambia-Malawi-Mozambique border. Gwaza led one of the groups to the Henga valley area in Malawi and here he offered the leadership to Mtwalo. Mtwalo declined the offer and, instead, recognised his young brother Mbelwa as leader saying, in the words of a Ngoni historian, Chibambo: 'I choose you as chief, tomorrow you may if you wish it, make an end of me'. The offer was accepted by Mbelwa and he did not kill Mtwalo, as the latter had feared. Instead, what resulted was a spirit of Ngoni reconciliation which was to play an important part in future Ngoni politics.

Mbelwa proved to be an able military leader, conquering a number of peoples including the Tumbuka-Kamanga and, as seen already, killing the Chikulamayembe (page 38). The Tumbuka, Henga and Thonga were taken captives. The raids were carried out as far as the Lake Malawi region, Kazembe's country and Lubemba. Mbelwa was, however, defeated by Mwase Kasungu, who had guns. But Mwase Kasungu later became a friend and ally of Mbelwa's. One of Mbelwa's raiding expeditions was led by Chiwere Ndhlovu, himself a Nsenga captive. Chiwere later broke away from Mbelwa to found his own Chiwere-Ngoni state in the Dowa district of central Malawi.

Meanwhile, Mpezeni had led his people towards Lake Bangweulo where they came into conflict with the Bemba in about 1850. After a very destructive battle, Mpezeni moved into the Nsenga territory taking with him many Nsenga captives – so many that his people became predominantly Nsenga-speaking. Around 1870 the Mpezeni-Ngoni settled in the Petauke district of eastern Zambia. From there they moved to the Chipata district where they defeated the Chewa of chief Mkanda in the late 1870s. Mpezeni's young brother who had also been defeated by the Bemba led his small group back to Malawi where he joined Mbelwa's kingdom.

Ngoni political and social organisation

In the Ngoni society the king was all-important. In the words of Chibambo: 'All the lesser chiefs and headmen received from him the leadership of the people ... they kept unity by messengers passing between them.' Once or twice a year the king called an *indaba*, or meeting of elders, to decide the laws. According to another Ngoni historian, Mwale, the Ngoni had 'one law for all people, and there were courts ... where this law was enforced'. These were the king's court and the village courts. There was a system of appeal fron one court to another.

An important feature of Ngoni society was the 'segment'. This was formed round a wife of the king. It included members of the king's family and their followers. Captives were added, and the segment grew bigger. As the sons of the king's wife became older they tended to split away and form households of their own. This led to fragmentation which was a source of weakness to the Ngoni.

In the village itself, houses were arranged in order of seniority. The most important group after the king were the *zansi*, the Nguni-speaking aristocracy. These normally took wives from among the same group. Below the zansi were the captives. Mbelwa and Mpezeni had different ways of treating the captives. When Mpezeni had conquered a group such as the Nsenga he sent them to different parts of his kingdom. This kept them apart and so prevented rebellion. Later he modified this policy, leaving some groups in their villages to carry out hunting and agricultural work and allowing others such as the Nsenga, Chewa and Kunda, who had resisted Ngoni rule, to pay tribute for not being raided.

This had been Mbelwa's policy from the start. The Tonga, Henga and Tumbuka living in Mbelwa's country had been allowed to live as separate communities paying tribute to the Ngoni king. This meant that they kept their identity and often rebelled. In 1875, for instance, the Tonga fled

Ngoni warriors at Hopa Mountain, Mzimba district

to Chinteche and Bandawe on the shores of Lake Malawi where they built stockaded villages. Mbelwa sent an army to crush the rebellion, but the Tonga, under their leader, Kazizwa, defeated Mbelwa's force. This was a bitter blow against the Ngoni. Mbelwa sent smaller forces which kept the Tonga penned in against the Lake. By 1878, according to missionaries in the area, the Tonga were in a pitiful condition.

In 1879 there was a rebellion by the Henga and Kamanga. Mbelwa crushed it, but a small group of Henga and Kamanga carried on the rebellion from a hill top. They were defeated only with the help of Mwase Kasungu and his guns. A few of the rebels escaped and lived a miserable life on islands of the Lake. In 1880 the Tumbuka escaped into the Hora mountains, but they were weakened by starvation and were easily crushed by Mbelwa.

The Maseko and Msene Ngoni
After their defeat by Soshangane in about 1831, the Maseko-Ngoni of Ngwane and the Msene-Ngoni of Nxaba split. Neither of the two travelled with Zwangendaba. The Maseko-Ngoni crossed the Zambezi at its mouth and settled somewhere in the country between Lake Malawi and the western coast of the Indian Ocean in the south-eastern section of Tanzania. Some time in about 1860 they were defeated by Zulu-Gama's Gwangwara-Ngoni living in the Songea district. The leadership of the group had now passed on to Mputa, Ngwane's son. They fled the Songea area and went to the Ncheu district of southern Malawi where, it would appear, the group was plunged into a civil war. This was a result of a succession dispute in which both Chikusi and Chifisi claimed the throne. Chikusi was successful in the fighting and he got the throne. Chifisi was not destroyed however and he remained in the kingdom as a potential threat to Chikusi.

Maseko-Ngoni's greatest success and achievement was during the years 1870 to 1885. At this time they carried out raids into areas east of Domwe. Ntumba, Chipeta, Nyanja and Mbo villages were brought under control. The Maseko-Ngoni even raided the Yao communities, forcing them to run to hilltops. The Yao were, however, assisted by the Kololo of the Shire Highlands area, who possessed guns (page 76). They were also helped by the white missionaries who were based at the Livingstonia Mission station.

By the mid-1880s, Yao slave traders were very active in the region. The southern end of the Lake was occupied by these people and many Yao chiefs possessed firearms. The Maseko-Ngoni on the other hand still relied on their short stabbing spear, clubs and bows and arrows. As time went by, the Maseko-Ngoni fell more and more under Yao influences. After the deaths of Chikusi and Chifisi another succession war broke out between their sons. Chikusi's son, Gomani, was successful, largely because of assistance from Mponda's Yao. The Maseko-Ngoni had also absorbed a lot of Chewa people into their society and as a result they were losing their original cohesion. There were differences in family units and raising children. When white people came to settle in the area the Maseko-Ngoni were more ready to join them as plantation labourers and domestic workers. Many more went to work for Mponda, the Yao chief. A lot of them also came under missionary influence. Raiding had now become less profitable and it was now more difficult for Ngoni chiefs to recruit for their regiments.

The Msene-Ngoni of Nxaba went towards the Mwene Mutapa kingdom after being beaten by Soshangane in 1831. As we have seen, Nxaba and Zwangendaba clashed in that area and Zwangendaba was defeated and forced to march towards the Zimbabwe high veld (page 78). Nxaba's people remained in Zimbabwe during most of the 1830s raiding the Shona for cattle and grain. They crossed the Zambezi into Zambia in the early 1840s. The Msene-Ngoni clashed with the Kololo of Sebetwane and Nxaba and most of his men were killed.

PART V
Nineteenth Century Traders, Explorers and Pioneer Missionaries

15 Nineteenth century traders and hunters

The nineteenth century witnessed a growing interest in the Central African interior, first among the Portuguese in Mozambique and in Angola as already seen (pages 64–5), and then among the East African coastal traders. The course of Central African history might not have changed very much had it not been for increasing interest from outsiders especially Europeans in the south during the last half of the century.

It was the activities, reports and writings of the European traders, explorers, hunters and missionaries which helped to focus Europe's interest in the African interior in the nineteenth century after centuries of association with the west and east coasts of Africa. The result of this growing interest in the African interior was the ultimate colonisation of the continent during the last decades of the nineteenth century by various European powers. This part of the book deals with the activities of the fore-runners of European occupation of Central Africa.

Swahili traders and the organisation of the caravan trade
Ivory, slaves and copper were by far the most important items of trade between the East African coast and the Central African interior. The main traders were Swahili from the east coast, the Yao of the Lake Malawi area and the Chikunda from the Zambezi valley area. The Central African interior also traded with the Angolan coast in the west and the Mambari and the Swahili were the main agents of this trade. The Mambari came from Angola. European traders, mainly Cape colonists and Boers from the Transvaal, were also to join in this trade.

Central Africa had been trading with the centres on the east coast for many centuries but it was not until the nineteenth century that traders from the coast actually ventured into the interior. The exception was the area to the south of the Zambezi where, as already seen, Swahili traders had established themselves at the courts of the Mwene Mutapa and other rulers even before the arrival of the Portuguese in the area. Otherwise, north of the great river, it was the people of the interior who took goods to the east coast. For instance, the Bisa are known to have carried ivory and copper from the state of Kazembe to the Portuguese in the Zambezi valley area and to the Swahili trading cities on the coast. This pattern, however, was altered some time towards the end of the eighteenth century and by the first two or three decades of the nineteenth century traders from the coast were seen in large numbers in the interior – in Zambia, Zaire and Malawi.

By 1831 Swahili traders, sometimes referred to as Arabs, were trading in Kazembe's kingdom. Nine years later in about 1840 Swahili traders were found in many parts to the north and east of the Shaba or Katanga region. They were also buying slaves from the Ila to sell on the West African coast. In 1850 two of them crossed the continent to Banguela. By this time they were also trading in the Congo Basin area

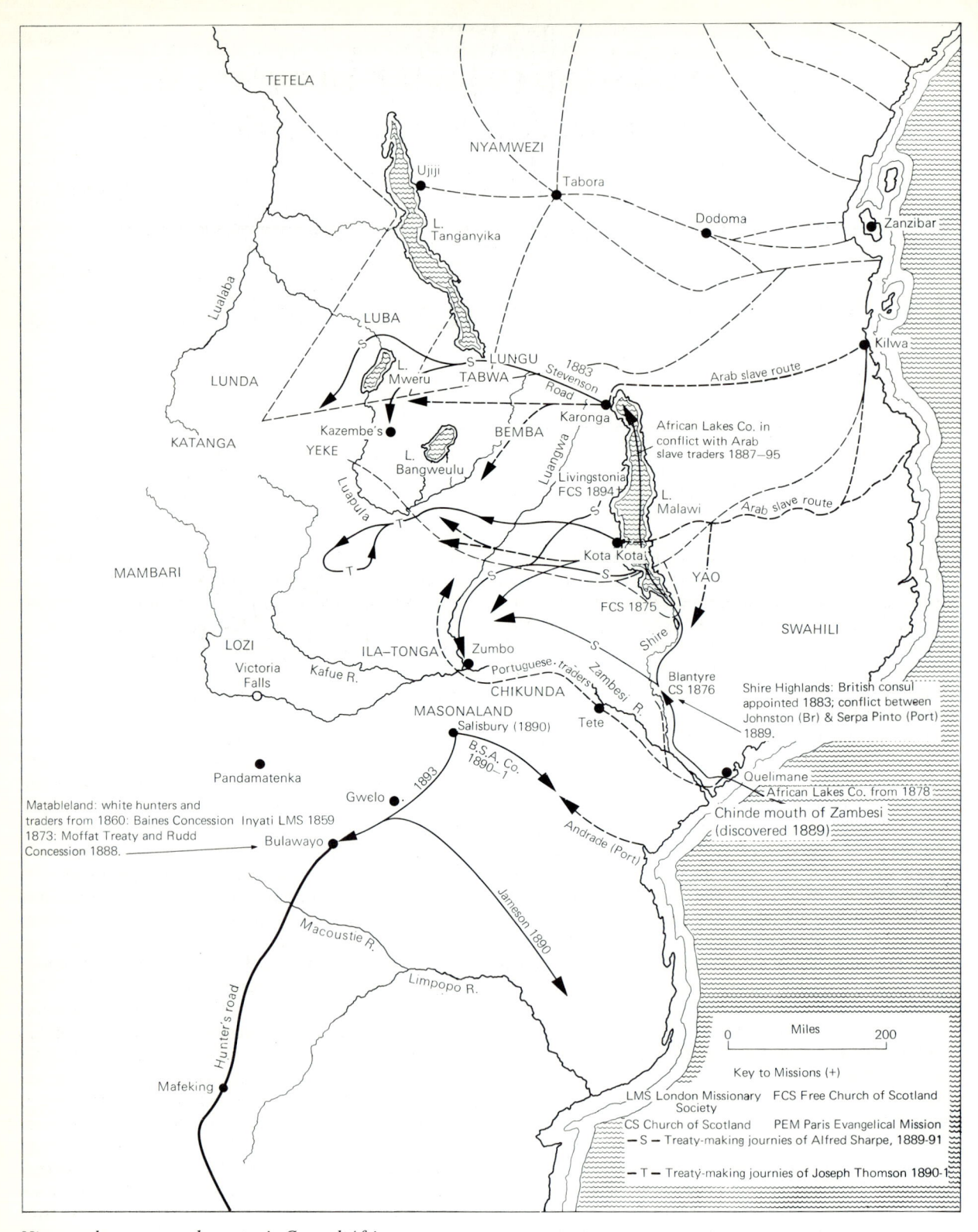

Nineteenth century trade-routes in Central Africa

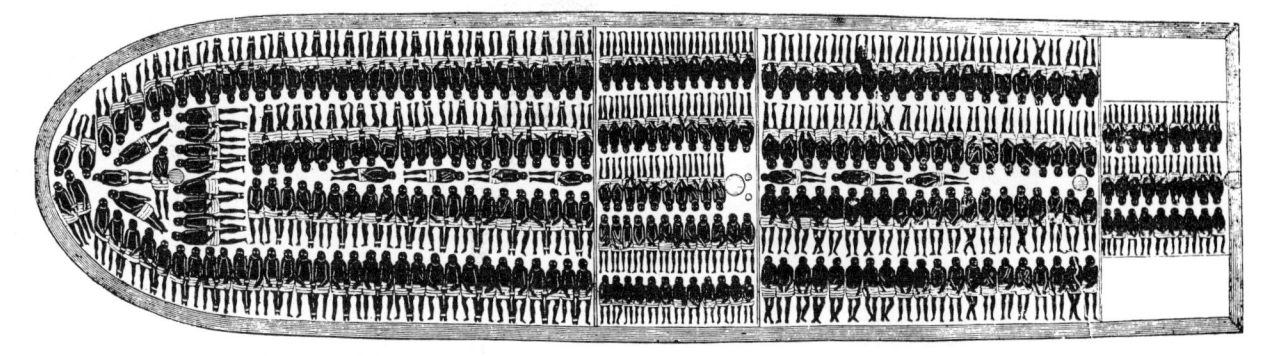

Diagram of a slave ship, 1844, showing how slaves were packed

from their base at Ujiji on the east shores of Lake Tanganyika. They were doing a great deal of trade with Nsama, the Tabwa ruler.

We have seen that the Portuguese became keen to establish contacts with Kazembe as early as the last decade of the eighteenth century. By October 1798 the Portuguese had reached the capital of Kazembe and in 1831 some Portuguese explorers and travellers met Swahili traders at Kazembe's (page 65). Yet, in spite of this early start, from the middle of the nineteenth century on it was not the Portuguese but the Swahili who were important traders in the Central African interior in general and in the Kazembe state in particular. The rulers of Kazembe preferred the Swahili traders to the Portuguese for a number of reasons. The Swahili, most of whom were a mixture of African and Arab or Asiatic elements, seem to have been seen as less of a threat to the rulers of Kazembe. Moreover, unlike the Portuguese who travelled with large armed parties, the Swahili came in smaller numbers at first and did not seem to have had any political ambitions. Secondly, the Swahili did not show any sense of superiority over the local people whereas the Portuguese were very arrogant. Swahili traders mixed easily with the locals and some of them married Central African women. The third reason for their preference was possibly the fact that the Swahili were very patient bargainers.

It is important to point out that the policy of non-involvement was not always observed by Swahili traders some of whom later meddled in local politics. This was done only for the purpose of improving their commercial position, and only after gaining the confidence of local rulers.

As will be seen, the Swahili did use force when it was necessary. Their usual method was firstly to build walled villages or stockades in the area. From these defensive centres they also sent ivory, slaves, copper and other trading goods to the East African

A typical dhow used in the slave trade

coast. If and when it became necessary they would invade neighbouring villages and areas killing men and capturing women and children who were driven to the east coast. Some villages and areas would send ivory, slaves and copper to the Swahili leaders as tribute. In this way many Swahili leaders built themselves strong settlements in the Central African interior. These settlements were, of course, not kingdoms as such because the Swahili were, first and foremost, traders.

The Swahili developed good communications to the east coast. Staging posts were built in Tanzania at such places as Ujiji, Tabora and Dodoma. Nominally the Swahili traders were subjects of the Sultan of Zanzibar, Seyyid Said, although in fact he had little control over them. In the period between 1837 and 1840 the Sultan moved his capital from Muscat in Arabia to the island of Zanzibar on the Indian Ocean. Thus Zanzibar became the centre of the slave and ivory trade. Some of the slaves were required to work on the clove and sisal plantations on the islands of Zanzibar and Pemba. Many more were also sold to the French colonies in the Indian

Sultan of Zanzibar, Seyyid Said

Ocean, Madagascar, and Reunion, where they worked on sugar plantations. The needs of Zanzibar, Pemba and the French Indian Ocean colonies increased the volume of the slave trade between the Central African interior and the East African coast. Slaves were also used to transport ivory, copper and other trade goods from the interior to the coast.

The demand for ivory was increasing in the nineteenth century especially in India, Europe and the United States. In India ivory was used mainly in the manufacturing of bangles, while in Europe and the United States it was used to make billiard balls, piano keys and handles for table knives and forks.

Trade between the coast and the Central African interior was a matter of cooperation between various groups. The Swahili traders organised and were in charge of caravans which travelled between the two areas. Indian merchants on the coast and on the islands provided money in the form of long-term loans with which the Swahili traders bought guns, cloth, beads, alcoholic drinks, axes, swords and other goods. These were valued by the chiefs in the interior who paid for them in ivory, slaves, copper and other Central African products. It was Indian money in the form of loans to the Swahili traders, therefore, that kept the storehouses and warehouses at Dodoma, Tabora and Ujiji well-stocked with goods. The arrangement about long-term loans was found to be most convenient by the caravan owners who could stay in the interior for many months or even for over a year before returning to the coast to sell their slaves and goods. A third group that cooperated in the trade were the chiefs in the interior, including the Nyamwezi who provided porters and guides.

Swahili traders and the decline of Kazembe

As the Swahili were building up their economic influence and power, the rulers in the African interior were becoming weaker and their states declining. This was true of the state of Kazembe which had become by far the strongest and wealthiest kingdom in the interior by the beginning of the nineteenth century. There were, of course, both external and internal factors responsible for the decline of Kazembe. For instance the various Kazembes were not always efficient rulers, especially those who came after the death of Kaleka. Kaleka, one of the most able Kazembes died some time in the 1840s and after his death, up to the 1880s there was a great deal of instability in the kingdom. Four of Kaleka's six successors, for instance, died violently. Succession wars had also reduced the kingdom. Swahili traders took advantage of these internal weaknesses to improve their own position. Furthermore, as he began losing the revenue from salt, copper and ivory, the Kazembe found it difficult to reward some of his chiefs, especially those on the Zambian side of his kingdom, who needed to be rewarded for the tribute which they paid to the king. He may have desperately tried to press other chiefs for more tribute while rewarding them with imported cloth and other foreign manufactures. This, in turn might have encouraged such chiefs to think of breaking away from the king's control. The Swahili traders, as may be expected, were always ready to play on such feelings, even if they had not directly influenced them. Up to the middle of the nineteenth century, the Swahili traders had benefited from Kazembe's trade monopoly, but from that time on they found prices at the capital too high. Thus they now preferred to buy at cheaper prices from the subordinate chiefs. This practice was particularly easy during a succession dispute, or when a weaker Kazembe was on the throne. Ironically, on more than one occasion, the reigning Kazembe had to appeal to one or other of the Swahili leaders for support. In fact, it was during the reign of a weak and aged Kazembe, Chinyanta, that the powerful Swahili trader, Msiri, was allowed to settle in the kingdom of Kazembe.

Msiri and other Swahili traders

Msiri was a Nyamwezi. His father was Kalasa Muswiri, a trader who had been attracted to Central Africa by the copper mines in the Shaba (Katanga) region. In the 1850s Kazembe Chinyanta allowed Msiri to settle in his territory west of Lake Mweru. The area was rich in both copper and ivory. Msiri became friendly with some of the local chiefs, especially those of the Lamba and Sanga who had been unhappy with Lunda economic dominance and also with the Kazembe's inability to protect their people against Luba raids. To these chiefs Msiri seemed to be offering an opportunity to regain their independence from the Kazembe. Eventually, Msiri and his Yeke followers were becoming more powerful than the king. The Yeke were a Nyamwezi group from Tanzania who had worked with and for Swahili traders as carriers, porters and guides. They knew the Kazembe kingdom too well.

After establishing himself in the area, Msiri demanded tribute from the chiefs, such as those of the Kaonde and the Lamba people. He also raided the neighbouring Ushi, Bisa and Unga areas. Some of the Luba chiefs were defeated, and by 1869 a great part of the Shaba (Katanga) area of the kingdom of Kazembe had been taken by Msiri. He had also effectively cut Kazembe's communication with Mwata Yamvo's capital to the west and broken Kazembe's control of the copper trade. He had opened trade with the Portuguese on the west coast and with the Swahili on the shores of Lake Tanganyika. The Kazembe's capital was no longer the centre of Central African trade as now all routes were leading to Msiri's stockaded village of Bunkeya. Msiri even raided across the Luapula River threatening the capital of Kazembe. The Lenje of the Kabwe district were also regularly raided by Msiri's armies. By this time he was undoubtedly one of the most powerful traders and rulers in the interior.

There were disturbances in Central Africa during the years 1860 to 1875 and, as a result, trade declined markedly. Recovery did, however, come during the reign of Sultan Barghash (1870–1888). Also the activities of some of the Swahili traders contributed to the economic recovery. Among these traders were such men as Salim bin Abdullah, well known in Central and East African history as Jumbe, Hamed bin Muhammed el Murjebi and Milambo.

Around 1845 Jumbe, or Salim bin Abdullah, settled at Nkhotakota on Lake Malawi. He protected the local people from Ngoni raids, and by 1860 had been given the title of Jumbe or chief. The Jumbe family was to continue ruling this area until 1889. The Jumbes were basically trading leaders sending their goods and slaves to Zanzibar.

Hamed bin Muhammed el Murjebi, otherwise well known as Tippu Tip, was another brilliant Swahili trader. Some time around 1860 he led about 600 men into Central Africa, spending a few months among the Lungu who lived around the southern end of Lake Tanganyika. He soon entered into trade agreements with senior Bemba rulers and received large quantities of ivory from them in exchange for cloth, silks and beads. Later he defeated the Tabwa chief, Nsama, in 1867. Then he returned to Lubemba and back to the East African coast. In 1869/70 he returned to Central Africa and established a permanent trading post at Nsama's. Tippu Tip did not, however, remain at this post long and he left it in charge of his brother Kumba Kumba while he moved westwards to establish

Three captured Arab slave traders, Jumbe is on the left

Swahili trader, Tippu Tip

himself in Zaire among the Totela people. Here there was a good ivory supply. Tippu Tip soon gained political power over the Totela by claiming to be a descendant of a Totela chieftainess. He established a powerful trading state in Zaire.

Tippu Tip's success attracted more Swahili traders into the interior. Most of these settled in the Tabwa and neighbouring areas. For instance, Hamis Wadi Mtao, settled among the Lungu with his 200 followers. Another one, Said bin Habib, settled at the northern end of Lake Mweru. Milambo's kingdom gained strength in the Mansa district partly at the expense of the power and influence of Kazembe. In fact by the late 1880s the once vast and powerful Kazembe state had been reduced to a very small territory in the Kawambwa district.

The Yao
The Yao originally came from northern Mozambique around 1850. It appears that their migration into Malawi was a result of wars with their Makua-Lomwe neighbours and also of the Maseko-Ngoni invasions (page 80). In Malawi the Yao came into conflict with the Mang'anja and Nyanja peoples.

But in some areas they seem to have lived in peace with their Malawi neighbours and hosts for some time before food shortages compelled them to follow a course of raiding. In this they were helped by the fact that some of them possessed firearms, which their victims did not have.

The Yao did not enter Malawi as a single group, under one leader and by one route. Their migration and subsequent settlement in Malawi were due to more complex processes than that. There were many migrant groups, some of which were under powerful leaders and equipped with modern firearms. Some groups were also made up of desperate and destitute fugitives in search of new homes and safety among Malawian peoples. Such groups often intermarried with their hosts, copying Malawian languages, religious beliefs and culture.

One group, the Amachinga, settled at the south-east corner of Lake Malawi in about 1860. In the 1870s the Yao chief Makanjila built a powerful kingdom in this area. Other Yao groups settled in the Shire Highlands under such chiefs as Mponda, Mataka, Nyambi, and Jalasi. They controlled the trade from Malawi to the east coast, buying ivory and slaves from the Bisa. More slaves were taken from the Nyanja peoples, and sold to merchants at Kilwa on the Tanzanian coast. The trading Yao came very much under Swahili influence. Many of them became Moslems which may have been seen as a way of modernising society and obtaining education for the majority of the people. Chief Makanjila, for instance, built dhows to sail on Lake Malawi, planted coconut palms on the shore of the lake, and built schools where many children went to receive Moslem education and religion. His Yao learnt Arabic too. They wore Arab dress, and their houses were similar to those found on the east coast.

The Yao, however, did not build a centralised political state under a paramount chief or ruler. Their chiefdoms depended on the personal following of individual Yao leaders who became chiefs. The chiefdoms were built through war and trade. Not only did the chiefdoms raid their non-Yao neighbours, they also raided one another for slaves. Thus Yao slaves were taken to the coast along with Malawian slaves.

Chikunda and Mambari traders
The Chikunda were Portuguese-speaking people from the Zambezi valley area. They were a mixture of Portuguese, Goan and African. They organised raids into the area from the Shire Highlands to the Luangwa valley either for themselves or on behalf of Portuguese prazo-holders in the Zambezi valley

area. In the 1860s the Ngoni of Mpezeni settled east of Luangwa compelling the Chikunda to direct their raids further west. The Kunda, Nsenga, Ambo and Soli were raided and were also encouraged to fight one another. In this way many slaves were captured, more especially in the Central and Southern Provinces of Zambia.

The worst of the Chikunda raiders were perhaps Mariano Francisco Vaz dos Anjos, Jose d'Aranjo Lobo, and Manoel de Soutana. In the 1850s Mariano Francisco Vaz dos Anjos defeated a Portuguese expedition sent against him in the Lower Shire area where he had established his own fortress and prazo. Jose d'Aranjo Lobo, an ex-colonel in the Portuguese army, carried out raids in the lower Luangwa valley area in the 1890s. Manoel de Soutana defeated Mbuluma, the Nsenga chief.

The Mambari were yet another Portuguese-speaking group. They came from Angola where they were also known as *Pombeiros descaldas*, or barefoot traders. They were also attracted to the Central African interior during the first half of the nineteenth century, and by 1850 the Mambari were trying to establish trade relations with the Kololo ruler of Bulozi, Sebetwane. But Sebetwane would not sell them slaves, perhaps partly because their prices were too low, and partly because the guns they offered were of poor quality. There is also no doubt that Sebetwane did not have enough slaves to sell to anybody as he himself needed labour to work on the flood-plain which was the mainstay of the economy of Bulozi. When the Mambari found Sebetwane uncooperative they began to buy slaves from private individuals in Bulozi, as well as from the Tonga, in return for iron hoes. This type of trade increased during the reign of Sekeletu, son and successor to Sebetwane, who tried to stop the Tonga from selling slaves to the Mambari. He sold hoes to the Tonga himself in return for ivory.

The Mambari also faced competition and opposition from the Luvale. Although lacking a centralised government system, the Luvale were by now the most commercially active people in northwestern Zambia. They possessed guns which they used to carry out slave raids on the Lunda states of Ishinde and Kanongesha. These states were more vulnerable as they no longer had the support of the Mwata Yamvo who was now too weak. The Luvale also raided the Kaonde who were by now no longer part of the Lunda kingdom of Musokantanda. Slave raiding and trading among the Luvale were the work of individuals not of the chiefs, just as among the Bisa. The Mambari also traded with the Lenje of the Central Province of Zambia. There were trade contacts with the Swahili and the Chikunda as well.

White hunters and traders

From the mid-1850s Central Africa attracted white hunters, traders and travellers from South Africa. Unlike the Swahili, the whites concentrated upon the area to the south of the Zambezi. But like the Swahili they were also interested in ivory. These whites were not involved in the slave trade.

The first white ivory hunters and traders from the south entered Matabeleland in western Zimbabwe

European hunters in Matebeleland. Tainton, Philips, Sam Edwards and van Rooyen. It was Sam Edwards who took Robert Moffat to see Mzilikazi in 1854

in the mid-1850s. Sam Edwards, one of them, arrived at Mzilikazi's court in 1854 in the company of the missionary Robert Moffat. That visit was the beginning of a long career as a trader in Matabeleland, and also a long relationship with the Ndebele court. Another early name connected with both the mission at Inyati and the Ndebele capital was Edward Chapman, who came to Matabeleland in the 1860s. Chapman used to bring supplies and mail for the London Missionary Society mission station at Inyati near the capital. Jacob Hartley and another fellow Transvaal farmer, George MacCabe, also hunted in Zimbabwe regularly from about 1861. The limping Hartley is said to have killed about 1200 elephants in one year. Piet Jacobs and Jan Viljoen, two Boers, were also among some of the most destructive hunters. For instance it is said that on one single expedition, one of many, they returned to the south with 10000 lbs of ivory.

Most of these hunters' activities were in the Ndebele-occupied part of Zimbabwe as Mzilikazi did all in his power to prevent whites entering Mashonaland where the elephant herds had now gone. There were special reasons why Mzilikazi took this line. First, to ensure that the Shona bought no guns from the whites. Secondly, because he wanted to protect the elephants for himself since he was also doing a lot of ivory trading. The restrictions could, however, be removed in favour of certain trusted white hunters. For instance in 1865 Jan Viljoen, Piet Jacobs and Hartley were allowed into Mashonaland. On that occasion the hunters went as far as the Mfuri river. Hartley found old gold mines now abandoned. His report and that of another hunter, the German Karl Mauch, caused a great deal of excitement about the possibilities of rich gold deposits in Mashonaland.

One of the most well-known travellers and fortune seekers who came to Zimbabwe was Thomas Baines, famous for his beautiful paintings of Central African scenes, plants and animals. Baines was attracted to Zimbabwe by stories about stone buildings and gold markings. He visited Matabeleland in 1868 and three years later in 1871 he was granted a concession by Lobengula (who had succeeded Mzilikazi in 1870). The concession allowed him to prospect for gold in the general area between Gweru River and the Hunyani in Mashonaland. Baines found gold but could not raise money to found a mining company. He died in 1873, by which time gold mining had begun in the Tati area of eastern Botswana.

Hunters, traders and gold seekers continued their activities in Zimbabwe during the 1870s and 1880s and up to the time of British occupation of the country. One of the most notable big game hunters was Frederick Courteney Selous. He arrived in Matabeleland in 1872 at the age of eighteen and, thinking him to be too young to be an effective big game hunter, Lobengula allowed him to hunt wherever he pleased in Zimbabwe. In this Lobengula was terribly mistaken as Selous turned out to be the most destructive hunter, killing thousands and thousands of elephants and other animals of Zimbabwe. Selous spent most of his time in Mashonaland's Mazoe valley area and he also hunted briefly across the Zambezi in the Ila or Mashukulumbwe area. Selous was so successful in his business that he made a suggestion for the cutting of a road between Bulawayo and the Chegutu Hills area to facilitate the transportation of ivory. This road, known as the 'Hunters' Road' was cut.

North of the Zambezi the most notable of the hunters and traders of the time was George Westbeech who lived and traded among the Lozi during the years 1871–88. A very brave and friendly man, Westbeech had no difficulty in gaining the confidence and respect of the Litungas of his time – Sipopa and Mwanamwina II. He also made friends with the young Lobosi who was to become the famous Litunga Lewanika of Barotseland. Westbeech established his base south of the Victoria Falls at Pantamatenka. He was a very successful big game hunter and ivory trader exporting not less than 30000 lbs of ivory from Bulozi and neighbouring areas between 1871 and 1876. Westbeech was joined by other hunters and traders, men like Walsh, Bradshaw and Oates. His influence at the Lozi Court was so great that he even became adviser to the Litunga. He introduced Litunga Lewanika to such Christian missionaries as Coillard and Arnot whom we shall discuss in the next chapter. In trade Lewanika preferred Westbeech's guns to those of the Mambari traders because they were of a better quality and because Westbeech used ox-wagons, not slaves, to transport his trade goods.

Malawi did not have white traders and hunters until 1878 when two Scotsmen, John and Frederick Moir, established the Livingstonia Central Africa Company Ltd. The Company, later to become the African Lakes Company, was founded as a result of Livingstone's plea that good trade in the area would bring an end to the slave trade. The company was thus not allowed to sell firearms or ammunition to Africans. The Moir brothers did explore the area but not to the same extent that David Livingstone had done.

16 David Livingstone and the exploration of Central Africa

Although David Livingstone is the most well-known of Central Africa's explorers, he is by no means the only one; there were others before and after him. We have already referred to some of them in the previous chapters and shall not, therefore, deal with their activities in any detail in this chapter.

As already seen, the first white explorers were the Portuguese who penetrated Central Africa from the Mozambican and Angolan coasts almost immediately after they established themselves in these two countries. Antonio Fernandez, for instance, went as far as Zimbabwe in 1513, and there are indications that he might have made more than one expedition (page 58). He may have even entered Malawi and perhaps Zambia too, although there is no record of that. Another Portuguese, Gaspar Bocarro, traversed Malawi, south of Lake Malawi, on the way from Tete to Kilwa on the Tanzanian coast.

We have also seen how Portuguese interest in Central Africa's interior increased towards the end of the eighteenth century. The result of this growing interest was the organisation of both private and official expeditions aimed at establishing a trans-Central African route, via Kazembe, linking Mozambique and Angola (page 65). An expedition under Dr Francesco José da Lacerda reached the capital of Kazembe on the Luapula river in October 1798. Lacerda himself died a few weeks after his arrival there. Two *Pombeiros*, José and Baptista, succeeded in crossing Central Africa from Luanda to Mozambique during their 1806–14 expedition. Three years of this period were spent at Kazembe's capital as royal guests. Gammitto and Monteiro also reached Kazembe's capital in 1831 and went as far as Lake Mweru.

However the Scotsman, David Livingstone, was by far the most notable Central African explorer. He came to Africa as a Christian missionary under Dr Robert Moffat of the London Missionary Society in 1841. For some time he worked with Moffat at Kuruman Mission among the Griqua people. His experience as a missionary, though not very long, was enough to open new vistas and create more ambitions and challenges which later completely altered his views about mission work. In short Livingstone soon abandoned the traditional idea of mission work which was limited to the establishment of mission stations and the converting of African people to Christianity. He became an explorer.

Shaping of Livingstone's aims
Livingstone worked at first in the Cape Colony and in Botswana among the Tswana people. He founded a mission station at Kolobeng north of

David Livingstone

Kuruman in 1847. He and his family lived there for some time. It was at this post that the vastness and challenges of the African continent struck him for the first time, and he remarked: 'All my desires tend forwards, to the north ... Why, we have a world before us here.' His Tswana Christians had told him about the Kalahari desert and the land beyond it with its forests, grass lands and rivers. The mention of great rivers and many tributaries suggested to Livingstone that there were waterways which could be used by boats to reach the heart of Africa. His mind was filled with thoughts about the vast, unexplored areas and their peoples. He made up his mind to be the first Christian missionary and the first white man to reach them. From that time on, Livingstone was convinced that geographical discovery and exploration should precede the establishing of mission stations and the converting of people to Christianity. Thus it has been observed elsewhere that for Livingstone 'the end of the geographical feat (was) the beginning of the missionary enterprise'.

Livingstone's preliminary expeditions were made in 1849 and 1851. In 1849 Livingstone and two white companions went as far as Lake Ngami. In 1851 he was accompanied by his wife and children and a friend, William Oswell. On this occasion the party reached the Chobe river. Livingstone was visited by the Kololo king, Sebetwane, who had travelled about one hundred miles to meet him as it had been his wish to see a white man before he died. The two men were greatly impressed with each other.

Livingstone's expeditions

The 1851 expedition is usually regarded as marking the end of Livingstone's career as a missionary and the beginning of a new career as an explorer. Subsequent expeditions by Livingstone were strictly speaking for geographical and scientific discovery. At the end of 1851 Livingstone also decided that from then on his efforts would be concentrated upon the areas to the north of the Zambezi and not in the south.

First exploratory expedition 1852–56

Livingstone's main objective in this expedition was to explore the Zambezi and to see if it was navigable. He left for the north in June 1852 arriving at Linyanti, the Kololo capital, in May 1853. His old friend Sebetwane had by this time died. Sekeletu, Sebetwane's son, had succeeded to the throne. Livingstone had no difficulty in establishing good relations with Sekeletu. The Kololo ruler of Bulozi

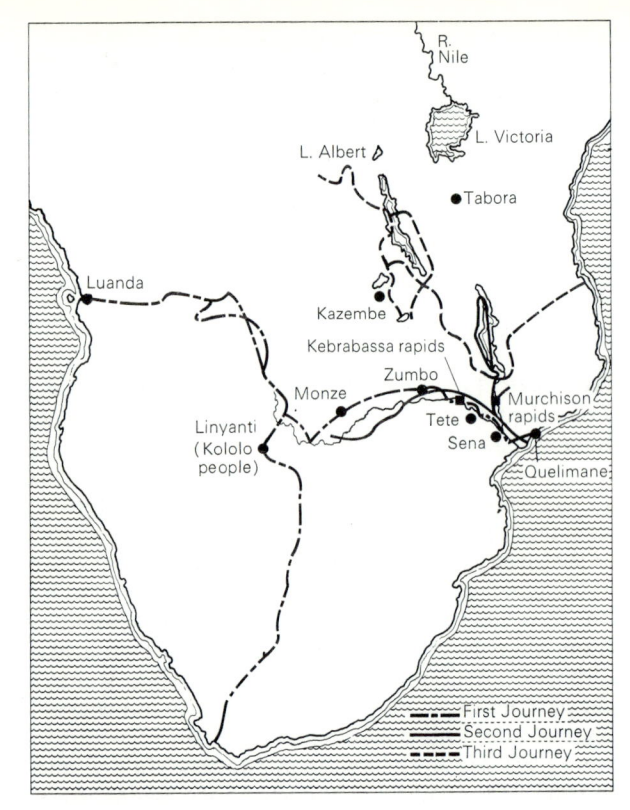

Livingstone's journeys

gave Livingstone twenty-seven men, most of whom were to serve him faithfully for many years (page 76). Livingstone and his party travelled up the Zambezi to a point near its source in the Lunda kingdom of Ishinde. Livingstone met Ishinde before proceeding westwards to Luanda on the west coast. Livingstone also had his first glimpse of the devastating effects of the slave trade on his way to the west coast. The journey to the coast owed as much to the enterprise of the Kololo as it did to Livingstone. The Kololo's interest was to establish direct contact with the Portuguese traders in Angola in order to cut out the Mambari middlemen who were unpopular in Bulozi (page 87).

May 1854 saw the expedition at Luanda. Livingstone was already ill with fever and for this reason the party remained four months while Livingstone, under the care of the British Commissioner for the Suppression of the Slave Trade, recovered his health and strength. The British official failed to persuade Livingstone to take a ship to England and in September Livingstone led his party back to the Central African interior. By October 1855 they were happy to be back in Bulozi. The expedition had established that after the Zambezi there was no waterway to Luanda on the west coast. For Livingstone there was still the thousand miles of the Zambezi to Quelimane on the east coast to be explored and to this he turned his attention.

Again, Sekeletu gave great assistance. Porters, guides and supplies were provided. As in the westward expedition, the Kololo ruler hoped that this mission might establish external trade relations for his kingdom. After leaving Bulozi the party came upon Mosi-o-tunya, the most spectacular waterfall on the Zambezi, which Livingstone decided to call the Victoria Falls. From here Livingstone's party travelled overland avoiding the difficult gorges. They were in the Tonga country for most of the journey crossing the Kalomo river. Livingstone had an opportunity to visit the Tonga chief, Monze. The Tonga plateau impressed Livingstone so much that he thought that it might be suitable for European settlement and Christian missions.

Up to now, on the downward Zambezi exploration, Livingstone had not seen any slave trade activity in the Zambezi valley area. This happy picture changed however after the expedition had crossed the Kafue river into the Chirundu area. Here Chikunda slave raids had not only disrupted communities, they had also made the people suspicious of and even hostile to strangers. It has already been noted how the Chikunda slavers were concentrating their activities upon the area of the lower Luangwa valley. After leaving the lower Luangwa valley area, Livingstone and his party passed through the Portuguese trading post of Zumbo on the Zambezi. A few days' hard walking brought them to Feira and Tete. Tete, once a prosperous trading centre on the lower Zambezi, was now almost in ruins. Nevertheless, Livingstone received a warm welcome from the Portuguese commandant, Sicard.

From Tete down the Zambezi by boat, they were at Sena, another Lower Zambezi trade centre which, like Tete, was now in ruins. As the party bypassed the Cabora Bassa rapids on the way down, Livingstone wrongly concluded that the Zambezi was navigable from the Victoria Falls to its mouth at Quelimane. By now, Livingstone was very sick with dysentery and malaria and the expedition finally ended at Quelimane. He left for England in the middle of 1856 with the mistaken view of the Zambezi's navigability.

Back in England Livingstone was given a hero's welcome. He published his African observations and experiences in a book called *Missionary Travels and Researches in South Africa*. His expedition had covered over 4000 miles. The book was widely read in England where more than 12000 copies were produced and sold within a short time. Livingstone also addressed the British public on a number of occasions. He also spoke to university students and communities appealing to them to take up the challenges of mission work in Africa. Special appeals were also made to business people to open up trade in Africa. At Cambridge University, Livingstone told his audience: 'I go back (to Central Africa) to try to open up a path to commerce and Christianity. Do you carry on the work that I have begun?' Livingstone hoped that Christianity and commerce would bring the Central African slave trade to an end.

Second expedition
Livingstone's book and the public talks not only impressed the British public, but also Government officials. Thus on his second journey to Central Africa he led an official expedition which was supported by the Government. He needed this backing as his links with the London Missionary Society had been broken as a result of serious disagreements. This expedition, which also included a number of white people, was thus much better equipped and had greater funds than the first one. Livingstone was given boats and a steamer to sail the rivers of Central Africa. He was also appointed Britain's Consul at Quelimane with specific instructions to open up communication lines with the Central African interior, and to establish contacts with the African rulers of Central Africa. The expedition left for Africa in March 1858 and by the end of May they were at the mouth of the Zambezi to carry out the objectives of the mission.

The immediate aim of the expedition was to find out exactly how navigable the Zambezi was. Unfortunately the expedition was beset with many difficulties. First of all, Livingstone himself proved to be a poor leader of such an important mission, and quarrelled with his British colleagues. It was also realised that the Zambezi was not as navigable as Livingstone had reported after his 1852–6 journey, because of the Cabora Bassa rapids. Also the main steamboat broke down many times. Livingstone suffered a big personal loss when his wife died from malaria in 1862.

Having explored the lower Zambezi the expedition moved on to the Shire river where it met with a measure of success and encouragement. The Shire river proved to be more navigable than the Zambezi, at least as far as the cataracts which Livingstone called the Murchison Falls. In April 1859

Livingstone was in the Shire Highlands where he saw for the first time Lake Chirwa. In June he saw Lake Malawi and it was here in the Lake region that he also came across slave traders who were using the lake as a route. The main slave traders were the Yao chiefs whose armed gangs were raiding the Mang'anja and other peoples of the area.

In 1860 Livingstone sailed up the Zambezi to go to Bulozi both to return his Kololo servants to their country and to see if he could contact a London Missionary Society group which was expected to have arrived in Bulozi to start mission work. He finally arrived at Sesheke where he was warmly received by Sekeletu. Sekeletu's idea this time was that a white settlement should be established on the Toka plateau and that such a settlement should be under Livingstone's direction. The project did not appeal to Livingstone however, who was now thinking of the proposed mission in Malawi's Shire Highlands.

Livingstone returned to the east coast by way of the Zambezi, arriving there at the same time as his new boat also arrived from England. This was the *Pioneer*, on board which were members of the Universities Mission to Central Africa (UMCA), under Bishop Mackenzie. The missionary party was on its way to establish a mission in the Shire Highlands according to Livingstone's wishes. Bishop Mackenzie's party however failed to establish a permanent mission station in the Shire Highlands. Many members of the group, including Bishop Mackenzie himself, died. We shall turn to this later but for now we should note that the failure of the UMCA to establish a mission in the Highlands added to Livingstone's misfortunes. He was also very depressed by the destruction caused by the activities of the slave traders among the societies of the Central African interior. He returned to England in 1863, his second expedition having failed.

Third and final expedition

In England Livingstone published another book, the *Narrative of an Expedition to the Zambezi and its Tributaries*. At the same time preparations were being made for yet another Central African expedition. This time Livingstone was to undertake the expedition with his African assistants as no white man would accompany him to Africa because of the difficulties which he had had with his British companions during the second expedition.

Geographical and scientific discovery were the main objectives of this expedition. Among the important geographical factors to be investigated were the African river and lake systems; especially the discovery of the sources of the Nile and the Congo rivers. Livingstone was not alone in his search for the source of the Nile; many British and European explorers were investigating the same problem. Another objective of the third mission was to further expose the evils of the slave trade. Livingstone arrived at Zanzibar in March 1866 and immediately made arrangements to travel to the interior of Central Africa.

From the outset this expedition promised to be full of problems. This time Livingstone did not have the financial backing of the British Government and the London Missionary Society which had been so important in the previous missions. The little money he had, had been raised by friends and from the sale of his books. Secondly, when Livingstone left for Africa on what was going to be the longest expedition of his career, he was fifty-three years old. Before leaving for the Central African interior, Livingstone lost most of his transport animals. Also along the route all except nine of his carriers and porters deserted him. But Livingstone was not the type of person to admit defeat and so the expedition continued its journey along the Rovuma.

They reached the present Chipata area where they found Mpezeni's Ngoni fighting the Nsenga

Bishop Mackenzie of the Universities Mission to Central Africa

people. From there they crossed the Luangwa emerging into the Muchinga hills area. Livingstone's most valuable possession, his medicine box, was stolen in January 1867. But even without his medicines and with his life in danger, Livingstone continued his expedition. Wherever he went Livingstone made interesting observations about some of the peoples of the interior. For instance, he wrote about the Bemba, Tabwa, and the Lunda of Kazembe. He noticed that the Bemba, now under Chitimukulu Chitapankwa, were 'decidedly more warlike than any of the tribes south of them.' Bemba villages were stockaded and surrounded by deep, dry ditches. He also noticed that the Lunda, now under Kazembe Muonga Sunkutu, were losing much of their trade to the Swahili. The region was now very much affected by the activities of slave traders, so much so that Livingstone had to spend a longer time than he had intended at Kazembe's capital.

Livingstone was quite ill and since he had lost his medicine he had to depend, ironically, upon the same Swahili traders whose activities he denounced in letters to friends in Britain. The letters, in fact, never reached the east coast because they were intercepted and destroyed by the Swahili traders. In 1868 Livingstone even stayed with one of the Swahili traders, Said bin Habib, who had established his headquarters north of Lake Mweru (page 86). Later in 1869 he travelled with another Swahili trader, Mohamed Bogharib and had greater opportunity to see for himself the worst aspects of the Central African slave trade. He and his Swahili companions sailed a section of Lake Tanganyika to Ujiji. At this Swahili trading depot on the eastern shore of Lake Tanganyika, Livingstone noticed that caravans from the east coast made regular calls there. From Ujiji, Livingstone crossed the lake and travelled westwards through Manyuema country. Making very slow progress he reached the Lualaba at Nyangwe. What he saw of the activities of the slave traders, together with his deteriorating health, depressed his spirits very much. At Nyangwe, for instance, he witnessed one of the worst atrocities of the slave trade in the interior, usually referred to as the Manyuema massacre. Here Swahili traders shot at three hundred people – men, women and children who were attending a market. Many were killed and the few that managed to escape from the musket balls were drowned in the Lualaba river.

Horrified and depressed, with greatly deteriorated health, Livingstone returned to Ujiji hoping to find his mail, medicine and other supplies from England. Nothing but further disappointment

Slaves being taken to the coast, from a drawing by Livingstone himself

Stanley meets Livingstone, 28 October 1871

awaited him; there were no letters and no supplies. The few possessions which he had left behind had been stolen. He decided to wait at Ujiji for a while and it was during this time that relief and help came to him from an unexpected source. This was the surprise meeting with Henry Moreton Stanley, a journalist working for the *New York Herald*. This was in November 1871.

Since leaving the east coast in 1866, Livingstone had not been seen or even heard of by any white person. Fears and rumours were growing in Britain and in the United States that the explorer might be dead. Thus the *New York Herald* commissioned Stanley to find Livingstone, dead or alive, and bring back whatever news about him he could find in the Central African interior. Stanley's expedition was very well equipped and had been generously supplied with medicines and other necessities. After their meeting, Livingstone's health improved markedly and, for about two weeks, the two men explored parts of northern Tanzania together before Stanley left, having failed to persuade Livingstone to return with him to Europe. Livingstone still wanted to prove his theory that the source of the Nile lay somewhere in Central Africa, possibly in the Shaba region of Zaire. At Nyangwe he had noticed that the Lualaba was flowing northwards and had thought that it might be leading into the Nile. Accordingly, he left Ujiji for the Shaba region to go and explore the Lualaba. He had also heard that the river had its source in Lake Bangweulu so he planned to explore this lake as well.

When Livingstone left Ujiji for the south he was already very weak. Also he was caught by the rainy season while still crossing the Bemba plateau. From here he had to be carried most of the way to the Shaba area. He finally died at Chitambo's village on the edges of Lake Bangwuelu on 1 May 1873. With great difficulty his African companions and servants carried the body to the East African coast for shipment to England. This was probably the wish of Livingstone's two most trusted assistants, Cuma and Susi, and a freed slave who had become part of the Livingstone group; his name was Jacob Wainwright. This man accompanied the body to England and was there when it was finally buried at Westminster Abbey in London.

Conclusion

It is extremely difficult to provide an appropriate

comment upon Livingstone's activities in Central Africa. One thing is clear, however: Livingstone was not a great success as a missionary in the traditional and narrow sense of the word. But this was probably because Livingstone did not see his main role as that of building mission stations and converting a few local people to Christianity. In his opinion, although this was important, this would come later and only after Africa's resources and potential had been explored.

Thus he became an explorer seeking to understand Africa's river and lake systems with a view to establishing whether they could be used to provide effective and cheaper transportation and communication networks. Such communications and systems, he thought, would be useful not only to Christian missionaries but to all agents of European development and commerce as well. It was with these ideas in mind that he explored the Zambezi and the Shire rivers, Lakes Malawi, Tanganyika, Mweru and Bengwuelu and adjacent areas. Livingstone, however, failed in his main objectives – to find the sources of the Nile and the Congo. He also made a number of geographical errors.

Yet it still is true that Livingstone was one of the greatest explorers of the nineteenth century. His observations about the peoples of Central Africa, their beliefs, customs and traditions, although often restricted by his Victorian and Christian views, are useful to our understanding of Central African societies in the nineteenth century. This is equally true of his reports and observations about plants, insects and animals of the region.

Livingstone did not immediately have an effect on the slave trade. But it is true that his writings and speeches did much to focus Europe's attention on this inhuman trade and its destructive effects upon the societies of Central Africa. The Zanzibar slave market was closed not very long after his death and it was only a matter of time before the trade was eliminated from the Central African interior.

David Livingstone's contribution, as a scientific observer and a writer of Central Africa during the nineteenth century, was great. He was content to leave the practical work of establishing mission stations and converting people to Christianity to those who felt this to be their particular mission. But Livingstone was also a forerunner of European colonists of Central Africa because he appealed not only to Christian agents to come to Africa, but also to European businessmen to come and settle. This was because he believed that only Christianity, European commerce and development could bring an end to the slave trade. Whether or not Livingstone would have agreed with the manner in which African colonisation took place towards the close of the nineteenth century is a rather different matter.

17 Pioneer Christian missions in Zimbabwe and Zambia

Big game hunters, gold seekers, traders and explorers were not the only whites interested in Central Africa during the pre-colonial period. Equally interested were Christian missionaries whose enterprise began almost at the same time as those of the others. Livingstone regarded his exploratory efforts as an extension of mission work. Several missionary societies began work in Central Africa during Livingstone's time and many more came after his death. Missionary efforts were mainly in Zimbabwe, Zambia and Malawi.

Zimbabwe

Strictly speaking, the first Christian missionaries to Central Africa were Portuguese who came to the Kingdom of Kongo in the fifteenth century and to Mozambique and Zimbabwe in the sixteenth century. Their efforts which extended in to the eighteenth century do not, however, seem to have achieved much in any of the three areas.

The London Missionary Society
One of the first missionary societies to enter Central Africa after the Portuguese was the London Missionary Society (LMS) whose missionaries entered the region in the nineteenth century. As seen already, Dr Robert Moffat, head of the LMS's mission at Kuruman, established a friendship with Mzilikazi, the Ndebele king, in 1829 while the Ndebele were still in the Transvaal (pages 68–9). It was because of this friendship that Mzilikazi allowed John Smith Moffat, his old friend's son, to establish a mission at Inyati near Bulawayo in 1859. Following his father's example, Lobengula allowed the LMS to open a second station at Hope Fountain in 1870.

The missionaries at Inyati and Hope Fountain devoted a great deal of their time and energy to teaching, preaching and literary work. Within a few years Sindebele books were printed for Ndebele children to read. More missionaries arrived to join or replace the original team. Other missionaries working in the area included such men as Thomson, Sykes, Charles Helm, David Carnegie and their families. Mzilikazi and Lobengula were both kind and generous to the missionaries providing some of their needs in the early days. They also made generous land grants to the mission to enable the missionaries to grow their own food and to carry out their work. They also used the missionaries to repair guns, inoculate cattle, treat the sick and write the king's letters. The missionaries in turn were allowed to preach to the Ndebele people.

Yet, in spite of all their efforts, the pioneer missionaries of the LMS made little impact on the Ndebele. Until 1894 when Matabeleland was colonised by the British South Africa Company the LMS had not produced any following among the Ndebele over thirty years of effort. Because of the nature of Ndebele society and its own religion which greatly influenced its political and military systems, it was almost impossible for them to accept Christianity.

The economy of the Ndebele nation was largely based on raiding. Trade, though practised, was not very important. Ndebele society was also organised into inferior and superior classes which Christianity's principle of equality seemed to threaten. Potential converts were therefore mistrusted and were often punished and sent to areas far away from the missions. Missionary efforts to convert the Ndebele were therefore frustrated.

The LMS missionaries were later joined by Roman Catholic missionaries in Matabeleland. In 1882 prior to the occupation of Matabele land by the British, Jesuit missionaries under Father Bartholomew Kroot arrived at the Ndebele capital. One mission was opened at Empandeni and another one near Bulawayo. But like Inyati and Hope Fountain, the two Jesuit missions also made no impact upon the Ndebele.

African evangelists and catechists
Among the Shona people most of the pioneering work was done by African evangelists and catechists, mainly from the Transvaal and Lesotho. The

Dutch Reformed Church of South Africa, the Paris Evangelical Mission of Lesotho, and the Berlin Missionary Society, all sent many expeditions under leading evangelists to the south and the south-eastern parts of Mashonaland in the period from the late 1860's to 1890.

African evangelists and catechists were preferred at that stage because it was feared among missionary circles in the south that Lobengula would not permit white missionaries to enter the Shona country. The evangelist expeditions reached as far as the areas of Matibe, Mposi, Mudavanhu, Chingoma, Nyamhondo and Chiri, east of Bulawayo; and Zimuto, Mugabe, Chilimanzi and Dzike in the south-eastern part of Mashonaland.

In some cases the evangelists were so successful in their work that some Shona chiefs requested that permanent missions be established in their areas. This, for instance, was true of the work of evangelists Madzima and Samuel of the Berlin Missionary Society among the Pfumbi of Matibe and Varemba of Mposi. Evangelist Sehahabane of the Paris Evangelical Mission in Lesotho and his fellow Basotho evangelists also convinced Chief Chivi of the need to have a permanent mission station at his capital, just as the Dutch Reformed Church's evangelist Michael Buys and his companions had also convinced the Govera chief, Zimuto, near modern Masvingo, that he needed resident missionaries. Chief Mugabe, near the Zimbabwe Ruins, also assured evangelist Makgatho and his companions that a mission would be welcomed in his area.

In fact it was the successful preliminary work done by the Mosotho evangelist Sehahabane and his friends that persuaded the French missionary Francois Coillard of Leribe in Lesotho to undertake the founding of a branch of the mission at Chivi's in 1876/7. The Chivi centre was, however, very short-lived because Lobengula arrested Coillard and his party, which consisted of Basotho evangelists and their families, and some white missionaries. They were charged with using a forbidden route into the country and also with going there without Lobengula's permission. It seems likely, however, that the party would have been allowed to continue their mission work at Chivi but for the fact that the group included Basotho evangelists. The Basotho of Lesotho were not particularly liked at Bulawayo because one of their chiefs, Molapo, had betrayed

Coillard's mission party, 1884

Langalebalele, the Hlubi chief, to the British in Natal in 1873. Coillard and his party were thus expelled and warned never to return to Zimbabwe again.

Another group that entered Zimbabwe were the missionaries of the Berlin Missionary Society. After some ground work by evangelists Madzima and Samuel in the areas of Matibe and Mposi in the Mwanezi and the Mberengwa districts respectively, it was felt that permanent mission centres should be established in the two areas. Thus in 1886/7 German missionaries, Knothe and Schellnus of Tshakoma Mission in the Transvaal, accompanied by the two evangelists and other Venda Christians, went to establish mission centres at Matibe's and Mposi's. The two centres were established as planned but they were abandoned later on account of disease and famine. Lobengula did not interfere with them.

In 1879 a Roman Catholic pioneer expedition under Father Law perished from malaria while trying to establish a mission in Mzila's land in the border region between Zimbabwe and Mozambique. The Anglican pioneer, Knight-Bruce, led an exploratory expedition to the Zambezi via Matabeleland and Mashonaland in 1888. On that occasion he visited many Shona chiefdoms and spoke to a number of Shona chiefs. These visits were to prove useful to the Church of England three years later when Knight-Bruce returned to Zimbabwe to found the Diocese of Mashonaland.

Failure of the Missions in Zimbabwe
The work of missions in Zimbabwe differed from that in other parts of Central Africa in at least one important aspect. In other parts of Central Africa missions were successfully established during the pre-colonial period and were able to prepare people in those areas for the problems of colonisation. In Zimbabwe, as seen above, pre-colonial missionary efforts failed completely. Missions only began to have an impact upon both the Ndebele and the Shona after the establishment of colonial rule. It has been suggested, perhaps with justification, that missionary failures in the pre-colonial period, contributed to the violence with which the Ndebele and Shona responded to the imposition of colonial rule.

It has also been suggested that because of the frustration resulting from their failure, the missionaries became hostile to the Shona and Ndebele during the introduction of colonial rule. For instance, J. S. Moffat, first head of Inyati Mission, turned strongly against the Ndebele. Charles Helm, Lobengula's own trusted *Umfundisi* (teacher), helped the imperialist, Cecil John Rhodes, to obtain a mining concession from Lobengula by deceitful means, and did not protest when the whites killed Africans with the maxim gun. The Catholic Father Prestage also supported the crushing of the Ndebele in 1893.

Zambia

In Zambia, as in Zimbabwe, the LMS was the first society to try to establish a mission. The first attempt was made in Bulozi and, as in Matabeleland, the LMS was unsuccessful. In 1859 James Helmore and Roger Price, accompanied by their families and African workers from the south, arrived in Bulozi to found a mission among the Lozi.

The Kololo ruler of Bulozi, Sekeletu, had once hinted to Livingstone that he might welcome a mission in his land and Livingstone had advised the LMS accordingly. But on arriving in Bulozi the Helmore-Price mission was informed that Sekeletu would not tolerate them in his country.

When Sekeletu had hinted to Livingstone he had intended that Livingstone himself or Moffat would be in charge of the mission. He wanted an experienced resident missionary who would act as an adviser to him, and one who would also have sufficient influence upon the Ndebele king to persuade that king to stop organising raids into and against Bulozi. Helmore and Price were a great disappointment to Sekeletu because they were inexperienced and ignorant about the people's language and customs.

When the missionaries arrived in Bulozi most of them were tired and ill with malaria. The journey had been long and difficult since the party had travelled across the Kalahari Desert. Sekeletu would not even allow them to go to Sesheke or to the Toka plateau where conditions were healthier. To make matters even worse, Livingstone whom they had expected to meet in Bulozi had not arrived and, in fact, he did not arrive until after their departure for the south (page 92). While negotiations with Sekeletu continued in an attempt to change his mind about the mission, Helmore, his wife, two of their children and some of the African servants died of malaria and exhaustion. Price and the remainder of the party were forced to retrace their way back to the south and across the Kalahari thirstland. Many more perished including Price's wife.

In the meantime Livingstone arrived to be greeted with the news of the tragic fate of the missionaries. He expressed his disappointment at the way Sekeletu had treated the missionaries.

C.S.	—	Church of Scotland.
F.C.S.	—	Free Church of Scotland.
L.M.S.	—	London Missionary Society.
U.M.C.A.	—	Universities Mission to Central Africa.
J.	—	Jesuit Missions.
P.E.M.	—	Paris Evangelical Mission.
W.F.	—	White Fathers.

Christian missions in Central Africa

Although he thought that Sekeletu was partly responsible for some of the misfortunes befalling the party, it was also his opinion that such disasters could have been minimised or even avoided if the expedition had included someone with medical knowledge. Accordingly, he recommended that in future every mission going into the Zambezi area should not only have enough medical supplies, it should also have a medical person.

A decade was to pass, however, before another missionary expedition visited Bulozi. In the meantime Livingstone had died and his death was followed by a revival of missionary activities and interest in the lands and peoples visited by the great explorer. The next missionary group to go into Bulozi was that of the Paris Evangelical Mission in Lesotho. That was after its failure to establish a permanent mission in Chivi in south-eastern Zimbabwe (page 97).

On their way back to Lesotho after being released

99

from arrest at Bulawayo, Coillard and his companions had stopped for a rest at Soshong, the Ngwato capital. Here they had learnt from King Khama and his people about the Kololo, a Sotho-speaking people living in Bulozi. Bulozi seemed attractive to the missionaries from Lesotho for many reasons. The expedition turned northwards across the Kalahari reaching Bulozi in August 1878. This was a period of uncertainty in the political history of Bulozi (see Chapter 13). Litunga Lewanika was still battling to secure his authority in the country (pages 75–6). Thus, although willing to have the missionaries in his land, Lewanika thought it necessary to advise them to come back later when his country was more stable. Besides, as he also told them, he was still building his new capital. Coillard and his party left Bulozi as advised.

The party returned to Bulozi in 1885 and negotiations with the Litunga were facilitated by several factors. First, Coillard and his team of Basotho and French missionaries spoke Sesotho which was close to the language spoken in Bulozi. Secondly, the Ngwato ruler, Khama, who had by now accepted British 'protection' and had missionaries in his country, did much to persuade Lewanika to accept Christian missionaries. Thirdly, Frederick Arnot of the Plymouth Brethren, and an admirer of Livingstone, had spent some time at Lewanika's capital during which he had impressed the Litunga with his medical skills. Arnot supported Coillard's efforts to establish a mission in Bulozi. Finally, it is likely that Lewanika wanted to avoid creating a bad impression like Sekeletu two and a half decades earlier.

The first mission was established on the Sefula river a few miles from Lealui, the Litunga's capital. A church and school were built. Children from the community, including Lewanika's own son Latia and other members of the royal family, attended the school. Another mission centre was established at the capital and more missionaries joined the team. They experienced initial difficulties and some members, including Coillard's wife, died of malaria. Coillard died later in 1904 and was buried next to his wife in Seafuli.

Like the Ndebele rulers to the south, Lewanika's initial acceptance of the missionaries was to some extent motivated by a desire to benefit from their skills. He was suspicious that they might have hidden intentions which were likely to threaten his authority, but he also hoped that the presence of missionaries in his country might help to create external trade contacts. He also knew that missionary people had medicines and doctors who would be able to help the sick. The Lozi ruler had also been impressed by certain individuals among the settlers and wished to further his friendship with them. George Westbeech, for example, a resident game hunter, had impressed Lewanika with his marksmanship, and Westbeech's friend Arnot who arrived in Bulozi in 1882 proved to be a very skilled medical man.

The Paris Evangelical Mission shared the field with other missionaries. The Jesuits, for instance, arrived in 1879. They did not, however, work exclusively in Bulozi. They moved to the area of the Ila people who were subject people of the Lozi. Lewanika felt insulted by the Jesuit presence there and, when they were forced to leave the Ila country because of malaria, he refused them permission to settle in his country. No other missionaries went into the Ila area until 1893, when the Wesleyan Methodist Missionary Society sent an expedition headed by Arthur Baldwin. He established a mission on the Nkala river and later their work extended beyond the Kafue river.

In northern Zambia

The Plymouth Brethren pioneer, Frederick Arnot, left Bulozi in 1883 and went to Angola where he worked for some time. From there he visited the Yeke trading chief, Msiri, in 1886. Like Lewanika, Msiri was very much impressed by Arnot's medical skills. By 1891 the Plymouth Brethren had established a mission station on the shores of Lake Mweru and later the work was extended to the area of the western Lunda people.

Also active in northern Zambia was the London Missionary Society which had arrived in the region in the 1880s. LMS activities were mainly among the Lungu, south of Lake Tanganyika, and also at Kambole and Kashinde in Mporokoso's area. The mission also worked at Mbereshi in the area of Kazembe. Again, as in Matabeleland, LMS efforts were not very successful in northern Zambia. Conditions here were no more favourable than those in south-western Zimbabwe. For instance, the Lungu and Mambwe were being constantly raided for cattle and slaves by both the Bemba and the Tuta. Like other groups, the LMS also suffered from tropical diseases which claimed the lives of eleven men in the first sixteen years.

The most successful society in the northern parts of Zambia was a Roman Catholic Church order usually known as the White Fathers. The society had been founded in 1848 by Cardinal Lavigerie. Its work in Zambia was an extension of the activities in Uganda and Tanzania. A mission had been established at Ujiji on the eastern shores of Lake

Tanganyika in 1879, and in 1891 another was established at Mambwe on the Stevenson Road. It would seem that the Mambwe accepted the mission, believing that the missionary presence would deter Bemba invaders and slave hunters.

Through Mambwe Mission, the White Fathers missionaries were able to move further south in to Lubemba. They knew that the reigning Chitimukulu, Sampa, had given strict orders that white men were not to be allowed to enter Lubemba. However, with the co-operation and assistance of some of the Chitimukulu's lesser chiefs and headmen, the missionaries successfully entered Lubemba and eventually established missions there. For instance, in 1892 Fathers Van Oost and Lechaptois of Mambwe Mission visited chief Chilingwa. In 1894 Father Oost visited yet another chief, Chitika. The same year, with Chitika's assistance, the Fathers reached the village of Mukasa, one of the most important lesser chiefs under the Chitimukulu. Mukasa was at that time very much involved with slave trade and the missionaries found Swahili traders at his village. In spite of this, Mukasa gave them a warm welcome and allowed them to build in his village. A mission was founded at Kayambi Hills close to Mukasa's capital in July 1895.

Moreover, Musaka offered to assist them in their negotiations with the Chitimukulu. This challenge was readily accepted by Father, later Bishop, Dupont then in charge of Mambwe Mission.

Several headmen and sub-chiefs visited Father Dupont at Kayambi Mission. Even Sampa's attitude to the missionaries was gradually changing for the better. In any case at this time the situation was rapidly changing on the Zambian plateau. It was now expected among the missionaries that the British South Africa Company would invade and take over Lubemba at any time. Chitimukulu Sampa, ill and weak, died in May 1896. His death was followed by a long period of uncertainty, caused by succession disputes, violence and confusion. This instability was advantageous to the missions and the British South Africa Company, both of which were trying to enter Lubemba.

In April 1897 Father Dupont visited Mwamba, the chief expected to succeed Sampa as the new Chitimukulu. But, partly because of Swahili presence and influence, the situation was unfavourable to the missionaries and consequently the expedition returned without achieving much. However, in October 1898, Father Dupont rushed back to Mwamba because the chief, who was seriously ill, had sent for him. Mwamba died shortly after Dupont's arrival, but not before he had had time to renew his permission for the establishment of a mission at his home. Mwamba is also reported to have offered Father Dupont part of his chieftainship if the French missionary successfully cured him of his illness, and the whole chieftainship in the event of death.

After Mwamba's death many Bemba people, anticipating violence which usually followed a chief's funeral, went to Father Dupont's camp which was a few miles away from the dead chief's town. It was here where a mission later grew; it was called *Chilubula*, meaning a 'place of escape'. After the founding of Chilubula Mission in 1898 the missionaries founded other missions in northern Zambia: Chilonga near Mpika in 1899, and Kambwili in the Luangwa valley in 1904.

18 Pioneer Christian missions in Malawi

The Livingstonia Mission

David Livingstone's ideals and activities in Central Africa, and the circumstances of his death in the heart of Africa became both an inspiration and a challenge to European Christian leaders and ordinary Christians throughout Europe. Response to the challenge was both positive and immediate and Malawi benefited directly from this response.

Within weeks after the burial of Livingstone at Westminster Abbey people like Dr. James Stewart of Lovedale, were already thinking that the Free Church of Scotland should preserve Livingstone's name and carry on his aims through an active memorial – a mission. The idea of a 'Livingstonia' was proposed and it was suggested that such an institution should be founded in a very 'carefully selected and commanding spot' somewhere in Central Africa. The institution was to be both industrial and educational so that it could teach the truths of the Gospel and the arts of civilised life to the natives of the country. Thus in 1875 the Livingstonia Mission was established by the Free Church of Scotland in Cape Maclear at the south end of Lake Malawi.

The area selected proved to be difficult in a number of respects. Firstly, it was hot and uncomfortable. Also the Machinga Yao, who lived in that region, were a very strong and independent people who had no desire for Christianity. Moreover, their own religious and educational needs were being satisfied by Islam which had been established there before the arrival of the missionaries (page 86). The Yao were also unwilling to give up the slave trade which was the basis of their economy and disliked the missionary practice of giving refuge to people escaping from slave traders.

In spite of these difficulties the missionaries, under the leadership of Dr Robert Laws, continued their work. Schools, industrial and medical centres were opened and attracted many people to the mission. Trade was also established. But in six years of effort at Cape Maclear the missionaries did not convert many people to Christianity.

Apart from the problems discussed above, Cape Maclear was not suitable in yet another major respect. It was too remote from the most populous areas of Malawi to serve as an effective mission centre in the region. Thus in 1881 the mission was moved north to Bandawe on the western shore of Lake Malawi. Here in the Tonga area, Dr. Laws and his colleagues were more successful in their effort to establish a permanent 'Livingstonia' mission. There was no slave trade, and no Islamic influence. The Tonga, unlike the Machinga Yao, welcomed the missionaries, as they arrived at the time when the Tonga were looking for allies against Mbelwa's Ngoni from whose control they had broken loose. Also because of their economy which

Dr Robert Laws, missionary leader

was based on agriculture, the Tonga were less opposed to mission work than the Yao and Ngoni.

Schools, industrial centres and medical centres were established and the Tonga availed themselves of all these opportunities. By 1890 about 2,000 Tonga children were attending school. Western education was very much valued because it provided the necessary skills for participation in the western-type economy already developing in the country. For instance by 1886 the Tonga were taking positions as clerks, interpreters and foremen in the Shire Highlands, where the African Lakes Company (page 88), an adjunct of the Livingstonia Mission, had established the first white settler-type economy north of the Limpopo. The desire for education generally preceded conversion to Christianity itself among the Tonga. Thus, while still suspicious of Christianity, many Tonga were prepared to take advantage of the education provided by the mission schools. Large-scale Tonga conversion to Christianity did not come until about 1895–8.

Among the Ngoni
Dr Laws and his colleagues also approached Ngoni chiefs and the initial response was not encouraging. In 1878 Laws and James Stewart were kept waiting for four days before Chief Chikusi would agree to see them when they visited his headquarters. Stewart was similarly treated by Mbelwa, another Ngoni ruler, when he went to see him in 1879. This was because the Ngoni rulers felt the missionaries a threat to their positions. Eventually in 1887, Chikusi did allow the missionaries to establish a centre, possibly for the same reasons as the Lozi ruler in Zambia. He thought the mission would bring material goods through trade to his land. A mission was founded at Livlezi to the east of the chief's village. Its first missionaries were Drs Henry and McIntyre. Another was later established at Mapondera's.

Mbelwa, on the other hand, was very angry with the missionaries because they had established a mission among the Tonga whom he still regarded as his subjects. He tried without success to prevent the missionaries from associating either with the Tonga or with other Ngoni groups. He was at this time under considerable pressure. His rivals, such as the Chewa chief Mwase Kasungu and the Tonga chief Mankhambira, had obtained guns from Swahili traders and were becoming more powerful and a threat to his position. N'gonomo, the Ngoni commander, informed Mbelwa that he would not raid Mkhambira without the help of the Senga who possessed guns. Mbelwa decided that the missionaries might be useful as allies against the Tonga and Tumbuka and therefore agreed in 1882 to receive a mission at Hoho village near Njanyu hill. The first missionaries here were William Kayi, a Lovedale-trained evangelist, and James Sutherland. At first they were not allowed to open schools or even to preach. But by selling calico they were able to demonstrate to Mbelwa and the Ngoni that they had brought material goods as well as Christianity. Mbelwa was anxious to share these benefits among Ngoni sub-groups so as not to appear to be keeping them to himself.

Mbelwa was in fact being pulled in two directions. On the one hand, the missionaries were trying to persuade him to stop raiding the Tonga, and on the other his own advisers were asking him to turn the missionaries out of the country. It was only by chance that Mbelwa's advisers were finally won over to the pro-missionary view. There had been severe droughts in the country during the years 1882–86. Ngoni rain-makers had failed to bring rain and, as a last resort, the Ngoni appealed to the missionary Dr Elmslie to pray for rain. He complied with their request at one of his Sunday services and the following day rain fell in the area. The Ngoni advisers now dropped their opposition to schools and in 1889 permission was granted for a second centre at Ekwendeni.

By 1890 schools had been opened in many parts of Mbelwa's kingdom and children from all sections of Ngoni society attended them. Work centres were also established to shift the emphasis away from cattle and slave raiding. In time, the Ngoni became just as keen for education as the Tonga. The young Ngoni especially wanted this education; the same group which by Ngoni tradition should have been recruited into the raiding regiments. The Livingstonia Mission besides converting the Ngoni to Christianity, trained and prepared some of them for responsible positions in their society. In accordance with this policy the Overtoun Institution was opened in 1895 at Kondowe further up the lake. Eventually the name 'Livingstonia' was given to this institution and it is still known by that name today. The Livingstonia Institute trained Africans to be pastors, evangelists, schoolteachers, medical assistants and craftsmen. It soon became famous for providing the most advanced education and professional training for Africans in Central Africa. Its guiding spirit was Dr Laws, who was himself an extremely talented and practical man. Not only did he preach and teach, he also performed surgical operations and worked as a carpenter, joiner, printer, photographer, farrier, boat-builder, engineer and druggist.

The success of 'Livingstonia' cannot be attributed solely to Laws or, for that matter, to the missionaries. Certainly Mbelwa, though initially suspicious and uncooperative, later contributed greatly to its success. This was also true of many ordinary Ngoni who cooperated with the missionaries in several ways. It took skilful diplomacy on Mbelwa's part to overcome the initial difficulties facing him. Once he had decided to support the missionaries he was also able to convince his traditional advisers that this was the right thing to do. This also reflects the flexibility of Ngoni society.

The Scottish Mission
About a year after the Free Church of Scotland's pioneers had established themselves at Cape Maclear, the Established Church of Scotland, another branch of the Presbyterian Church, also sent a mission to Malawi. The Established Church of Scotland was also committed to the fulfilment of Livingstone's ideals and dreams. Its missionaries arrived in Malawi under Henry Henderson and founded a mission centre in the Shire Highlands. The mission was called Blantyre after the Scottish town where Livingstone was born. The land on which the Blantyre Mission was built had been granted by a Mangoche Yao chief, Kapeni. Blantyre Mission was more successful than the 'Livingstonia' mission at Cape Maclear because, unlike the Machinga Yao, the Mangoche Yao cooperated with the missionaries. In fact the missionaries were seen as allies against the Machinga Yao who had driven the Mangoche Yao to the south where now they were exposed to attacks by the Maseko Ngoni from Dedza.

Unfortunately, however, Blantyre Mission suffered greatly, in the initial years, from a number of scandals, some of which almost caused its collapse in 1879–1881. But under the leadership of D.C. Scott the situation improved. Scott was joined in 1883 by Alexander Hetherwick, and together the two men worked hard to restore the people's

The Presbyterian Church at Blantyre, Malawi

confidence in the mission. But unfortunately in their enthusiasm they also involved themselves in local politics and administrative matters creating yet another damaging scandal. They made themselves into 'chiefs' over local people, charging, trying and imprisoning people accused of such crimes as murder, theft etc. There were instances of brutal flogging, torture and even one case when an African was executed. The two men promoted themselves to 'paramounts' assuming the authority to preside over disputes between chiefs.

The activities of the two missionaries, which were damaging Blantyre Mission's image in the eyes of the local people, ended when the Foreign Mission Committee of the Established Church ordered the Blantyre Missionaries not to involve themselves in the political and administrative affairs of the local communities. As soon as the missionaries decided to concentrate upon their proper work, they were very successful – especially in the field of education. Hetherwick and Scott were among the few pioneer missionaries to recognise the potential of African culture and society. In their opinion African society was something upon which to build rather than something to break or destroy. Furthermore, as successful tradesmen themselves, the two men worked hard to train and prepare Africans for the Industrial Revolution which they were certain would also reach Africa. Their views were put into practice by placing a measure of responsibility upon such men as Matecheta, Chisuse and Kinje. In Scott's words: 'Africa for the Africans has been our policy from the first.'

The UMCA

The formation of the Universities Mission to Central Africa was itself a direct response to Livingstone's Cambridge appeal that university students and teachers should regard missionary work in Africa as their responsibility (page 91). As already seen, the first expedition of this society arrived in Central Africa in 1860 under Bishop Mackenzie. A mission site was selected at Mogomero not far from the modern city of Zomba. The mission was abandoned in 1863 when the UMCA was compelled to leave Malawi altogether after losing several members including Bishop Mackenzie himself. The survivors, under a new leader Bishop Tozer, finally settled on the island of Zanzibar.

The UMCA however returned to Malawi in 1881 when W. P. Johnson travelled around Lake Malawi. A permanent station was established on the Likoma Island in 1885. Likoma Island later became the centre of missionary activities on both sides of the lake. According to a map drawn in 1899 there were seventeen sub-stations on the eastern side and five on the western. The building of Likoma mission is attributable to Chauncy Maples as Johnson devoted most of his time and energy to travelling and itinerant work. He was fortunate in that the mission owned a steamship, the *Charles Jansen* which enabled the missionaries to bring the necessary stores and supplies from Matope on the Shire River, and it also gave them contact with the Scottish missionaries at Bandawe, where medical supplies and care were available. This meant that the UMCA missionaries no longer had to rely upon the dangerous route to Zanzibar for most of their immediate needs.

The Nyanja peoples, however, were now being raided by the Gwangwara Ngoni, so Likoma Mission, like Magomero before it, became a place of refuge for displaced people. There was also the recurring problem of malaria which, in the first thirty years of the mission, claimed the lives of fifty-seven missionaries out of a total of two hundred. Furthermore, Islam had been firmly rooted among the local communities making Christian conversion rather difficult. Nonetheless the UMCA went ahead with its work, opening schools, translating the gospels into the Chinyanja language, and carrying out some medical work, especially after the arrival of Dr Robert Howard in 1889.

Very soon the UMCA had its greatest impact, especially among rural communities. Most of its missionaries had had experience in dealing with the worst effects of the Industrial Revolution as they had worked in the slums of London, Manchester and Birmingham before going to Malawi. They were determined that Africa should avoid the same mistakes made by Europe in dealing with the problems resulting from industrialisation. They tried to preserve the structures of rural societies and their way of life as much as possible, and to this end they offered, as part of their educational programme, instruction in such practical subjects as agriculture, building and carpentry. In spite of the emphasis on practical things, however, literary education remained the most important activity, second only to Christian conversion. Whether or not they succeeded in their efforts to prepare the Africans for the Industrial Revolution is an open question. The UMCA missionaries began the training of the African clergy quite early, their first African priests being men like Johanna Abdallah and Leonard Kamungu. Kamungu later worked at Nkhotakota in Zambia.

The Dutch Reformed Church of South Africa

The Dutch Reformed Church was not interested in missionary work until the 1880s. For instance, Stephanus Hofmeyr, in charge of the mission's work among the non-white communities in the Zoutensberg area of the Transvaal in the 1860s and 1870s, tried unsuccessfully to make the leaders of the DRC interested in starting work among the southern Shona of Zimbabwe. He did send some of his Buys, Venda and Pedi evangelists to spend some time teaching and preaching among the Shona (page 97). After 1885/6 this attitude changed. A missionary society was formed to take charge of the Dutch Reformed Church's missionary work. In 1888 the first DRC missionary to Malawi, A. C. Murray, left for the north to start mission work in Malawi. Before starting his own independent missionary activities he worked with Elmslie of the 'Livingstonia' (pages 102–3). Having gained sufficient experience, Murray went to start a DRC mission among Chiwere's Ngoni. Chief Chiwere gladly allowed Murray to work in his area as the missionary's presence helped to maintain Chiwere's prestige among his people and especially the counsellors some of whom were known to be plotting against their chief. Chiwere also expected Murray to be in possession of supernatural powers, especially after Dr Elmslie had successfully prayed for rain at Mbelwa's request (page 103). On one occasion rain also fell in Chiwere's area after Murray's prayers for it. This, of course, confirmed Chiwere's belief.

Murray was joined by another missionary, Vlok, and in 1890 schools were opened at Mvera and Ndwide. More missionaries also came in the 1890s enabling the DRC to open even more schools. It was, however, uphill work. The Ngoni often threatened the missionaries and malaria was rife. Murray himself was savaged by a leopard. However, the work expanded slowly, and in 1894 nineteen Africans were baptized. The work was extended to the Chewa under chief Mazengera in 1896. Mazengera had been troubled by invasions from both the Ngoni and the Yao and in accepting the DRC he hoped that the presence of the missionaries would deter these invasions. By 1900 the DRC had eighteen white missionaries in Malawi running its centres at Mvera, Kongwe, and Nkhoma. The mission also had an African, Albert Namalamba, in charge of its fourteen schools, forty-eight teachers and 1300 pupils. The educational work expanded further after 1900.

Effect of Mission work in Malawi

The missionaries brought many changes to Malawi. The missionary activities in Malawi during the two decades before European rule were more successful than they were anywhere in Central Africa. By the end of the century there were many schools teaching young Malawians to read and write, and how to speak and write foreign languages such as English, French and Swahili. Schools also prepared many Malawians for the arrival of Western ideas. For instance, most missionaries were traders as well and encouraged Africans to be interested in European manufactures. Africans were also taught such practical skills as carpentry, tailoring and printing. The missionaries introduced new methods of farming and are thought to have brought the plough to the people of Malawi. The missionaries introduced and grew fruit such as pineapples and oranges, and a variety of vegetables. Once they accepted them, the African people of Malawi became successful growers of these new fruit and vegetables. The Africans also copied new methods of building houses from the missionaries.

As we have already seen, in some areas the missionaries became too involved in local politics and this made their work among local communities rather difficult and even dangerous at times. Once this involvement in local affairs stopped, missionaries became more acceptable to the African societies.

Missions such as Blantyre and Livingstonia helped to produce potential African leaders and a more literate population. The Northern Province of Malawi became the most educationally advanced in the whole of Central Africa. Some of the graduates of Blantyre and Livingstonia were to play significant roles in the rise of Malawian nationalism. Many others were to play similar roles in the rise of African nationalism in Zambia, Zimbabwe and South Africa.

PART VI
The Scramble, Conquest and Colonisation

19 Leopold and the establishment of the Congo Free State

By about the middle of the 1870s most of Central Africa had been visited by one or more agents of European enterprises mainly interested in establishing themselves in the region: big game hunters, traders, explorers, and missionaries. Few African and European leaders alike could have foreseen the revolutionary changes which would come to the region within the next decade. Although some missionaries, explorers and traders did ask their home governments to intervene in Africa on their behalf to protect their interests, no government was prepared to be directly involved in Africa.

This policy of non-involvement in Africa by European governments and their leaders did, however, change at the end of the 1870s and by the middle of the 1880s European powers were competing for colonies in Africa. There were historical reasons for this turnabout at the end of the 1870s. By that time, possible routes into the African interior had been found. It was now known that the African interior had great lakes and healthy uplands which added to the continent's beauty and economic value. There was also a growing demand in Europe and North America for raw materials to keep the home manufacturing industries well supplied. Markets were also needed for the goods manufactured by these industries. In Europe itself, there was a new power struggle following German unification after the Franco-Prussian war of 1870.

The beginning of Europe's change of attitude towards Africa is usually dated from around 1879 after Stanley's Central African expedition of 1876–79. Stanley had traversed the continent and had also sailed down the Congo River collecting valuable information about Central Africa's economic potential. His ideas about Central Africa's economic future appealed to the opportunist Belgian king, Leopold II.

Leopold II was a very ambitious man. As a constitutional monarch he had no active role in the politics of his little kingdom. It is not surprising therefore, that this active young head of state looked for something to relieve his boredom. Thus, when Leopold became king in 1865 his personal expansionist ideas had already been vaguely formed. He had travelled widely and read the writings of explorers and hunters about Africa with great interest. His idea was that industrialised Europe should take over the undeveloped parts of the world in order to exploit their resources. Markets should also be opened in these areas for European manufacturers.

To give practical meaning to his ideas Leopold formed the African International Association in 1876. The Association would establish trading and scientific centres attached to mission stations in Central Africa. These centres would be given military protection. The first of them were established in 1878 and 1879 at the White Fathers's missions at Tabora and Ujiji respectively. Up to this time, however, the activities of the African International Association had had no real impact in the area as they had been mainly concerned with collecting information. A major shift in emphasis came in 1879, when Leopold became more openly interested in building up a personal empire in Africa.

In 1879 Leopold began his close association with Stanley, the journalist and explorer who, as already seen, had met Livingstone at Ujiji in 1871. Stanley had since made another trip to Central Africa to try and carry on Livingstone's work by exploring the Lualaba area. He had also travelled down the Congo River and had formed the opinion that the great river could be developed or used for the development of the basin. Stanley had first turned to the British Government for financial support, but when the Government showed no interest he approached the Belgium king, Leopold II. An agreement was signed between the two men under which Stanley was provided with large sums of money to help him take over the Congo River basin for the Belgian king.

What later came to be called the 'scramble' for and 'partition' of Africa among European powers had, in fact, begun. The 'scramble' meant the competition between agents or representatives of European powers for territorial gains in Africa. 'Partition' on the other hand refers to the division of Africa among the competing powers. While the scramble was going on within the African continent among representatives of the European powers, the partitioning was done on paper or maps by European diplomats who were thousands of miles away. In some cases the scramble caused such bitter competition that some European countries came dangerously close to open military conflict. But wars were avoided through conferences and discussions. One of the most important diplomatic initiatives made to avoid conflicts over African colonial claims was the Berlin Conference of 1884–5 which was called by the leading diplomat of the day, the German Chancellor Otto von Bismarck. Before the Berlin meeting, the representatives of each European country involved in Africa were allowed either to occupy portions of Africa, or to enter into treaties with local rulers.

As Leopold's representative in the scramble, Stanley concentrated his activities in the Congo Basin. In 1879–84 he explored the Congo River and the adjacent area where he established road and river communications from Kisangani to the Atlantic coast – a distance of over 1000 miles. The idea was to bring this area under Leopold's authority to enable him to control all the trade in the Congo Basin. Leopold wanted all the goods to be exported by his own river steamers, and later on his railway from Kinshasa in the interior to the west coast.

There was, however, opposition to Leopold's plans in the area from a number of European powers, especially France. In 1882 Savorgnan de Brazza, a French agent, obtained a treaty from the Teke chief, Makoko. Makoko, who controlled territory north of the Congo, ceded his land to France. This situation prompted Leopold to take quick political and diplomatic steps in Zaire in order to secure his economic objectives. Thus, Stanley was instructed to make treaties with African rulers south of the Congo River, and this Stanley did. But Leopold still had to take further steps to protect his interests from rivals and competitors.

Leopold's diplomacy

Leopold's ultimate objective was to take over Zaire for himself. In this he showed himself to be a skillful diplomat. He claimed that it would be in the best interest of all the powers concerned with Central Africa if the whole Congo Basin was maintained as a free trade area under the control of his African International Association rather than let a particular power have it. He had to convince the French, Germans, British and the Americans about his suggestion. A secret agreement was signed with France according to which Leopold promised that France could have Zaire in the event of his failure to administer it; which at the time appeared quite likely for financial reasons. German support was gained by backing Bismarck's claims to Togoland, Cameroun, Tanganyika and Namibia. In return the German Chancellor supported Leopold's claim to Zaire. American support was achieved by promises to fight the slave trade in the Congo Basin.

None of the countries mentioned above was, however, more interested in the area than Britain. There were British traders doing business in the area and British Baptist missionaries had been working there since 1878. In addition, Britain had signed a treaty in 1884 with Portugal allowing the Portuguese to control the Congo estuary thus cutting off Leopold from the coast. Leopold countered by offering profitable contracts to British merchants, and by persuading the British Government that he would be more 'liberal' in Zaire than either the French or the Portuguese. His diplomatic efforts were in part successful when Britain abandoned the Anglo-Portuguese agreement of 1884, but the British refused to support Leopold's plans for Zaire.

In the meantime the Berlin Conference was called in November 1884. The Conference decided that a free trade zone across Central Africa, from the mouth of the Congo in the west to the Zambezi delta in the east, should be created. Britain thus no longer had the power to keep Leopold out of the Congo estuary as this had become part of the free navigational area. The Berlin Conference allowed Leopold to retain the rest of the Congo Basin as far as the Congo–Zambezi watershed, including the mineral-rich Shaba province. Leopold called his new acquisition the Congo Free State, and it was his personal empire, not that of the Belgian Government. France was also allowed to keep the area to the west, from Stanley Pool (Malebo Pool) to the Atlantic Ocean, which was later known as French Congo, now the People's Republic of Congo (Congo-Brazzaville).

Congo Free State 1885–1908

Leopold did not have enough money to both develop and administer his new empire. No trading company would risk moving into an area in which no trading between Europeans and Africans had been developed. Leopold had to demonstrate that something was being done to develop the Congo Free State in terms of the requirements of the Berlin agreement. Thus he attracted companies by offering them huge rewards in land grants. These companies were known as *concessionaire* companies and they undertook certain projects, for example, building roads or a railway line in return for land or mineral rights.

One of the *concessionaire* companies was the Compagnie du Congo pour le Commerce et l'Industrie (CCCI), whose contract with Leopold was signed in 1886. The company agreed to build a railway line from Kinshasa to Matadi on the Congo estuary. For every kilometre of railway built Leopold was to give the CCCI 1425 hectares of land. When in 1898 the company completed its work it was granted 777000 hectares of land. Two other railways were similarly constructed, one from the Congo to Lake Tanganyika, and the other from the Kasai River to the Shaba province.

In 1891 a contract was made with another company, the Compagnie du Katanga, under which the company was to occupy and develop the Shaba (Katanga) area. This company would be paid or granted ownership of one third of the province. It was opposed by the Swahili. The strongest of these

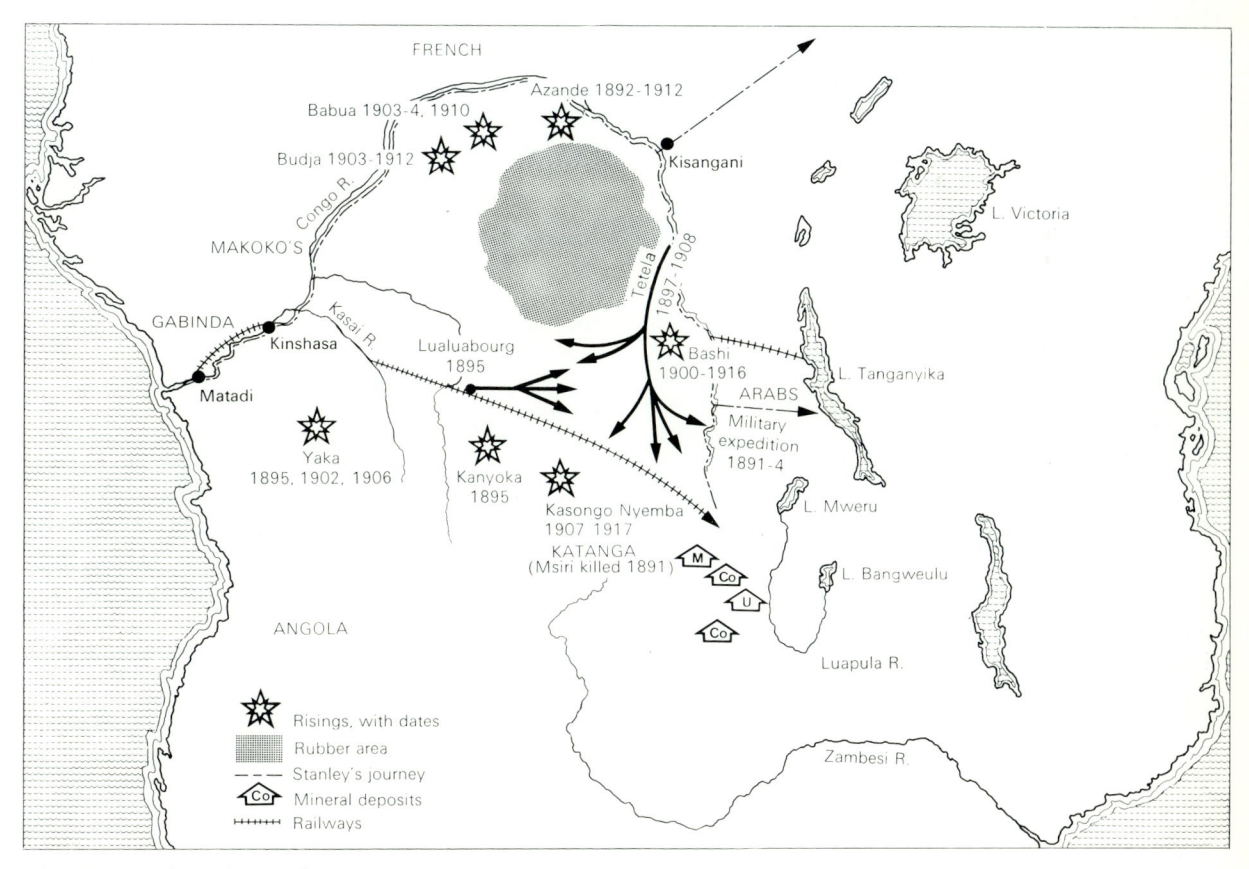

The Congo under Belgian rule

states was Msiri's Yeke kingdom. Msiri and his Yeke people resisted the Compagnie du Katanga for over three years (1891–4). Msiri told the Belgians: 'I am the master here, and as long as I live Garenganja (his Yeke kingdom) shall have no other.' He however allowed the company to establish a post not far from his capital, Bunkeya. In 1891 Msiri was shot and fatally wounded during fighting with some Belgian soldiers under Captain Stairs.

The areas granted to the companies were supposed to be waste land on which no African communities lived. But in reality many African communities were compelled to abandon their land which was taken by the companies and people were forced to work for these companies building roads and railways and, during the period 1895–1905, tapping rubber from rubber trees in the forest. There was, during these years, a big demand for rubber in Europe. The African labourers were paid very meagre wages, and sometimes no wages at all. They were recruited by a system of forced labour and were virtual slaves. Although the Congo Free State was not the only colony practising the system of forced labour, it was the worst of its kind throughout colonial Africa.

For a time Leopold made good profits from the rubber trade. Some areas were owned and run directly by him as 'Crown land', and the rest of the land was leased to companies on a profit-sharing basis. From 1906 to 1910, however, the demand for rubber from Zaire fell as rubber plantations had been established in South-East Asia. There was also growing international condemnation of the Congo Free State's forced labour system which supported the rubber trade in the country. In 1908 Leopold was made to hand over his Congo Free State to Belgium and from that date until 1960, when it gained independence, the country was known as Belgian Congo.

Effects of Leopold's occupation

Leopold left behind many problems after nearly two and a half decades of the most oppressive and most exploitative colonial administration in the history of colonisation. The *concessionaire* companies owned vast areas under contracts made with Leopold. They still controlled trade in many parts of the country. There were debts to be paid by the Belgian Congo as Leopold had borrowed large sums of money on the account of the colony. This money, however, was never used to develop the country, but to build and support expensive palaces in Belgium. Moreover, interest on these debts took as much as twenty per cent of the Government's revenue. The Belgian Congo remained very poor as its people had no income to pay for further development.

The people of Zaire had resented Leopold's personal rule and they had no reason to accept Belgian colonial rule either. So the hostilities continued after the Belgian Government had taken over the colony. The main opposition came from groups remote from the main centres of Belgian power, where the chief was a military leader. These included such peoples as the Azande on the Sudan frontiers, who opposed colonial rule from 1892 to 1912; the Bashi of eatern Zaire who fought against the Belgians from 1900 to 1916; the Luba of Kasongo Nyemba from 1907 to 1917, and the Yaka on the Angolan border who fought in 1895, 1902 and 1906. There were also uprisings as a result of the forced labour system and the cruelty of Belgian officials; in 1903/4 by the Babua in the north, and by the Budja from 1903 to 1905. In the first seven months of 1905, 142 'sentries' were killed.

20 Rhodes and the occupation of Zimbabwe

Rhodes

Cecil John Rhodes was not a king like Leopold II. He was a self-made businessman. Rhodes went to South Africa at the age of seventeen, a sickly young man who had been advised that his weak lungs might benefit from the warm and clean atmosphere in Africa. He joined a brother who was growing cotton in Natal. In 1868 diamonds were discovered in west Griqualand and by 1871 Rhodes had crossed the Drakensberg mountains and joined the diamond diggers in Kimberley, where he bought many diamond claims and became one of the richest mine owners. Rhodes was a great money-maker and became a multi-millionaire, and he wanted to use his money to gain power. He was a strong believer in the superiority of the British society, its systems of government and justice and its principles of peace and liberty. His purpose in life was, therefore, to spread these principles to other parts of the world and he was prepared to spend his personal fortune to achieve this. Since such ideas could only be put into effect through the colonisation of foreign lands, Rhodes was, therefore, an advocate of British imperialism. Indeed, he became one of the biggest Empire builders of the nineteenth century. In this respect he was like Leopold II.

Rhodes's dreams and aims about Africa were vast. He wanted Britain to take the whole territory roughly stretching from the Orange River in the south to the Great Lakes area in the north. But such dreams were, of course, in direct conflict with those of the Boer republic of the Transvaal and the Germans who had established themselves at Angra Pequena on the Namibian coast since 1884, and were claiming Damaraland and Namaqualand. The Portuguese also had plans in Malawi and in Zimbabwe's eastern districts while, as seen already, Leopold was in occupation of the mineral-rich Shaba or Katanga region. The Transvaal was now extending its frontiers westwards, thus threatening the 'missionary road' which was the vital link between British Cape Colony and Central Africa. Moreover, the Transvaal president, Kruger, was busy persuading the Germans to cooperate with the Transvaal in frustrating any British plans to reach Central Africa.

Such schemes were intolerable to Rhodes who had already successfully persuaded the British Government to make 'missionary road' secure by establishing a Crown colony in southern Botswana, and by declaring a protectorate over the northern part of Botswana as far as the Zambezi River in 1885. In 1887 Rhodes learnt that Lobengula, the Ndebele king, had signed an agreement with the Transvaal's agent, Peter Grobler. The Grobler Treaty, as the agreement is also known, was an

Cecil Rhodes

agreement of friendship between the Transvaal and Matabeleland. The Transvaal was allowed to maintain a permanent representative at Bulawayo. Rhodes, who expected that there would be some rich gold deposits in Zimbabwe's Mashonaland area, had to act quickly to persuade Lobengula to withdraw the Grobler Treaty. Once more, he managed to persuade the British High Commissioner to intervene.

The Moffat agreement
Rhodes was successful as the High Commissioner sent the new Assistant Commissioner for British Bechuanaland on a mission to Bulawayo to go and ask Lobengula to drop the Grobler agreement. The man sent was John Smith Moffat, who knew Lobengula well since his days in Matabeleland as head of the Inyati Mission. Not only did Moffat succeed in persuading Lobengula to cancel the Grobler Treaty, he also got the king to enter into a new agreement with the British. This agreement was reached in February 1888. Under this treaty Lobengula agreed to be a friend of the British Queen and promised not to enter into any agreement with any other country or group without the knowledge and approval of the British High Commissioner. Lobengula had entered into this agreement because he regarded Moffat as an old friend. Little did he realise that by this time Moffat was no longer a real friend to the Ndebele who he now regarded as 'a miserable people' and thought 'it will be a blessing to the world when they are broken up.'

John Smith Moffat c.1880

At the time of Moffat's arrival in Matabeleland, Lobengula was under a lot of pressure from white negotiators at his court, each of them wanting mining concessions for himself or for a particular group of exploiters. Lobengula was, of course, aware that behind these white men were strong powers which would one day invade his land. He did not know what to do in order to prevent this from happening. It was clear to him that a war against these people would worsen the situation, or even hasten the destruction of his kingdom. Lobengula compared his position to that of a fly before a chameleon that 'advances very slowly and gently, first putting forward one leg, then another, until at last he darts out his tongue.' The position of the Ndebele king was further complicated by the growing impatience among his regiments who were eager to fight and drive away the whites.

The white population staying at Bulawayo at this time was growing. It included such people as Renny Tailyour, the representative of Edward Lippert, a wealthy Johannesburg merchant, and E. A. Maund, representing the Exploring Company in South Africa, and several ivory hunters and traders as already seen (pages 87–8). All these people wanted the gold of Zimbabwe, and in their efforts to obtain concessions from Lobengula they pretended to be friends of the Ndebele people. They advised that the British would be better to deal with than, say, the Boers or the Portuguese, both of whom were after Lobengula's land. Lobengula was persuaded that the best way to prevent either the Boers or the Portuguese from taking his land was to grant British groups mining and trading concessions, and in return they would help to defend the country.

Lobengula played his part cleverly. He tried to delay his decision as long as he could, and gave away as little as possible. He also restrained his regiments from provoking a war with the whites. Moreover, it was well known at Bulawayo that the Zulu had defeated the British at Isandhlwana in 1879; and the young Ndebele soldiers thought that they could also do the same. But Lobengula knew that the British had the Maxim gun, and that they were supported by the South African railway and telegraph systems. But he used his diplomatic skill to prevent the inevitable destruction of his kingdom for as long as he could.

The Rudd mission
The Moffat agreement of 1888 had opened the way to the north. But to Rhodes it was still clear that this was a temporary measure as Lobengula might soon realise that he would not be able to conduct his

foreign policy freely and might therefore cancel the treaty. To make the position more secure Rhodes sent his own mission to Lobengula to negotiate a mineral concession. The mission consisted of three very carefully chosen men. The leader was Charles Rudd, an associate at Kimberley and a member of Rhodes De Beers Consolidated Company. The other two were Francis Thompson, also called 'Matabele' Thompson, a fluent Nguni speaker and an expert in Nguni customs; and Rhodes' friend from Oxford days, now a lawyer – Rochford Maguire.

The three men arrived at Bulawayo in September 1888. At that time Lobengula was trying to restrain his young *majaha* (soldiers), who wanted to drive the whites out of the country by force. It was very difficult to arrange an audience with Lobengula, and so Rudd and his companions had to wait for five weeks before they could speak to the Ndebele king. Even then they might not have had the opportunity but for local assistance and support from the British Commissioner for Bechuanaland, Sir Sydney Shippard. Sir Sydney Shippard, respected

Charles Rudd, leader of a mission to Lobengula

Sir Harry Johnston at Kimberley, May 1890. Standing left to right, J. A. Grant, J. W. Moir, Joseph Thomson; seated, left to right, J. Rochfort Maguire, Harry Johnston, Cecil Rhodes, A. R. Colquhoun

by Lobengula as the British Queen's representative, did more to influence the Ndebele ruler's decision to consider dealing with Rhodes' emissaries than any one else. Local support for the Rudd mission came from such people as Charles Helm, now heading the LMS in Matabeleland, and whom Lobengula had always regarded as his trusted missionary. It was Helm who persuaded Lobengula that Rhodes was a reliable man and one who could be trusted. Similar recommendations came from Lobengula's own senior indunas and trusted advisors, Lotshe and Sikombo. Without realising that the three men had been bribed by Rhodes' men, Lobengula listened to advice from Helm, Lotshe and Sikombo.

During the negotiations Rudd emphasised that if granted mineral rights, Rhodes would 'protect' Matabeleland from European colonisation. He also said that Rhodes would put notices in the newspapers notifying white people that they should keep out of Matabeleland. Rudd also lied that no more than ten men would be brought to Matabeland and that these would abide by Ndebele laws. He also assured Lobengula that their firearms would be surrendered to the Ndebele king when they arrived in Zimbabwe. On the strength of such empty promises and assurances, and at the advice of Helm, Lotshe and Sikombo, Lobengula put his mark on the document later known as the Rudd Concession

Lobengula, chief of the Ndebele

on 30 October 1888. Helm was witness to this and also added his signature to the document.

According to the document which Lobengula signed, the Ndebele king, his heirs and successors were to be paid a monthly sum of one hundred pounds. The Ndebele rulers were also to be supplied with 1000 rifles and 100 000 rounds of ammunition, and a gunboat to patrol the Zambezi (nothing was ever heard of this boat). In return Lobengula agreed to grant Rhodes and his group 'complete and exclusive charge over all metals and minerals in my kingdom... together with full power to do all things they may deem necessary... to procure the same... and undertake to grant no concession of land or mining rights...' without Rhodes' concurrance.

Lobengula had been tricked into signing a document which did not include most of the things emphasised and promised during the negotiations, and a document that was to lead to the colonisation of Zimbabwe by Rhodes. Although he soon discovered that he had been tricked, it was too late to reverse the trend set in motion by the Rudd Concession. He did, of course, complain to the Queen of England. This only made Rhodes move with more calculated care and speed to frustrate Lobengula's efforts. In South Africa he was in a strong political position, and was soon to become Premier of the Cape. He also had substantial influence among some leading personalities, including government officials, in Britain. Above all, Rhodes owned millions of pounds of the De Beers money. He could, and did, use his money to buy or bribe rivals and opponents in both southern Africa and Britain. Rhodes moved to the next stage of his plans, the formation of a commercial company with the power and authority to colonise Zimbabwe and to exploit the mineral and other resources of the land.

The British South Africa Company and the Charter
Rhodes had in mind a company that would give him the authority to colonise and administer Zimbabwe on behalf of Britain. Such a company, therefore, had to have a special charter, which was a document bearing the Queen's signature and clearly setting out what the British Government required Rhodes' company to do in Zimbabwe.

The British South Africa Company (BSA Company) was formed in early 1889 but it took a great deal of effort to obtain a royal charter for it. There was opposition, not to the extension of British imperialism in Central Africa, but to the idea of a commercial group exercising political power in the region. This opposition came from Christian missionary groups and philanthropic circles both in South Africa and in Britain. The opponents wanted Britain herself to colonise and administer Central Africa under a system of protectorates. Such a responsibility, however, was not favourable to the British Government as the administration and development of the region would cost money.

For his part Rhodes argued that if his company was granted a royal charter it would colonise and 'develop' Zimbabwe on behalf of Britain but without requiring the British taxpayer to pay for all these things. All expenses would be met by taxes from share holders of the BSA Company. This seemed possible as the Company was backed and supported by some of the richest groups including Rothschilds, De Beers and Consolidated Goldfields. Also at this time Rhodes' efforts to gain a royal charter were more likely to be favourably received by the Conservative party who governed Britain at this time. Lord Salisbury, the Conservative Prime Minister, strongly believed in British imperialism, but he was also aware that any attempt to make the British taxpayer pay more for the administration and development of overseas colonies would be resisted by the population. He therefore agreed to Rhodes' plan and in October 1889 a royal charter was granted, in spite of Lobengula's efforts to prevent it. The Charter affirmed Rhodes' entitlement to the Rudd Concession. It in fact went beyond this as Rhodes' Company was granted royal authority to colonise the rest of Central Africa, including Malawi and Zambia. The Charter also authorised the Company to raise a powerful police force to maintain 'law and order' in the region.

Clearly, once Lobengula had put his mark on the Rudd Concession the odds against him were simply too great. Rhodes, on the other hand, had entered a period of success. Many of his rivals and opponents were being won over to his side. Maund, for instance, who had advised Lobengula that he had been tricked and that he should complain to the British Queen about it, later supported Rhodes. While Maund was in London accompanying Lobengula's ambassadors, Induna Babiyane and Commander-in-chief Mtshane, who had been sent to complain to the Queen, Rhodes had bought the Exploring Company and instructed Maund to stop assisting Lobengula's mission in its efforts to prevent the British Government from granting the charter to the BSA Company. Thus, Maund kept the two Ndebele leaders in London until such time as Rhodes had won sufficient support for the granting of the charter.

In October 1889 Rhodes sent three more of his respresentatives to Bulawayo, Dr Leander Starr Jameson, Maxwell and Doyle, to ask Lobengula to let the BSA Company go into Mashonaland in accordance with the Rudd Concession. Of course, whether Lobengula's permission was granted or not, the Company was determined to go into Mashonaland, by force if necessary.

The Pioneers and the colonisation of Mashonaland

Having obtained the charter for his company, Rhodes went ahead with the recruiting of a pioneer group that was to occupy Zimbabwe. The first white settlers would also be accompanied by a police/military force, not only to keep order among the white population but to crush any resistance by the people of Zimbabwe.

The white settlers and the members of the police force were carefully selected from over two thousand applications. The pioneers had to include both English and Afrikaner elements, and they had to have South African experience. Only two hundred were needed, most of them below thirty years of age. They represented a wide variety of trades which would be needed in a new country – blacksmiths, carpenters, builders, printers, bakers, miners, farmers and traders. Each of the two hundred men was promised 3000 acres of land on arrival in Mashonaland, and up to fifteen gold claims.

The colonising party was to be led by Major Frank Johnson, with Heany and Borrow as his

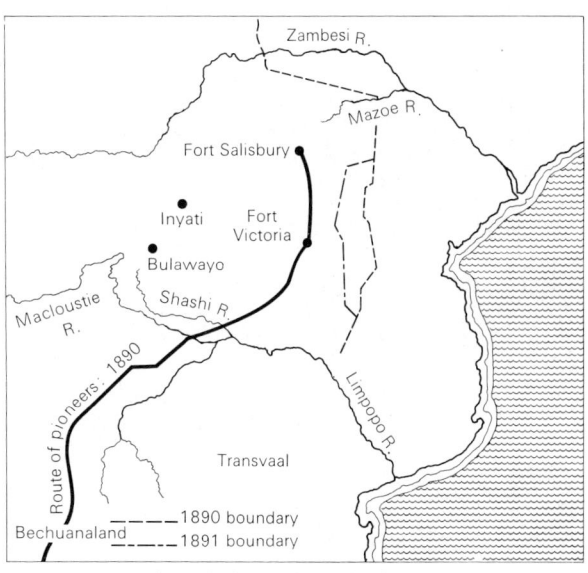

The invasion of Zimbabwe (then Rhodesia), 1890

seconds in command. The march to Mashonaland was to assume the form of a military operation and for this a squadron of four hundred mounted men and over a thousand auxiliaries provided by Khama of the Ngwato was organised. This force, which formed the nucleus of the British South African Police after the occupation of Zimbabwe, was commanded by Colonel Pennefeather. Major Johnson was to be paid a sum of fifteen thousand pounds while Khama was to be rewarded with some of Zimbabwe's land. The guide of the Pioneer column was the hunter and scout, F.C. Selous, whose knowledge of the land was excellent. The Pioneer column was generously equipped and supplied. Its provisions and supplies were transported by a fleet of one hundred and seventeen ox wagons.

The expedition crossed the Matloutsie river on 27 June 1890, and the Shashi on 11 July, travelling at the pace of about twelve miles a day. By August of the same year the column was in the Masvingo area. The Ndebele regiments wanted to fight, but Lobengula restrained them. Finally, on 12 September 1890 the Pioneers made their settlement at a place which the leaders called Fort Salisbury, in honour of the imperialist British Prime Minister. It was soon clear to the Shona people that the whites had not come to trade or to look for gold, but to settle in Zimbabwe permanently.

The Anglo–Ndebele War and the occupation of Western Zimbabwe

The white settlers did not take long to establish themselves in that part of Zimbabwe which they called Mashonaland. They soon claimed large farms on which tents were hurriedly put up to provide temporary homes, soon to be replaced by solid houses built of locally made bricks. A number of newly established town centres were also rapidly taking shape as houses now took the place of temporary shelters along neatly laid out streets and roads. Many settlers were also seen in many parts of the Shona territory searching for gold and other precious metals. Wherever these were found mines were established and shafts were sunk. However, very little gold was found.

Similar progress was being made on the political and diplomatic fronts. Among the most important achievements in this respect was the declaration by the High Commissioner at Cape Town in early 1891 that the area north of the Transvaal, between Portuguese Mozambique and German South-West Africa, was British. To Rhodes and his BSA Company this was very encouraging news as they had always been wanting to take Manicaland and Gazaland. A separate treaty had been signed on 14 September 1890 with the Manyika chief, Mtasa, in which he had granted mineral rights, and had also

The Pioneer column crossing the Lundi River

permitted the stationing of a white resident and a police force in his area. Missions and schools were to be introduced. Other treaties had also been negotiated with a number of Shona chiefs in the area lying between the Sabi and the Odzi river valleys. The significance of the treaties with Mtasa and other Shona rulers of eastern Zimbabwe must be noted. Firstly, the treaties belied Lobengula's claim that he was king of the Shona, and secondly, by negotiating with these rulers, Colquhoun and those Company officials with him had acknowledged the fact that Lobengula had no authority over the Shona in these areas. By implication, therefore, the Rudd Concession, which was based on the assumption that Lobengula was king of the Shona, was seriously undermined.

Another diplomatic achievement by the Company and the white settlers was the final settlement of the boundary line between the British and the Portuguese spheres in East-Central Africa in 1891. This settlement had been made in favour of the British South Africa Company. Also, Rhodes and his commercial company had been granted authority, if they so wished, to enter Zambia and exploit its resources, on condition that a sum of £10000 was paid annually to the British administration in Malawi. Eventually, in 1891, the Company was given power over all the whites living within its territory. In June that year magistrates were introduced and Archibald Colquhoun was appointed Acting Resident Commissioner. He was later replaced by Dr Leander Starr Jameson who preferred to be called Chief Magistrate.

Communications were soon established with the outside world. In 1892, for example, the telegraph line reached Fort Salisbury from Cape Town and a printed newspaper was produced regularly. This helped establish the settlers further and made them feel more secure.

Lobengula and the Ndebele could do little to check the rapid progress. He protested to the High Commissioner with no effect and finally, in desperation, offered land and mineral rights to a Johannesburg businessman in an effort to weaken Rhodes' position. Unfortunately, Rhodes himself knew of this transaction and persuaded Lippert, the businessman, to sell his concession, thus strengthening Rhodes' position even more. Lobengula came under increasing pressure from his military and government leaders to declare war on the whites and the BSA Company. This pressure on the Ndebele leader, his army's frustration and the white's desire to extend their control over the whole of Zimbabwe lead us to the war of 1893.

Causes of the war of 1893

In August 1891, Coloquhoun resigned as Acting Resident Commissioner of Mashonaland and was succeeded by Dr Jameson. While the entire causes of the 1893 war do not rest with him alone, Jameson must share a great part of the responsibility as Ndebele relationships with the white settlers rapidly deteriorated soon after he came to power.

Moreover, after the occupation of the eastern part of Zimbabwe in 1890 and the establishment of a Western-type state, friction between this state and the Ndebele kingdom was almost inevitable. The two states pursued opposite interests. For instance, while the Ndebele regarded the eastern part of Zimbabwe as raiding ground, the Company and the white settler farmers saw it as a source of cheap labour. Soon the two states would clash. Both Lobengula and Colquhoun and later Jameson were aware of this. Jameson thought that the solution lay in the establishment of a boundary between the area under Company control and Matabeleland. Thus he spent a great deal of time drawing and defining boundary lines which he persuaded Lobengula to recognise and respect. He asked white hunters and prospectors not to venture beyond the west of the border line. Similarly he asked Lobengula to give instructions that his army should not raid areas east of the border.

There had never been a boundary line between Western Zimbabwe (Matabeleland) and Eastern Zimbabwe (Mashonaland) before the white settler occupation of Eastern Zimbabwe. Also, the boundary line was never the same as it kept on shifting. More importantly, Lobengula, for all his willingness to cooperate with Jameson in preventing war, never shared Jameson's views about the need to confine Ndebele raids to the western side of the 'border'. As far as the Ndebele were concerned, white settler occupation of Eastern Zimbabwe had made no difference to the fact that it was their traditional raiding ground.

Although Ndebele rule did not extend beyond Western Zimbabwe, there is no doubt that many areas of Eastern Zimbabwe were raided by the Ndebele regiments. Some Shona leaders thought that with white settler occupation of their areas, Ndebele raids had ended. Some of them even stopped paying their annual tribute to Lobengula. Lobengula did not share this view and several Shona leaders were punsihed severely. In 1891 chiefs, such as Nemakonde (Lomagundi) and Chivi (Chibi) were actually killed by Lobengula. These acts were unacceptable to the officials of the British South Africa Company and white settler farmers because they frightened the Shona who were their main source of cheap labour to work on the mines and farms. It is in this light that Jameson's and the white settlers' response to the behaviour and activities of the Ndebele in what is now known as the 'Victoria Incident' must be understood. This is usually regarded as the spark of the 1893 war.

The Victoria Incident
Following the killing of chiefs Nemakonde and Chivi in 1891, Jameson pleaded with Lobengula to keep his army under strict control to prevent further occurrances. Lobengula assured Jameson that the whites had no reason to fear for their lives but his position regarding the Shona remained unchanged; they were his subjects and he had authority to punish them if they defied his orders. Indeed, from the middle of 1892 onward a number of raids and incidents took place, most of them around Masvingo, which was in the middle of a potentially wealthy agricultural, ranching and mining region. Already, white settlers were engaged in farming and mining, and were employing a Shona labour force. The whites wanted to protect these economic activities. However in May 1893 some men under headman Gomara, between the Tuli and Fort Victoria, cut and carried away about 500 yards of the telegraph wire – possibly to make snares. Gomara was ordered to either hand over the culprits or to pay a fine in the form of cattle. He paid in cattle which he claimed to be his own but later proved to belong to Lobengula. He demanded their immediate return. Jameson complied with the demand, but warned that there would be serious consequences if the telegraph wire was interfered with again.

While this was going on, reports reached Bulawayo that another Shona headman, Bere, some fifteen miles west of Masvingo, had taken cattle belonging to Lobengula. The angry Lobengula decided that the Shona in the Victoria district had to be taught a lesson. Thus a raiding army was despatched under the command of Manyao assisted by the young commander, Mgandani. The force consisted mainly of young warriors, *amajaha*, about 3000 of them. Manyao and Mgandani were given strict instructions to avoid clashes with white people in carrying out their mission.

The expedition left Bulawayo in June, and Jameson and Lendy, a magistrate at Fort Victoria, were informed of this and the purpose of the raid. Lendy in particular was told to inform the white inhabitants in the area not to be alarmed as the expedition would have nothing to do with them.

Unfortunately, however, Jameson's telegram and Lendy's letters were delivered after the trouble had already started, thus frustrating Lobengula's diplomatic efforts to prevent a war with the whites. By July the Ndebele were in the Masvingo district. On 9 July many were seen burning homes, killing men and driving away women and girls in the areas of Bere, Zimuto and others in the neighbourhood of Fort Victoria. It is said that farm and mine labourers were also attacked, and hundreds of white settler-owned cattle were driven away by the raiders. Within a day or two white farms and mines in the Masvingo district had been deserted by their African labour force. The district's economic activities were brought to a standstill and many local Africans were either taking to the hills or streaming towards the little town centre of Masvingo. The leaders of the raiding expedition demanded that they be handed over to them for punishment, but Lendy would not agree to this.

Jameson, at Salisbury, was informed of the situation in the Victoria district and he decided to go and see for himself. He also sent instructions to Lendy that he should demand from the Ndebele the return of all the cattle taken from white farmers and that the raiders should withdraw beyond the 'border'. He also authorised Lendy to drive away the raiders by force if they proved to be uncooperative. In preparation, the small police force at Fort Victoria was supplemented by over 400 settler volunteers.

Meanwhile, on 14 July, Lobengula's letter to Lendy arrived and was delivered by a messenger escorted by Manyao, Mgandani and several raiders. The Ndebele repeated their demand that all Shona refugees at Fort Victoria should be handed over to them. Again, Lendy refused to comply with the demand. Jameson himself arrived on 17 July and held an *indaba* (meeting) with the leaders of the raiding expedition the following day. He told Manyao and Mgandani that no refugees would be surrendered and ordered them to lead their army away across the 'border' immediately. In reply to this order they pointed out that it might be difficult to move such a large body of people all at once, but Jameson warned them that he would use force if they failed to comply. 'Very well', replied Mgandani, 'we'll be driven!' The *indaba* had lasted only twenty minutes. In fact Jameson had already made up his mind that the Ndebele should be driven away by force. Shortly after the end of the *indaba* he instructed Lendy to be ready with a mounted patrol within two hours and see to it that his orders to the Ndebele leaders were carried out.

At about 2.30 pm Lendy's mounted patrol rode towards the west, as instructed by Jameson. By this time the Ndebele army had already started to retire towards its country. Unfortunately the rear part, under Mgandani was still within the area slowly marching westwards. Lendy's patrol soon caught up with this section and concluded that Mgandani was defying Jameson's orders. Somebody fired a shot, possibly one of Lendy's men, although later it was alleged that the shot came from the Ndebele. The shot gave Lendy an excuse to order his men to attack. In the ensuing skirmish Mgandani and eleven of his compatriots were killed. The rest of the Ndebele fled.

Encouraged by Lendy's apparently easy victory, the white settlers now demanded a full-scale war to destroy the Ndebele kingdom once and for all. Jameson shared this sentiment and he wasted no time in informing Rhodes and the High Commissioner of this feeling among the whites. He had given his own account of the Victoria Incident to Lobengula adding a warning that another raid would lead to war. He also demanded that Lobengula should make good all losses suffered by the settlers. Lobengula had not only accepted Jameson's account of what had happened, he also apologised to the white settler government and promised to pay for the damages done to white property by his army. Clearly, Lobengula was anxious to prevent a war with the British South Africa Company.

Jameson's account of events leading to the Victoria Incident had been given to Lobengula before Manyao's arrival with his own version of the same incident. In time, however, the induna gave his own report which was very different from that of Jameson. Naturally Lobengula was enraged by what seemed to be treachery and cowardice on the part of his white neighbours. He, accordingly, informed the High Commissioner that no compensation would be paid for any damage to white property although he still wished to avoid war.

Preparations for war
The fact that Lobengula was still determined to avoid war with the British South Africa Company even at this latest hour was demonstrated when in early August he sent an ambassador to Queen Victoria. Jameson however, now at Salisbury, was already preparing for war with Lobengula. Volunteers were being recruited and organised into a military force. Although at first not happy about the timing of the war against the Ndebele, Rhodes was soon persuaded to accept Jameson's judgment of the situation. In time even Henry Loch, the British High Commissioner, was also persuaded to accept the necessity of a war to destroy the Ndebele kingdom. The only remaining obstacle seemed to be the Secretary of State for Colonies, Lord Ripon, whose view was that there should be no war unless the lives of the white settlers in Mashonaland were in real danger. Ripon, however, agreed that precautionary measures, including increasing the Bechuanaland Police at Macloutsie near the border with Ndebele territory, be taken without delay in case the Ndebele invaded the Protectorate.

It did not seem to matter what the Secretary of State in London thought of the matter. War was inevitable because all the relevant people in Africa, from the ordinary white settler to the High Commissioner, now wanted it and were busy preparing for it. As part of the war preparation, Jameson made the 'Victoria Agreement' of 14 August 1893.

This was a secret arrangement between the British South Africa Company (Jameson) and white settler volunteers under which any settler volunteer who enlisted for action against the Ndebele was entitled to 2469 hectares of land in any part of Western Zimbabwe, twenty gold claims, and a share of Lobengula's cattle. By September 700–800 volunteers had registered for the Anglo–Ndebele war. Preparations for the war also took the form of collecting as much information about the Ndebele as possible. Scouts and spies were sent to Western Zimbabwe to find out what preparations the Ndebele were making for the war, and ascertain how many men Lobengula was going to put on to the field against the whites. Reports gathered indicated that, although still committed to a peaceful solution, Lobengula was also preparing for any eventuality. However, most of Ndebele preparations were for the defence of their land and not for attacking the whites. Thus regiments were being placed in various positions along the border with Botswana in the west, and in the east along the western boundary of the sensitive Victoria district.

The preparations for war made Ripon and Queen Victoria rather anxious about the situation in Zimbabwe. Both the Secretary of State and the Queen made appeals to Lobengula through Loch, High Commissioner. 'You can tell (Lobengula) from me', wrote the Queen to the High Commissioner, 'that I have no intention of invading his country'. Such assurances were of little use because the country was invaded. At the beginning of October 1893 Ripon instructed the High Commissioner to request Lobengula to withdraw the Ndebele regiments from their positions and send ambassadors to Cape Town instead, 'to talk matters over so that there may be peace.' Lobengula responded by sending three ambassadors, his own brother Ingubungubu, and chiefs Mantusa and Ingubu. By the middle of October they had reached Tati on their way to Cape Town. By this time the white settler volunteer forces in Eastern Zimbabwe (Mashonaland) were ready to invade Matabeleland. Suspecting the three Ndebele leaders to be spies, Goold-Adams, in charge of the Imperial Police at Tati, arrested them. Mantusa and Ingubu were killed while trying to escape. Ingubungubu was never heard of again.

Diplomatic efforts by Lobengula and Ripon could only delay but not prevent war. The British South Africa Company had been disappointed by the little amount of gold in Eastern Zimbabwe and share prices had fallen. It was now widely expected that Western Zimbabwe might have more gold. The white settlers now coveted the healthy and excellent cattle country in Western Zimbabwe. If the Company and the white settlers were to achieve their respective objectives, therefore, the Ndebele nation had to be destroyed. 'We either had to have that war', admitted Rhodes later, 'or to leave the country (Zimbabwe)'.

The war, in Jameson's opinion, had to begin and end before the rain season. Provocative incidents were created in such a way that the Ndebele would appear to have started the war while the whites were simply fighting to defend themselves. This plan worked for on the strength of such 'provocative incidents' the High Commissioner formally agreed to the war.

The war and its results

The war began in October. There were about 18 000 Ndebele men on the field. The other side had about 3500 fighters including about 1100 whites, 2000 Tswana auxiliaries provided by Khama, and about 400 Shona and Cape auxiliaries (mainly employees of whites). Although numerically heavily outnumbered by the Ndebele, the Company's forces were better equipped and could move faster than the Ndebele. They had about 800 horses and their modern firearms included about 16 heavy machine guns such as Maxim guns and 7-pounders. Wagons ensured continued supplies. The Ndebele regiments, on the other hand, used their traditional spears as they did not trust modern firearms.

The Company's forces were organised into three columns – the Salisbury and the Victoria columns, and the Tuli column. The general command of the volunteer forces was given to the magistrate of Salisbury, Patrick William Forbes. On 16 October the Victoria and the Salisbury columns met at Iron Mine Hill, between Gwelo and Umvuma. From there began the westward march towards Bulawayo. On 24 October, after several minor skirmishes with Ndebele units, the combined force crossed the Shangani River south-west of Gwelo. All its movements had been carefully watched by Ndebele intelligence units. Having crossed the Shangani the volunteer army established a laager in which to rest for the night. At dawn, on the morning of 25 October, the Ndebele struck killing many African refugees sleeping outside of the laager. But by about 10 o'clock in the morning the Ndebele had been driven away leaving many of their men dead. Company losses in the first major battle of the war were slight.

The advance towards Bulawayo was continued until 31 October when it was halted on the Mbembesi River where another laager was hurriedly built. In the afternoon of 1 November the Ndebele made their second most determined attack against the invaders. The Ingubo, Imbizo, and the Insukamini regiments very bravely fought the enemy. The 7-pounder guns cost many Ndebele lives. When the march continued on 2 November four Company men had been lost and about seven badly wounded. The plan was to storm Bulawayo and capture Lobengula thus demoralising the Ndebele army. But Lobengula set his capital on fire and fled northwards towards the Zambezi valley. On 4 November the Company's forces took over the burning city and hoisted the Union Jack over its ruins, thus completing the conquest of Zimbabwe. Among the residents of Bulawayo who witnessed its capture by the white forces were European traders, Fairbairn and Dawson whom Lobengula had strictly instructed should not be killed by the Ndebele.

Although to all intents and purposes the Ndebele had now been defeated, it was felt necessary to find and capture Lobengula because as long as he was still at large the Ndebele would not easily submit to the new authority. First, Jameson sent a message to Lobengula asking him to surrender himself and promising that he would not be harmed. Lobengula replied that he would go back to Bulawayo to meet with Jameson, but he never did. It was therefore decided that Lobengula should be pursued by a police force led by Major Forbes. He managed to reach Lobengula's camp on the southern bank of the Shangani on 3 December. But Lobengula had just left to continue his northward flight. Realising that his pursuers might capture him any time,

Fairburn and Dawson. Lobengula gave instructions to see that they were to be kept safe

Lobengula sent two of his chiefs to them with a peace message and a bag of gold, pleading: 'White men, I am conquered. Take this and go back'. Two troopers received both the message and the gold but never passed them over to their leaders. Instead they stole the money and perhaps destroyed the letter. So Forbes never knew of Lobengula's last peace plea until much later.

Forbes camped on the Shangani River and sent Allan Wilson with twenty-one men to investigate the direction taken by Lobengula's fleeing party. Wilson and his men soon caught up with Lobengula's party on the other side of the river. He sent for reinforcements, but Forbes was unable to comply. Instead he dispatched Captain H. J. Borrow with twenty men, without making it clear whether this was a supporting unit in the event of striking against the Ndebele army. When by daybreak on 4 December Borrow's unit arrived, Wilson and Borrow decided to attack the Ndebele to capture Lobengula. There were not more than thirty-five men for the dangerous task. Needless to say, they were easily overpowered and were all, except three scouts who escaped, cut to pieces by the Ndebele. It was impossible for the main body to reach them because the Shangani river was dangerously flooded.

On 5 December Forbes and the rest of the expedition were compelled to retreat. The expedition had been costly in men, horses and cattle and it had failed in its objective – the capture of Lobengula. Jameson had by now decided that no further military campaigns could be organised because of rains. Instead, he decided to persuade the Ndebele to surrender and assured them that not only would they be protected, they would also be given seed to plant as the rainy season had already begun. The Ndebele, most of whom were tired of living in the forest, agreed to down arms and enter peace negotiations with the BSA Company.

The story that Lobengula had died of smallpox on his northward flight was spread by the Company officials in order to persuade the Ndebele to lay down their arms. The assumed death enabled the BSA Company to effect a number of things in Zimbabwe, especially in the western areas. Having convinced the British Government that Matabeleland should become part of the Company's territory, Rhodes and Jameson went ahead with rewarding the white settler volunteers for their service during the war. Among other things, they threw open the area for white settler farming and many hundreds of farmers received large areas of land there. On the other hand only two very poor reserves were set aside for Ndebele settlement. These were the Shangani and the Gwaai Reserves, dry, infertile and generally hot and unhealthy. White settler military volunteers were also rewarded with some of Lobengula's cattle. The rest of Lobengula's cattle, the royal herds, were converted into Company property on the principle that the Company had succeeded Lobengula as the Ndebele ruler.

Having successfully claimed Western Zimbabwe for the British South Africa Company, Rhodes and Jameson took the necessary steps to introduce the white administrative machinery. In short, the whole of Zimbabwe had now been placed under colonial rule. By 1895 the new British colony was known in colonial circles and records as 'Rhodesia', after Rhodes, the imperialist whose money and expansionist schemes had enabled Britain to acquire Zimbabwe. For administrative convenience Rhodesia or, as it was also called later, Southern Rhodesia, was divided into two main provinces: Mashonaland (Eastern Zimbabwe) and Matabeleland (Western Zimbabwe). White occupation brought not only colonial administration, but also forced taxation, forced labour and other forms of political oppression and economic exploitation.

21 Ndebele and Shona uprisings 1896–97

Ndebele rebellion
After acquiring Western Zimbabwe at the end of the war in early 1894, the British South Africa Company encouraged white settlement in the area. Bulawayo was rapidly developing into an important urban centre with many traders and skilled workers. Because of its easier and more efficient communications with South Africa, Bulawayo was certainly becoming more attractive than Salisbury. Hardly a year after its occupation by whites, there were over a hundred traders, twelve hotels, three banks and three regularly printed newspapers. Bulawayo could now boast over two hundred white residents. Equally impressive and encouraging was the speed with which the Ndebele seemed to be accepting not only the new political authority, but also European employment. They were cooperating with law-enforcement authorities too. Many of them even joined the police force, and a corps of Ndebele police was formed immediately after white occupation of Western Zimbabwe. Significantly, the majority members of the new force were elements of Lobengula's crack regiments, the Imbizo and the Insukamini.

Although the 1893/4 war had not yet been completely forgotten among the settlers, nobody seriously thought that the Ndebele could one day rise up in arms against the new order. For this reason there was no serious effort on the part of the Company administration to raise and organise an army. There was a force known as the Rhodesia Horse, but it had been formed because of a dangerous situation caused by the unfair treatment of non-Boer (especially English-speaking) residents of the Transvaal by the Boer government of President Paul Kruger. In Zimbabwe itself, there was an atmosphere of security, confidence and complacancy among the whites which continued up to the end of 1895 when the settlers were shocked to learn that their Administrator, Dr Jameson, had been captured with his force trying to invade Johannesburg on behalf of the *uitlanders* or foreigners.

Then came reports on 23 March 1896 that a number of African police men had been killed by armed Ndebele at Dawson's Store, east of Bulawayo. These reports, however, caused no general panic among the white residents of Bulawayo as only blacks had been involved. But more reports were received the following day and were coming from such districts as Insiza and Filabusi in the east. This time the victims included white people living in isolated centres. Alarm and anxiety began to grow at Bulawayo that there might be a general rising of the Ndebele. Indeed, from the evening of 23 March, fires were started in isolated white communities. Stores, mines and farms were targets and their occupants and owners were now in real danger. In fact, within weeks of the outbreak of the uprisings about 100 were killed. Those that managed to escape were running towards Bulawayo, Gwelo, Belingwe and Mangwe where laagers had been hurriedly constructed. By April the rebellion had spread all over Western Zimbabwe.

In the initial stages the uprising was assisted by the fact that the white settlers and the Government had been taken completely by surprise. Also Jameson had on 29 December 1895 secretly taken most of the military men to the Transvaal to assist the uitlanders (foreigners) to overthrow the Boer Government of Paul Kruger. This unsuccessful venture, known in history as the Jameson Raid, led to the capture of Jameson and his raiding army by the Boers. Thus, when the uprisings began in March, the Administrator of Rhodesia and most of those men that could handle guns were prisoners. Although there were still about 900 men capable of fighting, most of the horses had been captured with their riders in the Transvaal. Only a mere 100 were available for use in the search to bring any settlers that might still be in danger to safety.

Within a week the white settlers had organised themselves sufficiently to deal with the situation. Relief patrols of 30 to 40 mounted men began to ride out daily into areas around Bulawayo to rescue

122

whatever settlers were found. In most cases, however, these relief parties were too late. All they could do was bury the bodies of victims. These included children. The whole operation was extremely risky because well-armed Ndebele units attacked the patrols with great determination.

End of Ndebele resistance
By about the end of May it was clear that Ndebele resistance was weakening, while the white forces were gaining an upper hand. By July the rebellion was almost over. The whites' success is attributed to several factors. One of these was, no doubt, the superiority of firepower which had proved so crucial in the 1893 war. Equally important was the lack of Ndebele strategy. For instance certain vital areas and routes were left open. While Ndebele forces were concentrated on the eastern, south and north of Bulawayo, the western side was left open. The road to South Africa, via the Matopo Hills and the Mangwe area was also left open. It is important to note that this route was the most vital line of communication with the south, and that through it Bulawayo continued to receive food, medicines and other needs.

The Ndebele were not supported by other subject people, especially the Kalanga, who remained uninvolved. One of the Kalanga chiefs, for instance, is said to have given the following reply when he was asked to cut off the road to Botswana: 'The people don't want to fight; they want to sit still.' However most of the Shona-speaking peoples of eastern Matabeleland cooperated with the Ndebele. There were divisions and disagreements within the Ndebele ranks. There were two broad divisions; the old and the younger groups. The younger faction wanted to see Nyamanda, one of Lobengula's sons, succeed as king in the event of the rebellion being successful. The other faction, which was supported by Mlugulu, the chief priest and the majority of senior chiefs, favoured Mfezela, a senior kinsman of the former king. The younger group received the active cooperation of the officials of the Mwari cult as officials of two of the Mwari shrines helped to organise the rising. The Ndebele were aided by men like Mkwati, Siginyamatshe and Tengera. The importance of the Mwari cult and its officials in the war of resistance is demonstrated by the fact that after the last battle on the Umgusa river, when the leading ndunas and Mlugulu hid in the Matopos, Mpotshwane and most of the younger warriors went to Mwari's shrine near Thaba zi kaMambo. Here, under Mkwati's influence bitter fighting continued before the hill was captured by Plumer and his forces in July. Although the younger group wanted to continue the struggle, Mlugulu and the old group wished to negotiate with the enemy.

A similar movement in favour of negotiation and peace was also growing among high circles in the British South Africa Company. Rhodes, who had arrived in the country in March, did not want to continue with the costly war. He had been advised by Major-General Carrington, supreme commander of white forces, that 6000 troops would be needed to win the war against the resisting Ndebele. To bring these soldiers and all the necessary supplies from the south, a railway line would have to be built quickly, linking Cape Town and Bulawayo. It was

Laager at Bulawayo

Ndebele kraal in the 1890s

Lobengula's envoys at Fort Tuli, 1890

clear to Rhodes that the scheme would cost the Company and himself a great deal of money at the time when the Company was experiencing financial hardships. He decided instead to call an *indaba* or a peace conference with Ndebele leaders. Even then, he had to wait for six weeks in the Matopo Hills before the suspicious ndunas agreed to meet with him.

Rhodes was accompanied by a friend, a journalist, an interpreter, and two Cape Colonial servants. The Ndebele leaders insisted that the Rhodes party should be unarmed. Chief priest Mlugulu and Senior Nduna Sikombo led the Ndebele delegation consisting of about 40 chiefs and headmen. The negotiations which began in August ended on 13 October. The Ndebele leaders agreed to suspend all military operations against the settler forces. Briefly, the main terms of the final agreement were: that all the Ndebele who had committed murders and other crimes should be tried; that the officials of the Mwari cult should be punished for their part in the rebellion; and that all the assegais and guns should be handed over to the Government. (About 13 000 spears and 2 500 guns were surrendered later). For his part, Rhodes agreed that white forces would be withdrawn, their place being taken by a permanent police force; that no African police, especially Shona, would be used in the province without the authority of the Ndebele chiefs; and that leading Ndebele chiefs and headmen would be granted official recognition and would receive a regular salary. Since the immediate need for most of the people in Western Zimbabwe was food, Rhodes also promised grain to see the Ndebele through the rest of the year. (About 5 000 000 lbs of grain were later delivered). The Ndebele were also promised seed for the next planting season.

Causes of the Ndebele Rising

What is clear from the beginning is that the rebellion cannot be attributed to a single cause. A number of factors combined to persuade the Ndebele to take up their guns and spears against the people who had defeated them three years earlier.

The Ndebele not only lost their state but their land as well after the war of 1893–4. The loss of their land continued to be an irritation to the Ndebele, the majority of whom were now crowded in the dry, impoverished and unhealthy Gwaai and Shangani Reserves assigned to them by the 1894 Land Commission. Many Ndebele families and communities had also been compelled to squat on white farms providing cheap, semi-slave labour in exchange for permission to remain on white property.

Very often the owners of the farms did not hesitate to move squatters off their land. This situation provided constant irritation, especially as the Ndebele had owned this land up to just two and a half years earlier. 'One cause of dissatisfaction and unrest", explained Chief Gambo, 'is that after we have lived many years in a spot, we are told that the white man has purchased it and we have to go.'

It has been noted elsewhere that some chiefs who had lost their traditional land did not get involved in the uprising. But when seen together with other causes such as the loss of cattle, the land question becomes very important. It has been estimated that before the 1893–4 war Lobengula had owned about 250 000 cattle. After the assumed death of Lobengula and the fall of the Ndebele state, the royal herds were taken over by the Company administration (page 12). Most of the cattle were given to the Volunteers while others were used as rations for the police. It is also said that many more were taken to South Africa. Only about 40 930 were left in the hands of the Ndebele, mainly senior ndunas and not the young men. This distribution of cattle showed a total disregard of Ndebele customs. Even those cattle left in the hands of the senior chiefs could still be taken by the Government as their ownership continued to remain with the administration.

Then there were other causes, such as forced labour, oppressive administration and natural disasters, which will be discussed later in this chapter since they were also largely behind the Shona uprising. Before turning to the Shona rising, we should point out that the Ndebele would have probably revolted against white rule anyway. Most important, they had lost national independence which meant the destruction of their way of life. For instance, the age-regiment system and the raiding of neighbours had been abolished by colonial administrators. Ndebele indunas had lost their powers and importance among the people. The Ndebele felt very insulted by arrogant Government officials. Perhaps the biggest insult was the use of black policemen, especially the Shona, in Ndebele areas.

Shona uprising 1896–7

If the outbreak of the Ndebele rebellion had been a surprise to the white settler community and their government, the news of the Shona uprising in the middle of June 1896 was even more puzzling and mysterious. Nobody had suspected trouble from Eastern Zimbabwe as the Shona had always been regarded by the whites as 'cowards' quite incapable of taking up arms against their colonisers and oppressors. Besides, the whites saw themselves as

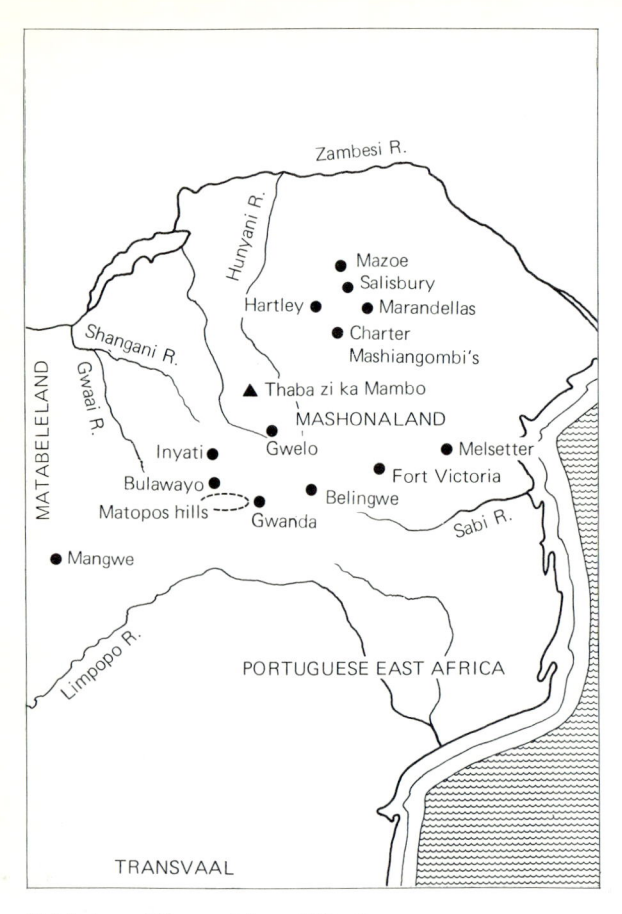

Ndebele and Shona risings, 1896–7

'liberators' of the Shona from Ndebele oppression. It was this view of themselves that made the settlers unable to realise that the Shona people had had their own way of life and their own political independence before 1890.

The white settler government had taken all the troops to Western Zimbabwe to cope with the Ndebele uprising. Thus the Shona enjoyed similar military advantages at the start of their revolt in June as had been created for the Ndebele earlier by Dr Jameson when he took most military men on his abortive raid in the Transvaal. When the Shona did decide to take up arms against their colonisers they carried out the war with determination. Those areas or chiefdoms that were involved appeared to have risen up in arms almost as if they were responding to a special signal or call to act on a certain day or week. Marshall Hole has described the time as the 'blackest hour in all Rhodesia's chequered history'. Indeed, within about a week of the outbreak of hostilities nearly 120 Europeans, including a number of their Cape Colonial servants, had been killed.

The first day of the uprising seems to be 14 June when two Indian traders were killed near Mashayamombe's capital in the Chegutu district. One of the traders escaped and later reported the killings to the authorities. Shortly afterwards the local commissioner of Hartley (Chegutu) was killed, again by Mashayamombe's people. The officials at Salisbury had hardly grasped the gravity of the situation when reports reached them on 17 June that Nyamweda's people had killed two white traders. Many more deaths were reported during the rest of the week as traders, farmers, prospectors and miners in the Harare and Mazoe districts were attacked. By 19 June the war had spread as far as the Charter district to the east of Salisbury. The war cry, *Chimurenga!*, was heard as signal fires burned at night on mountain tops in the Marondera, Rusape, Nemakonde and other affected districts of Eastern Zimbabwe.

The whites in Eastern Zimbabwe responded in similar ways to those of their friends in Western Zimbabwe. Laagers were hurriedly constructed at main urban centres. Mounted patrols were organised to ride into remote areas to rescue beleaguered families, groups and individuals and bring them to safety. Many whites were rescued in this way.

As in Western Zimbabwe, some chiefdoms refused to join in the war of resistance in Eastern Zimbabwe. This was true of people living in the extreme north and south of Eastern Zimbabwe. The whole of Victoria district and several chiefdoms in the Buhera and Chikomba areas also stayed out of the *Chimurenga*. In spite of these abstentions, however, the uprisings were very difficult to end. Imperial forces had to be brought in from the south, in addition to the forces that had already been transferred from Western Zimbabwe. The forces were under the command of Lieutenant-Colonel Alderson and they arrived at Beira in Mozambique towards the end of July 1896. From there they marched westwards to Umtali and then to Salisbury. But on the way to Salisbury Alderson's forces went to Gwindingwi, Paramount Makoni's fortified mountain headquarters. They tried, unsuccessfully, to dislodge Makoni and his resisters from their fortress. Gwindingwi was, however, burnt down and its defensive walls were pounded to the ground with machine guns and seven-pounders. Makoni's people, armed with muskets, a few captured rifles and spears, were forced to go into caves. As it would have cost him a lot of his men to force Makoni out of his caves, Alderson decided to go on to Salisbury leaving the Maungwe Paramount in control of the fortress – at least for the time being. There was another fortified mountain headquarters, that of Paramount Mangwende at Maopo. But Mangwende and his people managed to hide in their caves before the arrival of the invaders. In anger and frustration, Alderson instructed his infantry to destroy large quantities of grain and any food that could be found before proceeding to Salisbury. Again, Mangwende was left safe in his mountain.

Seeing that the whites had the advantage of superior firepower, the Shona were avoiding open clashes with them. They were now resorting to the tactics of guerrilla warfare. As ordinary or conventional army units, no matter how well-armed, could not effectively deal with this type of situation the police force was increasingly involved during the later part of the war, which proved to be the most difficult and most brutal stage of the 1896–7 war of resistance. The police were now having to use dynamite and other explosives to blow up the caves and crevices in which many people were hiding. This is one major difference between the Ndebele and the Shona risings. In Western Zimbabwe, where there was a kind of professional army, the civilians were more or less unaffected.

In spite of all the cruelties committed by the colonisers against the Shona, it was difficult to bring the war to a formal end. This was because in Eastern Zimbabwe there was no single authority with whom Rhodes or his representatives could hold an *indaba* or peace conference. The Shona were under their various chiefs each of whom was independent. For this reason the white forces were forced to deal with, and defeat, each of the fighting chiefs separately. And since the resisting chiefs and their people, men and women, had become guerrilla fighters contact with chiefs was almost impossible. Eventually, towards the end of 1897, however, resistance was gradually weakening as the leaders were either killed or captured.

Causes of the Shona Rising
Some historians have rightly pointed out that Rhodes and Jameson, two key men in the colonisation of Zimbabwe, were uncontrollable territorial expansionists. Indeed, after the occupation of Eastern Zimbabwe (Mashonaland) the two men were vigorously planning the extension of the young colony in various directions – eastward towards

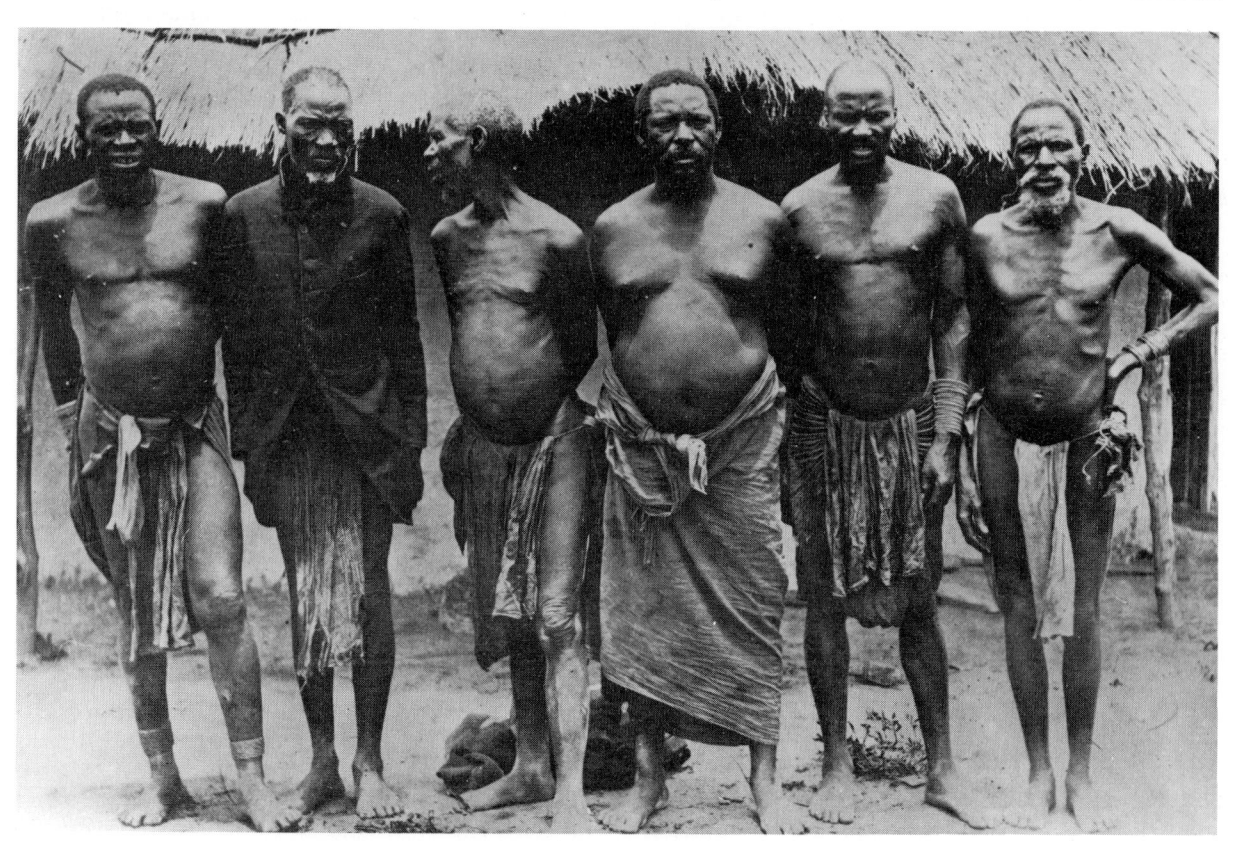

Sons and councillors of Chief Makoni, captured at the end of the 1896 war

Gazaland, and westwards to include the land inhabited by the Ndebele. Plans were also being drawn to link the new colony with the east coast and with the south by railway, road and telegraph. Unfortunately, however, both men were hopelessly poor administrators and cared little for the people whose land they colonised.

It is not surprising therefore that from 1890 until the outbreak of hostilities in 1896 no plan or system for the governing of the Shona had been clearly worked out. No doubt, African administration was not a priotiy and for this reason Rhodes and Jameson were not going to spend money on it. A department of Africans was formed in 1894, but its role was to facilitate the collection of the Hut tax and step-up the recruitment of cheap labour for the mines, settler farms and public works. This department soon became unpopular among the African people. There were cases of officials seizing cattle, goats and grain from people failing to pay their taxes and arresting defaulters who were sentenced to long terms in jail with forced labour. Even before the outbreak of the 1896–97 war of resistance, some areas, like those under Makoni and Nyandoro had been in revolt against the Native Department.

The Government promoted many injustices. Although magistrates had been appointed in the various districts to administer justice, there was little justice for the African people. Often the men appointed were untrained and unsuited for the type of work. There were too few magistrates to cope with the number of incidents concerning blacks and whites and being largely from the white community, it was in their own interests to protect those of the white settlers at the expense of the black people. Thus, they conceded the white settlers' demands for cheap African labour and turned a blind eye to the many instances of cruelty towards the African servants. Punishments for whites in comparison to those dealt out to blacks were minimal.

A related aspect of bad African administration and white injustice concerns the activities of the field cornets. Dr Jameson had reduced the Police Force in 1892 in order to save money. The few policemen that were left were working in urban centres while the rural areas were served by field cornets. Field cornets were usually recruited from among white settlers, prospectors and traders. Cases involving Africans (desertions, stock-theft, quarrels between settler farmers and their African neighbours etc.) were often dealt with on the spot by farmers and field cornets. Again all this was done at the expense of Africans as the field cornets naturally protected white interests.

Shona response to the pressure arising from the white settlers' activities might have taken a different form were it not for certain natural disasters which were attributed to the presence of the whites in their land. In 1895–6 a severe drought occurred, killing most of the crops and those that seemed to survive were then devoured by swarms of locusts. The result was widespread famine in the districts. Added to this a devastating cattle disease, rinderpest, killed hundreds of cattle. The Government veterinary officials in their efforts to eradicate the disease ordered that all cattle showing signs of rinderpest should be killed and people were not allowed to eat the meat of the dead cattle. This made the Shona people very bitter.

Natural disasters meant only one thing to the Shona people; it was an expression of God's or Mwari's anger. Indeed, this was confirmed by traditional religious authorities all over the country who blamed the white people for having angered Mwari. They warned that unless the whites were fought and driven out of the land, the Africans would continue to suffer. Thus, religious leaders in Eastern and Western Zimbabwe played a major role in the war of resistance. The uprising was inevitable because colonial occupation had seriously undermined the Shona way of life. Although some areas were under Ndebele rule the vast majority of the chiefdoms had been independent until the arrival of colonial rule. Institutions holding each of the various Shona chiefdoms together, traditional religion and chiefly authority, were now in great danger both from the consolidation of colonial authority and from the activities of Christian missions. White occupation had also brought to an end trade relations with the Portuguese to the east and in the Zambezi valley area, which had been maintained for generations before, and had continued after Ndebele settlement in the country. The Shona had been selling ivory and gold dust to the Portuguese in return for firearms and a variety of cheap goods. After stopping the Africans from participating in the gold trade (in order to protect European gold-mining), and after ending Shona trade with the Portuguese, the white government was doing all it could to force the Africans to buy goods from colonial traders. Unfortunately, however, their goods which came from South Africa, were more expensive than goods supplied by the Portuguese.

The role of religious leaders in the uprisings
The outbreak of the risings in both Western and Eastern Zimbabwe, and the campaigns of resistance by both the Ndebele and the Shona were to a large

extent attributable to the working relationship between the political leaders and the Mwari and the Mhondoro cults. As already seen, the Mwari cult had its main shrines in Western Zimbabwe. The Mhondoro cult, on the other hand, had more influence in the eastern part of the country.

For some time after the occupation of Zimbabwe by the whites it had been feared that one day the spirit owners of the land (ancestors) and Mwari would express their disapproval of white occupation and the many wrongs committed by the foreigners through a terrible act or acts. Thus when the natural disasters occurred the officials of both the Mwari and the Mhondoro cults thought the time had come and interpreted these disasters as expressions of Mwari and the ancestors' anger at white colonisation. They consequently ordered the expulsion of the foreigners from Zimbabwe.

The Mkwati and other officials of the Mwari cult worked closely with Ndebele military and political leaders during the Ndebele revolt. Similar cooperation existed between Mkwati and his colleagues and also between a number of Shona political leaders in eastern Matabeleland and western Mashonaland. This was before the outbreak of hostilities in Eastern Zimbabwe and this cooperation continued even after the Shona had taken up arms against the whites. For example chief Mashayamombe of Chegutu is said to have maintained communication with the Mwari shrine at Taba Zika-Mambo under Mkwati. When asked by Government officials why he did this the chief explained that the Mwari shrine was a source of medicine used to drive locusts out of his country. Bonda and Tshiwa, also officials of the same cult, are reported to have travelled extensively in Mashayamombe's area, and in the territories of chiefs Maromo and Mtekedza in the Chikomba district and even as far to the east as the Sabi Valley area.

At the same time Mhondoro spirit mediums were busy in most of Eastern Zimbabwe including some of the areas visited by Mkwati, Bonda and Tshiwa. For instance, the Kagubi medium, Gumboreshumba, later to be remembered as one of the greatest heroes of Shona resistance against white occupation, worked with many chiefs: Chinamora, Chikwaka, Nyandoro, Zvimba, Mangwende, Mashayamombe, Rusike, Seke and several others in the Hartley and Charter districts. He was also working in close cooperation with the famous heroine of Shona resistance in the Mazoe valley area, Chargwe the Nehanda medium. She in turn had a great deal of influence upon the chiefs in her region; Chiweshe, Hwata, Nyamweda, Negomo, Nyachuru etc.

Nehanda and Kagubi, after their arrest in 1896

Thus, the religious leadership gave religious sanction to the risings. They also contributed to the success of the organisation of campaigns as their centres were used for intelligence purposes. It took government officials a long time to discover that war information was passing between various paramount chiefs through messengers belonging to the two cult systems. Sometimes chiefs or their representatives actually visited shrines of the cults pretending to be collecting medicine for various problems in their lands – locusts, rinderpest, scabies etc. There, the officials in charge of the shrines would tell them about the war in other parts of the country, and about the need for them to take up arms against the white people. On returning to their countries they would organise the people at night meetings, sometimes disguised as rain-making ceremonies. War fires would be lit on mountain tops while special messengers were sent to neighbouring areas to go and make the war cry, *Chimurenga*!

22 Lewanika and the Barotseland Protectorate

Lewanika and concession seekers

Lobosi or Lewanika was firmly restored to the Lozi throne in 1885 after having been deposed for a year by a rival, Tatila Akufuna. The Litunga's restoration to his position came at the height of the European 'scramble' for territorial possessions in Central Africa and, indeed, in the whole continent, (page 108). Lewanika was anxious about the future of the Lozi monarchy. Lewanika was also afraid of a possible Ndebele invasion of Bulozi. Thus, after his installation as Litunga, he asked his missionary friend and adviser on European matters, Francois Coillard, to write to Queen Victoria requesting her to extend her protection to his country. Lewanika, a great admirer of Khama, knew that the Ngwato chief had obtained British Protectorate over his land. Thus in 1889 he wrote a letter to Sir Sydney Shippard, Administrator for British Bechuanaland. 'Lewanika is most anxious to solicit the Protectorate of the British Government', Coillard wrote on behalf of the Lozi ruler.

The Ware Concession

In the same year that Lewanika approached the British Government for the Queen's protection, a Kimberley business man, Henry Ware, arrived at Lewanika's capital to seek the Litunga's permission to search for minerals in Bulozi. As he was expecting a reply from the British Government to his request for protection, Lewanika did not respond to Ware's request immediately. However, when no reply came from the British, Lewanika finally decided to grant Ware's request in June 1889. This was a limited concession allowing Ware to prospect for minerals in Bulozi and, if any were found, to mine for them for a period of twenty years. The concession excluded the area inhabited by the Lozi. In return Lewanika was to receive an annual subsidy of £200 and mineral royalties.

Lewanika had defined the extent of the area under his rule during negotiations with Ware. He claimed that his territory extended from the Lovale country in the north-west to Katanga in the north. To the east it included all the territory as far as the countries of the Ila and the Zambezi valley Tonga north of the Falls. This, of course, was an exaggeration of the extent of Lozi political authority and effective control. Lozi control, such as it was, had never gone beyond occasional raiding of the Ila and Tonga. But, it benefited both Lewanika and Ware to lay exaggerated claims, just as it had benefited Lobengula and Rhodes to claim that the whole of Zimbabwe was under Ndebele rule.

The news of Ware's exploits soon reached Rhodes' ears, at the time when he was busy negotiating a Royal Charter for his British South Africa Company. Rhodes acted quickly to frustrate any rival trying to establish himself north of the Zambezi. Fortunately he soon received the all-important Royal Charter authorising his British South Africa Company to colonise over half of Central Africa. The northern limit of Company activities and territorial acquisition ran roughly from Lake Mweru eastwards across the southern part of Lake Tanganyika, and as far as the northern shores of Lake Malawi. The western limits were determined by the claims of Leopold's Congo Free State and Portuguese Angola. Effectively, therefore, the vast land mass north of the Zambezi, stretching from the upper Zambezi in the west to Lake Malawi in the east, was open to Company occupation. As can be seen, the area included Bulozi and other territories claimed by the Litunga to be under his authority.

Rhodes then bought the Ware Concession for £9000 from King and Nind, two miners to whom Ware had since sold it. Rhodes was already preparing for the next strategic move.

The Lochner Treaty

As a follow-up to the purchase of the Ware Concession, Rhodes sent a personal agent to Bulozi in early 1890. This man was Frank Lochner. He was to tell Lewanika that the Ware Concession had since been bought by the British South Africa Company and that this company had in its possession the Queen's Charter. Lochner was further authorised to negotiate with the Lozi ruler for a wider concession than the Ware agreement.

By March 1890 Lochner was at Lealui, the Lozi capital, where he found several other concession seekers and traders bothering Lewanika. One of these was a Mafeking business man, George Middleton, who seemed to have substantial influence among some of Lewanika's chiefs and members of the opposition faction at the Litunga's Court. Lochner had both advantages and disadvantages in the negotiations with the Litunga which began almost immediately after his arrival at Lealui. His first disadvantage was that he did not know the country, its people and their languages and customs. Secondly, he had to compete with people like Middleton, who already had a great deal of influence among Lozi leaders. In fact the strongest opposition to his proposals came from the Sesheke chiefs and leaders among whom Middleton had a lot of influence.

Lochner's advantages however, were many and of great substance. Firstly, like Rudd at Bulawayo in 1888, Lochner soon gained the confidence and support of resident missionaries, especially Coillard. As already seen, Coillard, who advised the Litunga on matters concerning Europeans, had a lot of influence upon Lewanika – just as Charles Helm had on Lobengula. Moreover, he was now convinced that Bulozi's connections with the Company might benefit the missionaries in the form of security, the suppression of slavery, raiding and the system of tribute. He also thought that such connections would prevent German expansion (from South-West Africa) towards Bulozi. Lochner's second advantage was that Lewanika himself was eager to establish some kind of link between his kingdom and the British, whom he thought would bring protection for his people. It was, therefore, up to Lochner to convince the Litunga that the British South Africa Company could provide such protection. Thirdly, Lewanika did not fully understand the nature of the relationship between, say, the British Government and Rhodes' Chartered Company. The fourth advantage for Lochner lay in the nature of the Lozi society. Unlike the Ndebele, the Lozi were not just soldiers; they were farmers, craftsmen, hunters and fishermen. The introduction

Negotiations between Lewanika and Lochner

of Western ideas was less likely to threaten the Lozi way of life. In fact Lewanika saw advantages in accepting a measure of westernisation and moreover he had a stronger desire for peace than Lobengula.

Since he knew that Lewanika wanted Queen Victoria's Protectorate, Lochner pretended that he was the Queen's or the British Government's envoy and that the Company on whose behalf he was negotiating with Lewanika was linked to the British Government by the Charter signed by the Queen. Lochner responded to Lewanika's request for direct protectorate by assuring the Lozi ruler that an agreement with the Company was in many ways a treaty entered into with the Queen herself. This, of course, was a lie but was compounded by a messenger from Khama. His name was Makoatse and he assured Lewanika and a great gathering of leaders (*pitso*) that the Company which Lochner represented was indeed linked to the British Crown. Makoatse's intervention on behalf of Lochner came at the right time and it had a dramatic effect upon Lewanika and the faction opposed to the establishment of relations with the British. Thus on 27 June 1890 the Litunga signed an agreement with Lochner. The document was also signed by many of his chiefs and witnessed by Coillard and some of the missionaries present. It later turned out that Makoatse had been paid by Lochner to enumerate and emphasise the advantages of a Protectorate. With this treaty Lewanika had, in fact, delivered his kingdom into the hands of the British South Africa Company. The Queen's Protectorate, such as it was, was accepted but Lewanika carefully managed to retain constitutional authority as the ruler of his people. He also tried to safeguard his people's lands, villages, pastures and cattle from the Company's interference. Witchcraft and slavery were to be suppressed.

On behalf of Rhodes and the British South Africa Company, Lochner agreed to pay Lewanika an annual subsidy of £2000 and four per cent royalty on minerals. He bound the Company to provide schools for Lozi children and to promote trade and industry in Bulozi. It was also agreed that the people's rights to certain iron mines were to be respected, and no mining or prospecting would be carried out in territories actually inhabited by the Lozi proper. Above all, the Chartered Company would protect Bulozi from outside threats and attacks. To see this was carried out a special officer called a Resident would be appointed to reside in Bulozi and he would also look after the Company's interests in Bulozi.

A typical prospector's license issued in 1891

Seven years of neglect and growing doubt
Lewanika had asked for the Queen's protection in the face of external threats upon his kingdom from the Ndebele and European concession seekers from the south and, no doubt, the now fast expanding Cape-centred British imperialism. The Lochner Treaty of 1890 or, as it is also called, the Barotseland Treaty had instead delivered Lewanika and his kingdom into the snares of the Cape-based British commercial company. Like Lobengula in 1888, Lewanika would soon realise that he had been tricked into signing a death warrant for his monarchy. But by the end of the year no such appointment had been made. Lochner himself had left for the Cape, already a sick man. His departure had created an opportunity for rivals such as George Middleton to give their own explanation of the Lochner agreement to Lewanika. They told the king that he had been tricked and that Lochner did not represent the Queen or the British Government but a mere

commercial company whose main interest was profit and not the protection of Bulozi. Naturally, Lewanika was angry with those that had misled him, especially Coillard and other missionaries.

Lewanika was angry and disappointed and in October 1890 he instructed Middleton to write to the British Government informing it that he had decided to cancel or withdraw the treaty partly because he had given away more than he had intended to, and partly because he had since discovered that he had not entered into an agreement with the Queen's or the British Government's representative. The British Government replied through the High Commissioner at Cape Town, Henry Loch, reassuring Lewanika that he would have British protection. Lewanika was also told that the British South Africa Company had the Queen's recognition and that the Queen had signed the Charter under which the Company was operating. The letter added that the Queen's own Commissioner would soon visit Bulozi. In spite of all these assurances no such appointment was made, and no Resident or Queen's Commissioner arrived in Bulozi. Rhodes and the Company were too absorbed by more urgent matters, as Rhodes was now the Premier of the Cape and the Company was preoccupied with taking possession of Eastern Zimbabwe.

After the occupation of Eastern Zimbabwe came a series of events some of which seriously threatened the future of the Company and Rhodes' own political career. In fact one of them actually ended Rhodes's premiership of the Cape. In 1893–4 there was the war against the Ndebele, followed a year later by the abortive Jameson Raid which resulted in the arrest of Jameson and his fellow-raiders. The affair was so bad that Rhodes was compelled to step down as Prime Minister of the Cape, and the Charter was nearly withdrawn. The Company was now facing grave financial problems. Then, as we have seen already, the Ndebele and the Shona took up arms against the Company and the white settlers in Zimbabwe.

The suggestion that Bulozi might come under the authority of the Commissioner of the British Central African Protectorate fell through on account of difficult communications with the Protectorate. Also the Commissioner himself was very much preoccupied with trying to crush Yao and Swahili resistance against British penetration of their areas. Rhodes requested Coillard to act as Resident, but the French missionary declined. In 1896 the resident magistrate of Salisbury, Hervey, was appointed to the position but could not go to Bulozi because of the 1896–7 risings in Zimbabwe. He was in fact, killed during the risings. It was not possible, therefore, to send anybody to Bulozi before 1897. Meanwhile the question of the boundary between Lewanika's area and Portuguese Angola had arisen and a provisional agreement was reached between Portugal and Britain.

A Company Resident was finally sent to Bulozi in 1897. He was Robert Coryndon, a Police Major and formerly of the Bechuanaland Border Police. He had also seen service during the 1893–4 war against the Ndebele, and had been Rhodes's personal secretary from 1895 to 1896. Coryndon arrived at Kazungula in September 1897 and was met by Lewanika's mission-educated son, Letia, who led him to Lealui to meet the Litunga. After a long journey through the desert-like and hot Botswana and having lost most of their oxen, Coryndon and his little party were weary, dusty and unimpressive. The party's appearance and the fact that Coryndon was not accompanied by an army was a great disappointment to Lewanika who had awaited the 'Great White Queen's Representative'. But Coryndon was formally welcomed by the Litunga and his chiefs and councillors at Lealui on 20 October. Coryndon took this opportunity to allay the Litunga's fears about the decision to seek British protection: 'You were afraid that you had sold your country. Do not believe this. You have not sold your country.'

The Company Resident established his headquarters at Sesheke and immediately took steps to cultivate the Litunga's confidence in preparation for another round of negotiations for a new agreement with the Lozi ruler. This was not an easy task as none of the clauses of the Lochner Treaty had been fulfilled, including the payment of the £2000 annual subsidy. As already pointed out, the Company was in a bad state because of its involvement in the Jameson Raid, and also it was being severely criticised both in South Africa and in Britain for the way it had handled the Ndebele and Shona risings. The total effect of all this was that the British Government was no longer confident that the Company could be left to exercise political power north of the Zambezi without some form of supervision or control from the Colonial Office. However, Coryndon was so successful in his efforts to restore the Litunga's confidence and goodwill that a new agreement was signed on 28 June 1898.

The Lawley Treaty
The 1898 agreement was negotiated by Arthur Lawley, Administrator of Matabeleland, in his

Coryndon at Lealui. Middle row, left to right: Letia, Lewanika, Worthington, Coryndon. Sykes, the missionary, is second from right, back row

capacity as a senior representative of the Company. The agreement included most of the clauses of the Lochner Treaty and it also contained new additions. For instance, it allowed the Company administrative authority and powers over most of the areas which Lewanika claimed to be under Lozi control. As will be remembered, the Company already had administrative powers given it by the Royal Charter. It was also agreed that Lewanika would continue to exercise his administrative powers in the territory, between Sesheke in the south and Lealui in the north which was occupied by the Lozi. No prospecting and mining for minerals was allowed in this area and powers of jurisdiction were reserved to the Litunga except in cases involving white people. Also the Company lost the trade monopoly granted under the Lochner agreement.

As already pointed out the British Government had lost confidence in the Company's competence to exercise political power in the area without some form of Government control. Alfred Milner the new High Commissioner held the view that more control was necessary. Thus, before the Lawley Treaty could become effective the nature and extent of the Company's political involvement and responsibility had to be carefully spelt out. This was done by passing a special law called an order-in-council. Under this law Bulozi was called North-Western Rhodesia or Barotseland. The Barotseland/North-Western Rhodesia order-in-council of 1899 stated that the country would be under an administrator nominated and appointed by the Company, but subject to the approval of the British Government through the High Commissioner at Cape Town. The position was further clarified by yet another agreement usually called the Coryndon or Victoria Falls Treaty of 1900.

The Coryndon Treaty 1900
The 1900 treaty's main objective was the clarification and confirmation of the Lawley Treaty and the British Government's responsibilities over the Company's administrator for Barotseland Protectorate. Administrative expenses were the responsibility of the Company. The Company was also required to provide schools, industries, postal and telegraphic communications and transportation services. There was also a new clause authorising the Company to make land grants for farming purposes in the Ila and the Tonga areas of North-Western Rhodesia. Needless to say, the Ila and the

Tonga chiefs were never consulted. The clause was meant to benefit white settler farmers who had already established themselves in the Choma and Kalomo districts on the Tonga Plateau.

Also Lewanika's £2000 annual subsidy was reduced to £850. Certain traditional rights – rights to game, ironworkings and tree-felling for building canoes were safeguarded. The iron rights were particularly important as the Lozi were getting their iron hoes and axes from the Totela. These were cheaper than European-manufactured ones from South Africa. Like the Lawley agreement before it, the Coryndon Treaty also closed the Lozi-inhabited part of the Protectorate to European prospecting and mining.

The Coryndon Treaty, however, did nothing to solve the boundary dispute between Barotseland and Portuguese Angola. As we have already seen, the Portuguese and Lewanika had never agreed about the western extent of the territory under Lozi control. Going by Lewanika's evidence the Company had been claiming 20° west longitude as the dividing line while, for their part, the Portuguese also claimed that some areas to the east of that line were under them. The matter was submitted to international arbitration in 1903. The arbitration commission led by the King of Italy settled the boundary dispute in 1905. This was a turning point in Francois Coillard's attitude to the British South Africa Company. He and some of his missionary companions were so opposed to the growing power of the Company that they refused to witness the signing of the agreement.

More and more white settlers came into the Barotseland Protectorate. Although Lewanika became popular with the Company administration and among white settlers, his influence upon non-Lozi African communities living outside the Lozi territory began to decrease rapidly. Several chiefs

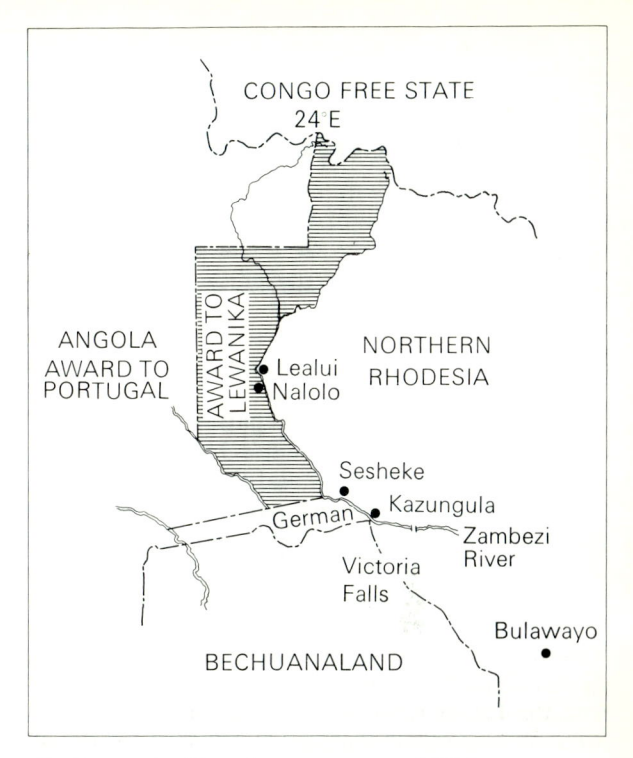

The Barotseland boundary agreement of 1905

stopped paying annual tribute to him as they now felt protected by the Company.

Before discussing the colonisation of the rest of Zambia (i.e. the territory between the Kafue valley area and the western borders of Malawi) we must turn to events taking place in Malawi while North-Western Rhodesia was being taken over by the British South Africa Company. This will make it easier for us to follow the progress of the colonisation of North-Eastern Rhodesia as the area was colonised from Malawi rather than from North-Western Rhodesia.

Mlozi's stockade, destroyed by the whites and their Ngonde and Mambwe allies

British occupation of Malawi

The occupation of Malawi was achieved through a series of treaties, most of them dubious, entered into with a number of chiefs and headmen. The 1889 agreement with the Swahili leaders which has been mentioned above was one such treaty. The negotiator of most of the treaties was Harry Johnston, hence they are usually referred to as the 'Johnston treaties'. Like Cecil John Rhodes, Johnston was a very strong believer in Britain's superiority. He was, therefore, prepared to work for, or cooperate with, any group furthering British expansion in Africa. Before taking up his post at Mozambique, Johnston had been to several parts of Africa, including north Africa, Angola, Zaire and East Africa. He was also a very keen student of African societies, languages and plants.

Johnston was appointed as British representative in Mozambique at a time when someone like him was needed to promote and protect British colonial interests in East and Central Africa as these were being threatened by the German and Portuguese advances. Johnston decided to achieve his objectives through agreements with African chiefs and headmen in the regions concerned. The treaties had three objectives: the establishment of some sort of legal basis for taking away African land; the securing of rights for white commercial groups to prospect and dig for minerals in African territories; and, in the case of Malawi in particular, to enable British agents to end the slave trade. Johnston also cooperated with Rhodes whose main interest was to secure treaties with chiefs in the Luangwa valley area and in the Zambia-Tanzania border region so as to improve his British South Africa Company's communications to the north. Also Rhodes did not want to see the Germans taking over the Tanganyika plateau and so he gave Johnston £2000 to buy treaties from chiefs in the area when the two men met in London in 1889. Rhodes was then busy negotiating a Royal Charter for his Company and Johnston was preparing to take up his appointment as Britain's Consul in Mozambique.

Johnston arrived at Mozambique in July 1889 ready to travel to the interior to make the various treaties. The strongest opposition to his determination to take over as much of Malawi as possible came from the Ngoni. Only one chief, Chiwere Ndlovu of Dowa, signed a treaty with Johnston. He met with more success in the Shire Highlands, however, where Kololo and some Yao chiefs cooperated with him. The Kololo chief and the Yao leader, Mponda, signed treaties. The latter had been promised an annual payment of £100.

From the Shire Highlands Johnston travelled through Chewa country northwards to Nkota Kota where the Swahili chief, Jumbe, agreed to sign a treaty in return for an annual payment of £200. Jumbe had been warned that if he did not accept British protection, the Germans or the Portuguese would take his land. Travelling through Tonga territory, Johnston reached Karonga where, as already seen, a treaty was signed with Mlozi in October 1889. Then he travelled north-west towards the Lake Rukwa area in western Tanzania. He passed through the Zambia-Tanzania border area. It was while he was on the shores of Lake Rukwa that word reached Johnston that the Portuguese were threatening British interests back in southern Malawi. He immediately rushed southwards to attend to the Portuguese problem.

The Portuguese problem
The Portuguese had been laying claim to the Shire Highlands in southern Malawi since 1884. Their position was strengthened in that they had agents south of the Zambezi, Paiva d'Andrade and Antonio de Sousa, who had already signed treaties with a number of chiefs. Also from the port at Quelimane, the Portuguese were in a position to control most of the Zambezi trade, because British ships wanting to go up the Zambezi into southern Malawi had to call at Quelimane first. Thus, the Portuguese at Quelimane could interfere with British trade on the Zambezi, if they wanted to. In fact, this happened in 1887 when supplies were prevented from reaching the British missionaries in Malawi. However, the discovery of the Chinde mouth of the Zambezi in 1889 significantly reduced Portuguese interference with the British river traffic bound for the interior. British ships could now sail up the river without having to report at Quelimane first.

Naturally, the missionaries in Malawi were against Portuguese occupation of the Shire Highlands and they knew that the only effective way to prevent it was to encourage Britain to move into the area. The British Government had, in 1888, sent Johnston to Lisbon to negotiate with the Portuguese. At first his view was that the Portuguese could have the Shire Highlands provided that they were willing to abandon their age-old claim to the area between Mozambique and Angola, a claim made since early in the century when the Portuguese conducted expeditions between the two coasts in a bid to establish a trans-Central African route. As a result of missionary demands and the discovery of the Chinde mouth the British became less compromising. They were now even more determined to keep the Portuguese out of the Shire Highlands.

In 1889 a crisis developed which demanded Johnston's early return from his treaty-making mission in the north. A Portuguese expedition was sent up the Shire River under Major Serpa Pinto. Officially the Pinto expedition was in search of scientific information, but it aroused a great deal of excitement and suspicion because it had several thousands of military personnel including Zulu warriors. The expedition was resisted by Chief Mlauli's Kololo who attacked it south of the Ruo. But the attack did not prevent the Portuguese from crossing the river into the Shire Highlands. This Portuguese advance prompted David Buchanan, Acting British Consul, to declare British protectorate over the countries of the Kololo and the Yao, which was almost the whole Shire Highlands. Pinto also claimed on 26 December 1889 that he had established Portuguese authority over the Shire Highlands. He moved 600 Zulu warriors to Katungu, the port for Blantyre on the Shire River.

British response to this challenge was even more decisive. In January 1890 the Portuguese were warned that Pinto's activities north of the Rou should be stopped immediately, or the British navy would take over Mozambique Island. The ultimatum produced the desired results as the Portuguese withdrew south of the river thus accepting the Rou as the boundary line between British and Portuguese spheres of influence. This position was subsequently confirmed in the Anglo-Portuguese agreement of August 1890 and again in the Convention of June 1891.

Treaties of Sharpe and Thomson
In August 1889 while on his way to the north, Johnston had met a big-game hunter and ivory trader, Alfred Sharpe, in the Shire Highlands. Sharpe had also taken part in the fighting at Karonga in the Anglo-Swahili war of 1887–9. Johnston was impressed by Sharpe, indeed so much so that he appointed him to act as a temporary vice-consul with special responsibility over the lower Luangwa valley area. In that capacity Sharpe was authorised to negotiate treaties with local chiefs and headmen. Thus, when Johnston had to return to southern Malawi to deal with the Portuguese problem in January 1890, Sharpe was continuing the treaty-making activities. Unfortunately, however, Sharpe had very little success in the lower Luangwa valley area. Sharpe's difficulties in the lower Luangwa area arose from the people's fears and

Sir Alfred Sharpe, big-game hunter and ivory trader

suspicion created by the slave-raiding activities of the Chikunda and prazo owners from the Zumbo district of the Zambezi valley. The Ngoni chief, Mpezeni, was friendly but equally suspicious of the real purpose of the white men's treaties and flags. Moreover, he thought himself and his state so powerful and secure that he found the suggestion that his country might need the British Queen's protection both amusing and insulting. He had rebuffed the Portuguese earlier and was prepared to do the same to Sharpe. Sharpe travelled through Nsenga and Chewa countries where he seems to have met with a bit of success.

Having successfully persuaded only two chiefs to sign treaties, Sharpe decided to go northward to the Luapula valley. Treaties were signed with Nsama, the Tabwa chief and then with the Lunda ruler, Kazembe. Under the treaty with Kazembe, the Lunda ruler accepted British protection and agreed to grant mineral rights to the British South Africa Company. It will be remembered that Sharpe was also representing this Company through Johnston's agreement with Rhodes (page 138). The treaty did not, however, include the mineral-rich Katanga to the west of the Luapula, which Sharpe had really wanted for Rhodes's Company. Since 1884 when samples of Katanga's copper were tested, Katanga was believed to be potentially one of the richest parts of Central Africa. This area, as we now know, had become part of King Leopold's Congo Free State. In terms of African states most of it was under Msiri's Yeke kingdom of Garenganja (page 110). The Congo Free State's claim to the Katanga area had even been recognised by Britain in 1889. In spite of this however, and as late as 1891, Rhodes still hoped that Msiri could be persuaded to grant the British South Africa Company mineral rights. Without realising that Johnston had already engaged Sharpe and that Sharpe was now busy in the Luapula valley area, Rhodes sent his personal agent to Katanga in 1890. This was Joseph Thomson, an explorer of great African experience. Sharpe and Thomson however met in Malawi before going to the Luapula valley area and agreed between themselves that Thomson should travel through Central Zambia. Thomson however failed to reach Msiri's area.

As a general rule the treaties negotiated by Johnston, Sharpe and Thomson bound African chiefs not to enter into agreements with any other group or power without British knowledge or consent. But they did not, however, authorise Britain to establish protectorates over such areas. The treaties were, to say the least, very doubtful since in most cases the contracting chiefs in the Lungwa valley area, Central Zambia and in the Luapula valley did not have any neutral interpreters like Lobengula's and Lewanika's missionary witnesses during negotiations. In spite of their dubious nature, however, the treaties were later accepted and used by the British authorities as a legal basis for setting up British protectorates. For instance Johnston's treaties were used in settling the Zambia–Tanzania border, that is the boundary line between British and German spheres of influence. In the Anglo-German agreement of July 1890 the northern end of Lake Malawi beyond the Songwe river was given to Germany, and on the strength of Johnston's treaties, Britain got most of the Tanganyika plateau. Although the treaties generally purported to give Britain mineral rights in the areas concerned, this was not so. Thomson, for instance, was never granted mineral rights in the Copperbelt or Kabwe, yet his treaties were the only 'legal' title that the British South Africa Company ever obtained to the upper Kafue region, the economic heart of Zambia.

The establishment of the British Central African Protectorate

Although constituting a very important step towards the colonisation of Malawi, the treaties of Johnston, Sharpe and Thomson discussed above represented a mere partition of the area on paper into the Nyasaland Districts. Effective rule as such was still to be formally commenced. In fact, at first the British Government was reluctant to move in this direction because they were aware that before colonial control could be established the slave trade and the system of military raids in the area would have to be ended. In Lord Salisbury's words, this was 'risking tremendous sacrifices for a very doubtful gain.'

Unlike Rhodes' British South Africa Company, the African Lakes Company, operating in the country since 1879, was unable to end the slave trade and raiding and to establish political authority in Malawi. Even if Rhodes had wanted to establish his authority there, the missionaries were passionately opposed to the idea of creating another 'Southern Rhodesia' in Malawi. However, in 1890 Rhodes, whose company had bought up £20000 worth of shares in the African Lakes Company and was keen to participate in the economic exploitation of Malawi, offered the African Lakes Company an annual payment of £9000 towards the ending of the slave trade and the protection of Christian missionaries.

The African Lakes Company spent the £9000 paid by Rhodes but never succeeded in ending military raids and the slave trade. The disappointed Johnston correctly observed and remarked that the African Lakes Company was 'entirely unfitted' to end the slave trade and to exercise political control in the area. In 1891, however, the British Government and the British South Africa Company reached an agreement on the future of the Nyasaland Districts. Under this, the Government would provide a police force to maintain order in the country, and Rhodes' company would pay £10000 annually for the maintenance of the police force. Rhodes' company was also granted trade and mineral rights in the area. The administration of the area would be the responsibility of an officer appointed by the British Government with the title Commissioner and Consul–General. The Commissioner's salary was the responsibility of the Government although the British South Africa Company met most of the expenses of the administration of the country. The Commissioner was to be independent of the British South Africa Company and he was not its agent either. The new appointment was given to Harry Johnston in February 1891 and in May of the same year the area was formally called the 'British Central Africa Protectorate'. The name changed in 1907 to the Nyasaland Protectorate.

In theory, therefore, Johnston's new territory was vast, extending from the Zambezi in the south to Lake Tanganyika in the north, and from Lake Malawi in the east almost to the border with Bulozi in the west. However, his effective control was exercised on a much smaller area because, for several reasons, he was in a very difficult position. He had been appointed to his position by the British Government, but the expenses of his office were paid by the British South Africa Company which also bore the financial burden of maintaining the police force which kept order in the Protectorate. This complicated arrangement created great friction and tension between Johnston and Rhodes, and also between the Commissioner and the missionaries who incorrectly regarded Johnston as Rhodes' agent. Then there was a chronic shortage of staff which also hampered Johnston's work and some of the men employed by Johnston were not suited for their work as they had been 'picked up by the countryside and appointed on the spot.'

Johnston's own racist ideas brought about friction between the Commissioner and the African people. The Protectorate's population consisted of Africans, Europeans and Asians and it was the Commissioner's idea that each of the three racial groups should have a specific role to play in the development of the Central Africa Protectorate. The whites were rulers or administrators, the Asians would develop the country's economy and the Africans would provide cheap, unskilled labour. Accordingly, Johnston encouraged whites to come as administrators and coffee farmers, and Asians – mainly Sikhs and Zanzibaris – as policemen, shop owners or traders. The Africans provided labour for these two groups. At first Johnston had also thought that some Swahili could help in the development of the Protectorate's agriculture – a view that had been influenced by Jumbe's successful farming producing, as it had done, 'magnificent crops of rice ... of which he sells quantities to the passing caravans.'

If African administration was to be effective, however, it was clear that Johnston had to work closely with local chiefs. Indeed, on occasions he relied upon chiefs like Mponda, Mbelwa, Kapeni and others. Unfortunately, however, the continued slave trade and Johnston's own intolerant attitude towards Africans led him to fight rather than cooperate with the chiefs, even killing some of them. In doing this he destroyed the basis on which Protectorate government was to rest; that is administration through strong chiefs. This system is also known as indirect government.

24 Yao and Ngoni resistance to the establishment of British rule

It was one thing to declare protectorate over Malawi and yet another one to establish an effective administration in the country. This could only come after the suppression of the Yao slave trade and the ending of Ngoni raids upon their neighbours. Such objectives could either be achieved by persuasion, if possible, or if necessary by war. It must be noted that the Yao and the Ngoni who had never had any intention of accepting British rule were unwilling to abandon their respective ways of life. The only way open to the British, therefore, was to force them to accept British authority. Hence the Yao and the Ngoni wars.

The Yao Wars

Not only did the Yao continue their slave trading activities, they also refused to submit to the Commissioner's authority. Now, Johnston's instructions from the British Government were bound to bring him into conflict with local rulers. He had been instructed to do four things: to establish British authority in the British Central Africa Protectorate; advise local chiefs and headmen on their relations with each other and with foreigners; ensure peace and order in the country and end the slave trade. With a force of 200, the Commissioner had a relatively strong military base. The force, led by Captain Cecil Maguire, was made up of two other British, Sikhs, Zanzibaris and local recruits. Rhodes' annual grant of £10000 (in actual fact £17000) enabled Johnston to increase this force substantially.

Johnston arrived in Malawi in July 1891 to find that the Yao were busy intensifying their slave trading activities. Within a few months of his arrival, Johnston authorised his force to fight the Yao. In October 1891 it attacked and defeated Chikumba and the Mount Mlanje area. From there it went on to the southern end of Lake Malawi where it engaged and defeated Mponda's Yao. Fort Johnston, named after the Commissioner, was established at the site of Mponda's destroyed

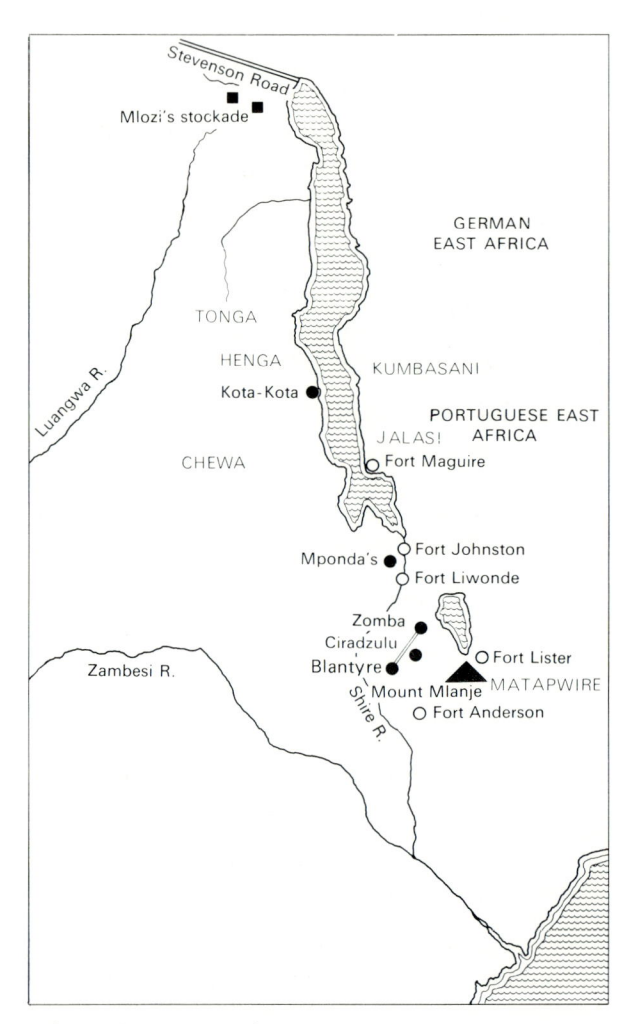

Johnston's wars in Malawi

headquarters. Makanjira, the leading slave trader, was driven away from the eastern shore of the lake. A number of Yao chiefs, including Jalasi, Liwonde and Kawinga, surrendered and were forced to sign treaties of submission to the British Queen.

In December 1891 Makanjira's village was at-

Maguire's attack on the slave dhows, 1891

tacked once again but in this battle things went rather badly for the invaders who lost their leader, Captain Maguire. The two civilian assistants, Buchanan and Sharpe, were away on leave in England and the people of Chiradzulu and Ndirande also chose this time to carry out raids along the Zomba-Blantyre road. Johnston tried to weaken African resistance by deliberately creating divisions between the Yao and their subjects, especially the Nyanja. This step was particularly aimed at destroying the power and states of Makanjira and Jalasi which were predominantly Nyanja. Johnston's strategy was to win the Nyanja away from the Yao by praising them as 'industrious people ... well worthy of our protection.' Also in November 1983 Johnston supported Kumbasani, a female rival to Makanjira, who had substantial Nyanja support. In August 1893 when the Yao chief, Chiwaura, rebelled against Jumbe he was encouraged to flee to Fort Johnston. The British later restored Jumbe to his position but when his successor, Mwene Kheri, became hostile to them he was deposed.

By the end of 1893, however, Johnston's position had improved greatly. A special £10000 grant from Rhodes had enabled him to employ 100 more Sikhs. He could also now put three gunboats on the lake and more forts had been built. Late in 1893 a third campaign was mounted against Makanjira who was forced to flee and cross into Mozambique. Fort Maguire was built on the site of his deserted village.

Yao resistance was, however, far from being completely crushed for in the following dry season, supported by Jalasi, Kawinga, and Matapwiri, Makanjira made his last and even more daring effort to expel the British from southern Malawi. This campaign failed partly because of lack of coordination and partly because of the anti-Yao activities of the Portuguese across the border. Finally, in 1895 Johnston was able to defeat the Yao. In September Matapwiri submitted to British rule. Kawinga was defeated and Jalasi fled into Mozambique. In November the villages which Makanjira had re-built were destroyed and all the slaves in them were set free. The administration's forces were greatly assisted by the forts which Johnston had established: Lister, Anderson, Liwonde and Maguire. By 1896, when Johnston was succeeded by Sharpe as Commissioner, the Yao wars were over. For some time, however, Jalasi and Makanjira continued their opposition to British rule in Malawi from Mozambique, but this opposition was not very effective.

Sikh at Fort Johnston. His uniform of black, yellow and white was designed by Johnston and was supposed to represent harmonious race relations. Compare this with his racist opinions on how Africa should be developed

Ngoni wars

At the end of Yao wars British authority was still threatened by a number of powerful Ngoni chiefs opposed to colonisation. These included Chibisa, Chiwere Ndlovu, Gomani, Kachindamoto, and the senior induna of Mbelwa's Ngoni, Ng'onomo. In 1895, the British defeated the Chewa ruler, Mwase Kasungu, who later committed suicide rather than live as a British subject. Chibisa fled to Hora where he was given asylum by Ng'onomo who was enjoying the support of resident missionaries. This angered Johnston who thought that the missionaries were in league with uncooperative chiefs. Through Swann, the District Resident, Johnston instructed the missionaries to hand Chibisa over to him. Dr William Elmslie of the Livingstonia Mission's Ekwendeni station refused to comply with the demand. However, feeling unsafe, the fugitive Chibisa escaped and went on to Mpezeni's.

A similar problem arose for Chiwere Ndlovu in 1895–6. Like Chibisa, Chiwere was greatly alarmed at the defeat and fall of so many African rulers. He came under increasing pressure from both his wives and headmen to wipe out the missionaries of the Dutch Reformed Church of South Africa working in his country. Although he successfully resisted these demands, the British authorities, fearing for the safety of white missionaries in Chiwere's land, sent uniformed policemen to guard the mission – a move which led to the souring of relations between the missionaries and Chiwere. Chiwere concluded that the missionaries were in league with the authorities and were planning to turn him 'into a slave'. Accordingly, he decided that all Government officials and whoever cooperated with them should be removed. This threat, however, was not carried out and later he accepted Robert Codrington, the magistrate/tax collector from Nkhota Kota, in his area.

Chiwere's change of heart was due to missionary influence and advice. For instance, the chief was frankly warned that the British were simply too strong for him to drive away. At the same time he was also assured that the British would never harm him and his people unless they were forced to do so by Chiwere's Ngoni. For instance, missionary W. H. Murray of the Dutch Reformed Church assured him: 'If Codrington were to arrest your chiefs he would have to arrest me too. If he kills Chiwere he will have to kill me too.'

The chief of the Maseko Ngoni, Gomani I, was very anti-European, both administrators and Christian missionaries. He did not want his people to pay tax because, he argued, the Maseko Ngoni had never asked for British protection. The chief did not want his people to take up European employment whether at the mission, as porters or in Government departments. It is not surprising, therefore, that confrontation with the British in 1896 was sparked off by Gomani's demand that all his people working for whites should be released immediately. On 6 October, he and his headmen called upon all the Ngoni working for missionaries to leave their employers. When this was not done Gomani ordered the burning down of certain Ngoni villages. This led to his arrest by Captain Ashton. He was marched to Blantyre but never reached there as he was shot on the way.

Gomani's former succession rival, Kachindamoto, had readily given up raiding and had also accepted British rule over his people. Unfortunately, however, having stopped raiding, Kachindamoto no longer had any regular supply of cattle. So to make up for this loss therefore he began to sell slaves to Makanjira. The administration would not allow this and so they fought and captured him.

Kachindamoto finally committed suicide.

Finally, Mbelwa's Ngoni, who were already under the influence of the Livingstonia Mission, had been greatly weakened socially and economically by the rinderpest outbreak of 1893 which had killed most of their herds. Chimtunga, the new chief, was incompetent and very unpopular. Yet all these disadvantages did not deter Mbelwa's Ngoni from resisting the British. Indeed, their resistance continued until 1904 when tax collectors came to their area illegally and burnt the homes of those who refused to submit to British rule. The administration moved in during October 1904 and finally brought northern Ngoni-land under British rule. In that year the Government entered into an agreement with the Ngoni chiefs.

The 1904 Ngoni settlement
According to the settlement of 1904 the British administration agreed and stipulated that no Tonga policemen would be used in Ngoni-land. It was also agreed that some Ngoni chiefs would be paid regular wages by the Government of the Central Africa Protectorate; no Ngoni cattle would be confiscated; people would not be scattered too far away from their chiefs' control; and new land would be provided for those who wanted it. The terms of the 1904 agreement between the administration and the Ngoni had been very much influenced by missionaries, but this did not prevent some Ngoni people and their leaders from blaming the missionaries. For instance, the old warrior Chief Ng'onomo is said to have bitterly told the missionaries: 'You have spoiled the country. You have just come from Marambo. The people there were once mine. There at Kasungu you see people running to the Consul with tusks which should have been brought to me as of old. You have caused me and my country to die.'

Land, labour and taxation
Johnston strongly believed in white settlement in Malawi and land ownership. He encouraged white settlers to build a plantation economy based on such crops as coffee, tea and tobacco. Then, there were traders and Christian missions also owning a large portion of land. The third group was the Government itself, which held large areas called the Crown Land. The fourth land-holding group were commercial companies such as the British South Africa Company and the African Lakes Company. A greater part of the land, however, still remained in African hands. Within two years of the establishment of Protectorate rule in Malawi the land position was as follows: planters, traders and missions one fifth; commercial companies one fifth; the British Crown one fifth; and the African people of Malawi two fifths.

It is clear from this land distribution that the Africans' total share of Malawi's land mass was smaller than the share held by minority groups. There was a strong danger that unless the trend was stopped, the Africans could easily lose much of their share, especially to individual white planters who were claiming to have 'bought' large tracts of land from Africans. To control this practice of 'buying', Johnston devised a system known as 'Certificates of Claim' according to which any planter claiming to have 'bought' land from an African was required to prove that the African concerned knew what he was doing, and that the price paid for the land was reasonable. The system seems to have worked satisfactorily with individual planters, but not with commercial companies, especially Rhodes' British South Africa Company which usually made claims that Johnston often found hard to accept. For instance, the African Lakes Company once claimed that it had bought 57201 hectares of land for only fifty-three shillings from four people who were not even chiefs! Johnston was also pressurised by Rhodes who demanded more favourable treatment, because his Company paid money towards the administrative expenses of the Protectorate. Rhodes seemed to have wrongly assumed that Johnston was an employee of the British South Africa Company because of this payment. This view was, however, rejected by Johnston who resisted Rhodes's influences. There were times, however, when Rhodes was given land to which his Company had no claim as, for example, in Mpezeni's country.

As already pointed out, Johnston never envisaged any role for Africans other than as subsistence farmers and a source of cheap labour for white plantation owners. It must be said, however, to his credit, that he tried to prevent the African farmland being incorporated in to the planters' estates. The policy did not take into account the African system of shifting cultivation, but it did stop the whites having complete control over African labour, as was the case in Southern Rhodesia. For instance, discouraged by the meagre wages on the plantations (five shillings or even less per month), some Malawian labourers went to Southern Rhodesia, and later to South Africa, thus beginning the country's migrant labour tradition. Some of those who remained in the country were employed by the Government.

The question of land and labour is directly linked to the problem of tax revenue. Johnston's administration was in great need of money. Rhodes' British South Africa Company was providing £10000 annually (later increased to £17000). In addition, Rhodes had also given £10000 towards the defeat of the Yao slave traders. Johnston decided to impose a five per cent import tax on all goods, but this only raised £300. He then began to consider raising a poll tax on all Africans. The poll tax came in to effect in 1892. Every adult was required to pay six shillings annually, or pay in livestock, farm produce or labour. Most Africans could not afford this and with the support of the missionaries complained that they had not been consulted.

Although taxes were not meant to be levied on people who had not been conquered or who had transferred their allegiance to the Protectorate, there were cases of tax collectors forcing people to pay. A village in the Malanje area was destroyed when the people refused to pay. Often women were taken hostage and were only released when their husbands paid the tax.

25 Occupation of North-eastern Zambia

Before white occupation

We have already seen in previous chapters how North-western Zambia (Barotseland Protectorate) and the Central Africa Protectorate were colonised by the British. Between these two colonies, and lying between the Zambezi to the south and the Tanganyika plateau in the north, was a vast land mass untouched by white colonisation. North-eastern Rhodesia, as the area was also known, was the home of some of the most powerful African peoples in Central Africa north of the Zambezi: Mpezeni's Ngoni, the Bemba, the Luapula valley, Lunda of Kazembe and a few Swahili groups. The area fell within the British sphere of influence in terms of the paper partitioning of Central Africa, yet there was no effective occupation until the end of the nineteenth century.

Several reasons account for this late colonial occupation. Firstly, the chief colonisers in the region, Rhodes and Harry Johnston, were busy elsewhere and were unable to turn their attention to this area. Secondly, it was also known that the organised African states of the region would offer very stiff opposition to the forces of colonisation. Another reason for this delay was that some diplomatic questions about who should colonise the area had to be settled. There were several British agencies that could be used to colonise African areas, and there were also Portuguese agents that were laying claims to parts of Central Africa.

Unsuccessful attempts were made in 1890 and 1892 to establish administrative centres at Chiengi, north-west of Lake Mweru, and on the Kalungwisi River, but these two centres were quickly abandoned because of malaria. From 1895 onwards, the territory was formally placed under the control of the British South Africa Company. As we have seen already, Sharpe and Thomson had earlier travelled through most of the area trying to persuade some of the chiefs and leaders to sign the Company's treaties. But as will be remembered Mpezeni and several other rulers had rejected their offers.

The first Company Administrator of North-eastern Rhodesia was Major Patrick Forbes. Forbes had great experience in Southern Rhodesia as an administrator and as commander of the Mashonaland and Shangani columns in the war against the Ndebele in 1893–4. Forbes' administrative centre was not in the territory during the first four years of his term; he administered North-eastern Rhodesia from Zomba in Malawi. Partly because of this, the impact of white rule upon Mpezeni's Ngoni, the Bemba, the Lunda and the Swahili slave trading communities of the territory was very slight until towards the end of the century. As time went by, however, and as the British sought to make their power more effective, tension and open conflict with the Africans were inevitable.

Mpezeni and white rivalry

Although Mpezeni had rejected Sharpe's and Thomson's treaties he was not totally anti-white. This is clearly demonstrated by his cordial relations with Carl Wiese, a tough German Jewish adventurer who had lived and traded in Ngoni country since 1885. This man exercised a lot of influence upon old Mpezeni. Wiese was a very fluent Ngoni speaker and was married to a Portuguese-speaking black woman from the Zambezi valley area. Because of this marriage, Wiese tended to see himself as a representative of Portuguese interests in Ngoni country and in other areas in the neighbourhood.

Because of his friendship with Mpezeni, Wiese had very easily obtained a vast concession giving him mineral rights over 2590000 hectares in 1891 in return for Portuguese protection of Mpezeni's country. But, as already pointed out, Mpezeni's land was within the British sphere in terms of the Anglo-Portuguese agreement of 1891. In spite of this set-back, Wiese was still determined to legalise his concession. For instance, he also asked for Johnston's 'Certificate of Claim' in 1891 (page 145), but, arguing that Wiese was a slave trader and that Mpezeni was only an immigrant chief with no rights over the land, Johnston had rejected the request.

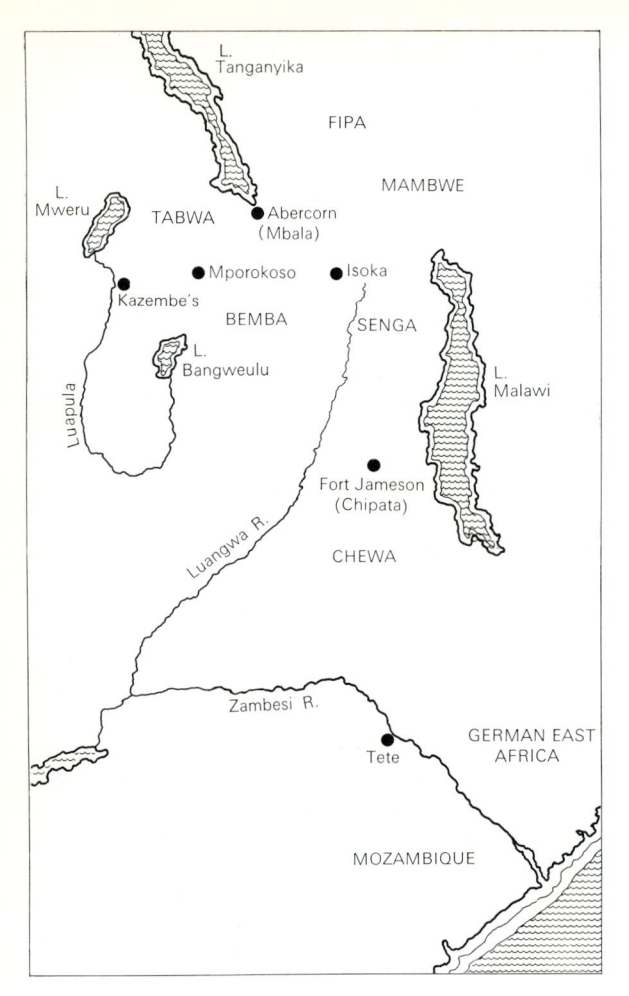

North-eastern Zambia in the 1890s showing how the territory was surrounded by white powers

The real reason however for Johnston's refusal was that he did not like Mpezeni and did not want to do anything that might promote Portuguese interests in the region. Wiese was not deterred by Johnston's attitude. He went to Europe to sell his concession and was paid a sum of £1500 for it by the Mozambique Gold Land and Concessions Company Limited which was formed to make use of the concession.

Developments in North-eastern Rhodesia and in London were now disturbing Rhodes and other leaders of the British South Africa Company. It will be recalled that since the visit of Sharpe and Thomson to the Luangwa valley area in 1889–90, (pages 139–40) the Chartered Company was claiming that it had rights over Mpezeni's and other areas there. Thus, in the face of competition from the Mozambique Gold Land and Concessions Company, the BSA Company moved rapidly and initiated negotiations with the rival group. A settlement was reached whereby the Mozambique Company was granted mineral and land rights in an area which included Mpezeni's country. Also a new company was incorporated in the same year called the North Charterland Exploration Company. Rhodes was behind the formation of this company and his BSA Company held vast shares in it. Thus, Rhodes had at long last found a way of participating in the exploitation of whatever mineral wealth was to be found in the area.

Many whites believed that there was plenty of gold and other minerals in Mpezeni's country. Wiese himself was largely responsible for stirring up these wild hopes. In fact, except for a little at Sassare, there was no gold in the area. Mpezeni's was, however, excellent cattle country, and it was also thought that the Ngoni would be a source of cheap labour for the Shire Highlands area.

White prospectors arrived in Mpezeni's country in 1896 and established themselves at Chinda's, some 48 km from Loangweni, Mpezeni's capital, and not very far from Fort Jameson (Chipata). Old Mpezeni, who was still determined to reject British rule, resisted tax collectors sent by Johnston, and, unwilling to end traditional raids against neighbours, believed the white prospectors to be Portuguese. But he soon realised that he had been tricked into believing this and was very angry. To make matters even worse, Wharton, the prospectors' leader, was involved in quarrels with Mpezeni and Nsingu, the chief's son.

War and the destruction of the Ngoni state

By the middle of the 1890s, Mpezeni, ruler of the powerful Ngoni of the Luangwa valley area, was an old man – perhaps too old to be in full control of his state. Mpezeni, powerful as he was, was very much aware that sooner or later the British, who had destroyed the Ndebele state, Yao and other Ngoni states in Malawi, would attack his own kingdom. Mpezeni's policy was to avoid war with them, if possible, but at his age he was no longer in complete control of his military forces. Moreover, there was a war party at court led by Nsingu his son, who was determined to see the British driven out of the country by force.

As already mentioned, Nsingu was complaining that Company officials had insulted him. In the absence of resident Christian missionaries, there was no 'neutral party' to assist Nsingu and the whites to settle whatever differences existed between them. Thus, by 1897 both groups were preparing for what they saw as an inevitable confrontation. The whites had by now persuaded themselves that no stability could be established in the region until Mpezeni's Ngoni kingdom had been completely destroyed. All this tension was developing at a time when changes were taking place in the administrative leadership of the territory. Forbes had been succeeded by Henry L. Daly as Acting Administrator for the Chartered Company's area in 1897.

By December 1897 relations between the Ngoni and the whites had deteriorated very dangerously. Rumours were reaching Daly's headquarters in Malawi that Mpezeni's men were killing white people working in the area. It was also reported that Wiese (now working for the North Charterland Exploration Company) and another Company employee had been killed. Alfred Sharpe, Johnston's successor as Commissioner of the Central Africa Protectorate offered Daly military assistance. An initial force consisting of fifteen Sikhs and over eighty Africans was sent to Mpezeni's under Captain Brake. In the meantime it was established that, although in danger, Wiese and his companion were alive and safe. In spite of this report, not only did Brake's force continue their advance towards Mpezeni's, they were followed by an even larger party led by Captain Manning of the British Central Africa Rifles. By January 1898 this expedition, made up of some fifty Sikhs and four companies of African warriors, and equipped with two seven-pounders and two Maxim guns was ready to tackle Mpezeni's military machine. For his part, Mpezeni could put on the field about 10 000 men. In addition to their numerical superiority, which was certainly an advantage over their fewer invaders, Mpezeni's men also knew their land better than the Protectorate forces.

The war began on 19 January when Brake's force attacked. The following day, 20 January, Mpezeni's army took the initiative. It was the first time that the Ngoni were fighting the whites and, as could be expected, they had no real answer to the seven-pounders, Maxims and automatic fire. They were soon forced to flee to the hills leaving their king behind. Most of their villages, including that of Nsingu, were burnt down. Within about a week, Mpezeni's village was reached and many leaders, including Nsingu, were captured in early February. Nsingu was accused of 'murder . . . and raiding in British territory', tried and found guilty. He was shot dead. About a third of the Ngoni cattle – 12 000 – were seized by the invaders. The old chief was also captured and taken to Fort Manning where he was detained until his death in October 1900.

The fall of Mpezeni has been attributed to several factors. Firstly, although large in number and certainly very courageous, like Lobengula's Ndebele four years earlier, the Ngoni were using traditional methods and strategies of warfare. For instance, not only did they rely heavily upon their spears, they also insisted on day-time attacks and preferred fighting in open areas rather than in thick bushes. Because of close range, the Ngoni also exposed themselves to ammunition fire. Secondly, it is also said that only half of Mpezeni's fighting men actually fought in this crucial war. The other half were involved in the Ngoni annual festival of the First Fruits. It is also said that over the decades of settled life the Ngoni had relaxed their military discipline and that there was disunity among the military leaders. Whatever the reasons for the defeat of Mpezeni's Ngoni, the British South Africa Company and British authorities in Central Africa were happy that at long last one of the menaces to their interests in North-eastern Zambia had been removed.

The defeat of the Swahili

We have seen already how Swahili trading communities and states were destroyed by the British in northern Malawi during the period 1887–95, (page 137). But the eight-year campaigns had not led to a complete destruction of Swahili power in Central Africa. They had simply driven some of the determined Swahili leaders and their followers out of Malawi towards the west and north-west where they soon re-grouped to form new trading communities or settled among other peoples. Thus, North-eastern Zambia was one of the few areas in Central Africa in which Swahili trading communities still existed until the late 1890's. Some of them established separate 'states' while others preferred to settle among existing chiefdoms in the Luapula/Katanga area. One of the Swahili traders Kambunda, for instance, established himself in the fertile Lofu valley south of Lake Tanganyika, among the Lungu. Kambunda raided his hosts for slaves whenever necessary, although he also assisted them to defend themselves against their Bemba neighbours. West of the Tanganyika plateau in Senga country was another strong Swahili centre. Also Swahili traders such as Nasoro bin Suleiman escaped westwards from the north end of Lake Malawi when the establishment of British Protectorate authority led to the fall of Mlozi's power in the mid-1890's and the killing of Mlozi himself by the British in 1895. Nasoro built himself a new centre in Mporokoso's area.

In the late 1890s, however, this Swahili power was being seriously threatened and eroded by the expanding British imperialism. In April 1896, for instance, a BSA Company official, Bell, ran into a caravan trying to cross the Choshi (Chozi) river into Bemba country. He fought and defeated the Swahilis, capturing large quantities of goods. Again, on 19 June, Bell met another Swahili caravan from which he confiscated a lot of ivory and many slaves. In July of the same year, another Company official, Drysdale, also broke up a large caravan making its way to Lubemba. He also freed many slaves and captured huge amounts of ivory. So, in order to check the slave trade from Senga, Forbes established a sub-station at Inyala, and a fortified post at Mirongo near present day Isoko. In September, Robert Young, an officer in the British South Africa Company's police force, was travelling near Mirongo when a Senga chief, Chiwara, who was expecting Swahili and Bemba attacks appealed to him for help. Young held off both the Swahili and the Bemba for five days before he followed them burning their villages and freeing the Senga who, in his words, were 'absolute slaves of the (Swahili) having to grow grain for them, kill elephants, etc.'

In 1898 an Assistant Collector stationed at Kalungwisi was recruiting labour in Mporokoso's area for the Lake Malawi telegraph line when he was attacked and driven off by the Swahili. In 1899, however, another official, H. T. Harrington, raised a force of three whites and a hundred African police and sacked Mporokoso's stockaded village where the Swahili trader Nasoro was, but he escaped. Nasoro, however, later surrendered to Company forces. In the same year the last Swahili caravan to the east coast was dispersed before reaching its destination. By this time it was clear that Swahili influence on the eastern part of the plateau had been largely checked. Farther north their power was limited by the *boma* at Mbala (Abercorn). They still had some influence, however, in Kazembe's country, at least until 1899.

Occupation of Kazembe's country

By the 1890's the Luapula valley Lunda under Kazembe were still relatively prosperous and politically well organised. The fertile valley area produced enough food – maize, millet, cassava, and beans – to feed a fairly large population. Fish and salt were also easily accessible to the Lunda, and trade with the Swahili brought cloth, guns and a variety of luxury goods. With a population of around 20000, Kazembe's capital on the Luapula was, without doubt, the largest urban centre in British Central Africa. It had a stockade 915 metres long, a deep ditch, and three defended entrances.

When, during the last years of the 1890s, Kazembe's Lunda were faced with a choice between two powerful groups, the British and the Swahili, they opted for the continuation of their alliance with the Swahili. Moreover, although the British South Africa Company had established a post at Mweru in the 1890s, this centre was not strong enough to affect the Lunda–Swahili trade in the area. Indeed, the Swahili continued with their slave trading activities as they had always done before the establishment of the British post in the area.

Yet by the late nineteenth century Kazembe's military power was rapidly weakening. For instance, when his country was attacked by the Yeke, Kazembe had to ally himself with the Bemba. Although in 1895 he had given the impression that he could resist the British, four years later Kazembe was prepared to negotiate rather than fight. But by this time the British had made up their minds that powerful African states in the region should be destroyed. Using the fact that Kazembe had once rebuffed a Company force under Watson in 1895 as a pretext, Robert Codrington, now Administrator of North-eastern Zambia, decided to attack the Lunda state in 1899. Thus, in October of that year a force of the British Central Africa Rifles was despatched to Kazembe's under Captain E. C. Margesson. But Margesson's force found no resistance when it marched upon the Lunda capital because Kazembe had fled across into Zaire, and so also had his Swahili allies.

While in Zaire, the Lunda ruler negotiated his surrender to the British through the missionaries of the Plymouth Brethren, who later brought him back to his capital in 1900. As for his Swahili allies, we are told that by that time there were only three of them on the Luapula who, according to Codrington, had been 'deserted by their followers ... and are on quite friendly terms with the administration ....' This was the end of Kazembe's independence.

British occupation of Lubemba

In 1895 the British South Africa Company had assumed formal control of North-eastern Zambia from the Commissioner of the British Central Africa Protectorate, and fundamental changes had taken place within Bemba society. These internal changes greatly facilitated the British take-over of Lubemba during the closing years of the century. By the 1890's the Bemba were no longer as united and as strong as they had been about a decade and a half earlier. For instance, the Bemba had fought and won many battles against the Bisa in a bid to take over from them the trade with the Portuguese. The Bisa country had valuable resources like salt and iron ore which the Bemba wanted to control. Indeed, the Bemba were so powerful that they had fought the Ngoni of Mpezeni during the reign of Chitimukulu Chitapankwa. It has been said that this military power had been created by an alliance among leading Bemba chiefs under the leadership of the Chitimukulu chieftainship. As a result of this alliance, succession to the paramount chieftainship was now limited to the Miti branch of the Bemba. Members of the Miti branch were also given the leadership of other Bemba chiefdoms. Trade with the Swahili from Zanzibar was bringing in cloth, silk, beads, and a variety of luxury goods which the Chitimukulu redistributed. The collection of ivory, as tribute, increased, and the Chitimukulu chieftainship was now assuming a more centralised character than it had before. Unfortunately, however, Chitimukulu was not the only important chiefdom in Lubemba. There was the Mwamba branch as well, which had become powerful and rivalled that of Chitimukulu. Among the well-known Mwamba chiefs at that time was Chileshe.

By the late nineteenth century internal rivalry and division was weakening the Chitimukulus. There was no standing army, nor were there centrally appointed administrators. The Chitimukulu had also lost control over trade and, as a result, lesser chiefs were now carrying on trade for themselves and increasing their influence. Mwamba was one of the most powerful of these.

Chitimukulu Chitapankwa and Mwamba Chileshe died in 1883. After the death of these two men it became increasingly clear that the Mwamba branch's power was a source of friction among the Bemba. Open conflict between the two branches came during the reigns of the two men's successors, Chitimukulu Sampa and Mwamba Chipoya respectively. Chipoya had a more forceful personality than Sampa. The two men did not appreciate the fact that now, more than ever before, their people needed unity to defend Lubemba's independence against British expansion.

Up to now, apart from the White Fathers, few whites had been into Lubemba since Livingstone's visit there. In 1893 Harry Johnston, Commissioner for the British Central Africa Protectorate, sent Hugh Marshall to Mbala on the south-east end of Lake Tanganyika, to open a Company post. The Mbala station, later called Abercorn, was opened both to make European authority felt and to protect whites in the area from possible Bemba attacks. Anxious to avoid military confrontation with the Bemba, Johnston strictly instructed Marshall to cultivate friendly relations with Bemba rulers. Marshall, who was accompanied by a small force of Sikhs, was soon able to build a three metre stockade at Mbala which received many refugees from Bemba civil wars and the activities of slave raiders. Naturally, by this time the Bemba were very much concerned about the presence of the whites. They felt very insecure and were no longer confident that their stockaded villages could provide sufficient protection against the white men's guns. The widespread insecurity was growing against the background of hostility and civil war between the two leading Bemba branches.

The expected clash with the British eventually came in 1897 in the upper Luangwa valley area. In this area, threatened by the Bemba, a Senga chief Chiwara appealed for British help. In response to this request, Forbes used Company forces to expel the Bemba from Chiwara's country. In order to impress them even more with the power of the British South Africa Company, Forbes destroyed and burnt down many villages in the neighbouring areas. He freed whatever slaves he found.

In 1898 Mwamba Chipoya died, leaving his people seriously divided by a succession crisis. It was this situation which Codrington, Forbes's successor, took advantage of in order to extend Company authority and influence into Lubemba. He was also helped by White Father missionaries. As already seen (page 10), Bishop Joseph Dupont had struck cordial relations with Mwamba Chipoya before the Bemba ruler's death. Chipoya, so we are told, had entrusted the control of his chieftainship to Dupont shortly before he died. In this position, Dupont was able to exercise a great deal of influence among Mwamba's people. However a few months later, Dupont's position was challenged by Ponde, one of Chipoya's kinsmen also claiming succession to the throne. The result was factional fighting which could only benefit Forbes and his Company administration. Charles McKinnon and Robert Young, two Company officials at Mirongo, easily defeated Ponde, marching into Mwamba's territory. Then they helped his rival Kalonganjovu to the throne as Chipoya's successor. A fortified Company post was built at Kasama and from it the rest of Lubemba, was easily forced to submit to British rule by the end of the century.

PART VII
Colonial Rule in Central Africa I

26 Colonial rule in Zimbabwe

The British Prime Minister Benjamin Disraeli once described England as 'The Two Nations,' rich and poor. In colonial times, Central Africa was also 'Two Nations,' white and African. The whites enjoyed the benefits of economic growth. They brought capital and sophisticated machinery from Britain and South Africa. They built farms, mines and big towns connected by roads, railways and telecommunications. They produced vast quantities of crops and livestock to sell locally and abroad. They enjoyed high living standards that were reflected in high salaries, nutritious diets, spacious homes in the suburbs and automobiles.

The Africans, on the other hand, suffered all the indignities of second class citizenship. Only a few benefited from the education and job opportunities offered by the colonial system. The majority remained poor. They lost their land and were crowded into Reserves. They were forced to leave home to earn money to pay tax. They were obliged to pay high prices geared to the high salaries of the whites and not to their own low wages. They could take no part in the political system and were made to feel inferior. They were offered little in the way of education. 'Do we not pay taxes to the government?' asked some Shona delegates to a meeting of Africans in 1929. 'Then we want a proper government school, we want to see something for our money, we want proper schooling for our children.' Yet twenty years later the white government of Zimbabwe spent just $6\frac{1}{2}$ per cent of its revenue on African education. It is hardly surprising that Africans became disenchanted with white rule and with the 'Two Nations' system on which it was based.

The white government in Zimbabwe
Zimbabwe was known to the whites as 'Southern Rhodesia' and had been created in 1901 by the joining of Mashonaland and Matabeleland. It was governed by the British South Africa Company, though the British government had ultimate responsibility for it. It had an Administrator appointed by the Company, and a Legislative Council chosen by the Company and the white settlers in Zimbabwe. In theory Africans could vote for members of the Legislative Council, but in practice few met the qualifications: in order to vote, they had to be able to complete an application form in English, occupy a house worth £75 or earn £50 a year. In 1912, when it looked as if Africans might begin to qualify, the property qualification was doubled.

'Southern Rhodesia' was governed almost entirely in the interests of the BSA Company and the white settlers. The British Resident in Salisbury could refer to Britain any bill that seemed unfair to Africans, as he did when the settlers tried to double the tax on Africans in 1901, but this power was rarely used. The Resident himself could take no major decisions; he had to refer these to the British High Commissioner in Cape Town, who was already burdened with the affairs of South Africa, Lesotho, Swaziland and Botswana. The day-to-day administration of Zimbabwe and the setting-up of a

A chief, stripped of his traditional powers, sits with a district officer

social and political colour bar was entirely in the hands of the settler-dominated white government, assisted locally by magistrates, Native Commissioners and chiefs. Magistrates dealt with issues affecting settlers such as land applications. Native Commissioners, scattered throughout the country, kept law and order among Africans, collected taxes, recruited labour and tried legal cases involving Africans. Chiefs, stripped of their traditional powers, were also officials of the white regime. They could be deposed and their chiefdoms divided or joined to other chiefdoms. Their work now was to assist the Native Commissioners. The chiefs were no longer the true leaders of their people. The BSA Company steadily lost interest in governing Zimbabwe. The administration was costly: revenue did not equal expenditure in 1908. The Company was disappointed not to have found gold in the quantities it had hoped.

The settlers on the other hand were eager to take over the government. By 1913 there were more settlers on the Legislative Council than Company members. In 1923 the Company gave up the government of Zimbabwe and the British Government offered the settlers the option of joining South Africa or governing Zimbabwe themselves; they chose the latter. On 1 October 1923 the settlers became responsible for all government matters except defence, mining royalties and African affairs, which were reserved to the British government. 'Southern Rhodesia' was now a fully-fledged white settler colony with a white Prime Minister, a white cabinet and a white parliament chosen by the whites. Voters had to be British subjects earning £200 a year, which excluded most Africans.

Land appropriation

Apart from their political power, the whites also took most of the best land in Zimbabwe. As white settlers had moved north through South Africa, they had destroyed African societies, taken their land and carved it into big farms for themselves. After the Ndebele defeat of 1896 their land was treated in the same way. Every white man who had fought in the war was given more than a thousand hectares of Ndebele land. Whites came pouring in from Britain and South Africa to buy farms. They charged the Ndebele rent for living on their own land, broke up Ndebele villages, and evicted the Ndebele in their thousands. Land companies bought big areas with the intention not of farming them but of reselling them later at a profit, so that

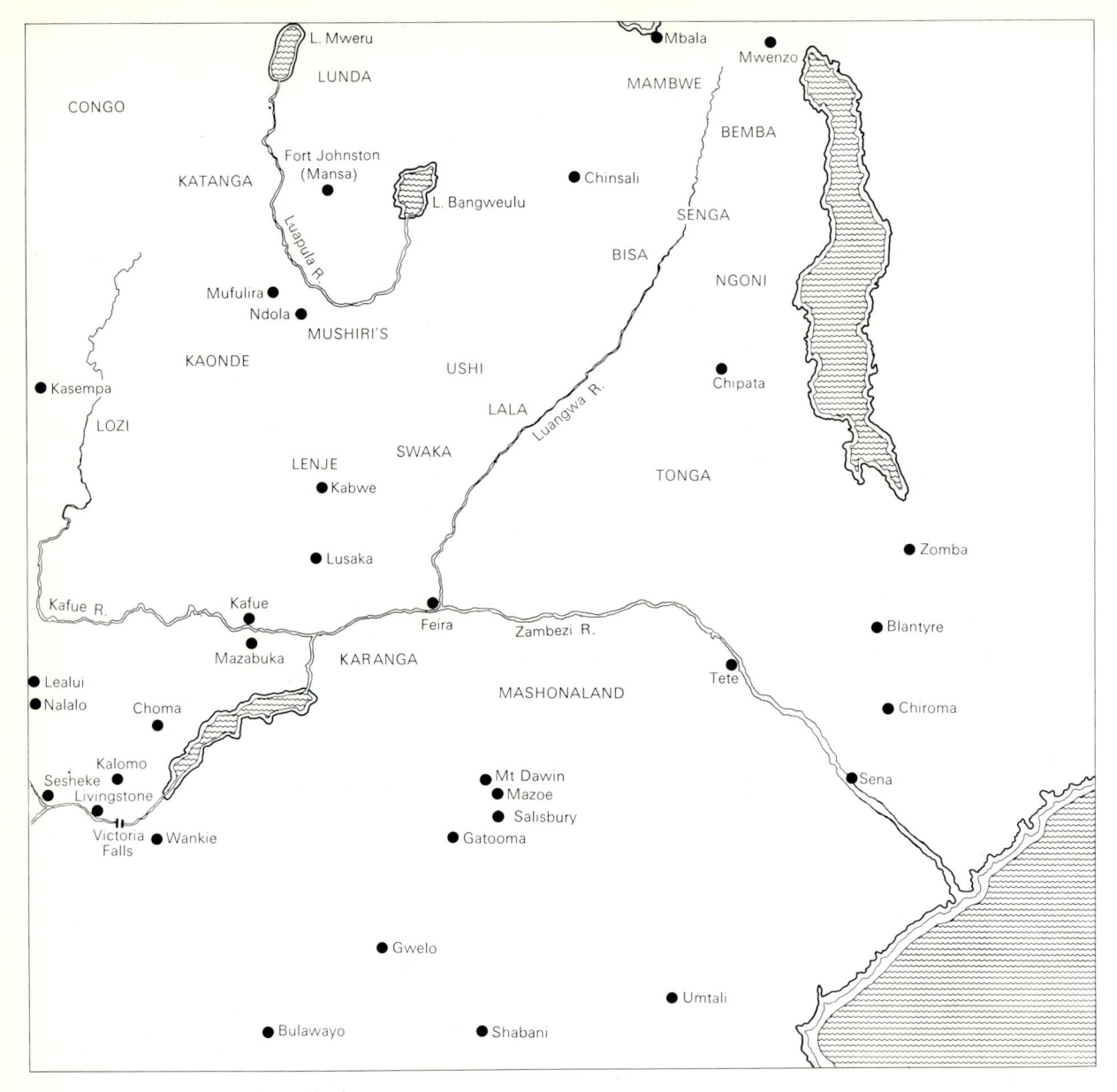

Administrative centres in Central Africa

although a sixth of Zimbabwe had been taken, only a fraction of it was being farmed.

In 1908 the BSA Company, disenchanted with Zimbabwe, began selling its land. It set up information offices in Britain and South Africa to publicise Zimbabwe as a land of farming opportunities. The result was a dramatic increase in the number of white farmers in Zimbabwe. By 1923 more than twelve million hectares of the best Zimbabwean soil had been taken by whites. In Matabeleland the whites took the red and black soils traditionally favoured by the Ndebele; in Mashonaland they put their tobacco farms on the sandy soils long-used by the Shona. The white farms were close to the markets along the railway line. Legally the Africans too could have bought land, but in practice few did. They could not afford it, the Company would not sell it to them, and the buying and selling of land was not an African tradition. Most Africans ended up in Reserves, large areas of relatively useless land infested with tsetse fly, without water, and miles from the line-of-rail markets.

27 Colonial rule in Zambia

Zambia, too, was administered by the British South Africa Company though, as in Zimbabwe, the British government had ultimate responsibility for it. The Company had even less interest in Zambia than it had in Zimbabwe, mainly because of tsetse fly and opposition from the Zambians. Fewer settlers went to Zambia than to Zimbabwe; by 1898 there were only a hundred whites in Zambia, most of them traders and missionaries.

Zambia was known to the whites as 'Northern Rhodesia'. 'Northern Rhodesia' was formed in 1911 by the joining of North-western and North-eastern Rhodesia. The capital in those days was Livingstone. The Administrator was appointed by the BSA Company. There was a British Resident but he spent most of his time at Salisbury and knew little about the day-to-day running of Zambia. Local administration was in the hands of District Commissioners, chiefs and police. Chiefs in Zambia did not lose as many of their powers as they did in Zimbabwe. The Company wanted to use them to control their people. Chiefly succession rules were upheld, though the Company took it on itself to create new chieftainships, especially among the Tonga. The chiefs were allowed to operate customary law, though in some cases they were helped by the District Commissioners. In return, the chiefs helped the District Commissioners to make roads and maps, locate tsetse fly, keep records of villages and prevent friction between Africans and whites. Chiefs were not rewarded for these duties, though some were allowed to keep part of the tax they collected.

There were several police forces in Zambia, made up of both whites and Africans, especially Ngoni and Yao. In 1911 these forces were combined to form the Northern Rhodesia Police. The police often used brutal methods to make sure the Company's wishes were understood. If Zambians refused to pay taxes or work for the Company, they were flogged and their houses were burned down.

The Company soon grew tired of administering Zambia, as it did of Zimbabwe. In 1924 it handed over its administrative role in Zambia to the British government. There were still not enough settlers in Zambia to justify their taking over the government, so Zambia became a 'Crown Colony' of the British government with an Executive Council appointed by Britain and a Legislative Council partly appointed by Britain and partly elected by the whites in Zambia. Few Africans were eligible to vote.

Land appropriation in Zambia
Before the First World War the British government, advised by its High Commissioners at the Cape, Lord Milner and Lord Selborne, thought that Zambia should not become a settler colony. Zambia was a tropical country with poor soils and deadly diseases. If settlers went there, they would always be turning to the British government for help, and that was a problem the British government could do without. Zambia should, so the British government believed, be developed in the same way as Uganda, Nigeria and other British colonies in the tropics, that is as an area of big plantations growing tropical products such as cotton and rubber.

The BSA Company, on the other hand, wanted settlers to go to Zambia to grow food for the white miners as food from South Africa was expensive to transport. The Company set aside two and a half million acres of Soli, Lenje and Tonga country on the Toka plateau and by 1911 there were 159 farms between Kalomo and Kabwe. The area was known as the 'maize belt'. These early white farmers were former officials, railway workers or Afrikaners from the Transvaal who employed poor whites known as 'bywoners' who lived in mud huts and gave a third of their produce to the 'baas'. The white farmers had little captial; they faced problems such as poor soil, poor communications and lack of markets; they had to compete with white miners for land, water and labour, and they generally came off second best as the miners could afford more money.

As in Zimbabwe, large areas of land were taken

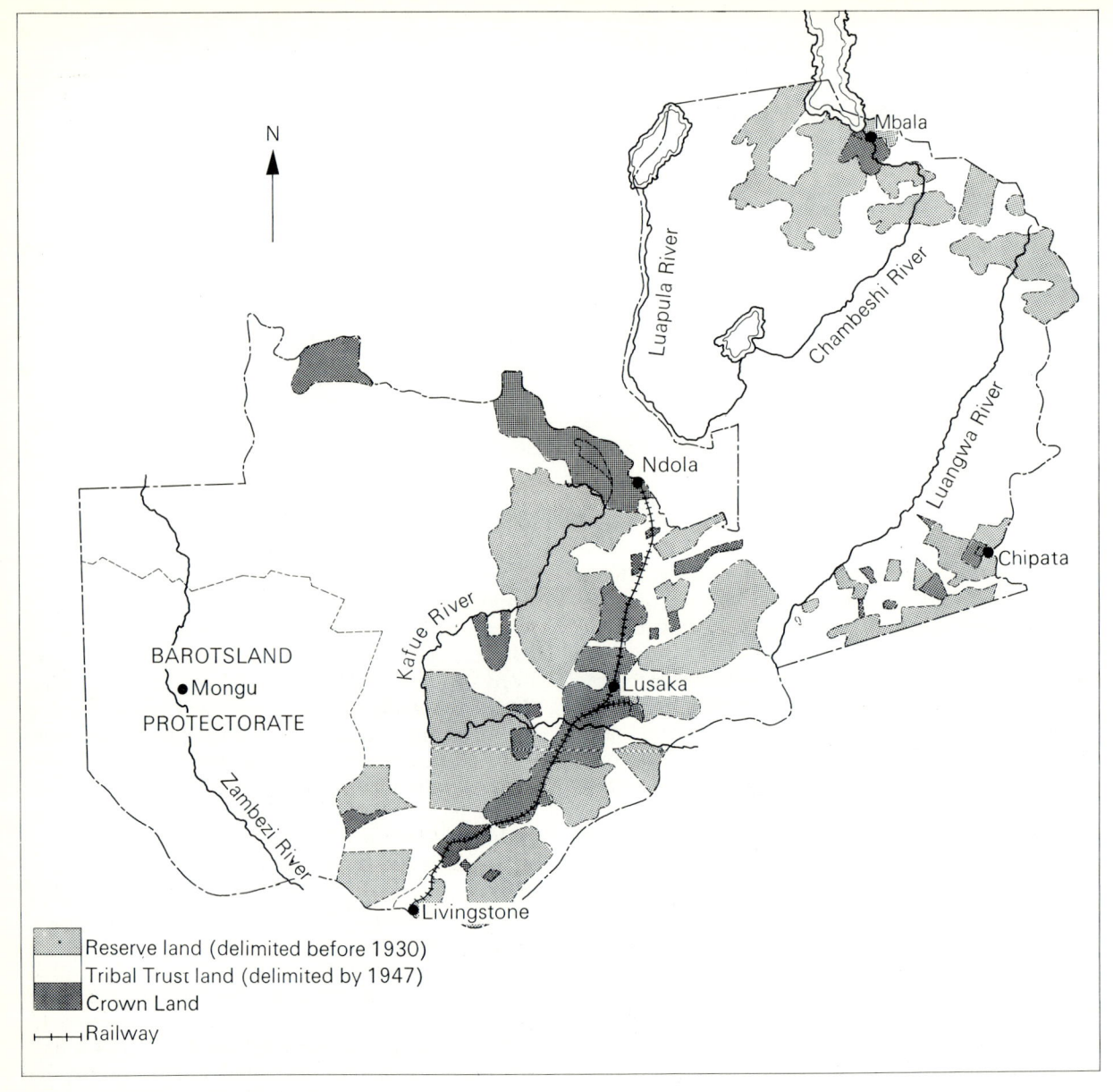

Land distribution in Zambia

by rich Englishmen who intended not to farm the land but to resell it later at a profit. Of four and a half million hectares of Zambian land owned by whites, only 28 840 hectares was being farmed. As in Zimbabwe, the Land Bank loaned money to white but not to African farmers and the Department of Agriculture advised white, but not African, farmers how to grow cotton and tobacco.

28 Colonial rule in Malawi

Malawi attracted even fewer white settlers than Zambia, though it did attract a fair number of missionaries, traders and planters. Malawi did not have many minerals and was never ruled by the British South Africa Company; it was a British Protectorate and was the 'poor relation' of Britain's colonial possessions in Africa.

Malawi was known to the British as 'Nyasaland'. It had a Governor, an Executive Council of three officials, and a Legislative Council of those three plus three other whites to represent the missionaries, traders and planters; the missionaries' representative was also to represent Africans, which one or two did so outspokenly that the government saw them as enemies.

The officials whom Malawis came most into contact with were the District Officers who kept law and order, collected taxes and acted as magistrates. Chiefs were allowed to keep most of their legal powers. Police duties were carried out by a military unit made up of Africans, whites and Sikhs and, when this was sent abroad, by *boma* messengers appointed by the District Officers.

Land appropriation in Malawi

Less African land was taken in Malawi than in Zambia or Zimbabwe: fifteen per cent in all. The earliest land-grabbing took place when a few whites 'bought' land from Malawi chiefs with such things as calico, beads, copper wire and liquor. The African Lakes Company was 'granted' three and a half million acres by Chief Kapeni. In these areas Africans were treated harshly; they had to pay rent either in cash or in labour under the *thangata* system, and some were moved out of the white areas, which caused overcrowding in other areas, especially around Blantyre. The overcrowding was made worse when a railway company took land in the overcrowded area, and later when Mukua-Lomwe people migrated into the Mlanje area to

Cotton farming in Malawi

escape from the harsh Portuguese regime in Mozambique.

The whites as usual took the best land, in the Shire Valley and Highlands, with small enclaves at Karonga in the north and Nchen in the centre of Malawi. On their big plantations the whites grew cash crops like coffee, tea, cotton and tobacco. Coffee was important around the turn of the century, when prices were high in England; 907 tonnes of coffee were produced in Malawi in 1900. Later production dropped because of drought, shortage of fertilizer, poor seed, and low wages causing unreliable labour supplies. Only 45 tonnes of coffee were produced in 1915. Tea in the Mlanje and Thylo areas was more reliable: by 1938 four and a half million kilogrammes of tea were being produced and by 1950 this had gone up to seven million kilogrammes.

As in the rest of Central Africa, African farmers were not given the same encouragement as whites. The missionaries encouraged them to grow cotton but until 1910 the colonial government would not supply enough seed; it also refused to finance an experimental farm and did nothing to alleviate transport difficulties which made marketing difficult. Middlemen could buy cotton from the villages at less than the market price and then resell it at a profit.

In 1910, because of demand for cotton in Britain, the British government granted £10000 a year for five years to encourage cotton-growing in all its Protectorates. The British Cotton Growing Association provided seed for African cotton-growers in Malawi; it also set up ginneries at Port Herald, Chiromo and Karonga and improved marketing facilities to cut out the profiteering middlemen.

29 Early African resistance and protest

African opposition in Zimbabwe
It was not easy for Africans to oppose white rule, still less to end it. In the early years the Shona were too shattered by the defeat of 1896 to want to take up arms again under the old political and religious leaders who had led them to that defeat. Among the leaders who did continue to oppose the whites were Kunzwi-Nyandoro and Mapondera. Chief Nyandoro opposed taxation but relied too much on old methods to lead an effective resistance movement; he continued until the 1930s when he was deported from Chiota Reserve. Mapondera of Mazoe, returning home from fighting the Portuguese in Mozambique, found that whites were killing his relatives and stealing his cattle; he led Shona fighters against the whites in Mount Darwin but was ultimately defeated.

The Ndebele, on the other hand, moved fairly quickly into a modern style of political protest. The leadership came from the *indunas*, who wanted to restore the Ndebele king. The indunas supported Lobengula's sons; they used modern methods such as petitions, and had the support of the younger Ndebele. They were advised by black South African lawyers to appeal to the British government and point out that the BSA Company had cheated them and they were the rightful rulers of Zimbabwe. These arguments made no impression on the British government. The Ndebele now saw that political power in Zimbabwe lay not with the British government but with the white settlers. They began to try to persuade the few African voters to vote for white candidates who would support African issues in the settler-dominated Legislative Council.

Churches also played a big part in early protest movements. Matthew Zwimba's Church of the White Bird, a Shona movement, combined Christianity with older Shona religions. The Watch Tower movement was brought to Zimbabwe by Malawi domestic servants; it was active in north-western Mashonaland, where hymns were sung in chiNyanja and nationalist heroes such as John Chilembwe and Eliot Kamwana were remembered. There was also an appeal to Shona history in such later churches as Guta ra Jehovah, led by the prophetess Mai Chaza. The future political leader Ndabaningi Sithole worked in a Church formed by Rev. E. T. J. Nempare. These churches gave voice to rural grievances and created a sense of national unity.

African opposition in Zambia
As in Zimbabwe, the earliest opposition in Zambia was to taxation. This opposition was not manifested among centralised communities such as the Bemba, Lozi and Ngoni, because in these societies the chief took a share of the taxation and so made sure it was collected. The opposition came from more disparate groups such as the Senga, Bisa and Lenje, some of whose people simply ran away from the tax-collectors and hid in the difficult part of the country.

It was a long time before a more modern form of political protest began to emerge. The reason for this was the slow development of a modern economy and education system. For many decades, political protest in Zambia was regional in character and confined mainly to the rural areas. The earliest opposition was led by Malawis who had received a better education than was available to Zambians and who now worked in Zambia as clerks and skilled workers. The Malawis were helped by people from north-eastern Zambia who had also been educated in Malawi. The breeding-place of these early Zambian politicians was the Scottish Livingstonia Mission at Mwenzo. From Mwenzo, promising students were sent to the Overton Training Institute in Malawi, where they received probably the best education then available in Central Africa. At Overton they rubbed shoulders with Africans from different backgrounds, which gave them a sense of African solidarity, and discussed social, economic and political problems which affected them as blacks and as a colonised people. Some Overton students went on to teach at a new school called Chinsali under their former fellow-student David Kaunda, father of Zambia's President Kenneth Kaunda. From Chinsali they launched many attacks on the racist attitudes of white people.

It was also at Mwenzo that the first African Welfare Association was formed in 1912. The aim of the Association was to put African viewpoints to the government. The Mwenzo Welfare Association was an isolated move, and though others were formed in the 1920s, they tended to be social clubs rather than political organisations.

As in Zimbabwe, religion played its part in Zambian opposition to white rule. Watch Tower preached about the end of the world, when whites would go to Hell and Africans to Heaven. The Jehovah's Witness was popular in the 1920s and 1930s.

African opposition in Malawi

The earliest Malawi opposition to white rule took two different forms. The less-westernised Malawis simply wanted the British to leave so that they could go back to their traditional ways. The mission-educated Malawis on the other hand saw the value of western institutions and churches but wanted to run them themselves. This latter sort of opposition was seen among the Tonga of North Province, who thought the Livingstonia Mission was too slow in promoting trained Africans. One African, Mwase, completed his theological studies in 1902 but was not ordained as a priest until 1914.

Religion played an important part in the Malawi protest movement. It was from Malawi that religious movements spread to other parts of Central Africa. Watch Tower sprang up among the Tonga in 1909 under the influence of Eliot Kamwana. Kamwana preached against taxation and within months had thousands of converts; he was deported but the Watch Tower movement spread. The desire for African churches to be separate from white churches grew. Charles Domingo started separatist churches among the northern Ngoni and condemned the treatment of Africans on European estates. These outbursts had no effect on the colonial government.

The most celebrated instance of early Malawi opposition to white rule was the Chilembwe rising of 1915. This was again based on an African desire to be left alone to run their own churches, combined with resentment against certain aspects of white rule in Malawi. John Chilembwe was a mission-educated Yao who had been to the United States with a radical preacher called Joseph Booth. He formed the Providence Industrial Mission in the Chiradzulu area, tried to persuade other Africans to join him in a single pro-African church, and for some years lived peacefully with his followers, running schools and working hard to grow crops.

It is not clear what made Chilembwe suddenly turn to violence. The rising may have been yet another protest against taxation by the whites or against Africans having to fight for the whites in the First World War. It may have been part of a personal vendetta between Chilembwe and the manager of the Bruce estates at Chiradzulu, W. J. Livingstone. Chilembwe seems to have wanted to become a martyr to the cause of African freedom: 'We must strike a blow and die,' he said, knowing the futility of his rising.

The rising began on 23 January 1915. Chilembwe sent men to Magomero, Mwanje and Blantyre to get arms and ammunition. The men sent to Blantyre failed to break into the armoury of the African Lakes Company but the other two groups attacked the settlements at Magomero and Mwanje, killing

Letter from Charles Domingo to Joseph Booth, 17 March, 1912. Joseph Booth had a large influence in Malawi in the early years of the twentieth century

Chilembwe baptising at Mbombwe, about 1910

Rhodesia Native regiment on a route march through Harare (Salisbury) during the First World War

W. J. Livingstone and his assistant, Duncan MacCormick; on Chilembwe's instructions their families were spared. On 24 January the insurgents set fire to the mission at Nguludi. The whites had by now formed a constabulary. They attacked Nbombwe mission where Chilembwe was hiding. He escaped but was later caught in the Mlanje area and shot dead. His followers were either shot trying to escape, executed, or sentenced to long terms of imprisonment. John Chilembwe became a symbol for later resistance movements. As Orton Chirwa said of him: 'He struggled almost in solitude for his people, determined to lay down his life as a price for human life and liberty.'

PART VIII
Colonial Rule in Central Africa II

30 Development and underdevelopment in Central Africa

Self-government enabled the whites to control the supply of African labour. In the early years labour was mostly used in the mines which were owned by outside companies. The settlers used their power to tax profits on minerals and some of this money was used to aid their own agricultural industry.

The value of gold mined in Zimbabwe increased from £36 000 in 1900 to £6 900 000 in 1940. Gold was the backbone of the economy; it helped the whites to finance their agricultural development. Other minerals mined in Zimbabwe included chrome, zinc, tin, iron, nickel and limestone. Asbestos mining started at Shabani in 1908 and Zimbabwe became the world's third biggest producer. Coal was exported to the copper mines of Zambia and Zaire. In 1949 beryllium was found in the Bikita district and Zimbabwe became the world's second biggest producer. These mining operations needed a lot of labour. The whites imposed a tax system to force the Africans to work in the mines. In other parts of Central Africa taxing Africans was a way of getting government revenue. In Zimbabwe the government had other sources of revenue such as land sales and mining royalties, but they still taxed the Africans to force them to work.

At first the Shona were able to raise their tax money by selling maize, millet, potatoes, rice and vegetables to those who were working in the mines or on the farms; thus they avoided having to work there themselves. The few Shona who did work at the mines did so only for three months at a time, just long enough to earn their tax money. The Ndebele, whose economy had been ruined by the wars of 1893 and 1896, found it more difficult to raise money in this way, and half of them had to work for whites.

The whites were still dissatisfied with the amount of labour they were getting. In 1902 the Chamber of Mines asked the BSA Company to raise the tax to £2. This was not allowed, but in 1904 the tax was fixed at £1. Anyone who failed to pay had to work for the whites for four months. The higher tax made it more difficult for the Shona to raise enough money by selling crops. Africans were now being forced into the Reserves, where they could not raise money by selling crops. More of them had to work in the mines. Yet even now the whites were not satisfied and they persuaded migrant workers to come from Malawi, Zambia and Zaire to the extent that there were soon more migrant workers working in Zimbabwe than there were Zimbabwean workers.

The whites did not think of taxing themselves until 1918, even though their salaries would have justified it more than African salaries did. The disparity between white and African salaries was enormous. Even in the 1960s white mineworkers earned twelve times as much as Africans and white farmworkers twenty times as much. The Africans began to look for ways of opposing, or even ending white rule in Central Africa.

Economic underdevelopment of the Africans and white development were most obvious in agriculture. After 1923 the land problem got worse. The Carter Land Commission, appointed to study the

Asbestos miners in Zimbabwe, 1928

British South Africa Company hut tax tokens, 1903–1916

land question, heard African complaints about having poor or insufficient land. The government's answer was the notorious Land Apportionment Act of 1931 which divided Zimbabwe into white and African areas and allocated to Zimbabweans only thirty-one per cent of their own country. More than a quarter of a million Africans were now forced to join the half million already in the Reserves. In the Reserves conditions deteriorated. There was a decline in crop production. For generations Africans had avoided soil erosion by practising 'shifting cultivation' and by using the hoe to break up the ground. Now they were forced to use the same land over and over again, which led to soil exhaustion and erosion. There was a high population rate increase among Africans already crowded in the Reserves. Yet another problem was cattle. By 1938 there were too many cattle in the Reserves. The whites asked the Africans to destroy their cattle, but the Africans refused, pointing out that overstocking was the result of the creation of the Reserves. It angered Africans that many white ranches adjoining the Reserves were still not being farmed, whilst Africans had nowhere to graze their cattle. They wanted this unused land opened up for their own cattle.

The whites used their political power to help white farmers but not Africans. White farmers could get easy loans from the Land Bank and advice on crops and soils from the Department of Agriculture. Laws were passed to protect white farmers from African competition, for instance in the selling of maize.

Zambia

After 1924 the British government decided that Zambia should, after all, become a settler colony. One Governor of Zambia, Sir Herbert Stanley, had worked in Zimbabwe and was influenced by the settler mentality. Stanley marked out huge areas of land along the line-of-rail as white farms: these farms were close to markets, which gave the whites an advantage over Africans. Africans were pushed into Reserves which were set up along the line-of-rail and at Abercorn and Chipata. These Reserves were on inhospitable terrain including swamp and barren mountainside. They had poor soils which were soon eroded because 'shifting cultivation' could no longer be practised. Food shortages soon occurred especially among the Lamba, Mambwe, Ngoni, Chewa and plateau Tonga.

As the copper industry grew in the 1920s and 1930s, some Zambians were able to sell food to the miners. The Tonga, Lamba and Lenje people sold maize and others who lived by rivers or lakes sold fish. On the other hand the copper industry drained labour away from the rural areas, leaving only women and children, or the aged and disabled, to work in the villages. This naturally increased the food shortages.

The Zambian copper industry
Copper mining became the main activity of white people in Zambia. There has been a big demand for copper throughout the twentieth century. Before the First World War, the demand for copper was for such things as telegraph wires, submarine cables, electric trams and lights. Later, the many wars fought in the century fueled the demand for copper to use in weaponry.

The earliest prospecting in Zambia was carried out by companies associated with the BSA Company. One company, the Zambezi Exploring Company, was given half a million hectares of land near

Copper miners at work in Zambia, early in the twentieth century

the source of the Kafue. Other companies discovered the Kansanshi, Sable Antelope and Silver King mines but they were unproductive. Yet another, the Bechuanaland Exploration Company, sent an agent into Lamba country where he found copper at Ndola's village and renamed the area Bwana Mkubwa. He then found Africans using malachite ore in the Kopopo area and named the area Roan Antelope, and finally discovered the copper deposits at Chambeshi. These early prospectors faced problems: they had little capital and found it difficult to get machinery from Britain and coal from Zimbabwe; they had to waste much time cutting wood. In fact for some years lead and zinc from Kabwe were more important than copper.

In the 1920s the BSA Company gave concessions only to companies willing to spend a minimum amount on their prospecting. The prospecting was now done mainly by South African prospectors who made aerial surveys and discovered rich sulphide ores which had three times the copper content of the oxide ores and were cheaper to work. At Nchanga both types of ore were found: oxide in the swamp and sulphide 180 metres below the surface. Sulphide ores were treated by a flotation process discovered in 1911.

By 1929, the smaller companies had merged into two powerful groups: the Rhodesian Anglo-American Company financed from Britain and South Africa and the Rhodesian Selection Trust financed mainly from the United States. There was now a big demand for copper in the motor-car industry and prices were high; capital came pouring into the Copperbelt and both the European and African population increased.

In 1929 there was a world monetary crisis. Copper prices fell suddenly. The copper market disappeared. The Copperbelt, already over-producing, was badly hit. In eighteen months the African population of the Copperbelt dropped from 32000 to 9000 and Europeans also left the area. The railway ran at a loss; trade with South Africa came to a halt. The only good feature of the period was that because of the reduced population, housing could be improved and Copperbelt towns were set free from the malarial mosquito.

After the Depression, the Copperbelt became a low-cost producer of good sulphide ores. White copper miners in Zambia had an advantage over their competitors in the United States in that they were able to use the Africans as cheap labour. There was now a market in Britain as the British government was preparing for World War II. Zambia's copper exports rose from £4 million in 1935 to £10 million in 1939. In the Second World War exports rose still further and by 1945 Zambia was producing an eighth of the non-communist world's copper.

After the war there were new problems. Because of war-time conditions it had been difficult to replace worn-out machinery. When the war ended there was a fall-off in demand. In 1950 the Korean War boosted demand again and by 1957 Zambia was second only to the United States as a copper producer. The biggest mines now were at Nchanga, Mufulira, Rhokana and Roan Antelope, and new mines were opened at Bancroft and Chibuluma.

Copper accounted for seventy per cent of Zambia's revenue. Because of this, Zambia's economy was subject to fluctuations in the world price of copper, which could vary from £420 to £181 a ton in just a few months. If copper became too expensive, importers turned to other minerals such as aluminium. Furthermore, much of the copper revenue did not remain in Zambia. It went overseas as profits to the copper companies, royalties to the BSA Company, and taxes to the British government. The British administration in Zambia took twelve per cent of the total profits of the copper industry in the form of taxation on the profits and on the royalties of the BSA Company, but there was no guarantee that the administration would use this money to benefit Zambians. The British government took £24 000 000 and gave back to Zambia in the form of development grants a mere £136 000: 0.056 of its total revenue from the copper industry.

The wealth and job opportunities created by the copper industry were not equally distributed between whites and Africans or between the Copperbelt and the rest of Zambia. The Copperbelt became a wealthy enclave in a country ridden with rural poverty. Zambians who learned skills on the Copperbelt could not use them elsewhere: the copper industry did not create offshoot industries in other parts of Zambia. The government's insensitivity to the problem was shown in 1957 when it allocated only 17 per cent of its development plan to the rural areas.

Malawi

Malawi's economic development was neglected by the British. The country simply remained as a supplier of cheap labour to Zimbabwe, Zambia and South Africa throughout the colonial period. The colonial government did little to develop the few minerals Malawi had, such as bauxite in Mt. Mlanje and asbestos, mica and corundum in the Nchen district. Because there were few minerals to export, the government was slow to build a railway to

A tea estate in Malawi

Malawi: the line from Beira was not completed until 1935.

There was some interest shown in cash crops – coffee, tea, tobacco and cotton. But nearly all the plantations were situated in the southern tip of the country – the Shire Valley and Highlands. The people who benefited were the white plantation owners. By the beginning of the twentieth century, 7000 hectares were under coffee cultivation. Such large scale production was encouraged by a spate of good prices in the United Kingdom. But towards the outbreak of the First World War, coffee production declined drastically in Malawi. For instance, coffee exports fell from 907 tonnes in 1900 to 45 tonnes in 1915 ending up at 15 tonnes in 1927. Low wages which made labour unstable, drought, lack of fertilizers and poor quality of seeds, all worked against coffee growing in Malawi.

Tea proved a little more stable as a cash crop than coffee. In 1938 four and a quarter million kilogrammes of tea were being exported from Malawi and this increased to seven million kilogrammes in 1950. But the tea industry was owned entirely by white planters and was therefore of little benefit to the Africans. It was also confined to the south in the Mlanje and Thylo areas.

Africans took an interest in growing tobacco and cotton. By 1914 Africans were producing 1100 tonnes of cotton for the British market. They also began growing tobacco for the British market: by 1926 1800 tonnes of tobacco were being grown. This sudden encouragement of African farmers, albeit motivated by a demand for tropical products in Britain, was never a wholehearted policy of the British government. The government could never decide whether Africans could be trusted to grow all the crops Britain needed from Malawi, or whether whites should not be encouraged to go to Malawi to grow them instead. After the Second World War both policies were followed in harness.

Although there was little mining in Malawi, Malawis were still needed as mineworkers in other countries, so they were taxed like other Central Africans to make them work. A few, mainly Tonga, worked for planters, but most worked in the mines of South Africa, Zimbabwe or Zambia. Between 1903 and 1907 the Witwatersrand Native Labour Association or 'Wenela', recruited some seven thousand Malawis to work in South Africa. This recruiting was then stopped, but Malawi nevertheless became the biggest supplier of labour in Central Africa.

This 'migrant labour' had a serious effect on Malawi society. By 1938 nearly twenty per cent of Malawis were out of the country and many of them had not been heard of since 1930; these were the *machona*, the lost ones. Their loss was severely felt in the villages, where no-one was left to do heavy work such as cutting trees, digging gardens, repairing buildings and carrying out the practice of *chitemene*. The migrant labourers themselves lived in poor conditions. They were treated harshly, paid low wages, and given poor houses with little sanitation. They had no medical services and many of them, including ten percent of those recruited by 'Wenela', died in epidemics. Because of these poor conditions, many workers stayed in the mine compounds for only a few months at a time, just long enough to earn their tax money and buy goods for their families.

31 The growth of African opposition

Causes of opposition in Zimbabwe
Africans in Zimbabwe had many grievances against white rule, many of which must now be obvious from the discussions in the previous chapters. In 1929 the Chief Native Commissioner observed that Africans suffered from economic stagnation. Consumer goods were scarce. Prices were high; they were geared to the white economy in which wages were far higher than in the African sector. Education was poor; Africans were educated for specific jobs. There was overcrowding in the reserves caused by a population increase and by effects of the Land Apportionment Act.

Land was indeed a big grievance. The Carter Land Commission appointed to hear evidence on the land issue, discovered in 1925 that the African community was unanimous in its demand for more land. But when the Land Apportionment Act was passed it still left the Africans with very little land. Africans were also against the Maize Control Board which discriminated against their maize on the market. The overstocking of cattle in the Reserves was by 1938 another great problem. Faced with underused white ranches the Africans were unwilling to heed the whites' calls to destroy some of their own cattle.

In 1929, at a meeting of Africans to attack the Land Apportionment Bill, some Shona delegates attacked the education system, which provided more schools for whites than for blacks. This scarcity of education meant that in an electorate of 54 000 only 400 Africans could meet the financial and educational requirements for voting. Clearly then African opposition to white rule was deeply rooted in their economic underdevelopment.

Growth of political and trade union movements in Zimbabwe
Because of the poor education system for Africans in Zimbabwe, political leadership often came from immigrants such as the black South Africans, Abraham Twala and Martha Ngano, who in 1923 helped to form the Rhodesian Bantu Voters' Association. The RBVA was an important step towards modern politics. It brought together Africans from different regional and ethnic backgrounds to discuss national issues, and it appealed to ordinary people by focusing on grievances such as land shortages, destocking and poor education.

Another important development in the 1920s was the formation of the first African trade union, the Industrial and Commercial Workers' Union (ICU), formed by Robert Sambo, a Malawian. The ICU had its origins south of the Limpopo in South Africa. Sambo was deported, but the South African trade union leader Clements Kadalie, who headed the ICU, wrote to the white Prime Minister: 'In spite of your ban, we shall find means, as we have done in the past, to get our message to our fellow-workers, and we shall find men and women to ... uphold ... freedom from all forms of oppression.' The ICU tried to organise both urban and rural workers and to overcome ethnic differences; the Shona leader Masoja Ndhlovu worked among the Ndebele, the Ndebele leader Charles Mzingeli, among the Shona. The ICU held weekend meetings in Salisbury and Bulawayo to attack white policies. Its effectiveness was however limited by its unwillingness to strike and by the imprisonment of many of its leaders.

In the 1930s more educated Zimbabweans took up roles in politics. They were aware of both urban and rural grievances but were as yet unable to translate their ideas into the form of a national mass party. The Southern Rhodesia ANC, formed by Aaron Jacha in 1934, was a moderate, middle class body of African teachers, ministers and clerks. It did not appeal to the mass of Africans living in the townships or the Reserves. After four years in existence it still had only 150 members. Its effect was also limited by its unwillingness to use other than constitutional means to oppose such manifestations of white rule as the pass laws and the Maize Control Act. The ANC was, nevertheless, a good training

Founder members of the Southern Rhodesia Bantu Congress, Bulawayo, in 1935

ground for African political leaders such as Joshua Nkomo and Rev. Samkange.

Causes of opposition in Zambia

As in Zimbabwe, Africans in Zambia had to put up with low wages, poor housing and education, a high cost of living and a colour bar imported from South Africa. Most Africans earned less than £1 a month in the 1930s and mineworkers' wages actually went down at one point. Because of low wages, Africans could not afford the high prices charged in shops or the high rents charged for land; at Choma the rent was £5 for just over 4 hectares. African housing was a disgrace. Europeans still thought Africans would not stay long in the towns and did not therefore need good houses. Yet at Ndola more than half the Africans said they intended to remain. Lusaka was planned as a garden city for the whites, with fine government buildings on the Ridgeway, but African compounds were located in swampy ground a long way from their places of work. The Lusaka City Council did not build houses for Africans until 1945.

Education for Africans was almost non-existent. The government saw no point in educating Africans as they were not allowed to play any political role or take skilled jobs. The only schools were those run by the missionaries. The government spent only a fraction of its income on education. Until 1930 the only government-built school was the Barotse School, built in 1906. The first junior secondary school, Munali, was not opened until 1939. A trades school was opened in 1932 but by 1948 it still had only seventy pupils. There was little point in Africans attending a trades school when they could

The first trades school at Sefula

Mufulira copper mine

not become industrial apprentices. In 1948 only $4\frac{1}{2}$ per cent of the government's revenue was spent on education and by 1953 this had been reduced to zero. Because of this inadequate funding, most Zambian children had to leave school before they had learned anything. In 1942 there were 86 300 Zambian children in school, but only 3000 of them were in fifth grade and only 45 were in secondary school.

Worse still was the colour bar. Africans were kept out of shops, hotels, clubs, cinemas, and swimming baths. It was socially unacceptable for Africans to walk on the pavement with whites or address them in familiar terms. In these circumstances, it is not surprising that Zambians, like their fellow-blacks in Zimbabwe, began to look for ways of opposing and ending white rule.

African politics in the Copperbelt
The growth of towns gave nationalism a boost. The Copperbelt towns attracted people from all over Zambia. These people became united by the common problems of the towns. Leaders emerged through whom the people could express their grievances. Migrant labourers carried this new political consciousness to other parts of the country.

Even so, real unity was slow in coming. This was due partly to the regional nature of some Zambian organisations and partly to the attitude of the colonial government. In 1933 there was an attempt to form a United Welfare Association of Northern Rhodesia. This came to nothing because the government refused to recognise it and because there was not the will among the people to make it a success. Most Zambians still thought in regional or ethnic terms: the Northern Rhodesia African National Congress formed in 1937 was, despite its grandiose title, essentially a Tonga organisation protesting about Tonga grievances.

In the Copperbelt towns, the colonial government and the mineowners refused to deal with the new political organisations. They preferred to deal with so-called 'Tribal Elders' appointed at the mine compounds. Africans were told to express their grievances, if they had any, 'in a reasonable manner' through these puppet-like government trustees. By denying Africans the right to choose their own leaders, the government and mineowners hoped to prevent Africans from forming trade unions, which would be a real economic threat to the mineowners who were using the Africans as cheap labour.

In 1935 the African workers ignored the 'Tribal Elders' and went on strike in Mufulira, Nkana and Roan Antelope. Yet still the government would deal only with the 'Tribal Elders', who were given the right to nominate members to so-called 'Urban

The headgear at Roan Antelope copper mine where miners went on strike in 1935

Advisory Councils'. In 1940 the Africans again went on strike for higher wages. In the disturbances, seventeen Africans were killed and sixty-nine wounded. The government now applied the time-honoured method of 'divide and rule'. Some Africans with greater responsibilities were given a wage increase so that they would lose interest in the plight of their more lowly-paid mates.

By 1942 Welfare Societies were being formed in the towns under the leadership of clerks and foremen. They were responsible for many local improvements. At Luanshya the Welfare Society was formed by Dauti Yamba; it contained people from both the mine compound and the municipal township, and persuaded the mining company to build a road between the two. Dauti Yamba visited South Africa and was impressed by the strength of the African Congress there; he dreamed of a similar movement in Zambia. In 1946 he formed the Federation of Welfare Societies. This was 'the first time an unofficial body of Africans had met together to discuss their problems at (national) level.' It was the beginning of a real nationalist movement in Zambia.

Dauti Yamba, founder of the Federation of Welfare Societies, 1951

Blantyre railway station. The train was for migrant workers journeying to Zimbabwe

Causes of opposition in Malawi

One of the biggest problems in Malawi was still migrant labour. Thousands were leaving the country to work on the Witwatersrand or the Copperbelt. A commission of enquiry in 1937 estimated that 18.3 per cent of the male population was out of the country, and that a quarter of them, the *machona* or the lost ones, had not been heard of since 1930.

In other respects, Malawi suffered in much the same ways as Zambia. Although Malawi did not have large numbers of whites, those who were in Malawi treated the Malawis with the same colonial condescension as the whites of Zimbabwe and Zambia. Malawis had to raise their hats to the whites but did not get the same courtesy in return. Whites overworked their Malawi staffs, did not provide housing or pensions, and often refused passes to leave the country. The colonial government provided little African education: even in 1948 it allocated only $3\frac{3}{4}$ per cent of its development funds to the education of Malawis. All these social injustices contributed to the dislike of white rule which Malawis shared with their fellow-blacks in Zimbabwe and Zambia.

Friction was increased by the land problem. One aspect of this was the immigration, mainly into the Mlanje area, of Mukua-Lomwe peoples from Mozambique. Though they were escaping the harshness of the Portuguese regime in Mozambique, they only added to the overcrowding already prevalent in Malawi. Many of them, without land rights of their own, simply became squatters on European farms. Another aspect of the land problem was that after the 1939–45 war Britain faced a food shortage, she tried to force Malawi farmers to produce more food for Britain. A National Resources Ordinance to this effect was passed in 1946 and was extended in 1949 and 1952. African farmers resented this interference in their methods, and chiefs such as Phillip Gomani at Ncheu instructed their people to disobey. In 1950, 7 per cent of Malawi was given to whites as 'Public Land.' Africans could be evicted from it under the thangata system; this caused great bitterness.

Forms of opposition in Malawi

After the First World War, Chilembwe's Providence Industrial Mission was refounded by Dr Malekebu and other separatist churches were

171

formed. In the Central Province there was Hanock Phiri's branch of the African Methodist Episcopal Curch; in the North Province, the African Reformed Prebysterian Church and the Church of the Black People of Africa (Mpingo wa Afipa wa Africa). The aim of these separatist churches was to improve African conditions and set up African schools, which the colonial government seemed reluctant to do. Unlike the prophets of Watch Tower, the leaders of the separatist churches were moderate, educated men like Mwase and Chinula.

Other avenues of protest in Malawi were Native Associations and Tribal Councils. The first Native Association was formed at Karonga in 1912 with the encouragement of Dr Laws. Others included the West Nyasa Native Association formed among the Tonga in 1914, the Mombera Native Association among the Ngoni in 1920 and some in the Southern Province. The members of the Native Associations were educated men – clerks, evangelists, teachers – and their aims were moderate. They did not want the British to leave, but wanted them to govern Malawi more fairly: to provide schools, roads and postal services; to end the social inferiority of the African. The methods of the Native Associations were moderate too: they used petitions, not violence. Levi Mumba said that the Chilembwe rising had been the wrong method because it was unconstitutional. The reward for all this patience on the part of the Native Associations was that the colonial government continued to take no notice of them.

Tribal Councils seemed an unlikely avenue for protest. In Malawi as elsewhere in Central Africa, the chiefs were used as part of the government system and were thought unlikely to criticise it. The Tribal Councils did, however, work closely with the Native Associations, and became an outlet for grievances, especially those connected with education. The Councils condemned mission schools for taking only selected pupils. In 1932 they demanded better educational facilities including a government high school. Like the demands of the Native Associations, those of the Tribal Councils met with a stony silence on the part of the colonial government.

PART IX
The Shadow of Federation

32 The shadow falls

In the 1930s many white settlers wanted to 'amalgamate' Zambia and Zimbabwe into one country. There were economic and political reasons for this. In the early 1930s the settlers in Zambia wanted to share in the profits of the Zimbabwe goldfields; later, when copper was more profitable than gold, they also wanted to share in the profits of the Zambian copper mines. As one settler put it, Zambia was 'a huge copper mine whose potential millions could swell the Southern Rhodesian revenues'. The settlers in Zimbabwe also wanted to make more use of Zambian labour. As one of them said, 'Northern Rhodesia's only value to Southern Rhodesia is as a big native reserve of cheap labour,' a comment which sums up the attitude of many white settlers to the black people of Central Africa.

Politically, the settlers argued that they were defending English-style liberalism against the racist doctrines of the Afrikaners in South Africa. It was true that the English-speaking settlers in Zimbabwe were not as overtly racist as their counterparts in South Africa, but it was a matter of degree, and it did not follow that the Africans would be better off if the settlers were allowed to dominate the whole of English-speaking Central Africa.

Not all settlers wanted to amalgamate. Colonel Stewart Gore-Browne, a settler in Zambia, said that Zambia should remain under the protection of the British government, which had at least taken on the responsibility of looking after African interests, which the settlers had not. The settlers in eastern Zambia, who exported their tobacco through Malawi, were more interested in co-operating with Malawi than with Zimbabwe. The Hilton Young Commission of 1938 said that if Zambia joined with anybody, it should be Malawi, not Zimbabwe, and that both Zambia and Malawi should co-operate with British colonies in East Africa. This terrified the settlers in Zimbabwe. They were filled with dread at the thought of co-operation between the 'black' colonies to the north of them.

Even the British government was opposed to amalgamation. When in 1931 the settlers demanded a conference to discuss amalgamation, the British Colonial Secretary in the then Labour government, J. H. Thomas, refused; Thomas did not want Zambians to fall under the sway of settlers in Zimbabwe. The settlers protested and held unofficial conferences at Victoria Falls. Their protestations got them nowhere. The Bledisloe Commission of 1938 reiterated that there could be no amalgamation until the settlers' policies on Africans were in line with those of the British government – and that meant never. The Bledisloe Commission pointed out that there were relatively few settlers in Zambia, so it would be unjust to the Africans to hand over power to the settlers there. African opposition to amalgamation was, said the Commission, 'a factor that cannot be ignored.' This was true: Africans in Zambia knew that if amalgamation took place, Zimbabwe would be the leading partner and the settlers' ideas of racial segregation would be extended to Zambia.

Events over the next fifteen years, however,

moved against the Africans and in favour of the settlers. During the Second World War there was closer co-operation among all three territories, Malawi as well as Zambia and Zimbabwe. An inter-territorial Secretariat was set up, and in 1945 a Central African Council, made up of the three governors and a politician from each territory. This body met twice a year to co-ordinate such matters as migrant labour; it helped to attune the British government to the idea of greater co-operation among the three territories.

After the Second World War the South African government introduced the system of *apartheid* (separation of the races) which gave credibility to the propaganda of white politicians such as Welensky and Huggins that there should be an English-speaking Dominion in Central Africa. In reality it was not the Afrikaners that Huggins and Welensky feared; it was the Africans. The Africans were by now forming trade unions and political parties; they were demanding a greater share in the running of their own countries. Huggins and Welensky wanted to enshrine white rule in Central Africa before the Africans insisted on African rule.

The economic arguments used by the settlers were, after the Second World War, more persuasive than ever. The Copperbelt was now finding it difficult to supply all its power needs; it could not afford all the coal and wood it required and it would benefit from a big hydro-electric scheme. Electricity was also needed for domestic use. The use of electricity had increased five-fold between 1940 and 1950. Railways were needed to supplement the outdated single-track lines to Capetown, Beira and Lobito Bay. Only a bigger economic unit in Central Africa would, so the settlers contended, attract the capital needed to develop these projects. Big business was in favour of joining the three territories together. The theory was that Malawian and Zambian labour would work the Zambian copper mines and the Zimbabwean industries, and the capital thus created would be used to develop the Zimbabwean industries. These would have ready-made markets in Britain and the enlarged Central African Dominion, to which white people would be attracted in droves.

The settlers realised that the British government would never agree to outright amalgamation, so they now demanded 'Federation'. In a Federation, each member state keeps some powers and hands over others to a central 'Federal' government. The settlers hoped that by leaving the British administrations in Zambia and Malawi with some of their powers, they would convince the British govern-

Huggins and Welensky, white politicians who wanted an English-speaking Dominion in Central Africa

ment that African interests would be protected. The settlers held a conference at Victoria Falls in 1949 to which no Africans were invited. It was here that Huggins and Welensky convinced the settlers that Federation, not amalgamation, was the answer. They now had to convince the British government.

The Colonial Secretary in the British Labour government at that time was Creech-Jones, and he was not to be convinced. Like J. H. Thomas before him, Creech-Jones respected the African wishes not to be part of any Federation. Unfortunately for the Africans, Creech-Jones was replaced by the less idealistic James Griffiths, who agreed that Federation should be looked into as a matter of urgency. Griffiths visited Central Africa and called another conference at Victoria Falls. Here he agreed that the settlers could have Federation on one condition: there should be 'partnership' between the settlers and the Africans.

This word 'partnership' became the theme-song of the British government. It was a word with which the British government could salve its conscience.

Three Colonial Secretaries: Creech-Jones (Labour); James Griffiths (Labour) and Oliver Lyttleton (Conservative)

As Griffiths defined it, partnership meant that Africans would 'take their full part with the rest of the community in the economic life of the territory.' African interests were no longer 'paramount' as in the earlier Passfield Memorandum. Welensky defined partnership a different way: the African, he said, 'can never hope to dominate the partnership.' The partnership was like that of a rider and his horse, the African being the horse. The African viewpoint was summed up by Robinson Nabulyato: 'Partnership is a ladder for Europeans to climb on us.'

In 1951 the Conservative Party was returned to power in Britain under Winston Churchill, who had made known his views on respecting the wishes of colonial peoples by opposing self-government for India despite the overwhelming desire for self-government by the Indian people. Churchill was not the man to stand in the way of Federation just because Africans did not want it. Nor was Churchill's Colonial Secretary, Oliver Lyttleton, who immediately said that Federation would be in the best interests of everyone in Central Africa, African as well as white.

Hell-bent on Federation, the Conservative government called a conference in London in 1952 to discuss the Federal constitution. It then sent a Conservative politician to Central Africa to see how the Africans liked the idea; this man reported, predictably, that most Africans had no objections and that the only opposition came from a handful of 'extremists'. Where now was the Bledisloe Report, which had said, 'African opinion is a factor that cannot be ignored?' The Conservative government had heard only what it wanted to hear. It called yet another conference in London to finalise the constitution.

The constitution provided for a Federal parliament of thirty-six M.P.s: eighteen from Zimbabwe, eleven from Zambia, seven from Malawi. Of these thirty-six only six would be Africans – so much for 'partnership'. There would also be three white M.P.s to look after African affairs: the whites had decided that Africans needed white men to speak up for them. The three white spokesmen plus three of the African M.P.s would sit on a so-called 'African Affairs Board' whose job was to examine legislation that might be unfair to Africans: it could theoretically veto such legislation, but since its veto could be set aside by the Governor-General or the British government, it was not much use.

The Federal parliament would control finance, trade, communication, industry and defence. The territories would control local government, African education, land, agriculture and health. 60 per cent of the income tax revenue would go to Zimbabwe, only 17 per cent each to Zambia and Malawi. The Federal capital would be Salisbury, the capital of 'Southern Rhodesia'. Salisbury became known to the Africans as *Bamba Zonke* which means 'Take All'.

The Federal constitution was approved by the British government, by the whites in Zimbabwe, by the Malawi Legislative Council (whereupon the African members, led by Henry Chipembere, walked out) and by the Zambian Legislative Council, seventeen votes to four. The four who voted against were the two African members and

*Bamba Zonke (*Take All*); Harare during the Federal years*

the two whites responsible for African affairs, Sir John Moffat and Rev. E. H. Nightingale, who said that Federation should not be forced on Africans against their wishes : these were voices crying in the wilderness.

Federation came into existence in October 1953. In the election of January 1954 the white Federal Party won a big majority and its leader, Godfrey Huggins, became Federal Prime Minister. For Huggins at least, Federation was a dream come true. The Confederation Party, whose policies included the South African doctrine of *apartheid*, won only one seat, but as an ominous sign of the future, it polled one-third of the votes in Zimbabwe.

33 African opposition to Federation

Federation was a bitter blow to Africans generally and to the growing African nationalist movement in particular. The nationalist movement had made good progress, partly because of the Second World War which had, all over the world, led to a weakening of colonial power and an awareness on the part of colonial peoples that if they were prepared to 'fight for their freedom' as James Sangala called on Malawians to do in 1943, they might just win it. Africans had fought in the war in India and Burma, Ethiopia and Madagascar; they had come home with a broader outlook, an awareness of the value of education, a new sense of urgency, a greater unity and military discipline. They would no longer put up with the tardiness of the colonial government in improving African conditions. They wanted to improve those conditions themselves. They wanted to form political parties and trade unions. Ultimately, they wanted to run their own countries.

Before the shadow of Federation fell across the land, there had been real political progress in all three territories. In Malawi the organisations connected with African welfare banded together in 1944 to form the Nyasaland African Congress. This body contained less ministers of the church than the pre-war Native Associations and more businessmen and civil servants. It was mainly located in the heavily-populated south. Its aims, as enunciated by Charles Matinga, were radical: they included African majorities on the Legislative Council and Township Management and Land Boards, an end to racialist practices in the towns, the recognition of rural grievances, more government aid to Africans and an expensive education programme. Membership of the Congress was extended to Malawians working in Zambia and the leaders made contact with Dr Kamuzu Banda, a highly-educated Malawian living in London. In 1948 Malawi's first trade union, the Association of African Motor Transport Workers, was formed.

In Zimbabwe too political parties were more radical than in pre-war years. They included the revived ANC, the Urban Welfare Association in Bulawayo, which attracted younger men who later joined even more radical parties, and the African Voice Association led by Benjamin Burombo, which was associated with the 1945 railway strike and united those urban Africans exasperated by low wages and poor conditions. Zimbabwean leaders were emerging who would no longer put up with the injustices of settler rule: among them were Charles Mzingeli, Stanlake Samkange, Enoch Dumbutshena, and Joshua Nkomo, now General-Secretary of the Railway African Workers Union and President of the Trades Union Congress.

In Zambia, the first political party, the Northern Rhodesia African Congress, was formed in 1948 at a meeting of the Federation of Welfare Societies at Munali School. The first Congress leader was the moderate Godwin Lewanika, a member of the Lozi royal family, and support came mainly from civil servants. Congress was not yet a mass movement, though younger men like Simon Kapwepwe helped to get support in the provinces. Kenneth Kaunda, who had joined the Mufulira Welfare Society in 1947, now went back to Chinsali and turned the local Welfare Association into a branch of Congress. He toured large areas on his bicycle and told Africans they were 'human beings as good or bad as any man.' This was the beginning of Kaunda's philosophy of humanism, which was to become the cornerstone of Zambian society.

The British Labour government sent out a trade union leader named Comrie to advise Africans. This led to the formation in 1948 of the Copperbelt Shop Assistants Union and in 1949 of the African Mineworkers Union which, under the leadership of Lawrence Katilungu, staged a long strike that brought copper production to a standstill. By 1954 75 per cent of African mineworkers on the Copperbelt were members of the Mineworkers Union.

White reaction to this growing African political activity varied with the nature of the government in

Police reservists and regulars watch a mass meeting at Bulawayo during the workers strike, 1948

each territory. In Malawi and Zambia, African political activity brought some reward as the British administrations there were committed to advancing Africans, even if more slowly than Africans wanted. In Zambia, the mineworkers' strike led to an African pay increase. In Malawi, the first African was appointed to the Legislative Council in 1949 and more were added in the 1950s. Two of the first to be elected were the 'Young Turks', Henry Chipembere and Kanyama Chiume, then in their mid-20s and known for their radical views on the future of Malawi.

In Zimbabwe on the other hand African political activity brought little reward. This was because Zimbabwe was ruled by the settlers, not by the British government. The settlers had not taken any responsibility for advancing Africans politically, economically or in any other way. They had no intention of giving way to African demands, however politely put. Instead of seeing African political activity as a sign that conditions needed improving, the settlers reacted with unpopular legislation like the Urban Areas Act of 1948, which provoked strong protest among Africans in Bulawayo. The white Prime Minister Huggins decreed that Africans in the towns must be tightly controlled: in 1951 he passed legislation that forced Africans to be registered and made regulations concerning their living standards. Huggins was trying to demonstrate that the whites were still running Zimbabwe. It came as a big relief to Huggins and the other settlers when the British government finally agreed to Federation: it would now be easier, so the settlers thought, to crush African resistance.

The new African political movements strove desperately to prevent Federation. It was hardly surprising that Africans did not want a Federation based on white supremacy, since there were eight million Africans in Central Africa and less than a quarter of a million whites; one white to forty Africans. The Africans, especially in Zambia and Malawi, felt that the British government had let them down, betrayed them to the settlers, and forgotten the principle of 'trusteeship' or protection of African interests implied in the Passfield Memorandum.

In Zambia, a group of young men at Ndola formed an Anti-Federation Committee. Its chairman was Justin Chimba, its secretary, Simon Zucas, and other members included Reuben Kamanga and Nephas Tembo. The Committee campaigned against Federation through such publications as *The Freedom Newsletter* and *A Case Against Federation*. The Northern Rhodesia African Congress was no longer led by the moderate Lewanika but by Harry Nkumbula, who was noted for his hostility to Federation. As early as 1942 Nkumbula had opposed the suggested 'amalgamation' of Zambia and Zimbabwe and in 1949, with Dr Banda of Malawi, Nkumbula had signed a memorandum attacking the proposed Federation. From its headquarters at Chilenje in Lusaka and through branches in the rural areas, Congress became for the first time a mass movement. In 1952 it formed a

Supreme Action Council with powers to call a general strike. One member of the Council was Kenneth Kaunda, now organising secretary in the Northern Province. Committees were formed to raise funds and delegates were sent to Britain to get support. Nkumbula burned the proposed Federal constitution. A national 'day of prayer' was declared, when no African was to work for a European. This failed because the copper companies said that anyone who did not work would be dismissed. In 1953 120 Zambian chiefs, including the Bemba and Ngoni paramounts, signed a petition against Federation. This led to the Mambwe chief being deposed and the Ushi and Bisa chiefs suspended.

In Malawi too there was widespread opposition to Federation. The Malawi chiefs feared that Federation would rob them of their powers. Malawi migrant labourers had experienced the social system in Zimbabwe – its pass laws and the lack of opportunity for Africans in skilled trades; they did not want the same system imported into Malawi. The leaders of the Nyasaland African Congress, especially Henry Chipembere and Kanyama Chiume, were outspoken in their opposition to Federation. Along with Zambian leaders, they refused to attend the London conference of 1952 which discussed the Federal constitution.

In Zimbabwe, the opposition to Federation was profound but less actively expressed, at least at first. Africans in Zimbabwe had for decades been suffering the indignities which Zambians and Malawians were now trying to fend off. To Zimbabweans, Federation would not greatly alter things: the same people – men like Huggins – would form the Federal government as they now formed the government in Zimbabwe.

Harry Nkumbula, leader of the Northern Rhodesia African Congress

African opposition was in any case to no avail. Federation was imposed in spite of it. The failure of the African political parties to prevent Federation was inevitable and no fault of their own, but they still lost credibility among their supporters. The imposition of Federation in October 1953 marked the nadir of African political fortunes in Central Africa in the post-war years.

34 The dark years in Central Africa

As the Africans had feared, white settlers in Zimbabwe reaped most of the benefits of Federation and Zambia and Malawi gained little. The main HEP project was located at Kariba in Zimbabwe, and thousands of Zambians were moved to make way for it. Kariba cost £110 million, but Malawi had to be satisfied with a proposed scheme at Nkula Falls that would cost a mere £2½ million. African political leaders rejected this outright. Malawi's contribution to the Federal economy was labour. It was not expected that Malawi would need much investment even though it had the biggest African population of the three territories. The subsidy to Malawi was only £4 million a year, and Malawi's share of development loans was only 6 per cent.

In all three territories, Africans gained little from Federation. The idea of 'partnership' was forgotten. The Federal Party made no attempt to win African support. Even the British administrations in Zambia and Malawi were afflicted by the Federal mentality. Their policy on promoting Africans was one of 'gradualism'; Africans were to be brought into the administrative system, but gradually. This fitted in nicely with the policy of the Federal regime in Salisbury.

Africans did not share in the economic boom that lasted for the first three years of Federation. They were taxed on things they bought in the shops such as clothing, footwear and dried milk, and they were charged high prices by white and Asian traders. As prices went up, so African wages came down. Godfrey Huggins had said in 1948 that 'the economic (African) wage is £5 a month and ... few natives, with their indolent habits, are worth that amount.' Now that Huggins was Federal Prime Minister, his ideas were put into practice. By 1956 the average African wage was £70 a year compared to the European average of £800, and the highest-paid African on the Copperbelt earned £540 a year compared to lowest-paid European salary of £1858.

Socially, things were no better. The Race Relations Board was ineffectual. The Moffat Resolutions of 1954 said that everyone had the right to progress according to 'character, qualifications, training, ability and education without distinction of race, colour or creed,' but these high-sounding Resolutions were never put into effect. There were many instances of racial discrimination. The Lusaka City Council tarred the road to the European hospital but not the 180 metres to the African hospital. A white man killed his African employee and was gaoled for only a year, but when an African robbed his white employer he was gaoled for five. At Ndola and Mufulira, restaurants refused to serve tea to African politicians; when they did, they charged £5. A white man set his dog on Fines Bulawayo, ANC propaganda secretary on the Copperbelt. In the notorious 'hatch' system as described by Wittington Sikalumbi. 'Africans either had to buy their often highly stinking meat at the back door of the shop or from a pigeon-hole opposite the European counter.'

The government did little for African education. As ANC pointed out, 'If the government ... had the principle of partnership at heart, it must give the Africans the same opportunity and standard of technical education and training as the Europeans ... the mass education of adults ... had been allowed to die out for lack of government support.'

The copper companies were slow in promoting Africans. The Afrikaners on the Copperbelt had brought their racial ideas with them from South Africa. The Dalgleish Commission recommended that some jobs be Africanised, but there was opposition from the white workers and the recommendation was never put into effect. The copper companies feared, however, that if they did not Africanise, the Africans themselves might Africanise – by violence. In 1955 RST and Anglo-American agreed that some jobs could be Africanised straight away and others after a period of time. To the Africans, this was too little too late.

In Zimbabwe, the position was slightly different. Here, the Africans appeared to be making some

Kariba Dam, built at a cost of £110 million

progress, but appearances were deceptive. The whites had been frightened by events in Kenya, where the 'Mau Mau' rebels had killed white people. They feared that unless they appeared to be doing something for the Africans, the same might happen in Zimbabwe. The new Prime Minister of 'Southern Rhodesia', Garfield Todd, was, by the standards of the whites, a liberal; that is, he wanted Africans to play a part in the white-run political system. In this, Todd was reflecting the views of other white 'liberals' such as David Stirling, founder of the Capricorn Africa Society, which wanted land reform, multi-racial trade unions and better representation for Africans (though not 'one man one vote' which lost Stirling support among Africans).

Todd therefore passed a string of reforms: a home ownership scheme, a multi-racial university college in the white area of Salisbury and trade union reform. Africans had never been allowed to form trade unions or even sit on the body that fixed minimum wages; after Todd's reform they could still not form trade unions but could join existing ones. The problem with all Todd's 'reforms' was that they were never put fully into practice. The government passed the legislation but the whites would not let it work. Their racial prejudices ran too deep.

All the time, African living standards were going down. There was overcrowding in the towns because of the government's harsh agricultural policy. When Huggins passed the notorious Land Husbandry Act in 1951, he said his aim was to encourage intensive farming among Africans – another way of saying that Africans must learn to live on small farms. The aim of the Land Husbandry Act was to turn the Reserves from communal areas to individual plots; its effect was to destroy the African way of life. Some Africans were given tiny plots of up to $8\frac{1}{4}$ hectares (compared to the thousands of hectares of European farms) whilst others were given nothing. They had no alternative but to drift to the towns to exacerbate the housing problem.

In these circumstances, African political parties found it very difficult to make headway. There were sporadic outbursts of anger like the disturbances in the Cholo district of Malawi in 1953 in which eleven Africans were killed and seventy-two injured. The younger leaders battled hard to maintain the unity created by the anti-Federation struggle of the early 1950s: as Nephas Tembo said, 'This nationalist movement to advance Africans politically, economically and socially must go on,' but most Africans felt that it was a lost cause.

In Zambia there were rifts between ANC and the Mineworkers Union, which was itself torn by internal schisms. The government reacted harshly to any African political activity. When Kenneth Kaunda, together with Titus Makupo and Wittington Sikalumbi, produced a monthly pamphlet called *Congress News*, the Governor, Sir Gilbert Rennie, branded Kaunda 'an agitator'. Police raided Kaunda's office and found there literature from an innocuous British MP called Fenner Brockway; Kaunda was gaoled for two months. In disturbances at Mbala, Luwingu and the Gwembe valley the riot police were used. When African miners on the Copperbelt went on strike in 1956 a state of emergency was declared, African trade union leaders were detained and racial tension ran high.

Hut No. 394, Chilenje. From here Kenneth Kaunda led the struggle for independence

Government action did not however stop Africans from complaining about injustice. In 1954 there was a seven-week campaign against the 'hatch' system when Africans refused to buy meat from butchers' shops in Cairo Road, Lusaka; the campaign spread to Livingstone and Mazabuka. There were boycotts against high prices, organised by Reuben Kamanga at Chipata and by Alex Masal and Dixon Konkola at Kabwe. A Youth League was formed by Wilson Chakulya.

In Zimbabwe, many Africans felt that it was pointless to go on fighting. The whites in Zimbabwe were far more numerous and powerful than those in Zambia or Malawi. They had enjoyed their power much longer, they were backed by the press and the financial power of industry, and they had erected Federation to give themselves an added layer of power. It seemed to many African leaders that the

Kenneth Kaunda speaking at a political rally in Chingola

whites would not be driven from their positions of entrenched power in the forseeable future, and that the best way forward was to co-operate with the whites for the time being and get the best deal they could for Africans, keeping African self-government as a long-term objective.

Not all Africans felt this way. Some wanted to go on fighting the whites to obtain better conditions for Africans and self-government within the forseeable future. Nathan Shamuyarira condemned the Bulawayo branch of Congress for becoming a social club with little political interest. For the moment, however, Africans who agreed with Shamuyarira were in a minority. By 1956, with Federation clamped down on Central Africa like a vice, and with Africans divided over how to deal with Federation, it looked as though the dark years in Central Africa would last for ever.

35 The collapse of Federation

The turning-point for Africans, at least those in Zambia and Malawi, came in March 1956 when the Federal Prime Minister, Godfrey Huggins, introduced the Federal Electoral Bill and the Constitution Amendment Bill. The aim of these two bills was to solidify white supremacy and prevent Africans from ever getting power over whites. The bills increased white membership of the Federal parliament to forty-five, compared to an African membership of twelve, and created new voting arrangements that were unfavourable to Africans. In passing the two bills, Huggins was inadvertently opening the door for a revival of African nationalism. Africans could now demonstrate to the outside world that they were getting a raw deal from Federation. In one of his last acts as Prime Minister before handing over to his cohort Welensky, Huggins was digging the grave of the Federation he and Welensky had conspired to create.

The African Affairs Board, which was meant to safeguard African interests, asked the Governor-General to refer both bills to the British government. But on Welensky's advice, the British government overruled the Board's objections. 'Political control,' explained Huggins, 'must remain in the hands of civilised people, which for the forseeable future means the Europeans.' Some whites even felt the bills were too generous to the Africans: in a by-election at Muwera in Zimbabwe the government candidate was defeated by Winston Field, leader of the Dominion Party, which wanted complete racial segregation as in South Africa.

In Zimbabwe, it was much more difficult for African parties to make progress. The whites were just too strong. The so-called 'liberal' government of Garfield Todd was passing just enough 'reforms' to keep African opinion at bay. In 1957 a new constitution was introduced into 'Southern Rhodesia'. A parliamentary commission had recommended that Africans earning £15 a year should be allowed to vote. Todd rejected this and said only Africans earning £60 a year should vote as he

Edgar Whitehead, Prime Minister of Rhodesia (Zimbabwe) 1958–62

wanted only educated Africans to do so. Naturally enough. Todd was not supported by the majority of Africans. If Todd was not liberal enough for the Africans, he was far too liberal for the whites. In 1958 he was discarded by the whites and replaced by Sir Edgar Whitehead, a former civil servant who was not a liberal and was regarded as tougher than Todd.

Yet even Whitehead found it necessary to pass some reforms. His reason for this was that in 1960 the Federal constitution was due to come up for review and Whitehead knew that the British government would not allow the whites to go on running the Federation if they were doing absolutely nothing for the Africans. So Whitehead launched what he grandiosely called his 'Build a Nation' campaign. He passed a string of reforms to improve African conditions. All Africans were to be in school by 1964; there would be multi-racial trade unions by

1960; separate counters at the Post Office were abolished; the urban housing programme was speeded up; all posts in the civil service were opened to Africans; Africans were admitted to swimming-pools and cinemas; the pass laws and the Immorality Act were repealed. It was also made easier for Africans to obtain land. Despite opposition from some whites, Africans were allowed to buy freehold land in African townships in white areas; five million acres were set aside for anyone, white or African, to buy. Two million acres were switched from the white to the African area. Whitehead claimed white supremacy was 'dead'.

The reality of this claim was shown in 1959 when, to stop the spread of African nationalism from Malawi following Dr Banda's whirlwind campaign of violence, Whitehead declared a state of emergency, had five hundred Africans arrested and passed six bills that restricted African liberties. One of these bills, the Unlawful Organisations and Preventive Detention Bill, gave the government power to put people in prison without trial, thus removing a basic safeguard of human liberty. This bill was to stay in force for five years and brought protests from white lawyers and churchmen.

The sheer strength of this white political system, combined with a ruthless police presence when necessary and subtle propaganda to make Africans think things were being done for them, conspired to make it very difficult for African politicians to convince people that the system could and should be altered so as to give Africans a bigger say in the government of Zimbabwe. The Bulawayo branch of Congress was once again engaging in political activity and in 1957 it joined with the Salisbury City Youth League to form the African National Congress under the leadership of Joshua Nkomo and George Nyandoro, who repeatedly drew attention to the difference between the wide European ranches and the crowded African farms. This new party was banned however in the Whitehead clampdown of 1959.

The next party to emerge was the National Democratic Party, NDP, which was supported by students, trade unionists, African traders, and young men with no land. NDP encouraged resistance to the Land Husbandry Act. It organised mass meetings like the great march through Salisbury townships in July 1960. Such rallies were attended by twenty to thirty thousand people. NDP was influenced by Marxism and by the ideas of the Convention Peoples Party in Ghana, but its roots were in Zimbabwean history, in the earlier Congress and ICU traditions, in the songs and memories of the 1896/7 rebellion, and in the name chosen for the new state that it hoped would one day emerge: Zimbabwe. The NDP leaders were the descendants of men who had taken part in earlier struggles, men like Nyandoro and Samkange. Joshua Nkomo was himself a link with the past.

Yet NDP faced many problems. It was concerned more with rural than with urban grievances and did not champion urban workers in their struggle for higher wages. It was, in fact, suspicious of Zimbabwean industry in which there were strong British interests. It believed, perhaps with some justification, that those interests would always stop Britain from giving Africans power in Zimbabwe. More importantly, NDP faced the problem of disillusionment among its supporters. A nationalist party must succeed or lose credibility. Conditions in Zimbabwe made it impossible for NDP or any African-led party at that time to succeed. Unlike the British Colonial Office regimes in Malawi and Zambia, which had to think of world opinion, the settler government in Zimbabwe had no qualms about suppressing Africans. If there was disorder, the government sent in the police. If a political leader became too strong, the government deported him. If a political party looked too dangerous, the government banned it. There was no way the whites in Zimbabwe were ever going to hand over political power to the Africans. After a few years of unrewarded protest, NDP followed ANC into oblivion. It was obviously going to take many years of struggle, and a more violent approach, to dislodge the whites from their positions of entrenched power in Zimbabwe.

PART X
Independence: Struggle and Achievement

36 The growth of nationalist parties in Zambia and Malawi

The revival of African parties in Malawi
In Malawi, the Federal Electoral Bill gave the younger, more radical leaders the chance to grasp control of the Congress movement. Older, more moderate leaders, like Wellington Chirwa and Charles Matinga gave way to the 'Young Turks': Henry Chipembere, Kanyama Chiume, Yatuta and Dundusu Chisiza, and T. D. T. Banda. The aim of the 'Young Turks' was to achieve 'one man one vote', self-government for Malawi and ultimately independence. To achieve this aim, the 'Young Turks' were prepared to use violence. As Chipembere said on 4 July 1958: 'Anything like moderation will never get us anywhere; whether we demand things in strong terms or whether we demand things in mild language we get nothing ... The only language which British imperialism can understand is the language of extreme conflict.'

Chipembere opposed all links with the Federation. He urged the Malawi representatives to the Federal parliament, Chirwa and Kumbikano, to resign. He did not want Africans to be seen associating with whites. In February 1957, when the Malawi Legislative Council was discussing a proposal to put European agriculture under Federal control, Chipembere walked out. The government thereupon withdrew its recognition of Congress. In April 1958 Chipembere boycotted the meeting of the Malawi Legislative Council that approved the Federal Electoral Bill.

Chipembere recruited support from all over Malawi. By April 1957 Congress had 60000 mem-

Dr Banda soon after his release from a year's detention

Dr Banda is welcomed back to Malawi after a 43 year absence, 6 July 1958

bers. They adopted the symbols of the mass party: the slogan of *Kwacha* ('the dawn'), the national flag, the weekly news-sheet. They built up the heroes of the past such as Charles Domingo and Eliot Kamwana; above all, they built up Dr Kamuzu Banda, then living in Ghana, as a national hero or *Ngwazi*. Dr Banda, a Chewa, had always been a staunch opponent of Federation and had left Britain in disgust when it was introduced. He had gone to live in Ghana, where he had studied the methods of Dr Nkrumah and the Convention Peoples Party. On 6 July 1958 Dr Banda returned to Malawi.

The 'Young Turks' intended Dr Banda to be merely a figurehead, a rallying-point. As Chipembere said, 'Human nature is such that it needs a kind of hero to be hero-worshipped if a political struggle is to succeed.' The real power was to stay with Chipembere and the 'Young Turks'. They called Dr Banda, the Saviour, the Messiah, and the Mahatma, but they themselves intended to keep control of the party. Dr Banda soon proved that he was no mere figurehead. In December 1958 he attended the first pan-African Congress in Accra and stressed that Federation must be destroyed. By January 1959 Dr Banda was talking of using violence and in February the violence began. There were strikes, demonstrations and riots, the worst being at Nkhata Bay. His whirlwind campaign of violence reached a climax in March 1959 when the Governor of Malawi, Sir Robert Armitage, declared a state of emergency. Dr Banda was imprisoned along with a thousand supporters.

The Nyasaland African Congress was banned, but a new party, the Malawi Congress Party, rose up in its place. The provisional Chairman of the new party, Orton Chirwa, was careful to say that constitutional means, not violence, would now be used, but the aims remained the same. On Dr Banda's release from prison in April 1960 he became leader of MCP. He at once reaffirmed that Africans in Malawi would be satisfied with nothing less than complete independence. It was becoming increasingly clear, even to the British, that Dr Banda and the MCP had the strength and support to free Malawi from the Federation.

The revival of African parties in Zambia

In Zambia too radical elements were taking control. Simon Kapwepwe and Munukayumbwa Sipalo, recently returned from studying in India, now found Harry Nkumbula's leadership too moderate. Nkumbula was known to be associating with whites: it was Harry Franklin, a white member of the Executive Council, who had persuaded Nkumbula to call off the 1956 boycott of white trading areas to give the Race Relations Board 'a chance'. Nkumbula was quite happy with the new constitution introduced in Zambia in 1958, which put eight elected and two nominated Africans on the Legislative Council and two Africans on the Executive Council, though both bodies would still have European majorities. Nkumbula said he would stand as a candidate in the 1959 elections based on the new constitution. 'We need the help and sympathy of all liberal-minded Europeans,' he explained, calling this policy the 'New Look'. The radical elements did not support either the new constitution or Nkumbula's decision to stand in the elections. They also felt that Nkumbula was spending too much of the party's money and refusing to let Kapwepwe, the treasurer, keep proper accounts. Nkumbula also demanded dictatorial powers and dismissed branch officials who were disloyal to him. He went to London but failed, for dubious reasons, to keep an appointment with the Colonial Secretary. The younger men felt that Nkumbula was giving the party a bad name. They decided to break away from ANC and form a party of their own.

On 26 October 1958, the Zambia Africa National Congress (ZANC) was formed. The President was Kenneth Kaunda, the Treasurer-General, Simon Kapwepwe, and the Secretary-General, Munukayumbwa Sipalo. Other members included the Lozi journalist Sikota Wina and Bemba businessmen Grey Zulu and Lewis Changufu. ZANC had support in the Northern Province, the Eastern Province and the Copperbelt. ANC support was now restricted mainly to the Southern Province.

Before the elections took place in 1959 Dr Banda had carried out the campaign of violence in Malawi. To stop nationalist fervour spreading to Zambia, Governor Benson acted swiftly. Before dawn on 12 March, ZANC officials and forty-five of their supporters were taken into custody. Dr Kaunda was sent first to Kabompo, then to prisons in Salisbury and Lusaka. Leaders were separated from their supporters: Kapwepwe was sent to Mongu, Wina's home district, and Wina was sent to Luwingu, Kapwepwe's home district. There was violence at Chilubi island in Lake Bangweulu and in other parts of the Northern and Luapula Provinces. More than a hundred Africans were arrested. ZANC was banned. The election itself passed off peacefully, Nkumbula duly winning his seat for ANC.

New parties at once sprang up to replace ZANC. The African National Freedom Movement was formed by Barry Banda, Dauti Yamba and Paskale Sokota. The United African Congress was formed by Dixon Konkola, President of the Railway Workers Union. In June 1959 these two parties combined to form the United National Freedom Party. The Vice-President-General, Solomon Kalulu, reminded the party that the real leader was Kenneth Kaunda, who was still in prison. A third party, the African National Independence Party, was formed by Paul Kalichini. In September 1959, this too joined with the United National Freedom Party to form the United National Independence Party, UNIP.

In the meantime a split had developed in ANC between Harry Nkumbula and Titus Makupo, who was supported by Fines Bulawayo and Mainza Chona, a London-trained barrister. In October 1959 Makupo, Bulawayo and Chona left ANC and

Kenneth Kaunda, President of the Zambia Africa National Congress

Dr Kwame Nkrumah; he had a large influence on the nationalist parties

joined UNIP. Finally, in January 1960, Dr Kaunda was released from prison and became President of UNIP with Simon Kapwepwe as second-in-command. Kaunda and Kapwepwe now turned their attention to the organisation of the party.

Dr Kaunda had been to both Britain and Ghana, and had studied the methods of the British Labour Party and the Ghanaian Convention Peoples Party. The organisation of UNIP was based on these two. Like MCP in Malawi, UNIP became a mass party. It adopted slogans that would appeal to the masses such as 'one man one vote'. It built up a network of regional organisations, constituencies and branches with thousands of regional workers. The party's aim was to achieve African majority rule, then leave the Federation, and finally win independence. The method was to be 'non-violent means plus positive action'. This shows the influence of Kwame Nkrumah of Ghana and Mahatma Gandhi who had helped India to achieve independence using non-violent means wherever possible. Like Gandhi, Dr Kaunda stressed that the struggle was against colonialism, not against the individual white people who were its agents. In spite of Dr Kaunda's insistence on non-violence, there was some violence in the dry season of 1960. Dr Kaunda visited London, Accra and Dar-es-Salaam to gain support and increase UNIP's international standing. UNIP thus acquired the support of world leaders such as Nkrumah and Colonel Nasser of Egypt, both key figures in the anti-colonial struggle throughout Africa. By 1960 it was clear that UNIP, like MCP in Malawi, had the strength and support to lead Zambia out of the Federation and into independence.

37 Independence in Zambia and Malawi

The settlers wanted the British government to make the Federation an independent, white-run state, but after the violence of 1959 it was clear that the British government could not do this if it was to respect the wishes of Africans. Africans had shown that they would not put up with white supremacy for much longer. The Devlin Commission, which was sent to Central Africa to investigate the violence, concluded that the violence reflected a genuine African desire not to be ruled by whites; it rejected the settlers' view that the violence was caused only by a handful of 'extremists'. 'The opposition to Federation,' said the Devlin Report, 'was deeply rooted and almost universally held.'

This view was supported by the Monckton Report on the future of the Federation. This report said that big changes were needed, especially in Zimbabwe. There should be more African voters and more African members of parliament. Unfair legislation such as the Land Apportionment Act should be abolished. The Federal parliament should be responsible only for defence, foreign affairs and the economy. The most damning conclusion of the Monckton Report was that 'partnership was a sham.'

The Monckton Report said that Zambia and Malawi should be allowed to 'secede' or break away from the Federation 'after a period of time.' This annoyed Roy Welensky, who had become Federal Prime Minister when Huggins retired. Welensky felt betrayed by Lord Monckton and by the British Prime Minister, Harold Macmillan. He claimed that he had only allowed the Monckton Commission to come to Central Africa on the understanding that it would not discuss secession. Dr Banda was annoyed that secession would only come 'after a period of time'. 'We want secession now,' said Dr Banda, 'not in five years time.'

Circumstances were on Dr Banda's side. The late 1950s and early 1960s was a time when colonial powers like Britain and France were being forced to give up their colonies all over the world. Among the reasons for this were administrative costs, opposition within the colonies, and a worldwide feeling, especially in the socialist movement, that colonialism was wrong. The process of decolonisation was seen at its most dramatic in Africa. By 1960 Ghana, Nigeria and many French colonies were independent. The British Prime Minister, Harold Macmillan, said in a speech at Cape Town that the 'wind of change' was blowing through Africa. In this light, it could only be a matter of time before Malawi and Zambia gained their independence and Africans in Zimbabwe stepped up their demand for African rule.

If Federation had to come to an end, it would not be without a bitter fight by Welensky. Welensky argued that the break-up of Federation would be a threat to British interests and a blow to the multi-racial idea. He claimed that his own Federal government and Whitehead's government in Zimbabwe had actually eased racial tension. He carried out a costly propaganda campaign in the British press and through his publicity agents, 'Voice and Vision Limited'. He spoke on British radio and television and addressed the British Institute of Directors in the Albert Hall, London.

None of Welensky's rhetoric had any effect on the British government. Having set up the Federation ten years earlier in spite of the Africans' protests, the British government was now going to dismantle it in spite of Welensky. In a conference held to discuss the future of the Federation at Lancaster House, London, in December 1960, Harold Macmillan said there was no question of the Federation becoming an independent white-run state until Africans took a bigger part in running the three territories. The conference was then adjourned so that the constitutions of the three territories could be discussed.

As a result of these discussions, new constitutions giving Africans greater representation were introduced in all three territories. The constitution introduced in Zimbabwe in February 1961, created a Legislative Assembly of sixty-five members, fifty of them from constituencies where most voters were Africans. There was to be a Bill of Rights and a constitutional council of lawyers to guard against unfair legislation. This constitution was approved by referendum, though there was opposition from both whites and Africans. The white-run Dominion Party thought the constitution too liberal; African political leaders like Joshua Nkomo and Ndabaningi Sithole did not think it liberal enough.

At the conference to discuss the Malawi constitution, the Colonial Secretary, Iain Macleod, agreed that Africans should enjoy a greater degree of self-government. The vote was given to Africans who could read and write English and earned £120 a year, to Africans who could read and write a vernacular language and had paid taxes for ten years, and to village headmen, councillors, pensioners, master-farmers and ex-servicemen. This satisfied Dr Banda but not Henry Chipembere who said that if Congress accepted it quietly, he and Kanyama Chiume would resign. Chipembere was imprisoned, and there were disturbances which were stopped by Dr Banda on his return from the London conference.

In elections held under the new constitution, the Malawi Congress Party won a sweeping victory, obtaining 94 per cent of the votes and twenty-two of the twenty-eight seats on the Legislative Council. In January 1962 Dr Banda became Minister of Land, National Resources and Local Government. In July he broke off negotiations with Salisbury for the HEP project at Nkula Falls. Britain guaranteed that in the event of Malawi becoming independent, Britain would finance Malawi's deficit. Malawi was moving rapidly to self-government. In January 1963 Dr Banda became Chief Minister with a cabinet of eight African ministers and two Europeans, one of them in charge of finance. The Governor retained certain powers relating to law and order. In May 1963 these powers came to an end and Malawi was granted full internal self-government. Dr Banda at once set about trying to achieve his two remaining objectives: to break away from the Federation and to win complete independence for Malawi.

In talks on the Zambian constitution, Dr Kaunda argued for concessions similar to those granted in Malawi. Welensky was determined to prevent this, but ranged against him were both Macmillan and Macleod. Welensky was especially bitter towards Macleod. When Dr Kaunda threatened action that would 'make Mau Mau look like a picnic,' Welensky called up the white territorials in Zambia without the permission of the Governor. This was an unconstitutional act.

A UNIP demonstration during Iain MacLeod's visit to Northern Rhodesia (Zambia)

In February 1961 Macleod suggested a legislature of forty-five members: fifteen from upper roll constituencies, fifteen from lower roll constituencies, and fifteen from constituencies on a new 'national' roll. This was reluctantly accepted by Dr Kaunda but bitterly denounced by Welensky. Welensky persuaded the British government to change it so that candidates had to get $12\frac{1}{2}$ per cent or 400 of the votes cast by Europeans, which would be impossible for Africans. In response, Dr Kaunda began a campaign of 'passive resistance'. In spite of Dr Kaunda's insistence on peaceful protest, bridges were blown up, roads were blocked, and buses were attacked. Twenty-one Africans were killed, mainly in the Northern and Luapula Provinces. The government said it would reconsider the constitution if the violence was stopped. By November 1961, all was quiet and the conference resumed. The new Colonial Secretary, Reginald Maudling, put forward a compromise solution: the $12\frac{1}{2}$ per cent requirement was reduced to 10 per cent and the 400 votes requirement was dropped. Welensky con-

Joshua Nkomo and Rev. Ndabaningi Sithole at the Lancaster House conference to review the constitutions of Rhodesia and Nyasaland, 1960

cluded that the British government was indifferent to the fate of the Federation and he was absolutely right.

Before elections could be held under the new Zambian constitution, there was friction between UNIP and ANC. ANC led by Harry Nkumbula was still prepared for gradual progress towards self-government; UNIP under Dr Kaunda was not. The situation was made worse by industrial trouble on the Copperbelt. In the election, UNIP won fourteen seats to ANC's seven. The white-run United Federal Party won sixteen seats, so Nkumbula could have formed a government with white support. To forestall him, Kaunda offered him an alliance: if Nkumbula allowed UNIP to form the government, Nkumbula and two of his followers could have seats on the Executive Council. Nkumbula accepted this.

In 1963 it was agreed that Zambia could become an independent Republic with a President and a Legislative Assembly of eighty M.P.s: sixty-five elected on a 'one man one vote' basis, ten reserved for Europeans, and five nominated by the President. There should be a House of Chiefs, a Bill of Rights, and a Constitutional Council of lawyers. Bulozi, which had secessionist leanings, should be part of the Republic, but as a sop to the Litunga, his council should have delaying powers over legislation.

By now it was clear to everybody (except perhaps Welensky) that Federation was on its last legs. The copper companies had already moved their headquarters from Salisbury to Lusaka in anticipation of the expected demise of Federation. The British government had set up a new department known as the Central Africa Office and had appointed as its head a leading Tory politician, R. A. Butler. Welensky thought that Butler's appointment showed Britain's renewed support for Federation, but Butler had, in reality, been appointed as an undertaker to see that Federation was properly buried.

In 1963 a conference was held to draw up the last will and testament of the dying Federation. This conference was ironically held at Victoria Falls, where many of the early Federation conferences had been held. At the conference it was agreed that after the death of Federation there should be joint management of Rhodesian Railways, Central African Airways and the Kariba Dam. The balance of the Federal debt was to be shared, Zimbabwe taking 52 per cent, Zambia 37 per cent and Malawi only 11 per cent; this was a generous agreement on Zambia's part. With these problems settled, Federation finally breathed its last on the last day of 1963. Welensky was the chief mourner.

All that remained was to give birth to the new nations, Malawi and Zambia. In Malawi there were no serious problems. Dr Banda was already Prime Minister and MCP was the only political party that could have taken power. On 6 July 1964 Dr Banda became President of an independent Republic which took the name Malawi as a reminder of that country's importance in the seventeenth century. In Zambia, things were not quite so simple. There was not one political party but two, and there was still friction between them. The issue was settled in the election of January 1964 when UNIP won fifty-five seats and ANC only ten. Dr Kaunda now had no further need of Nkumbula's support. He became Prime Minister and Zambia was given internal self-government.

To complicate matters, there was now a dispute between UNIP and the Lumpa Church, an anti-sorcery movement led by Alice Lenshina and supported by ANC. The dispute was bitter because both UNIP and the Lumpa Church had strongholds in the Northern Province; the Lumpa Church had started as a split from Lubwa Mission. In July 1964 troops moved in and at least seven hundred Africans were killed.

24 October 1964, the new Zambian flag is hoisted

Yet another problem was mineral royalties. These were currently valued at £7 million a year and the BSA Company was not due to hand them over until 1986. Shortly before midnight on 23 September 1964 the Company agreed to give them up in return for £4 million: £2 million to be paid by the Zambian government, £2 million by the British government. With this problem solved, Zambia duly became an independent Republic on 24 September 1964, with Dr Kaunda as its first President.

38 The liberation of Zimbabwe

There was to be no rapid progress to African self-rule in Zimbabwe. The settlers in Zimbabwe, unlike the British government, were not influenced by world opinion or the desire of Africans to govern the country where they formed the majority of the population. The whites felt no need to give up their privileged position as minority rulers; they were determined that they, and not the Africans, should go on ruling Zimbabwe. It was to take many years of armed struggle to make them change their minds.

After the demise of earlier parties like ANC and NDP, two African political parties were to emerge in the 1960s that became all-important in the struggle for liberation. These were ZAPU and ZANU. The first to be formed was the Zimbabwe African Peoples Union (ZAPU). Among its leaders were Joshua Nkomo, George Nyandoro, James Chikerema and Leopold Takawira. After protests in Bulawyo, ZAPU was banned and the government again passed emergency legislation in the face of protest from lawyers and churchmen. The Unlawful Organisations Act was strengthened and the Law and Order (Maintenance) Act was extended for five years. Joshua Nkomo went into exile and other leaders went underground and carried out arson and sabotage.

Meanwhile, among the whites, racist elements were gathing strength. In 1962 the segregationist Dominion Party joined with other racist groups to form the Rhodesia Front. The Rhodesia Front was to be the main vehicle of white racist opinion over the next two decades. Its policy was 'white supremacy ... for the forseeable future'. The Rhodesia Front wanted 'Rhodesia' to become an independent, white-run state. In December 1962 the Rhodesia Front gained power and its leader, Winston Field, became Prime Minister. He at once began putting Rhodesia Front policies into practice. He brought broadcasting under government control, made death the penalty for attempted arson, and provided the white security forces with the most modern military equipment to deal with the African nationalist movement.

This increasing white military strength led to still more vigorous action on the part of Africans. Some African leaders such as Rev. Ndabaningi Sithole wanted armed struggle against the whites. The ZAPU leadership was not prepared for this, so Sithole and others broke away to form the second big African party, the Zimbabwe African National Union (ZANU). ZANU attracted activist young blood such as Josiah Tongogara, who was later trained in conventional and guerilla warfare in Tanzania and at Nanking in China, and who was to become ZANU Chief of Defence. It was ZANU that first sent young men for military training, and these men were the first to launch military attacks across the Zambezi. ZAPU, on the other hand, was at this time so determined to gain independence by peaceful means that it dissociated itself from the ZANU attacks, calling the insurgents an 'illegal terrorist group'.

The whites took strong action against the new African military threat. They rounded up nearly all ZANU and ZAPU leaders in Zimbabwe and threw them into gaol or detention. By now Ian Smith had replaced Winston Field as Prime Minister, and on 11 November 1965 Smith illegally declared 'Rhodesia' independent. Because he did this without consulting the British government (which had ultimate responsibility for Zimbabwe) Smith's action was called the 'Unilateral (One-sided) Declaration of Independence' or UDI. UDI was the time-bomb that fifteen years later exploded in Smith's face.

The Africans hoped the British government would use force to bring the Smith regime back to legality. The British government, led by Harold Wilson, would not use force against its 'kith and kin'; it preferred less violent means such as economic sanctions. Wilson twice met Smith on board Royal Navy ships, but failed to persuade him to give up UDI. The Commonwealth, the United Nations and the Organisation of African Unity all opposed UDI. Many socialist countries like Russia

Ian Smith

and the Peoples Republic of China offered training facilities and material support to the Zimbabwe freedom fighters. Such training exposed the trainees to socialism, which was to determine the nature of the struggle for liberation in Zimbabwe. It did not mean simply striving to take over political power from the whites, it now meant a struggle for the total change of society. Instead of a few rich people running the country for their own further enrichment, all the people through their government and other organisations would control and own the means of production, distribution and exchange. This was a fitting ideology for Zimbabwe, whose rural population had for seventy years been systematically impoverished through exploitation by the whites. The socialism of the new nationalist movement promised liberation not only from foreign rule but also from poverty, hunger and disease. As the liberation struggle got underway, the rural population welcomed the fighters and afforded them shelter, clothing and food.

The Zimbabwe freedom fighters were also helped by their African neighbours. Zambia, now independent, allowed her territory to be used by the freedom fighters for operational and training bases. Tanzania also offered training facilities. After the Front for the Liberation of Mozambique (FRELIMO) had liberated the Portuguese country, Mozambique, it allowed Zimbabweans to use

Prisoners practice carpentry at a ZAPU refugee camp in Zambia

Zimbabwean leaders in detention at Sikombele. From left to right: E. Tekere, E. Zvobgo, E. Nkala, N. Sithole, Robert Mugabe, L. Takawira, M. Malinanga

Burial of a ZANLA soldier in Mozambique, 1978. Present were Robert Mugabe, E. Tekere, E. Zvobgo, J. Tongogara, R. Manyika, E. Kadungure, M. Urimbo

Mozambique for military campaigns. In due course Botswana also allowed Zimbabwe freedom fighters to use her territory. The liberation front now more or less encircled the country. Even ZAPU had realised that the whites would never be brought down by peaceful means and had joined in the fight. ZAPU fought mainly from Zambia and Botswana, while the more powerful ZANU used the vast territory of Mozambique.

The war was waged on two levels. First the guerillas attacked and defended themselves against white forces. Secondly they strove to win over what Mao Tse-tung, the Chinese Communist leader, had called 'the hearts and the minds' of the rural population; this was done through socialist propaganda. These tactics had helped Mao to win power in China and later helped the Viet Cong drive the powerful United States army from Vietnam.

The white government used both violence and propaganda to stop Africans from supporting the guerillas. Glorified concentration camps, called protected villages, were set up where people were herded together and surrounded by electric fences. The death penalty was introduced for anyone found assisting the guerillas with food or information or who refused to report the presence of guerillas to the nearest white authorities.

These methods were effective, but not effective enough. In the ten years from 1966 to 1976 it became increasingly clear that the whites were losing the war. Large rural areas had been taken over by the guerillas, and the people of Zimbabwe were participating in the war on the side of the liberation movement. As Dzinashe Machingura, Deputy Political Commissioner of ZANU, explained in 1976: 'We have the support of the mass of our people. All factors indicate that we are heading for ever-greater victories ... We have reached the point where we no longer speak of "support from the masses" but of their actual participation in armed struggle.' The leadership of ZANU had now passed to Robert Mugabe.

By 1979 the liberation movement had won the war. The whites as well as their African opponents were prepared to go to London to negotiate a peace settlement. An independence constitution was drawn up and independence elections were held in 1980. They were won by ZANU, whose leader, Robert Mugabe, became the first Prime Minister of independent Zimbabwe, ending ninety years of colonial rule. It would have saved a lot of bloodshed if the whites had agreed to give up their power peacefully when Zambia and Malawi had gained their independence, sixteen years earlier.

39 Post-colonial developments

Malawi

At independence, all three Central African countries faced problems caused by decades of white rule. In Malawi these problems included overcrowding, poor communications, and lack of mineral and industrial development. Malawi was, in fact, one of the poorest countries in Africa.

Malawi's transition to independence was not helped by a split in the government. Dr Banda believed that Malawi's poverty could only be overcome by maintaining friendly relations with the white regimes of Southern Africa. Dr Banda believed that this would bring aid to Malawi and guarantee jobs for Malawians in the South. Such policies did benefit Malawi but they were contrary to the most cherished principles of the African people and to the aims of the Organisation of African Unity. As such they were opposed by some of Dr Banda's own ministers, notably the 'Young Turks', Henry Chipembere and Kanyama Chiume.

Dr Banda's policies were a turnabout from his own one-time unshakable stand against racism. In 1963, when fighting for Malawi's independence, Dr Banda had said: 'As an African nationalist I hate the present regime in South Africa and will have nothing to do with it when this country is independent. There will be no diplomatic or commercial dealings between us.' Yet now that Malawi was independent, Dr Banda visited South Africa, entered commercial relations with the Portuguese, ridiculed African liberation movements in South Africa, Zimbabwe and Mozambique, and spoke of allying with the white racist regimes to defend Southern Africa. Dr Banda seems to have been taken in by South African propaganda that Southern Africa was ripe for picking by the Communists and that the white nations must club together to prevent this. Malawi was now to be counted among the 'white' nations thanks to Dr Banda's visit to South Africa, where he was regarded as an 'honorary white'. This grated with the younger ministers, who believed that Malawi should be supporting African liberation movements, not the racist regimes that were oppressing them.

Dr Banda's pro-South African policies were not the only cause of the split in his cabinet. The younger ministers disagreed fundamentally with some of Dr Banda's ideas about the kind of society they should be creating in Malawi. They wanted Malawi to take a socialist path as Tanzania was doing and as Zimbabwe would subsequently do. They disagreed with Dr Banda over domestic issues like a fee for health services, a pension scheme for civil servants, and the slow pace of Africanisation in jobs. They charged Dr Banda with listening too much to the advice of white civil servants.

The roots of the split perhaps went deeper still. The younger leaders of MCP had always wanted Dr Banda to be merely a figurehead in Malawi politics. They were alarmed when they found that he was an extremely capable leader who intended to exercise power and whose popularity was soaring in the country. They wanted therefore to curb his powers. Dr Banda himself perhaps worsened the situation by his reluctance to accept criticism. It seems that he interpreted any frank criticism of his policies as a sign of disloyalty to himself as Life-President of the MCP and indeed to the party itself.

Soon after independence, Dr Banda sacked three of his ministers, Kanyama Chiume, Augustine Bwanansi and Orton Chirwa. He accused them of plotting with the Communists to overthrow him and of accepting a bribe of £18 million to persuade him to recognise the Communist Peoples Republic of China rather than the United States puppet regime in Taiwan with which Dr Banda wanted to establish diplomatic relations so as to get aid. Three other ministers resigned in sympathy with their colleagues.

Dr Banda was in a strong position to deal with the sacked ministers and their friends. He had on his side expatriate civil servants, army and police officers, and organisations loyal to himself such as the Young Pioneers and the Youth and Women's

Leagues. The ministers had only localised support which was easily crushed by the police. By May 1965 all internal opposition had been suppressed and the rebels, including the 'Young Turks' who had brought Dr Banda back from exile to be the leader of MCP, had themselves been forced into exile. In 1967 one of the rebels, Yatuta Chisiza, crossed into Malawi from Tanzania, hoping to be hailed by a people's uprising against Dr Banda. He received no support in the country and in a clash with security forces, was killed. Dr Banda's position in Malawi was now secure.

In tackling the country's economic problems, Dr Banda's government devoted its main efforts to agriculture. It set up a government agency, the Agriculture and Marketing Board, to encourage better farming methods and to provide extension services. People were given farming units, provided with new crops, and taught new methods of cultivation. Irrigation facilities were provided. These efforts were best seen in the Lilongwe project, financed first by the British government and later by the International Development Agency. The whole area of the Lilongwe project was provided with new roads, drainage ditches, boreholes, a cattle ranch, and marketing facilities which were also the distributing centres of seed and fertilizers. The idea was to increase the production of maize, beef and groundnuts.

African farmers were encouraged to grow crops which in colonial times had been grown by white planters. These crops included tea and flue-cured tobacco. In the Central Region farmers trained for six years at Kasungu produced high grade tobacco leaf. In the Cholo, Mlanje and Nkata Bay districts, small-holders grew tea. These encouragements were extended to ordinary villagers. The result was a marked increase in the export of cash crops and the lessening of Malawi's dependence on imported foodstuffs.

Zambia

In Zambia too there were serious economic problems left behind by the Federal and colonial administrations. Zambia was too dependent on the export of copper, so that if the world copper price fell, the whole Zambian economy would suffer. Because of links with Zimbabwe during colonial and Federal times, Zambia was too dependent on Zimbabwe for the export of her copper, as well as for coal and coke from Wankie, electricity from the Zimbabwe side of Kariba and oil from Beira pumped through a pipeline through Zimbabwe. Too much foreign capital was invested in Zambian trade and industry.

Too many Zambians were living in the towns; 25 to 30 per cent, the highest percentage in independent black Africa. There was too little trained Zambian manpower because of the paucity of African education during colonial times.

To these inherent problems were added the problems caused by the liberation war in Zimbabwe. Because of Zambia's dependence on Zimbabwe, when Ian Smith declared his illegal UDI, Zambia wanted Britain to use force against him and not economic sanctions, which would hit Zambia as hard as they did Zimbabwe. Yet when sanctions were imposed, Zambia readily complied, much though sanctions damaged the Zambian economy. At the same time Zambia tried to reduce her dependence on Zimbabwe. Copper exports were re-routed through Zaire and Angola to the port of Lobito and through Tanzania to the port of Dar-es-Salaam, at first by road or by an oil pipeline completed in 1968, and after 1975 by the Tazara railway built by the Chinese. An HEP station was opened on the lower Kafue and a power station was built at the northern end of the Kariba Dam to reduce the need for electricity from the Zimbabwe side of Kariba. The Nkandwe and Maamba coal mines were opened to reduce the need for coal from Wankie and indeed to make Zambia self-sufficient in coal.

Zambia was able to achieve these spectacular strides in such a short time because of her copper exports. In the first five years of independence there was a big demand for copper, mainly because of the Vietnam War. The copper price was high and the Zambian government was able to increase its share of the profits made by the copper companies. The government tried to use these copper revenues to diversify the economy and so reduce the country's future dependence on copper. The manufacturing industries were expanded, especially those producing basic goods such as copper wire, explosives for the mines, chemical fertilizer, textiles, and car assembly. Between 1964 and 1974 Zambia trebled her manufacturing production. The need for such diversification was brought home after 1970 and especially after the ending of the Vietnam War when the world price of copper began to fluctuate violently and generally to be much lower.

In agriculture, the colonial and Federal regimes had left Zambia poorly equipped to feed her growing and increasingly urbanised population, which in 1974 numbered more than four and a half million. The production of maize trebled in the first ten years of independence but there was still not enough to feed everyone. The government tried to increase the land available for agriculture by buying it from absentee landlords and distributing it to African farmers. This did not always lead to increased production as the farmers lacked agricultural knowledge and Zambia in general lacks good soil and sufficient water, so that only a big capital investment will make the land productive. In the early years of independence, with so many other commitments, the government was not always able to make the sort of investment required.

In the field of manpower, Zambia tried hard to become self-sufficient and so end her dependence on expatriates. At independence, Zambia relied on foreigners for doctors, lawyers, managers, technicians and even clerks. These expatriates were highly paid and were therefore draining money out of the country. Zambia was poorly equipped to train her own people. There was no university and few secondary schools. At independence there were only a hundred Zambian graduates from universities in other countries and twelve hundred school certificate holders; a sad commentary on sixty-four years of colonial rule. Dr Kaunda's government set about rectifying this. It increased the number of secondary schools and by 1972 more than fifty thousand students had enrolled in them. The university, which opened in 1965, soon had two thousand students pursuing degrees in law, medicine and science, and training for the teaching profession. This led to Zambians replacing foreigners rapidly in the civil service, education, para-statal organisations, the army and the police. Steps were taken to train Zambians in engineering so that they could replace foreigners in the mining and manufacturing industries.

In spite of all these efforts, Zambia was still not able completely to redress the imbalance in the distribution of wealth between the urban and rural areas and between high wage earners and the mass of the people who found it difficult to make a living. The government had to maintain the high wages paid to mineworkers because of Zambia's dependence on copper. The expanded education system opened up opportunities for some Zambians to make money by getting well-paid jobs, and the government encouraged Zambians to go into busi-

The Zimbabwe Cabinet being sworn in by President Banana at Government House, Harare, 19 May 1980

ness. The net result was an enormous improvement in the standard of living of educated Zambians and urban dwellers with good jobs, whilst in the rural areas and in the areas of the cities where the unemployed lived the standard of living steadily decreased. This was one of the legacies of colonialism that was seen in many Third World countries, and whilst the former colonial powers were aware of the problem they were not able to suggest any remedies.

In foreign policy, Zambia, unlike Malawi, remained dedicated to the political liberation of the whole continent. Zambia allowed her territory to be used by liberation movements fighting white regimes in Zimbabwe, Mozambique, Namibia and Angola. This made Zambia a target for military attacks by white Rhodesian, South African and Portuguese forces. Zambia's unselfish foreign policy was an important factor in the eventual success of the liberation movements, and it won for Zambia a highly respected standing in the community of African nations. Dr Kaunda himself became a leading figure in the struggle to end racial discrimination throughout the continent. Dr Kaunda's stance on helping liberation movements was totally in keeping with the philosophy of humanism on which Zambian society was based.

Zimbabwe

Having won her independence through armed struggle, Zimbabwe faced problems arising not only from colonialism but also from the aftermath of war. These problems included the resettlement of refugees, the provision of land for peasants, the expansion of educational facilities, and the welding together of the different political and military organisations that had fought in Zimbabwe over the previous sixteen years. The new government, led by the Prime Minister Robert Mugabe, tackled these problems with energy and vision.

Military integration involved fusing together white forces with African forces that had fought against each other because of their different beliefs about how liberation should be won and the kind of society that should be created in Zimbabwe after liberation. These rival forces were ZNLA under ZANU command and ZPRA under ZAPU command. The formation of a new Zimbabwean army

Robert Mugabe, Prime Minister of Zimbabwe

out of these rival units was given top government priority and was completed in a relatively short time.

The government also began its programme of helping those who had suffered from the war or from years of colonialism. Refugees from Zambia and Botswana were provided with farming land and seed. The government acquired land from white farmers to resettle people crowded in the Reserves. It provided free health services for rural and other lowly-paid workers. It introduced free primary education with the facility of extending it to secondary education. It began training Zimbabweans to replace whites skilled jobs in mining, manufacturing and transportation. In all these ways, Mr Mugabe's government was making a start to the socialist programme to which Zimbabwe was committed.

Questions

Part I

Chapter 1
1. Who are the Bantu-speaking peoples? Give some account of how and why they may have moved into Central Africa.
2. What do you know of Iron Age farming in Central Africa?
3. What was the importance of iron in the development of the Bantu-speaking peoples? What other metals were found in Central Africa?
4. Give an account of some early Iron Age settlements. What is the importance of pottery found at those settlements?
5. What were the main features of the Iron Age culture at (a) Kalomo; (b) Leopard's Kopje; (c) Kangila? Write briefly on Iron Age sites in Malawi?

Chapter 2
6. Describe the Iron Age settlement at Ingobe Ilede. Make some general points about trade in the Iron Age.
7. How do we know that the people of Great Zimbabwe were involved in the regional and inter-regional types of trade?
8. Why do you think Great Zimbabwe may have had religious and military importance?

Part II

Chapter 3
9. Describe in outline:
   a) the rise and fall of the Luba kings
   b) the political system they developed
10. What were the origins of the Lunda? In what way was their political system different from that of the Luba?

Chapter 4
11. What was the nature of the Luba–Lunda expansion into Zambia?
12. Discuss the expansion of the Lunda peoples, with special reference to (a) the Luvale and (b) Kazembe's Lunda.
13. Outline the history of the Bemba down to the end of the 19th century.
14. Write briefly on the history of the Bisa, with particular reference to their trading activities.

Chapter 5
15. How and why were the Lozi able to establish themselves on the Bulozi flood plain? What part was played by the Lozi economy?
16. Examine the Lozi political system. To what extent was it influenced by religious factors?
17. Consider the part played in Lozi history by (a) Mboo and his relations and (b) Mulumbwa.

Chapter 6
18. Describe the growth of the Malawi chieftainship. What were the political and economic achievements of Karonga Masula?
19. What were the main causes of the rise and decline of Undi's kingdom?
20. Give an account of the Tumbuka-Kamanga and Ngonde chieftainships.

Chapter 7
21. Write an essay on two of the following:
    a) the career of Mutota and Mutope
    b) the system of government they established
    c) the break-up of the Mwene–Mutapa kingdom at the end of the fifteenth century.
22. Who were the Changamires? What was the nature of the economy of their kingdom?

Part III

Chapter 8
23. What were the aims of the Portuguese in Kongo?
24. Describe Affonso I's attempts at westernisation of his kingdom and give reasons for their failure.
25. Account for the decline and fall of the Kongo kingdom.

Chapter 9
26. What were the Portuguese aims in Angola and how did these lead to the eventual colonisation of that country?
27. Give an account of the slave trade in Angola down to its abolition in 1836.

Chapter 10
28. Describe how the Portuguese became interested in the Mwene Mutapa Empire.
29. What changes took place in the political, social and economic relations between the Shona and the Portuguese in the 17th century?

Chapter 11
30. Give an account of the *prazo* system as it operated in Portuguese East Africa.
31. Why did the Portuguese want to make contact with Kazembe in the 18th and 19th centuries? Describe some of their efforts to do so.

Part IV

Chapter 12
32. Describe Mzilikazi's course of migration south of the Limpopo and his relationships with some of the peoples he met there.
33. Describe some of the internal and external threats to the survival of the Ndebele kingdom under Mzilikazi north of the Limpopo.

Chapter 13
34. Give an account of Sebetwane's character. What were his military and political achievements?
35. What kind of political system was established by the Kololo in Bulozi? Why did it collapse?

Chapter 14
36. What kingdoms were established in Central Africa by the Ngoni? Describe their political systems.

Part V

Chapter 15
37. Give an account of the trading activities of the Swahili and Yeke in the second half of the 19th century.
38. Write short notes on the trading activities of
    a) the Yao
    b) the Chikunda and Mambari
    c) the white hunters and traders

Chapter 16
39. *Either* What were Livingstone's aims in Central Africa and how successful was he in achieving them? *Or* Give a short account of Livingstone's travels in Central Africa.

Chapter 17
40. How successful were the missionaries in
    a) Bulozi?
    b) Matebeleland and Mashonaland?
41. Outline the missionary work done in Zambia in the nineteenth century.

Chapter 18
42. Describe the aims and achievements of the Livingstone mission.
43. Write short notes on *two* of the following: the Scottish missionaries at Blantyre; the UMCA at Likoma; the Dutch Reformed Church mission. To what extent did the missionaries change the traditional way of life?

Part VI

Chapter 19
44. Outline steps by which Leopold II gained control of the Congo Free State.
45. a) Discuss the question of forced labour with special reference to the Congo Free State.
    b) What opposition was there to Leopold II and the Belgian Government in Zaire?

Chapter 20
46. What were the aims of Cecil Rhodes? How did he persuade Lobengula to give the BSA Company mineral rights in Mashonaland?
47. Write short notes on (a) the BSA Company's charter and (b) the Pioneer Column.
48. Write briefly on (a) the Victoria Incident and (b) the preparation for war by Jameson and Lobengula.
49. Give an account of the Anglo-Ndebele war of 1893.

Chapter 21
50. What were the causes of the Ndebele rising of 1896?
51. Give an account of the Ndebele rising, paying particular attention to the part played by the priests.
52. Outline (a) the causes and (b) the course of the Shona rising.

Chapter 22
53. What were the steps that led to the signing of the Lochner concession of 1890?
54. What were the main events in Bulozi between 1890 and 1905?

Chapter 23
55. *Either* Describe the background to the Swahili war at the north end of Lake Malawi. *Or* give an account of the Swahili wars 1887–95.
56. Describe the treaty-making expeditions of Johnston, Sharpe and Thomson. Discuss the significance of the treaties they obtained.
57. What was the Portuguese problem in Malawi? How was it solved?

Chapter 24
58. Describe either (a) the Yao wars or (b) the Ngoni wars in Malawi.
59. Discuss the question of land, labour and taxation in Malawi.

Chapter 25
60 Describe the resistance shown to colonial rule by Mpezeni's Ngoni.
61 How was the Swahili power eroded in northern Zambia?
62 Discuss the position of (a) the Bemba and (b) Kazembe's Lunda when the Europeans occupied north-eastern Zambia in the 1890s.

Part VII

Chapters 26, 27, 28
63 Describe the colonial administrative systems in Zimbabwe, Zambia and Malawi. What were the main differences between them?
64 Describe land appropriation in Zimbabwe, Zambia and Malawi. Why were there differences between the three territories?

Chapter 29
65 Describe early African resistance and protest movements in Central Africa including the Chilembwe rising. Why did they fail?

Part VIII

Chapters 30, 31, 32
66 Describe the economic development of the three territories, giving reasons for the differences between them.
67 Describe white efforts to use taxation to force Africans to work in the mines and on the farms. How successful were these efforts?

Chapter 33
68 Trace the growth of African political movements in Zimbabwe.
69 What were the reasons for the growth of African protest in Zambia and how was this expressed after the First World War?
70 What forms did African resistance take in Malawi after the First World War?

Part IX

Chapter 34
71 What arguments were put forward by the settlers for the amalgamation of Zambia and Zimbabwe? What progress was made towards amalgamation down to 1945 and what was the African attitude towards it?

Chapter 35
72 What were the postwar arguments used by the settlers in favour of Federation? Why was Federation opposed by the Africans?

Chapter 36
73 Describe the effect of Federation on African society and on the African nationalist movement.

Chapter 37
74 Describe the constitutional changes made in the Federation and in the three territories between 1956 and 1961. Why were they considered necessary?
75 What were the main differences between the policies of Garfield Todd, Sir Edgar Whitehead and Ian Smith in Zimbabwe?

Part X

Chapter 38
76 Outline the steps leading to the formation of UNIP. What were the aims of the party? Describe briefly its organisation.
77 Describe the part played in Malawi by the 'Young Turks' and by Dr. Banda.

Chapter 39
78 What was meant by the 'wind of change'? How did it affect the Federation? Describe the ending of Federation.

Chapter 40
79 Why did the Africans win the war of liberation in Zimbabwe?

Chapter 41
80 Describe (a) the cabinet crisis in Malawi and (b) Dr Banda's agricultural policy.
81 Describe the steps taken to reduce Zambia's economic dependence on Zimbabwe. How did Zambia's foreign policy compare with Malawi's after independence?

Further reading

The following list of books includes most of the standard works of history on the Central African past. No single textbook, such as *Iron Age to Independence*, can possibly describe every aspect of a country or region's past. Try to obtain and read at least a small selection of the books listed here. Choose a subject that interests you and read as much for enjoyment of the topic as for purposes of preparing for your examination. You might like to select a book which deals in some of its chapters with the history of your own area. Teachers will also find this a useful list of books for the preparation of lessons.

General histories

D. Birmingham and P. Martin (eds.), *History of Central Africa*, 2 volumes, London, 1983.
B. Pachai, *Malawi: The History of the Nation*, London, 1973.
T. O. Ranger (ed.), *Aspects of Central African History*, London, 1968.
A. D. Roberts, *A History of Zambia*, London, 1976.

Pre-colonial history

D. Beach, *The Shona and Zimbabwe 900–1850*, Gweru and London, 1980.
H. H. K. Bhila, *Trade and Politics in a Shona Kingdom: The Manyika and their African Neighbours 1575–1902*, London, 1982.
J. D. Clark, *The Prehistory of Africa*, London, 1970.
P. S. Garlake, *Great Zimbabwe*, London, 1973.
H. W. Langworthy, *Zambia before 1890*, London, 1977.
M. Mainga, *Bulozi under the Luyana Kings*, London, 1973.
J. D. Omer-Cooper, *The Zulu Aftermath*, London, 1969.
B. Pachai (ed.), *The Early History of Malawi*, London, 1972.
D. W. Phillipson, *The Later Prehistory of Eastern and Southern Africa*, London, 1977.
A. D. Roberts, *A History of the Bemba*, London, 1973.

Colonial and post-colonial history

N. Bhebe, *Christianity and Traditional Religion in Western Zimbabwe 1859–1923*, London, 1979.
R. Hall, *Zambia 1890–1964*, London, 1977.
K. Kaunda, *Zambia Shall be Free*, London, 1963.
F. Macpherson, *Anatomy of a Conquest: The British Occupation of Zambia 1884–1924*, London, 1981.
I. Mandaza, *Zimbabwe: From Colonial Domination to Independence*, London, 1984.
D. Martin and P. Johnson, *The Struggle for Zimbabwe*, London and Harare, 1981.
R. Palmer, *Land and Racial Domination in Rhodesia*, London, 1977.
R. Palmer and Q. N. Parsons (eds.), *The Roots of Rural Poverty in Central and Southern Africa*, London, 1977.
T. O. Ranger, *The African Voice in Southern Rhodesia 1898–1930*, London, 1970.
T. O. Ranger, *Revolt in Southern Rhodesia 1896–7*, London, 1967 and 1979.
R. I. Rotberg, *The Rise of Nationalism in Central Africa: The Making of Malawi and Zambia*, Boston, 1965.
N. Shamuyarira, *Crisis in Rhodesia*, London, 1965.
G. Shepperson and T. Price, *Independent African: John Chilimbwe*, Edinburgh, 1958.
L. Vambe, *An Ill-fated People*, London, 1972.
C. van Onselen, *Chibaro: African Mine Labour in Southern Rhodesia 1900–1933*, London, 1976.
C. van Onselen and I. R. Phimister, *Studies in the History of African Mine Labour in Colonial Zimbabwe*, Gweru, 1978.

Students and teachers may also be interested in two historical recreations by Stanlake Samkange, *On Trial for my Country* (London, 1967), and *Year of the Uprising* (London, 1978). The first book deals with Lobengula, the second with the events of 1896–7.

Index

Affonso, 46–7, 48
African Affairs Board, 184
African International Association, 107
African Lakes Company, 88, 103, 136, 137, 141, 145, 157
African National Congress (ANC), 177, 182, 188, 192, 193
African Voice Association, 177
Anglo-German Agreement, 140
Anglo-Portuguese Agreement, 108, 139, 147
Angola, 26, 51–6, 64, 100, 130, 139
Anti-Federation Committee, 178–9
Apartheid policy, 174, 176
Armitage, Sir Robert, 187
Arnot, F. C., 88, 100

Baines, Thomas, 88
BaKongo people, 45–6
Balowoka people, 37
Banda, Dr Kamuzu, 177, 178, 185, 187, 188, 190–3,198
Bandeira, Sa da, 56
Bantu-speaking people, 5–7, 25
Baptista, Pedro, 65, 89
Barreto, Francisco, 59
Belgian Congo, 110
Bemba people, 25, 28, 65, 79, 93, 147, 149, 150–1
Benguela, 53, 54
Berlin Conference (1884–5), 108, 109
Berlin Missionary Society, 97, 98
Bisa people, 25, 29–30, 64, 65, 151, 159
Blantyre Mission, 104–5
Bledisloe Commission (1938), 173, 175
Bocarro, Gasper, 60
Boers, 71, 81
Booth, Joseph, 160
Brazilian influence, 54–5, 64
British South Africa Company (BSA Company), 96, 114–15, 117, 119, 121, 122, 123, 131, 132, 133, 135, 140, 141, 145, 148, 150, 152, 155, 165, 193
Buchanan (acting Consul), 137, 139
Bulozi, 26, 31, 33, 74, 76, 87, 90, 92, 98, 100, 131, 133
Burton, Richard, 30
Butler, R. A., 192–3

Capricorn Africa Society, 182
Changa, 19, 43

Changamire people, 19, 43, 60–2, 78
Changufu, Lewis, 188
Chewa people, 35, 36, 65, 106
Chibisa, 144
Chikerema, James, 194
Chikulamayembe, 38
Chikunda people, 37, 81, 86–7, 91, 140
Chikura, 40
Chikuyo, 43
Chilembwe, John, 159, 160, 161, 171
Chimba, Justin, 178
Chinyama, 26
Chinyanta, 84–5
Chipembere, Henry, 178, 179, 186, 191, 198
Chipoya, 151
Chirwa, Orton, 187, 198
Chitmukulu, 29, 93, 151
Chiume, M. W. Kanyama, 178, 179, 198
Chiwere, 106, 144
Church of Scotland, 102, 104, 136
Codrington, R. E., 144, 150, 151
Coillard, Françoise, 75, 76, 88, 97–8, 100, 130, 131, 132, 133, 135
Compagnie du Congo pour le Commerce et l'Industrie (CCCI), 109
Congo, 20, 108–10
Congo Free State, 109–10, 130, 141
Constitution Amendment Bill (1956), 184
Copper, 10, 11, 15, 24, 28, 64, 81, 164, 165, 173, 199
Copperbelt, 165, 169–70, 174, 177, 180, 182, 192
Coryndon, Robert, 133
Coryndon Treaty, 134–5
Coutinho, Sousa, 56
Creech–Jones, 174

Dalgleish Commission, 180
d'Almeida, Francisco, 52
Dambarare, 62
de Sa, Salvador, 54
Devlin Commission, 190
Dias de Novães, Paulo, 51–2
Diogo I, 48
Diogo Cao, 45
Domingo, Charles, 160, 187
Don Pedro, 62
Dupont, Father, 101, 151
Dutch influence, 54

Dutch Reformed Church, 97, 106, 136, 144

Education, 102, 103, 105, 106, 152, 167, 168, 171, 172, 200, 201
Elmslie, Dr, 103, 106, 144
Evangelists, 97, 106

Farming, 106, 153, 158, 162–4, 166, 182, 199–200
Federal Electoral Bill (1956), 184, 186
Federation, 174–6, 178–9, 189, 190, 192
Federation of Welfare Societies, 170
Fernandez, Antonio, 58
Field, Winston, 184, 194
Forbes, P. W., 120, 121, 147, 149, 150
Fort Victoria incident, 118
Franklin, Harry, 188

Gatsi Rusere, 59, 60
Gibixhegu, 69
Gokomere, 11
Gold, 15, 37, 58, 60, 71, 88, 112, 116, 129, 148, 162
Gomani I, 144
Gomani, Philip, 171
Gore-Brown, Col. Stewart, 173
Great Zimbabwe, 15–19, 41
Griffiths, James, 174–5
Grobler Treaty, 111–12

Hawes, A. G. (Consul), 136
Helm, Charles, 96, 144
Henga people, 79
Hetherwick, Alexander, 104, 105
Hilton Young Commission (1938), 173
Huggins, Dr Godfrey, 174, 176, 178, 180, 184
Hunter's Road, 88

Imbangala people, 26
Industrial and Commerical Workers Union (ICU), 167, 185
Ingombe Ilede, 14–15, 17
Iron, 7, 15, 28, 35, 132, 135, 162
Islamic influence, 102, 105
Ivory, 15, 24, 29, 35, 37, 58, 64, 81, 83, 84, 87–8, 129, 136, 151

Jacha, Aaron, 167
Jaga, 48, 53, 54

Jameson, Starr, 117, 118, 119, 120, 122, 126, 127
Jehovah's Witnesses, 160
Jesuits, 48, 51, 96, 100
Johnson, W. P., 105
Johnston, Harry, 138, 139, 140, 141, 142, 144, 145, 151
Jumbe, 85, 139, 141

Kachindamoto, 144
Kadalie, Clements, 167
Kala Ilunga, 21–2
Kalomo culture, 13
Kalonga chiefs, 35–6
Kamwana, Eliot, 159, 160, 187
Kangila, 13
Kanyembo, 27
Kapararaidze, 60, 61
Kapwepwe, Simon, 177, 188
Kariba Dam, 180, 193, 200, 201
Karonga, 11, 136, 137, 172
Kasang people, 24, 54, 55
Katanga, 6, 25, 109, 140
Katilungu, Lawrence, 177
Kaunda, David, 160
Kaunda, Kenneth, 177, 179, 182, 188, 189, 191, 192, 193, 199
Kazembe, 27–8, 64–5, 83, 84, 93, 150
Khoikhoi, 7
Kibinda Ilunga, 23
Kilolo (Lunda chiefs), 24
Kinguri, 24
Kirk, John, 136
Kololo people, 34, 66, 72–6, 90, 138
Kongo, 45–50
Korekore people, 41
Kunda people, 21–2, 28
Kyungu (Ngonde chief), 38

Lacerda, Francisco da, 65, 89
Land Apportionment Act (1931), 164, 167, 190
Land Commission (1894), 125
Land Husbandry Act (1951), 182, 185
Laws, Dr Robert, 102, 103, 104
Lendy, 118–19
Lenje people, 87, 159
Lenshina, Alice, 193
Leopard's Kopje culture, 12, 13
Leopold II, King, 107–10
Lewanika, 75, 88, 100, 130–5
Likoma, 105
Lilongwe Project, 199
Livingstone, David, 30, 75, 76, 98:
 first journey, 89–91
 second journey, 91–2
 third journey, 92–4
Livingstone, W. J., 160, 161
Livingstonia Mission, 76, 80, 100, 103, 144, 145, 159, 160
Lobengula, 71, 88, 96, 97, 111, 112–115, 116, 117, 119, 120
Lochner, F. E., 130–2, 133–4
London Missionary Society (LMS), 71, 91, 92, 96, 98, 100
Lopez, Alvare, 47, 48

Lozi people, 31–3, 74, 75, 130, 131
Luanda, 52–6, 90
Luba, 21–2, 25–30, 110
Lubemba, 29, 88, 101, 150, 151
Lugard, F., 137
Luhanga people, 37, 38
Lumpa Church, 193
Lunda people, 23, 24, 25–30, 100, 147, 150
Lundu, 36
Lusaka, 10
Lusengi, 23
Lusu, 9
Luvale people, 26, 34, 87

Machili, 9
Mackenzie, Bishop, 92, 105
Macleod, Iain, 191
Macmillan, Harold, 190
Maguire, C. M., 142–3
Makanjira, 142–3, 144
Makasa, 29
Makoko, 108
Malawi:
 early settlements, 11, 35–8, 76
 religion, 102–6, 172
 colonisation, 115, 136–45, 157–8
 mineral development, 165
 African opposition, 160–1, 171–2, 178–9, 186–8
 constitutional changes, 191–2
 post-colonial developments, 198–9
Malawi Congress Party, 187, 188, 191, 193, 198
Malekebu, Dr, 171–2
Mambari people, 81, 86, 90
Mambwe, 100, 101
Mamochisane, 75
Mange, 31
Mani-Kongo, King, 45, 46
Manning, Captain, 149
Manuel I, King, 47
Manyuema Massacre, 93
Mapondera, 159
Margesson, Capt. E. C., 150
Maseko people, 80
Mashonaland, 115–16, 127
Massangano, 54
Masula, 35–6
Matabeleland, 87, 96, 112, 117, 121, 123, 154
Matamba people, 54
Matinga, Charles, 177, 186
Matope, 41, 43
Maudling, Reginald, 191
Maund, E. A., 115
Mavura, 60, 63
Mbanza, 46, 47
Mbelwa, 26, 78, 79, 103, 104, 141, 145
Mboo, 31
Mbunda people, 34
Mbundu people, 51
Mbuywamwambwa, 31
Mfecane, 66, 67
Migrant labour, 166, 171
Milner, Alfred, 134, 155
Mineral development, 132, 138, 140, 148, 162–5 (see also under specific commodities)
Missionaries, 49, 51, 58, 92, 96–106, 114, 136, 144, 150
Mlowoka, 38
Mlozi, 137, 139, 149
Moffat, J. S., 96, 112–13
Moffat, Sir John, 176
Moffat, Robert, 68, 71, 88, 89, 96
Moffat Resolutions, 180
Monckton Report, 190
Moslem influence, 86
Mozambique, 59, 64, 77, 137, 139, 195
Mpanza, 46, 47
Mpezeni, 78, 79, 87, 140, 147–9
Msiri, 84, 100, 110, 140
Mtwalo, 78
Mugabe, Robert, 197, 201
Mulambwa, 31, 33
Murray, A. C., 106
Murray, W. H., 144
Muteba, 27
Mutota, 18, 40–1
Mwamba, 29, 151
Mwanambinyi, 31
Mwansabamba, 30
Mwata Yamvo, 24, 26
Mwene Mutapa, 35, 40–1, 58, 59–62
Mzilikazi, 66–7, 68, 69, 74, 88, 96

National Democratic Party (NDP), 185
Native Associations, 172, 177
Naweji, 23–4
Ndebele people, 66, 71, 74, 88, 96, 98, 112, 114, 117, 119, 120, 121, 122–5, 132, 153, 159, 162
Ndongo, 48, 51
Ngano, Martha, 167
Ngola, 51–3
Ngoleme a Kitambu, 52
Ngonda Bilonda, 27
Ngonde people, 38, 137
Ngoni people, 66, 77–80, 103–4, 105, 106, 137, 138, 147, 160, 172
Ngoni Wars, 144–6, 148–9
Nkomo, Joshua, 168, 177, 185, 194
Nkrumah, Kwame, 189
Nkumbula, Harry, 178, 179, 188, 192
North Charterland Exploration Company, 148
Northern Rhodesia African Congress, 178–9
Nsingu, 148, 149
Ntabeni, 78
Nyahuma, 43
Nyakyusa people, 38
Nyamazana, 78
Nyambe, 33
Nyandoro, George, 159, 185, 194
Nyanja people, 105, 143
Nyasaland African Congress, 177, 179, 187
Nzinga Kuwu, 45, 46
Nzinga Nbandi (Anna), 53

Paris Evangelical Mission, 97, 99, 100

207

Passfield Memorandum, 175
Pereira, Manuel Cerveira, 53
Pereira, Nuno Alvares, 60
Phiri people, 35, 36
Phopo Hill site, 11
Pinto, Francisco, 65
Plymouth Bretheren, 100, 150
Police forces, 128, 144, 157, 200
Political movements:
    in Malawi, 178–9, 186–8
    in Zambia, 178–9, 188–9
    in Zimbabwe, 167–8, 178–9
    (see also under names of specific parties)
Portuguese influence, 24, 25, 35–6, 43, 45–8, 51–62, 81, 108, 128, 139
Pottery, 7–11
Prazos (land holding), 63–4
Providence Industrial Mission, 160, 171

Racialism, examples of, 180
Railways, 109, 110, 123, 141, 174
Regimento, 47, 48
Religious activity, 42–3, 46, 47, 96–106, 128–9, 159, 160, 172
Rhodes, Cecil J., 111–21, 127, 130, 133, 138, 140, 141, 145, 148
Rhodesia see Zimbabwe
Rhodesian Anglo-American Company, 165
Rhodesian Bantu Voters Association (RBVA), 167
Rhodesian Selection Trust (RST), 165, 180
Rozvi, 78
Rubber, 110, 155
Rudd, Charles D., 113–14
Rudd Concession (1888), 114, 115, 117

Sambo, Robert, 167
Samkange, Rev. D. T., 168, 185
Samkange, Stanlake, 177
San Salvador, 45, 46, 47, 50
Sao Thome, 47
Scott, D. C., 104–5
Sebetwane, 34, 72–5, 87
Sekeletu, 75, 76, 90, 91, 92, 98–9
Selborne, Lord, 155
Selous, F. C., 88
Senga people, 25, 30, 159
Shaka, 66–7
Shamuyarira, Nathan, 183
Sharpe, Alfred, 137, 139–40, 149
Shila people, 27, 28
Shippard, Sir Sydney, 113–14, 130

Shire Highlands, 92, 103, 104, 136, 138, 139, 148, 158, 166
Shona people, 16, 18, 39–43, 96–7, 98, 106, 116, 117, 118, 120, 125–9, 159, 162, 167
Silveira, Goncalo da, 58
Sipalo, Munukayumbwa, 188
Sithole, Rev. Ndabaningi, 194
Slave trade, 24, 28, 37, 47, 48, 51, 52, 55–6, 64, 75, 81, 83, 86, 90, 91, 92, 93, 136, 140, 141, 142, 147
Smith, Ian, 194
Songye people, 21
Stanley, Sir Herbert M., 94, 107, 108, 164
Stirling, David, 182
Stone Age San, 7
Swahili people, 57, 65, 81, 83, 84–6, 93, 109–10, 133, 136, 147
Swahili Wars, 149–51

Takawira, Leopold, 194
Tambo people, 30
Tawara people, 41
Taxation, 37, 145–6, 152, 155, 159, 160, 162, 165
Thomson, Joseph, 96, 140
Tippu Tip, 85
Tobacco, 154, 156, 158, 166, 173, 199
Todd, Garfield, 182, 184
Togwa, 19, 43
Tonga people, 25, 73, 79, 87, 102–3, 135
Tozer, Bishop, 104
Transvaal, 111–12, 116, 122, 126
Tribal Councils, 172
Tshikapa, 8
Tumbuka people, 25, 37–8, 79
Twala, Abraham, 167

Undi, 36, 64
Unilateral Declaration of Independence (UDI), 194–5, 199
United National Indepence Party (UNIP), 188–9, 192, 193
Universities Mission to Central Africa (UMCA), 92, 105–6, 136
Urban Areas Act (1948), 178
Ushi people, 28

Victoria Agreement (1893), 119
Victoria Falls Conferences, 173, 174, 193

Ware Concession (1889), 130
Watch Tower Movement, 159, 160

Welensky, Roy, 174, 175, 184, 190, 191, 192–3
Welfare Associations/Societies (in Zambia), 160, 170
Wene, 45
Westbeech, George, 88, 100
White Fathers, 100, 107, 151
Whitehead, Sir Edgar, 184, 185
Wiese, Carl, 147, 149
Wilson, Major Allan, 121
Wilson, Harold, 194
Wina, Sikota, 188

Yao people, 36, 76, 80, 81, 86, 92, 102, 106, 133, 146
Yao Wars, 142–3
Yembe Yembe, 27
'Young Turks' (in Malawi), 178, 186, 198, 199

Zaire, 8, 26, 81, 108, 110, 136
Zambezi, 12, 59, 60, 90, 91, 92, 139
Zambezi Exploring Company, 164–5
Zambia:
    early settlements, 12, 24, 25, 73, 74, 80, 81
    religion, 98–101
    colonisation, 115, 117, 147–52, 155–6
    mineral development, 164–5
    African opposition, 168–70, 178–9
    constitutional changes, 192–3
    post-colonial developments, 119
Zambia African National Congress (ZANC), 188
Zanzibar, 83, 85
Zimbabwe:
    early settlements, 12, 24, 25, 73, 74, 80, 81
    religion, 96–8
    colonisation, 111–21, 125, 134, 152–4
    African opposition, 167–8, 178–9
    constitutional changes, 194–7
    post-colonial developments, 201
Zimbabwe African National Union (ZANU), 194, 197
Zimbabwe African Peoples' Union (ZAPU), 194, 197
Ziwa site, 11–12
Zulu influences, 112
Zulu, Grey, 188
Zwangendaba, 77, 78
Zwimba, Matthew, 159